Asia after Versailles

Edinburgh East Asian Studies Series
Series Editors: Natascha Gentz, Urs Matthias Zachmann and David Der-Wei Wang

Covering language, literature, history and society, this series of academic monographs and reference volumes brings together scholars of East Asia to address crucial topics in East Asian Studies. The series embraces a broad scope of approaches and welcomes volumes that address topics such as regional patterns of cooperation and social, political and cultural implications of inter-regional collaborations, as well as volumes on individual regional themes across the spectrum of East Asian Studies. With its critical analysis of central issues in East Asia, and its remit of contributing to a wider understanding of East Asian countries' international impact, the series will be crucial to understand the shifting patterns in this region within an increasingly globalised world.

Series Editors
Professor Natascha Gentz is Chair of Chinese Studies, Director of the Confucius Institute for Scotland and Dean International (China) at the University of Edinburgh.
Professor Urs Matthias Zachmann is Professor of Modern Japanese Culture and History at Freie Universität Berlin.
Professor David Der-Wei Wang is the Edward C. Henderson Professor of Chinese Literature at the Fairbank Center for Chinese Studies at Harvard University.

Editorial Board
Professor Marion Eggert, Bochum University, Germany
Professor Joshua A. Fogel, York University, Toronto, Canada
Professor Andrew Gordon, Harvard University, Cambridge, Massachusetts, USA
Professor Rikki Kersten, Murdoch University, Perth, Australia
Dr Seung-Young Kim, University of Sheffield, UK
Dr Hui Wang, Tsinghua University, Beijing, People's Republic of China

Titles available in the series:
Asia after Versailles: Asian Perspectives on the Paris Peace Conference and the Interwar Order, 1919–33
Urs Matthias Zachmann (Editor)

Asia after Versailles

Asian Perspectives on the Paris Peace Conference and the Interwar Order, 1919–33

Edited by Urs Matthias Zachmann

EDINBURGH
University Press

Edinburgh University Press is one of the leading university presses in the UK. We publish academic books and journals in our selected subject areas across the humanities and social sciences, combining cutting-edge scholarship with high editorial and production values to produce academic works of lasting importance. For more information visit our website: edinburghuniversitypress.com

© editorial matter and organisation Urs Matthias Zachmann, 2017
© the chapters their several authors, 2017

Edinburgh University Press Ltd
The Tun – Holyrood Road
12(2f) Jackson's Entry
Edinburgh EH8 8PJ

Typeset in 10/12 Ehrhardt by
Servis Filmsetting Ltd, Stockport, Cheshire

A CIP record for this book is available from the British Library

ISBN 978 1 4744 1716 7 (hardback)
ISBN 978 1 4744 1717 4 (webready PDF)
ISBN 978 1 4744 1718 1 (epub)

The right of Urs Matthias Zachmann to be identified as the editor of this work has been asserted in accordance with the Copyright, Designs and Patents Act 1988, and the Copyright and Related Rights Regulations 2003 (SI No. 2498).

Grateful acknowledgement is made for permission to reproduce material previously published elsewhere. Every effort has been made to trace the copyright holders, but if any have been inadvertently overlooked, the publisher will be pleased to make the necessary arrangements at the first opportunity.

Contents

List of Illustrations	vii
Notes on Contributors	viii
Acknowledgments	xi
Introduction: Asia After Versailles Urs Matthias Zachmann	1

Part I

1	The Correlation of Crises, 1918–20 Mark Metzler	23
2	Muslim Asia after Versailles Cemil Aydin	55
3	From Versailles to Shanghai: Pan-Asianist Legacies of the Paris Peace Conference and the Failure of Asianism from Below Torsten Weber	77

Part II

4	A Cultural History of Diplomacy: Reassessing the Japanese 'Performance' at the Paris Peace Conference Naoko Shimazu	101
5	India's Freedom and the League of Nations: Public Debates 1919–33 Maria Framke	124
6	Dashed Hopes: Japanese Buddhist Perspectives on the Paris Peace Conference John LoBreglio	144
7	Particularism and Universalism in the New Nationalism of Post-Versailles Japan Kevin M. Doak	175

8 Versailles and the Fate of Chinese Internationalism: Reassessing the Anarchist Case 197
Gotelind Müller

9 The Impact of Versailles on Chinese Nationalism as Reflected in Shanghai Graphic and Urban Culture, 1919–31 212
Hiroko Sakamoto

Index 237

List of Illustrations

Figure 4.1	'Vive Wilson', an illuminated sign across Rue Royale, Paris, in front of Maxim's, December 1918 (Princeton University Library, Woodrow Wilson Coll., box 42, folder 5).	103
Figure 4.2	Diplomats and the Shadow on the Blind: The Problems of Peace – 'President Wilson arrives in Paris', *The Herald*, 21 December 1918.	104
Figure 4.3	The Japanese delegation photographed at the Hôtel Bristol, Paris, 1919 (Diplomatic Archives of the Ministry of Foreign Affairs of Japan).	107
Figure 4.4	Seating at the Plenary Session of the Peace Conference (Charles T. Thompson, *The Paris Peace Conference Day by Day*, New York: Brentano's, 1920, after p. 118).	108
Figure 4.5	The 'Big Four' or the 'Olympians' (Courtesy of the Woodrow Wilson Presidential Library, Staunton, Virginia).	113
Figure 4.6	The 'Big Four' in situ (Author unattributed).	114
Figure 5.1	'Funeral Procession of Wilson's 14 Points' (*Vyanga Chitravali: Caricature Album, A Collection of Political and Cocial Caricatures*, Cawnpore, 1925; in the collection of the British Library).	131
Figure 9.1	Women students taking part in a demonstration, *Shenbao*, 27 May 1919.	214
Figure 9.2	'Not exactly, but almost' by Huang Wennong, *Shanghai Puck*, vol. 1, no. 1 (1918).	218
Figure 9.3	*Shishi Xinbao* (Shanghai), 11 May 1919.	219
Figure 9.4	*Shibao* (Shanghai), 27 April 1919.	220
Figure 9.5	*Shibao* (Shanghai), 18 May 1919.	221
Figure 9.6	*Dagongbao* (Tianjin), 6 May 1919.	224
Figure 9.7	*Shenbao*, 7 June 1919.	225
Figure 9.8	*Shenbao*, 22 May 1919.	227
Figure 9.9	*Shanghai Manhua*, vol. 12 (7 July 1928).	229
Figure 9.10	Huang Wennong, *Shanghai Manhua*, vol. 5 (19 May 1928).	231
Figure 9.11	Huang Wennong, *Shanghai Manhua*, vol. 75 (28 September 1929).	232

Notes on Contributors

Cemil Aydin is Professor of History at the University of North Carolina at Chapel Hill. His research deals with global intellectual history and international history, with a focus on Asia and the Middle East. Cemil Aydin's publications include his book on the *Politics of Anti-Westernism in Asia* (Columbia University Press, 2007), "Regionen und Reiche in der Politischen Geschichte des Langen 19. Jahrhunderts, 1750–1924" [Region and Empire in the Political History of the Long 19th Century], in *Geschichte der Welt, 1750–1870: Wege zur modernen Welt* [A History of the World, 1750–1870], (C. H. Beck, 2016), and *The Idea of the Muslim World: A Global Intellectual History* (Harvard University Press, 2017).

Kevin M. Doak holds the Nippon Foundation Endowed Chair in Japanese Studies at Georgetown University where he is also Professor in the Department of East Asian Languages and Cultures. His major publications include *A History of Nationalism in Modern Japan: Placing the People* (Leiden, 2007) and *Xavier's Legacies: Catholicism in Modern Japanese Culture* (University of British Columbia Press, 2011). Doak's current research is on Catholicism in modern Japan, and he is currently working on a book, 'Kotaro Tanaka and World Law: Rethinking the Natural Law Outside the West' (under contract with Palgrave Macmillan).

Maria Framke is a historian of modern South Asia working at the University of Rostock, Germany. She has researched and published on the history of international organizations, imperial and nationalist politics, humanitarianism, and international relations and ideologies in the twentieth century. Her current research project focuses on 'South Asian Humanitarianism in Armed Conflicts, 1899–1949'. Framke received her doctorate from Jacobs University Bremen in 2011. Her book on the *Engagement with Italian Fascism and German National Socialism in India, 1922–1939* was published in 2013 with the Wissenschaftliche Buchgesellschaft Darmstadt.

John LoBreglio is Senior Lecturer in Japanese Studies at Oxford Brookes University where he teaches courses on modern Japanese history and Japanese religions. His primary field of research is Japanese Buddhism from the mid-nineteenth century through to the Second World War. His publications include 'Uniting Buddhism: The Varieties of *Tsūbukkyō* in Meiji–Taishō Japan and the Case of Takada Dōken', *Eastern Buddhist*, XXXVII:1&2 (2005), pp. 39–76, and 'Orthodox, Heterodox, Heretical: Defining Doctrinal Boundaries in Meiji-period Soto Zen', *Bochumer Jahrbuch zur Ostasienforschung* (*Bochum Yearbook of East Asian Studies*), 33 (2009), pp. 77–102. He is currently working on a monograph on Japanese Buddhist perspectives on international imperialism in the nineteenth and twentieth centuries.

Mark Metzler is Professor of History and Asian Studies at the University of Texas at Austin and, from 2017, Professor of History and International Studies at the University of Washington. His research is situated at the intersection of modern Japanese history, global history and historical political economy. He is the author of *Lever of Empire* (University of California Press, 2006), *Capital as Will and Imagination* (Cornell University Press, 2013), and, with Simon Bytheway, *Central Banks and Gold* (Cornell University Press, 2016).

Gotelind Müller-Saini is Professor of Chinese Studies at the University of Heidelberg, Germany. Her fields of research are history and history of ideas in China and East Asia with a focus on the nineteenth and twentieth centuries, paying particular attention to Sino-Japanese, Sino-Western and Sino-Russian cultural exchange processes. Her books published in English and German include monographs on Lin Yutang (1989), modern Chinese Buddhism (1993), Kropotkin and anarchism in China (2001), representations of history in Chinese media (2007) and an edited volume on designing history in East Asian textbooks (2011). Her most recent book is *Documentary, World History, and National Power in the PRC: Global Rise in Chinese Eyes* (Routledge, 2013).

Hiroko Sakamoto is Professor Emerita of Chinese Intellectual and Cultural History at Hitotsubashi University, Tokyo, where she taught at the Graduate School of Social Sciences until 2014. Prior to her appointment at Hitotsubashi, she had also taught at Tokyo Metropolitan University and Yamaguchi University. Her publications include: *Chūgoku minzoku-shugi no shinwa—Jinshu, shintai, jendā* [The myth of Chinese nationalism—race, body and gender] (Iwanami Shoten, 2004); *Chūgoku kindai no shisō bunka-shi* [The intellectual and cultural history of modern China] (Iwanami Shoten, 2016); 'The Cult of "Love and Eugenics" in May Fourth Movement Discourse', *positions: east asia cultures critique*, 12:2 (2004). She is currently working on a Japanese-language monograph on the representation of Chinese women in Manga magazines, 1920–50.

Naoko Shimazu is Professor of Humanities (History) at Yale-NUS College, Singapore. Formerly, she taught at Birkbeck College, University of London. Her major publications include *Imagining Japan in Post-war East Asia* (co-ed., Routledge, 2013), *Japanese Society at War: Death, Memory and the Russo-Japanese War* (Cambridge University Press, 2009), *Nationalisms in Japan* (ed., Routledge, 2006), *Japan, Race and Equality: The Racial Equality Proposal of 1919* (Routledge, 1998). She is currently writing a monograph, *Diplomacy as Theatre: The Bandung Conference and the Making of the Third World*. She is Honorary Professor at the Department of History, and Research Associate at the Asia Research Institute, at the National University of Singapore; Fellow of the Royal Historical Society, Fernand Braudel Fellow (EUI), and Japan Foundation Fellow (Waseda University), amongst others.

Torsten Weber is a historian of modern East Asia and a Senior Research Fellow at the German Institute for Japanese Studies (DIJ Tokyo) where he also serves as Head of the Humanities Section. His research focuses on different aspects of the history of Japanese–Chinese relations and interactions from the modern to the contemporary era. His publications include several articles and book chapters on Japanese and Chinese conceptions of Asia from the nineteenth to the twenty-first centuries which have appeared, among other places, in *Pan-Asianism: A Documentary History* (eds Saaler/Szpilman, Rowman&Littlefield, 2011) and *The Palgrave Encyclopedia of Imperialism and Anti-Imperialism* (eds Ness/Cope, Palgrave Macmillan, 2015). He is currently preparing the publication of a monograph that studies Asianism as a contested concept in the struggle for hegemony between China and Japan in the first half of the twentieth century.

Urs Matthias Zachmann is Professor of Modern Japanese Culture and History at Freie Universität Berlin. Prior to that, he was Handa Professor of Japanese–Chinese Relations at the University of Edinburgh. His fields of research are the history of international relations in East Asia, the intellectual and cultural history of Japan, and law and legal history in East Asia. Among his publications are *China and Japan in the Late Meiji Period: China Policy and the Japanese Discourse on National Identity, 1895–1904* (Routledge, 2009/2011) and *Völkerrechtsdenken und Außenpolitik in Japan, 1919–1960* [The Discourse on International Law and Foreign Policy in Japan, 1919–1960] (Nomos, 2013). He is currently working on an English-language monograph on the history of international law in Japan.

Acknowledgments

This book arose from the question about what non-Western audiences actually thought and felt about the Paris Peace Conference as seen from *their* perspective rather than through the traditional lenses of Europe and the US. Reflecting the regional orientation of the authors' expertise, the chapters focus on the impact of the conference and its aftermath on China, Japan, India and the Ottoman Empire/Turkey. Given that the impact on these regions was as crucial as it was for Europe, particularly in its long-term effects that still reverberate today, and assuming that Asia and the Middle East will remain the most dynamic and conflict-ridden regions in the world for some time to come, the findings of this book intend not only to complement existing scholarship, but also to stimulate the debate on the historical roots of today's international order in and beyond the upcoming centennial of the Paris Peace Conference.

As Editor, I would like to extend my most sincere thanks to those who made the project possible. Most importantly, my gratitude goes to the nine authors of the chapters for their enthusiastic cooperation and unflagging good will in seeing this project through to the end. The book originated from a conference of the same title that was hosted by the Japan Centre of Ludwig-Maximilians-Universität, Munich. I am deeply grateful to my colleagues at the Japan Centre, Klaus Vollmer, Evelyn Schulz and Peter Pörtner for co-organising the conference and the generous financial support from the Münchener Universitätsgesellschaft. At the University of Edinburgh, Roddy McDougall, Anna Aleksandrova and Richard Stevenson assisted me in editorial work, for which I am most grateful. My particular thanks go to Dr Hiromi Sasamoto-Collins at the Asian Studies Department of the University of Edinburgh for her painstaking translation of the chapter by Hiroko Sakamoto. I am indebted to Laura Williamson, Joannah Duncan, Rebecca Mackenzie and Richard Strachan from Edinburgh University Press for their most professional and kind assistance in seeing this manuscript to publication. On a personal note, I would like to thank all my colleagues in the Asian Studies Department at the University of Edinburgh for the wonderful time working together while this volume was still in the making.

The cover shows an illustration by Chen Juanyin entitled 'Watching the Sunrise over the East China Sea' (*Donghai guan richu*) that graced the cover of

Shidai Manhua (Modern Sketch) no. 24 of December 1935. Although somewhat outside the time frame of this book and more immediately referencing the threat that Japan posed to China at the time, we chose it to represent in a more abstract way the mixture of hope and dread, idealism and cynicism, which so peculiarly marked the emotional spectrum of the whole interwar period.

While seeking copyright permission, every effort was made to trace copyright holders; however, the editor would be glad to hear of any omissions.

Finally, a short note on Chinese and Japanese names in the chapters: these have been given in their traditional order, i.e. family name first, followed by the personal name.

Urs Matthias Zachmann
Berlin, February 2017

Introduction: Asia after Versailles

Urs Matthias Zachmann

The Paris Peace Conference and its impact on interwar Asia

When the victorious Allied Powers convened in Paris in January 1919, they set themselves an immense task: after the cataclysmic event that had cost millions of lives, laid waste to whole regions of Europe, shattered or contributed to the downfall of four empires (German, Austro-Hungarian, Ottoman and Czarist) and generally seemed to symbolise the 'suicide' of Western civilisation, they had no lesser purpose than to create a new world order that should be just, universal and enduring.[1] To this end, the Peace Conference and its five related treaties attempted to redraw the borders of half the world's continents, change the nationalities of millions of people in a brushstroke, reframe economic relations, create institutions that would contain or even outlaw war, and in general introduce a new style and ethos of doing international politics that was to be fundamentally different from the old balance-of-power imperialist politics.[2] Negotiations had to be conducted under severe time constraints and faced a multitude of political and economic restrictions:[3] soldiers and workers from all over the world were still stationed in Europe, waiting to be sent home; there were food shortages because of blockades; and revolutionary movements were springing up everywhere (such as the short-lived 'Bavarian Soviet Republic' that appeared during the Paris Peace Conference) and had to be contained, not to speak of keeping a wary eye on Bolshevik Russia. Time constraints were such that, famously, the representatives of the Allied Powers never saw the draft of the Versailles Treaty in full before it was printed and signed in the Hall of Mirrors in June 1919.[4] On top of this, the almost messianic hopes that Wilson and his Fourteen Points of 1918 had raised among the masses globally, and which could be seen in the frenetic welcome that the President received when entering Paris, added another layer of pressure to the negotiations.[5]

Considering these factors, it is probably understandable that the so-called Council of Four (but effectively just the 'Great Three' – Wilson, Lloyd George and Clemenceau) concentrated on what was most pressing on their minds – namely, peace and stability in Europe – and that non-European matters figured only as an afterthought. Thus, non-Western regions usually featured as simple extensions of the European powers' imperial presence in these regions, and their peoples' fate mattered only in so far as the demise of their former 'guardians' (Ottoman, German or Austro-Hungarian) required that they be given into the care of the remaining empires. Despite Wilson's Fifth Point, which promised to give the interests of the 'populations concerned ... equal weight', the latter were regularly found 'not yet able to stand by themselves under the strenuous conditions of the modern world'[6] and thus placed under the tutelage (mandate) of the British or French Empire. The British Foreign Secretary, Arthur Balfour (disgruntled by his perceived lack of influence on the negotiations), mocked the often cavalier and sometimes outrageously callous way in which the 'Council of Four' dealt with the non-Western world thus: 'I have three all-powerful, all-ignorant men sitting there and partitioning continents with only a child to take notes from them.'[7]

Given the Eurocentric atmosphere, it is not surprising that 'Asia' – the concept is used here and throughout this volume in a wide, non-essentialising sense – featured in Paris mostly as an absence, and quite literally so. The Ottoman Empire was absent as a defeated party, awaiting (like Germany) the verdict of the victorious powers on its fate. Its voice was drowned out by the Turkish War of Independence, anyway, and the emerging republic soon abolished empire and caliphate, thus also divesting itself of the huge pan-Islamic networks that spanned Africa and Asia.[8] India was granted two seats at the big table by virtue of belonging to the British Empire and having contributed a disproportionately high number of soldiers to the war in allegiance to the 'mother country'. For the same reason, however, its presence was seen as a mere token of Britain's generosity, and its voice best not be heard.[9] Japan was invited as a 'great power' to join the Conference. But it was not made part of the inner circle and, not being particularly fond of Wilson's 'new diplomacy' and having a rather limited agenda (territories and racial equality), assumed a marginal position at the Conference by choice and temperament anyway.[10] The once proud empire, China, finally, figured only as a 'small power' at the plenary table (being allocated the same number of seats as its former tributary state, Siam (Thailand)) and left it soon in protest, too, after having failed to recover occupied Shandong from Japan and thus come under pressure by the so-called May Fourth Movement at home.[11]

The historiographical literature on the Paris Peace Conference and its aftermath has, with few exceptions (such as Naoko Shimazu's seminal study *Japan, Race and Equality*), adopted the European preoccupation of its subject, paying little, or at best 'derivative', attention to the non-Western world.[12] Thus, the bulk of scholarly literature deals with European matters, focusing particularly on the central questions of whether the Paris Peace Conference had failed to create stability in Europe by imposing a 'Carthaginian peace' (the more traditional verdict that was already prevalent among contemporaries),[13] or to what extent it was relatively successful in establishing a modicum of stability by the mid-1920s, before other factors such as the Great Depression, growing American isolationism or practicalities of enforcement intervened (the more recent trend in historiography).[14] Even Erez Manela's *The Wilsonian Moment*, which focuses on the responses of non-Western audiences to Wilsonianism (and disillusionment with it), cannot help but maintain a certain Eurocentric angle, considering non-Western actors only in so far as they responded to Wilsonianism in a predictable manner, i.e. with anticolonial nationalism. As important as this response was for non-Western audiences, such a perspective none the less downplays the latter's agency, ignoring alternative agendas that transcended nationalism and – particularly in the case of Japan and Turkey – even complicities with the Western powers that cannot easily be subsumed under the reductive pattern of anticolonialism.

This volume attempts to break away from Europe as the epistemic closure and approaches the subject from the opposite direction: that is, it looks at Asian perspectives, sensibilities and motivations *in their own right*. It tries to gauge the impact of the Paris Peace Conference on Asian audiences in all its diversity by consulting a wide variety of non-Western voices and sources. As the more detailed outline in the next part of this Introduction will show, the various chapters of this volume address the impact of Versailles[15] on countries and regions such as Japan, China, India, Turkey and the regions of the former Ottoman Empire on a number of different levels (economic, cultural, political, social, religious) and from a variety of disciplinary perspectives (intellectual history, media, gender, cultural studies and so on). The chapters thus not only reincorporate a massive, but hitherto largely ignored, global constituency that was directly affected by the outcomes of the Conference into the research focus, but also are thereby able to shed new light on the consequences of the Conference and its repercussions into the 1930s on a global scale.

Despite the wide variety of experiences illustrated in these chapters, in their totality they give ample proof that World War I and the Peace Conference were as crucial for their impact on Asia as they were for Europe. The war and subsequent events brought about the integration of Asia into global affairs at unprecedented levels, for better and for worse. To name just one example, the actions of the Western powers had the effect of spreading the destruction of the war on a global scale, not only by moving Indian soldiers and Chinese labourers into the trenches of British and French camps, but also by spreading epidemics and food shortages back into the world. To indicate the scale of proportions, it should be kept in mind that, if we look just at the sheer number of victims produced by direct *and* indirect causes of the war, it was India, not Europe, that may have suffered the most deaths of World War I.[16]

The momentousness of the situation, often coupled with the millenarian belief in a 'new order' rising out of the Great Destruction, was observed throughout Asia. Japanese intellectuals such as Tanaka Kōtarō, for example, likened the events to the French Revolution, albeit on a global scale.[17] And as in 1789, the shocks and stimuli that emanated from Versailles were not merely political or economic; they also occurred on the ideational level. In particular, the Wilsonian ideas of national self-determination, the equality of nations and a liberal international order centred on a league of nations chimed deeply with aspirations throughout the world.[18] Soon local forms sprang up, such as a 'Muslim' or 'Ottoman Wilsonianism', an 'Asianist Wilsonianism' or even a 'Buddhist Wilsonianism' (although detailed studies of the underlying agendas show that these were anything but simple adaptations; rather, they were strategic appropriations).[19] Moreover, in February 1919, Japan proposed a racial equality clause for the Covenant of the League of Nations.[20] Of course, it has been argued that neither Wilson nor the Japanese government really intended these principles to be of such universal significance as they came to be understood by the public, and each pursued a particular political goal with it (criticising German authoritarianism, attacking anti-Asian immigration laws, or using them as pure leverage for territorial negotiations and so on).[21] Yet, the public did not see this, and the racial equality clause henceforth assumed such an iconic status in the minds of Asian audiences that it could be called, without too much hyperbole, 'Asia's Fifteenth Point'.

The 'Wilsonian Moment' (Manela) or, rather, 'Wilsonian Bubble' (Metzler)[22] lasted from autumn 1918 to spring 1919 and witnessed an inflationary idealism that was completely out of line with reality. It was thus also the product of two phenomena that characterised the new era of postwar politics: namely, the heightened importance of 'the masses' in industrialised democratic societies, and the role that the media played in connecting the hitherto relatively separate spheres of politics and people.[23] Politicians and diplomats began to 'perform' for the public, and the media amplified, reduced or interfered with the impact of their performance, depending on their own agenda. Appeals to 'common sense' and the 'common people' hence became standard, a practice that the historian E. H. Carr, in a contemporary analysis of the interwar years, derisively called 'the apotheosis of public opinion'.[24]

It should be noted, however, that the global convergence of ideas not only took place on the level of political ideas, but also enveloped mass audiences in a much more quotidian and palpable way with the spread of common aesthetics, new social concepts and changing gender relations. Thus, the 1920s saw a startling synchronicity of sensibilities in metropolises all over the world; in Japan, for example, these would be identified as 'Taishō chic',[25] but similar ideas could be found on the streets of London, Berlin, New York or, for that matter, Shanghai. A shift in the gender dynamic was part of this new culture, which sought to overcome the old social order. If Wilson came to champion female suffrage by 1918,[26] we can observe a similar surge and synchronicity of female empowerment – at least in the media – in 1920s Shanghai. Female activists played a conspicuous role during the May Fourth Movement in China 1919, and women gradually became associated with the nationalistic paradigm in popular media (including advertising).[27] Thus, again, popular expectations and sensibilities were amplified by the emerging role of mass media at the time.

Yet, neither politicians nor the media could control the reception of the ideas they were floating or 'spinning', particularly not in those far-flung regions that had never been the intended audience of their declarations in the first place. Thus, the story of the 'Wilsonian Moment' is also one of over-exposure to the seductive rhetoric of the 'new diplomacy' and of a mismanagement of expectations. It was almost inevitable that after the heady boom and exhilaration of the first moments, the 'bubble' would burst and depression set in – not only emotionally, but also in a quite literal economic sense in East Asia[28] – when it became clear to almost everyone that the Paris Peace Conference was, in many ways, but the continuation of the 'old order'.

Yet, contrary to previous historiography, ethnic particularism and anticolonial nationalism were not a foregone conclusion of this disillusionment. Regionalism and the emergence of wide-ranging pan-Islamic or pan-Asian networks in the first half of the 1920s seemed to offer a viable alternative.[29] Moreover, these movements were neither outright anti-Western nor opposed to the idea of universalism and Wilsonian ideals in principle. On the contrary, the failure of the Paris Peace Conference and the League of Nations in realising these only reconfirmed the belief – often shared in Europe – that Western civilisation had seen its last decline in the trenches of the war and that the Western powers had lost all claims to the moral and political authority to rule beyond Europe. 'Asia', on the other hand, became for the first time the pristine cipher for a truly new and moral order, a 'better Europe' (or better Wilsonian order), as it were, that would eventually save the world from the West, and Europe from itself. Similarly, intellectuals dreamed of a Muslim or Asian 'League of Nations' that would truly realise the promises of internationalism (ironically, Japan would reprise this internationalist rhetoric in the late 1930s when declaring the 'New Order in East Asia').

In fact, the case of Japan most clearly shows that politicians and intellectuals alike were rather reluctant to let go of the idea of a universalist concept of civilisation and commit themselves to ethnic particularism.[30] In China, too, the public outcry against the Allies' awarding of Shandong to Japan, which sparked the May Fourth Movement, did *not* mark an end to internationalism, but rather redirected the universalist enthusiasm of Chinese intellectuals to *other* forms of internationalism, such as anarchism.[31] The Indian subcontinent was a case on its own but here, too, the 'inner withdrawal' from the League of Nations, which soon set in among Indian intellectuals and activists, was more a reaction to the latter's perceived role as 'imperialist agent' rather than a renunciation of universalist notions.[32] Moreover, the Khilafat Movement, which sprang up in India and reached its peak between 1920 and 1923, demonstrated, with its support for the Ottoman–Turkish struggle for independence, a pan-Islamic concern that went well beyond national borders.[33]

At the same time, it cannot be denied that negative experiences with the Paris Peace Conference and the League of Nations considerably darkened the political outlook of many intellectuals and politicians in Asia. Thus, the Japanese quotation above, comparing 1919 with the French Revolution, made this reference not to emphasise the momentousness of the events (this hardly needed pointing out), but primarily to voice a profound scepticism: in the same way as the French Revolution had failed to realise its ideas for the mass of the people, so would the new Versailles order.[34] During the interwar period, 'hypocrisy' almost became a non-Western byword for the Western powers and their glib references to humanity, self-determination and democracy whenever the latter wanted to sugar-coat the wholesale redrawing of borders, the dislocation of populations and the placement of old colonies under new 'mandates'. This disillusionment was not, of course, particular to Asia, nor to the non-Western world, but was equally palpable, for example, in Germany, where people chafed at the 'dictate of Versailles'. However, the scepticism in non-Western countries may have been all the more visceral, as it saw racial bias as the root cause of the discrimination, a suspicion that only seemed to be confirmed by the rejection of the racial equality clause in April 1919. Thus, the notorious article of future Japanese Prime Minister Konoe Fumimaro, entitled 'A Call to Reject the Anglo-American Centered Peace' (1918), denounced the Western rhetoric of 'democracy' and 'humanitarianism' as an excuse for the continuation of nineteenth-century imperialist policies and was certainly not an extreme statement; rather, it was an excellent summary of the main arguments of non-Western opponents of the Versailles order in the 1920s.[35]

Yet, these interventions equally well illustrated the latent cynicism and hypocrisy of many *non-Western* actors. With astounding clarity and prescience, critics pointed out that the peace treaty forged in Paris would only recreate the old, conflicted order under new pretences: an armed peace precariously resting on a balance of power that would ultimately break down and result in another war.[36] Yet, ironically, their own governments– that is, 'Asian' powers such as Japan and the newly established Turkish regime in Ankara – were complicit in establishing this precarious order, so that the line between victim and perpetrator certainly did not run along the East–West divide. Thus, Japan and the new Turkish republic most actively demonstrated the sinister consequences of this 'dark Wilsonianism', as it were, particularly in forcibly relocating whole swathes of the population in the name of 'self-determination', or in occupying foreign territories (such as Manchuria) and establishing puppet regimes there with the self-same argumentation.

It is therefore no coincidence that the unravelling of the Versailles order began not in Europe, but in East Asia, and was set in motion by a radicalised part of the Japanese army stationed in Manchuria. However, from a non-Western perspective, the 'Manchurian Incident' of 1931 and Japan's subsequent withdrawal from the League of Nations in 1933 do not seem as momentous as Western observers would often have it. After all, the argumentative foundation for this manoeuvre had already been in place since the late 1920s, and its realisation was merely a matter of opportunity.[37] Moreover, considering the ingrained scepticism and even outright rejection that dominated non-Western attitudes towards the outcome of the Conference and particularly its institutional emblem, the League of Nations, it would be disingenuous to maintain the claim – as MacMillan, for example, does against her own evidence[38] – that there was no link between 1919 and the events of the 1930s. This assertion may hold true for European affairs, where a modicum of stability had been achieved by the mid-1920s, but the matter looks different from a non-European perspective. Thus, if we agree that the real failure of the Paris Peace Conference did not lie in its concrete results, but in the negative perception of it and in its failure to inspire trust and confidence in the new political order,[39] it is difficult to ignore the fact that Versailles failed most consistently and most durably not in Europe, but in the non-Western world. Moreover, it is only by taking this perspective that we can explain events that otherwise seem quite unrelated, but which, when added together, resulted in the truly global conflagration that is called the Second World War; this time, the conflagration was not limited to Europe, but truly encompassed all the regions on which Paris had had an impact.

Finally, we have to ask ourselves to what extent the failures of Versailles could be also considered the failures of our own time.[40] In 1994, a group of scholars commemorating the seventy-fifth anniversary of the Treaty of Versailles found their world 'saddled with a Versailles-era framework and Versailles-style rhetoric as it again confronts a Versailles-era reality'.[41] And, indeed, the end of the Cold War in 1989 brought back the same heady, inflationary idealism of 1918/19, including the notion that, with the death of one ideology (in 1919 imperialism, in 1989 Communism), the world had finally reached its destination (Francis Fukuyama), and visions of a 'New World Order' based on democracy and market capitalism (George H. W. Bush) abounded.[42] Consequently, the Gulf War of 1990–1 was cloaked in a 'neo-Wilsonian framework' of democracy and multilateralism to sanction what was arguably a rather unilateral agenda.[43] However, if the same scholars remarked that '[t]oday, Wilsonianism is triumphant,' they also agreed that the collapse of Yugoslavia put a severe damper on this triumphalism and that the euphoria had given way to disillusion and resignation.[44] Thus, the post-Cold War decade after 1989 followed the same pattern as the postwar decade after 1919, and it is probably no coincidence that the same disillusionment was caused by problems that – with the recognition of Yugoslavia – had been created in Paris in the first place.[45] Considering the general disillusionment, it is therefore not coincidental that justifications of the occupation of Iraq in 2003 referenced, in particular, neorealist security concerns rather than 'neo-Wilsonian ideals', and met with much fiercer global protest.

As we approach the centenary of the Paris Peace Conference in 2019, the continuing strife in the Middle East shows that we still carry problems with us that were seeded in 1919.[46] The same applies to the final failure of the Conference – namely, inspiring trust and confidence in the international order built by Western powers among the non-Western world; constant criticism of the allegedly 'Western-centric' human rights regime or Western-style democracy in East and Southeast Asia, or more radical anti-Western attacks in the Middle East and throughout the world remind us of that.[47] To overcome this mistrust in a dialogue that takes non-Western concerns, sensibilities and motivations seriously *on their own merits*, then, is the real challenge that Versailles still presents to us today.

The structure of this volume

The chapters in the first part of this volume aim to give a general overview of the impact that the Paris Peace Conference and the 'Versailles system' had on interwar Asia, synthesising a wide variety of regional perspectives as well as disciplinary angles. In a 'microhistory' of the global political economy of the years 1919 and 1920, Mark Metzler traces the economic shockwaves that went around the world after the war, and their simultaneous occurrence (and interference) with political, social and cultural developments in Asia. This sets the stage for studies of politics and identity, the entanglement of regional, religious, ethnic and national identities in transnational concepts, and their gradual suspension (but not extinction) in more nationalist agendas during the interwar period. Cemil Aydin discusses this complexity in relation to Muslim populations in the former Ottoman Empire, India and Southeast Asia, while Torsten Weber focuses on the network of pan-Asianists in East Asia.

Chapters of the second part zoom in, as it were, on geographically more narrowly defined perspectives of Versailles and study particular modes and practices through which the signals that emanated from Paris were transformed into beliefs, movements and fashions among national audiences in Asia. Naoko Shimazu leads with an investigation into the performative nature of the Paris Peace Conference and the role of media in Wilsonian politics, focusing particularly on the relative success of the Japanese delegation as 'actors' on the international stage. Studies in political, religious and intellectual history further demonstrate the differentiated responses to Versailles in various constituencies, such as Japanese Buddhists (John LoBreglio) and jurists (Kevin Doak), Indian activists (Maria Framke) or Chinese anarchists (Gotelind Müller). A chapter on the material culture and gender aspect of modern urban society, particularly 1920s Shanghai, finally demonstrates the responses to and convergence with the 'new order' on the cultural and social side of Asian societies (Hiroko Sakamoto). The following section will give a brief outline of some of the central arguments and observations of the individual chapters.

As Mark Metzler shows in the first chapter of this volume, the war and the years immediately following the peace triggered a veritable storm of globalisation, the repercussions of which still remain with us today. In the surprising transnational synchronicity of events, Asia not only was closely interlinked with European phenomena, but also, at times, even played a pacesetter role. This becomes particularly apparent when looking at the economic impact of the early postwar period, in turn closely linked to the social, cultural and ideological shockwaves that rippled through Europe, the United States and Asia. The chapter demonstrates this through a microhistory of the years 1919 and 1920, the boom-and-bust cycle of which prefigured *in nuce* the global cycle of developments until 1931.

Thus, although the First World War was concentrated on Europe in military terms, its destructive force spread all over the globe through indirect catastrophes such as pandemics and famines. With the end of the war and the sudden release of capital and labour, however, Asia experienced an economic boom, and China and India saw a brief but 'golden' age of capitalism. The end of war in Europe also marked the beginning of speculation in Asia, particularly in Japan. It is no coincidence that this 'bullish' economic phase was paralleled by the buoyant and heady idealism of the Wilsonian Declaration and the Bolshevik Revolution, as well as other political, social and cultural movements, such as Islamic nationalism (see Aydin's chapter in this book), pan-Asianism (see Weber), the Taishō democracy in Japan (see LoBreglio), and the May Fourth and New Culture Movements and female activism in China (see Müller and Sakamoto's chapters). In the same way as the 'Wilsonian bubble' and the 'world revolution' bubble burst soon after and gave way to more realism, disillusion and reactionary tendencies, however, the speculative bubble collapsed first in Japan and sent the country into deflation (a word that was coined at this time). This signalled the beginning of the international deflation that lasted into the 1930s. Thus the bubble-and-bust cycle of the years 1919/20 in many respects echoed through the following decade, not only on the economy, but also in many intertwined spheres of political, social and cultural developments on a global scale. The unprecedented synchronicity ended only in 1931 with the collapse of the gold standard that brought down the economic system, and the Manchurian Incident that equally signalled the end of the tenuously achieved postwar equilibrium after Versailles.

Cemil Aydin takes the discussion to the political sphere and studies the complex web of entanglements that politicians and intellectuals in Muslim-majority regions of Asia and North Africa had to navigate during the long years of war between 1911 and 1924, torn between multiple and often conflicting (imperial, both British and Ottoman, pan-Islamic and nationalist) identities. The study focuses particularly on the significant role that the institution of caliphate played in the modulation of these identities. Aydin thereby challenges a number of assumptions – most importantly, the linear decolonisation narrative of a straightforward progression from imperialism to nationalism – by re-emphasising the importance of pan-Islamic ideals in the transformation process and also by looking at the impact of Versailles from a long-term perspective that acknowledges the regionally and chronologically differentiated experience of World War I and its aftermath in the Muslim world.

Thus, it was the Italian invasion of Libya as early as 1911 that led to the pan-Islamic mobilisation of worldwide Muslim networks. Aid and solidarity (such as donations to the Red Crescent Society from countries stretching from Central Asia to India and Southeast Asia) continued throughout World War I, and the Ottoman Empire strategically sought to utilise pan-Islamism in its imperial war by interpreting the event as a Muslim liberation war against a new crusade on the part of, especially, Britain. The strategy was unsuccessful, however, as it particularly failed to address the complexity and entanglement of Muslim identities in different regions: Muslims in British India, for example, preferred to keep multiple loyalties, both to the crown and to the caliph, and trusted in an implicit contract that, in exchange for their loyalty to and military support for the crown, the latter would respect the sanctity of the caliphate and the holy cities in return.

In this, Muslims were disappointed when World War I ended. Not only were Istanbul and the holy cities occupied, but also the Ottoman Empire did not receive a Wilsonian deal like Eastern Europe, substantial parts of it being placed under the 'mandate system' as a continuation of Western colonialism. As we have already noted, the pan-Islamic Khilafat Movement in India, which reached its peak between 1920 and 1923 and supported the Ottoman–Turkish struggle for independence, was a direct expression of Muslim disillusionment with the Western powers' deceitfulness.

It is also against this background of pressure that the Turkish government could reject the Sèvres Treaty and negotiate the Lausanne Treaty of 1923. Ironically, however, the success of pan-Islamic pressure politics also led to its demise, as the Turkish government abolished the Caliphate in 1924 in a pragmatic power calculation, thus renouncing any transnational claims to Muslim solidarity abroad. Even after the abolishment of the Caliphate and the loss of its spiritual leadership, Muslim regionalist imagination continued to live on and influence various political changes in the Muslim world. Against the overwhelming dominance of the old imperialism and new nationalism, however, it never regained the status it had during the war and early interwar period.

Torsten Weber takes up the problem of regional identities in the face of Western imperialism and discusses various manifestations of an Asianist discourse in interwar East Asia as a positive and affirmative critique of Western modernity and globalisation. Thus, prior to World War I, the association of Japan with Asia was highly unpopular. It was only during the war that 'Asia' in different parts of East Asia became positively recharged as a critique of Western modernity and globalisation, not only in Japan, but also among Chinese intellectuals. The Paris Peace Conference, then, finally gave rise to an 'Asianist momentum of Versailles' in East Asia, not, however, as a direct positive response to its political outcomes, but rather as a revisionist critique of it and the underlying Western hypocrisy. Thus, grassroots movements in Japan, as well as in China, sought to promote an Asianism that was neither intrinsically anti-Western nor essentialising 'Asian'; a consciously constructivist approach was adopted that conceived of 'Asia as a method', seeking to develop an Asia that was a 'better West': that is, one that sought to overcome all of its shortcomings, as demonstrated in the cataclysm of World War I and the hypocrisy of the Western powers at the Paris Peace Conference. The slogan 'Asia for Asians' thus combined two Wilsonian ideals, self-determination and internationalism. Moreover, common to all Asianist thought was the idea of an 'Asian League' as a regionalised and *better* League of Nations, as well as the ideal of racial equality.

Japanese, Chinese and Indian intellectuals met in 1926 for the first Pan-Asianist Congress in Nagasaki with the declared aim of creating such an Asian League, with more or less the same goals as the League of Nations in Geneva. Moreover, racial equality provided another item of identification for pan-Asianists in East Asia. Japanese politicians kept their distance from these grassroots movements, although partly sympathetic to their goals. In general, Japanese imperialism did not fit comfortably with the pan-Asianist agenda. Thus, when the Pan-Asianist Congress met for the second time in 1927 in Shanghai, it was already against a background of Japanese–Chinese competition and Japanese aggression on the continent. Asianism as a counter-narrative to Western hypocrisy lost its credibility and the brief window of the 'Asianist momentum of Versailles' closed. All that remained was the rhetoric of pan-Asianism, which the Japanese state re-employed in the 1930s and early 1940s in a cynical propaganda bid for Asian solidarity among the 'member states' of the Greater East Asia Co-Prosperity Sphere.

The second part of this volume opens with Naoko Shimazu's study of the performative nature of the Paris Peace Conference and the new role of mass media in international (image) politics. Thus, World War I was also fought as a media battle, as a war to dominate the *interpretation* of the conflict. The Paris Peace Conference continued this struggle, all the more so as it was staged as a media spectacle under the eyes of the global public. In a way, this was the direct outcome of President Wilson's call for open diplomacy, which 'shall proceed always frankly and in the public view' (the first of his Fourteen Points) – however, with unintended consequences for its participants. Henceforth and until this day, international summits have turned into a pageant – a theatrical stage, as it were, on which not necessarily the better arguments, but the better performances of the actors decide who succeeds in the public eye and in national polls. Thus, the Paris Peace Conference can be seen as the first instance of modern global summitry.

Shimazu demonstrates the new importance of performativity and symbolic images in the case of Japan's role in the Paris Peace Conference. Despite the relative success of the Japanese delegation in securing its most important goals – namely, its newly acquired territorial possessions in Shandong and Micronesia, Japan's participation in the Paris Peace Conference was seen as a failure, which seemed to demonstrate that Japan was not yet ready to act as a global power in international politics. The rejection of the racial equality clause in particular was a tragic public relations debacle, which became symbolic of Japan's failure to live up to the public's expectations of its leadership. The disillusion, not only among the highly-strung Japanese public, but also among participants of the delegation, was fateful: it discredited the Japanese Ministry of Foreign Affairs and, by extension, diplomacy per se in the eyes of the Japanese public, and played to military circles. It also led to a profound embitterment with the new status quo in international politics among the younger participants of the delegation, who, upon becoming the leaders of Japan in the 1930s, had the ambition to overcome it and re-establish Japan's status as a leading power on its own terms.

Maria Framke's chapter deals with the Indian reactions to the Paris Peace Conference and particularly the founding of the League of Nations. India was a founding member of the League, but was in a very precarious and anomalous position. Although India was represented in the League, it had no voice of its own being its only non-sovereign state. And although 'self-government' had been the proclaimed dream of Versailles, as in many other cases, the reality soon demonstrated that the League seemed more of an instrument to uphold the status quo rather than change it in favour of weak and dependent states. India's experience, despite its anomalous position, can thus be read as representative of most non-Western members' experience of the League of Nations and the fateful reactions of their elites to it.

Framke examines the perception of the League of Nations in Indian newspapers and journals, as well as by Indian nationalists. Initial reactions to Versailles and the founding of the League of Nations resembled responses from small or oppressed peoples throughout the globe: namely, enthusiasm for Wilson's 'self-determination', which naturally corresponded with the Indian nationalists' call for *swaraj*: that is, 'self-rule' vis-à-vis the British. As in other parts of the globe, however, frenzied enthusiasm gave way to disillusionment as critics realised that the League, rather than improving India's situation, in fact *protected* the status quo and kept India in limbo. The Indian National Congress soon ceased bringing its demands to the League of Nations, and by the mid-1920s a decidedly negative view of the League prevailed among the Indian public. Opinion leaders such as Gandhi, Nehru and Bose all considered the League as just another imperialist agent on the side of Britain or France. Eventually, feeling utterly frustrated by both the unresponsiveness of Britain to their demands and the League of Nation's indifference, Indian intellectuals and activists resorted to new forms of political resistance: namely, the 'non-cooperation movement' first and then 'civil disobedience' after 1929. Thus, one could argue that, firstly, withdrawal from the League of Nations was an option considered long before 1933 in non-Western countries, and that, secondly, 'non-cooperation' and 'civil disobedience' also symbolised, in a way, an 'inner withdrawal' of Indian intellectuals from the League of Nations. As in many other non-Western countries, the League of Nations thus *did* eventually bring self-determination and self-government, but on an indirect and largely *negative* path of disillusionment and protest against its perceived imperialist agenda.

John LoBreglio's chapter studies the psychological impact that the Versailles Peace Conference had on parts of the Japanese public and the reasons why even moderately progressive, internationalist-leaning intellectuals of the time supported Japan's confrontational course of all-out war against the Allies in the 1930s. The author focuses on the writings of Japanese Buddhists on the occasion of the Paris Peace Conference and, in doing so, challenges two important assumptions in Japanese political and intellectual history: firstly, the rather simplistic juxtaposition of 1920s internationalism and 1930s ultranationalism; and secondly, the 'revisionist' view of the Paris Peace Conference (represented, for example, by Margaret MacMillan) that, contrary to its own evidence, seeks to dissociate the Conference from the developments of the 1930s, not even considering the profound psychological effect that the Conference and its results had on the rest of the world.

LoBreglio argues that Japanese Buddhists – like many others – interpreted World War I as a trigger for 'the profound reversal of world destiny'. As such, they invested – again in line with large parts of the global public – great hopes in the Paris Peace Conference as the chance for a new world order on the basis of Wilsonian principles. In a familiar pattern, however, the same writers soon became disillusioned and harshly criticised the Conference as a continuation of the war, the greed, hypocrisy and infighting of which had caused the conflict in the first place. The seemingly blatant hypocrisy in particular became the predominant motif among the Japanese public in the following decades. In reverse proportionality to the disillusionment with the West, Asia and its leading power, Japan, became invested with the 'spiritual' mission to heal the ills of Western civilisation and, thus, initiate not only the salvation *of* the West, but also, globally, the salvation of the world *from* the West. The Paris Peace Conference in 1919 thus had a profound psychological impact on the Japanese: it reconfirmed and deepened a long-standing mistrust of the Anglo-American nations, even among moderate, internationalist-minded Japanese, and made the public all the more receptive to the ultranationalist propaganda of the 1930s. Many Japanese observers therefore considered a war between Japan and the United States inevitable and bound to happen within a ten- to twenty-year range. Ironically, the same comments also betrayed a conspicuous blind spot in the Japanese perspective: namely, Japan's own imperialist conduct in East Asia, the unequal treatment of its colonial subjects in Korea and Taiwan in particular, and the unconscious hypocrisy of their own criticism. Thus, while Japan and the Japanese public prided themselves as the champions of racial equality (and discriminatory treatment of the Ainu domestically was criticised), national self-determination was anathema, and protesting Koreans were considered 'unpatriotic'.

Taking up a number of motifs from previous chapters, Kevin Doak further develops these in a study on the interplay of universalism and ethnic nationalism in Japanese post-Wilsonian visions of international order. Japanese intellectuals understood very well the momentous political and epistemic change that the Great War brought to the world. As such, they compared the war with the French Revolution but, typically for the Japanese perspective, with a negative twist: as the French Revolution failed to realise its ideas for the mass of the people, so would the new Versailles order, particularly in its Wilsonian insistence on 'peoples' and ethnicities as the basic political order, fail to bring the global peace it envisioned. Japanese politicians, too, were reluctant to let go of the idea of a universalist concept of civilisation and place their faith in ethnic particularism, which they saw as ultimately destructive for the state and as the seed of a new war. Throughout the 1920s, they grappled with new solutions to reconcile traditional universalism with the new tendency towards particularism.

According to traditional historiography, the 1930s seemingly witnessed a decisive and uniform shift in Japan towards ethnic particularism. However, as Doak argues, some intellectuals still tried to defend the concepts of universalism against the onslaught of nationalism by recourse to the concepts of Natural Law. Doak demonstrates this by examining the case of Tanaka Kōtarō, a law professor at Tokyo Imperial University (and later President of the Supreme Court), who, on the basis of a religiously founded Natural Law, developed the idea of a 'World Law' (*sekai-hō*). This was a critique of both Western international law and Japan's particularist 'New Order in East Asia' and sought to constrain both the state and the nation (*minzoku*) within the confines of a universally (and transcendentally) founded order. As such, Tanaka was in the minority, but his aim to contain ethnic nationalism through recourse to universalism was shared by many Japanese legal experts and intellectuals of the time.

Gotelind Müller similarly challenges orthodox (Chinese) historiography, which places the May Fourth Movement of 1919, as a catalytic event for the rise to Chinese nationalism and the birth of Communism in China, at the centre of Chinese responses to Versailles. This narrative, which is taught even today in Chinese history textbooks, reduces the responses of 1919 to a teleology that eventually leads to the founding of the People's Republic of China three decades later, thereby writing out of the picture a host of political and intellectual currents that existed or were even more dominant in China at the time. Such is especially the case with the Chinese anarchist movement, whose internationalism coexisted with – if not dominated – Chinese nationalism until well into the 1920s.

Chinese anarchism, from its beginnings in the first decade of the twentieth century, had very strong internationalist leanings and had particularly strong ties to Japanese as well as French anarchist groups. The Chinese anarchist community in Paris (which, among others, educated future leaders of the Communist Party such as Zhou Enlai and Deng Xiaoping) witnessed the Paris peace negotiations. When the news broke that Japan would keep Shandong, they too pressured the Chinese delegation to withdraw from the conference, in the same way as protesters did in Beijing and Shanghai. However, contrary to the orthodox narrative, internationalism did *not* end with the May Fourth Movement and was not superseded by nationalism. Wilsonian internationalism may have been discredited in China after 1919 but other brands of internationalism lived on. In fact, the Shandong disaster even confirmed Chinese anarchists in their belief that national governments could not be trusted. Consequently, they did not put much faith in the League of Nations either, which was seen as an aggregation of state egotism. In a way, the failure of Wilsonianism even boosted the status of anarchist internationalism. The early 1920s marked the peak of its influence in China, and Chinese anarchists maintained close connections with Japanese and Korean anarchists well into the early 1930s. Communism, too, was initially considered as truly 'internationalist'. It was only in the latter half of the 1920s that nationalism finally superseded internationalism as the dominant factor in the dynamics of Chinese reunification.

Hiroko Sakamoto, in the final chapter of this volume, readdresses the question of nationalism in post-Versailles China and, from the perspective of popular culture and media, demonstrates how various *forms* of nationalism could coexist with an intrinsically globalised, consumer-oriented cosmopolitanism in interwar Chinese urban culture. The May Fourth Movement, triggered by the Paris Peace Conference, and its cultural counterpart, the New Culture Movement, are routinely interpreted as the iconic response to these challenges of Japanese and Western imperialism, and as a symbolic starting point for Chinese nationalism.[48] However, as Mark Metzler has pointed out in the first chapter of this volume, the end of World War I also coincided with an extraordinary synchronicity of global developments, not only politically or economically, but also on a social, cultural and ideological level. Looking beyond the often simplifying interpretations of the origins of Chinese nationalism at the ways in which urban mass culture in particular changed during the 'political season' and its aftermath, we can observe a more sophisticated picture of different *forms* of nationalism penetrating Chinese society, which shared much in common with global trends just as it revealed significant changes in Chinese society itself.

Sakamoto demonstrates this with a close reading of cartoons and advertisements published in Shanghai magazines between 1919 and 1931, paying special attention to the gendered dimension of the illustrations. Thus, as was to be expected during the 'political season', illustrators routinely extolled democracy and the October Revolution, and lambasted the unsavoury redistribution of political and economic rights during the Paris Peace Conference. Advertisements appealed to the patriotism of consumers by calling for a boycott of foreign (especially Japanese) goods and for the purchase of domestic products. Moreover, commentators also criticised Western culture as materialist and argued for a reassessment of Asian cultures. Yet, the illustrations also registered more subtle and surprising changes. Thus, illustrations of the May Fourth Movement also showed female activists for the first time, and women became associated with the nationalistic paradigm. Advertisements began to show women smoking and pursuing urban pleasures in defiance of Confucianist gender roles. In the late 1920s, these 'modern girls' became icons of Shanghai's urban culture, often portrayed with much more strength and independence than men. At the same time, however, this also demonstrated a synchronicity of global urban culture that linked Shanghai with Tokyo, Berlin or New York, particularly during the 1930s. Thus in general, in contrast to the highly politicised and polarising atmosphere of the early 1920s, the illustrations of the late 1920s demonstrate a much more relaxed and confident attitude towards political and cultural issues and, particularly in the role of women, show that the earlier mass movements triggered by Versailles had, indeed, brought about substantial political and social change.

Notes

1. On the progress of the Paris Peace Conference and related peace treaties, see MacMillan, *Paris 1919*; Marston, *The Peace Conference of 1919*; Cohrs, *Unfinished Peace*, pp. 20–74; Steiner, *Lights that Failed*, pp. 15–130.
2. Kunz, 'A Comment', p. 523.
3. Boemeke, Feldman and Glaser, 'Introduction', pp. 3–4; Fischer and Sharp (eds), *After the Versailles Treaty*, pp. 1–3.
4. MacMillan, *Paris 1919*, p. 459.
5. Cf. MacMillan, *Paris 1919*, pp. 3–16 and illustration no. 1. See also Ch. 4 in this volume.
6. Article 22 of the Covenant of the League of Nations.
7. As cited in MacMillan, *Paris 1919*, p. 435. Balfour himself was not innocent of callousness, either, as MacMillan, *Paris 1919*, p. 443 shows.
8. See Ch. 2 (Aydin) in this book. On the end of the Ottoman Empire, see Reynolds, *Shattering Empires*; Macfie, *End of the Ottoman Empire*.
9. See Ch. 5 (Framke) in this book. On India's involvement in the war, see Singh, *Testimonies of Indian Soldiers*; Jarboe and Fogarty (eds), *Empires in World War I*, Chs 4 and 11.
10. See Ch. 4 (Shimazu) in this book. On Japan's role in the war and at the Conference, see MacMillan, *Paris 1919*, pp. 306–44; Shimazu, *Japan, Race and Equality*; Burkman, *Japan and the League of Nations*; Minohara et al. (eds), *The Decade of the Great War*; Frattolillo and Best (eds), *Japan and the Great War*; Dickinson, *War and National Reinvention*.
11. See Chs 8 (Müller) and 9 (Sakamoto) in this book. For China's role in the war and at the Conference, see MacMillan, *Paris 1919*, pp. 322–44; Xu, *China and the Great War*; Elleman, *Wilson and China*.
12. For exceptions, see also Burkman, *Japan and the League*; and particularly Manela, *The Wilsonian Moment*. Most recently, see also Xu, *Asia and the Great War*.
13. For a particularly influential contemporary assessment, see Keynes, *The Economic Consequences*. For a recent study, see Graebner and Bennett, *The Versailles Treaty and Its Legacy*.
14. Cf. Boemeke, Feldman and Glaser (eds), *The Treaty of Versailles*; Cohrs, *The Unfinished Peace*; Fischer and Sharp (eds), *After the Versailles Treaty*.
15. Apart from referencing the main treaty, this volume uses 'Versailles' in a metonymic way, i.e. to denote the Paris Peace Conference, the associated treaties, and even, in a wider sense, the 'new order' associated with it and the Wilsonian spirit it represented.
16. See Ch. 1 (Metzler) in this book.
17. See Ch. 7 (Doak) in this book.
18. For an outline of Wilsonianism and its emergence, see Manela, *Wilsonian Moment*, pp. 16–62.
19. See Chs 2 (Aydin), 3 (Weber) and 6 (LoBreglio), respectively.
20. Cf. Shimazu, *Japan, Race and Equality*.

21. Shimazu, *Japan, Race and Equality*; Manela, *Wilsonian Moment*, pp. 35–43.
22. See Ch. 1 in this book.
23. See Ch. 4 (Shimazu) in this book.
24. Carr, *The Twenty Years' Crisis*, pp. 31–6.
25. Cf. Brown and Minichiello, *Taisho Chic*.
26. Manela, *Wilsonian Moment*, p. 33.
27. See Ch. 9 (Sakamoto) in this book.
28. See Ch. 1 (Metzler) in this book.
29. See Chs 2 (Aydin) and 3 (Weber) in this book.
30. See Ch. 7 (Doak) in this book.
31. See Ch. 8 (Müller) in this book.
32. See Ch. 5 (Framke) in this book.
33. See Ch. 2 (Aydin) in this book.
34. See Ch. 7 (Doak) in this book.
35. Cf. Hotta, 'Konoe Fumimaro', with an abbreviated translation of the article (pp. 315–17).
36. See Ch. 6 (LoBreglio) in this book.
37. Cf. Zachmann, *Völkerrechtsdenken und Außenpolitik*, pp. 159–203.
38. MacMillan, *Paris 1919*, pp. 493–4.
39. Boemeke et al., 'Introduction', p. 17; Kunz, 'A Comment'.
40. Cf. Kunz, 'A Comment', pp. 529, 532.
41. Kunz, 'A Comment', p. 532. See also Steel, 'Prologue: 1919–1945–1989'.
42. Fukuyama, 'The End of History?'; Steel, 'Prologue', 23.
43. Steel, 'Prologue', 23.
44. Steel, 'Prologue', pp. 21, 24.
45. On the making of Yugoslavia, see MacMillan, *Paris 1919*, pp. 109–24; Lederer, *Yugoslavia at the Paris Peace Conference*.
46. See Ch. 2 (Aydin) and MacMillan, *Paris 1919*, pp. 347–455; Steiner, *Lights that Failed*, pp. 100–30, with further references.
47. Cf. Nasu and Saul (eds), *Human Rights in the Asia–Pacific Region*; Bell, *East Meets West*; Euben and Zaman (eds), *Princeton Readings in Islamist Thought*.
48. See also the critical discussion of this assumption in the chapter before (Müller).

References

Bell, Daniel A., *East Meets West: Human Rights and Democracy in East Asia* (Princeton: Princeton University Press, 2000).

Boemeke, Manfred F., Gerald D. Feldman and Elisabeth Glaser (eds), *The Treaty of Versailles: A Reassessment after 75 Years* (New York: Cambridge University Press, 1998).

Boemeke, Manfred F., Gerald D. Feldman and Elisabeth Glaser, 'Introduction', in Manfred F. Boemeke, Gerald D. Feldman and Elisabeth Glaser (eds), *The Treaty of Versailles: A Reassessment after 75 Years* (New York: Cambridge University Press, 1998), pp. 1–20.

Brown, Kendall H. and Sharon Minichiello, *Taisho Chic: Japanese Modernity, Nostalgia and Deco* (Honolulu: Honolulu Academy of Arts, 2001).

Burkman, Thomas W., *Japan and the League of Nations: Empire and World Order, 1914–1938* (Honolulu: Hawai'i University Press, 2008).

Carr, Edward Hallett, *The Twenty Years' Crisis, 1919–1939* (London: Macmillan, 1939).

Cohrs, Patrick O., *The Unfinished Peace after World War I: America, Britain and the Stabilisation of Europe, 1919–1932* (Cambridge: Cambridge University Press, 2006).

Dickinson, Frederick R., *War and National Reinvention: Japan in the Great War, 1914–1919* (Cambridge, MA: Harvard University Asia Center, 1999).

Elleman, Bruce A., *Wilson and China: A Revised History of the Shandong Question* (Armonk, NY: M. E. Sharpe, 2002).

Euben, Roxanne L. and Muhammad Qasim Zaman (eds), *Princeton Readings in Islamist Thought: Texts and Contexts from al-Banna to Bin Laden* (Princeton: Princeton University Press, 2009).

Fischer, Conan and Alan Sharp (eds), *After the Versailles Treaty: Enforcement, Compliance, Contested Identities* (London: Routledge, 2008).

Frattolillo, Oliviero and Antony Best (eds), *Japan and the Great War* (Basingstoke: Palgrave Macmillan, 2015).

Fukuyama, Francis, 'The End of History?', *The National Interest*, 16 (Summer 1989), pp. 3–16.

Graebner, Norman A. and Edward M. Bennett, *The Versailles Treaty and Its Legacy: The Failure of the Wilsonian Vision* (Cambridge: Cambridge University Press, 2011).

Hotta, Eri, 'Konoe Fumimaro, "A Call to Reject the Anglo-American Centered Peace," 1918', in Sven Saaler and Christopher Szpilman (eds), *Pan-Asianism: A Documentary History* (Lanham, MD: Rowman & Littlefield, 2011), vol. 1, pp. 311–17.

Jarboe, Andrew Tait and Richard S. Fogarty, *Empires in World War I: Shifting Frontiers and Imperial Dynamics in a Global Conflict* (London: I. B. Tauris, 2014).

Keynes, John Maynard, *The Economic Consequences of the Peace* (London: Macmillan, 1919).

Kunz, Diane B., 'A Comment', in Manfred F. Boemeke, Gerald D. Feldman and Elisabeth Glaser (eds), *The Treaty of Versailles: A Reassessment after 75 Years* (New York: Cambridge University Press, 1998), pp. 523–32.

Lederer, Ivo J., *Yugoslavia at the Peace Conference: A Study in Frontiermaking* (New Haven: Yale University Press, 1963).

Macfie, A. L., *The End of the Ottoman Empire, 1908–1923* (London: Longman, 1998).

MacMillan, Margaret, *Paris 1919: Six Months that Changed the World* (New York: Random House, 2001).

Manela, Erez, *The Wilsonian Moment: Self-Determination and the International Origins of Anticolonial Nationalism* (Oxford: Oxford University Press, 2007).

Marston, Frank S., *The Peace Conference of 1919: Organization and Procedure* (London: Oxford University Press, 1944).

Minohara, Toshihiro, Tze-Ki Hon and Evan Dawley (eds), *The Decade of the Great War: Japan and the Wider World in the 1910s* (Boston: Brill, 2014).

Nasu, Hitoshi and Ben Saul (eds), *Human Rights in the Asia–Pacific Region: Towards Institution Building* (London: Routledge, 2011).

Reynolds, Michael A., *Shattering Empires: The Clash and Collapse of the Ottoman and Russian Empires, 1908–1918* (Cambridge: Cambridge University Press, 2011).

Shimazu, Naoko, *Japan, Race and Equality: The Racial Equality Proposal of 1919* (London: Routledge, 1998).

Singh, G., *The Testimonies of Indian Soldiers and the Two World Wars: Between Self and Sepoy* (London: Bloomsbury, 2014).

Steel, Ronald, 'Prologue: 1919–1945–1989', in Manfred F. Boemeke, Gerald D. Feldman and Elisabeth Glaser (eds), *The Treaty of Versailles: A Reassessment after 75 Years* (New York: Cambridge University Press, 1998), pp. 21–34.

Steiner, Zara, *The Lights that Failed: European International History, 1919–1933* (Oxford: Oxford University Press, 2005).

Xu, Guoqi, *China and the Great War: China's Pursuit of a New National Identity and Internationalization* (Cambridge: Cambridge University Press, 2005).

Xu, Guoqi, *Asia and the Great War: A Shared History* (Oxford: Oxford University Press, 2016)

Zachmann, Urs Matthias, *Völkerrechtsdenken und Außenpolitik in Japan, 1919–1960* [The Japanese Discourse on International Law and Foreign Policy, 1919–1960] (Baden-Baden: Nomos, 2013).

Part I

Chapter 1

The Correlation of Crises, 1918–20

MARK METZLER

Hundreds of millions of people who missed the news of Sarajevo or of Versailles nevertheless felt the shocks generated by Europe's war and peace. Of all the effects of the war and its settlement, the economic shocks, transmitted by the great rise and then fall of prices, may have been most universal in their social incidence. They were also global in their geographical reach. These economic revolutions were connected inextricably with the political and ideational movements that have received the largest share of historians' attention.

World War I induced extraordinary transnational flows of masses of people (especially young men) and material supplies. With these masses of people on the move came an amplified interchange of ideas. With them came also an amplified flow of disease pathogens. At the same time, the war blockaded other, pre-existing flows of people, goods and so on. Among the flows of information was an enormous flow of financial messages designating the privilege of employing newly created *credits*, meaning also the future obligation to repay newly created debts. These monetary messages corresponded to flows of material resources – and they signified the greatest international transfer of claims to wealth that had yet happened in such a temporally concentrated way. Simultaneously with these flows and counterflows of material goods and immaterial promises to pay, wartime embargoes and restrictions blocked the actual physical shipments of the gold and silver specie then used to settle international debts.

These new flows and blockages entailed extraordinary shifts in the prices of goods and extraordinary shifts in the relative values of different kinds of money. 'At the margin', as economists like to say, these notational revaluations meant very real changes in access to material resources, including food. The consequences of these changes included hunger, industrial strikes and food riots.

At multiple time scales, this postwar moment formed a hinge in social time. In common with earlier wars, World War I was followed in 1919 and 1920 by a rapid sequence of postwar boom followed by postwar depression. Historians have devoted attention to many individual aspects of this globally synchronous movement, but remarkably, it has not been grasped comprehensively as either an Asian or as a global phenomenon.[1] This chapter aims to integrate historical understandings by sketching out some dimensions of region-wide correlation. To state one conclusion at the outset: the transnational flows, surges and crashes of this period demonstrate how important it is to look *laterally* in time and to collate local–national histories that are often studied separately. To do this requires close attention to the *timing* of events. It also requires attention to the timing of ideas and their shifting expressions. In this view, economic, cultural and political analyses are different ways of imaging a common process. (Whose life-course is not enmeshed in all of these?) In this view, Asian countries were less incidental participants in a Europe-centred process and more in the middle of a global current.

Flows and shocks

Europe's war itself may have been a distant foreign disturbance for most people in Asia, but in Asia, as in Europe, the years 1918–20 were extraordinarily dense in the types of events that we usually record as historically meaningful. One can begin to analyse this interval by picturing a series of shocks, happening in rapid succession and echoing across the region. Before going into detail, it will help simply to list them.

1. *Export booms; embargoes; price increases.* Across the world outside of Europe, Europe's wartime demand for goods raised prices and profits and induced great increases of agricultural and industrial production. The effects of this 'positive' demand shock began to appear in 1915 and 1916. This was also Asia's first modern boom in the export of factory-made industrial goods. A comparable boom would not recur in most countries of the region for another thirty-five years. At the same time, shipments of gold and silver were restricted by the combatant countries, as were various basic goods needed for war production, constraining the supply for civilian use. There were myriad shortages and bottlenecks, especially in transportation (and especially for India, from where the British took railway carriages and ships for the war effort). Enlarged export flows out of Asia were thus, to a significant extent, not repaid by direct return flows of goods or specie. They were paid for instead with promises, meaning the creation of huge short-term credits, which raised prices. Export booms in some sectors raised prices for all sectors.
2. A *grain supply shock*, from the spring to the autumn of 1918, came on top of these wartime shortages and price increases. In 1918, an El Niño drought caused harvest shortfalls in many parts of India especially. Shortages and soaring prices set off waves of rice riots in South India and Japan, where the Rice Riots of 1918 remain the greatest instance of mass civil unrest in modern Japanese history. There was a second rice supply shock in Southeast Asia in 1919.
3. A *pandemic shock*, in the spring, summer and autumn of 1918, coincided in time with the grain supply shock. The overlaying of the influenza pandemic and the provisioning crisis intensified the pandemic's effects, especially in India, where many millions died. Indian influenza deaths accounted for perhaps one-half or more of the world total.

4. An international *workers' revolt* came also in 1918 and 1919, in the form of a global and region-wide strike wave. This was the greatest wave of strikes yet in the industrial history of most Asian countries, where local industrial booms drew rural migrants into burgeoning urban centres. The inflation of the cost of daily necessities was a decisive factor in intensifying and synchronising these social struggles, and in fostering popular sympathy with them. Happening against the world news background of the Russian Revolution, these industrial actions took on a sharp political edge, as understood both by labour activists and by ruling and owning elites.
5. An *'armistice shock'*, economically speaking, happened after November 1918, when the end of the war threatened export prospects. This economic setback was followed in 1919 by a renewed boom based on pent-up wartime industrial and consumer demand, restocking of inventories and European reconstruction.
6. A series of *postwar political shocks* came in the spring of 1919, including those emanating out of the Paris Peace Conference. These events are remembered as the beginning of mass-based national awakening movements in countries across the region: the March First (1919) Movement in Japanese-occupied Korea; the May Fourth (1919) Movement in China, which echoed through overseas Chinese communities in Southeast Asia; and the simultaneous explosive development of national movements in Dutch-occupied Indonesia and in British-occupied India.
7. A second *inflation shock* occurred after June 1919. That was when the US government lifted its wartime embargo on the export of gold and silver specie, releasing a great outflow of monetary metals that helped restart an international inflationary boom. In a kind of snap-the-whip effect, this postwar boom developed into a speculative financial bubble, which came to a head in 1920 in Tokyo, Osaka, Bombay and elsewhere.
8. A *deflation shock* in the spring of 1920 abruptly terminated the inflationary postwar boom. The postwar bubble burst first in Japan in March 1920. In the late spring and summer of the year, deflation and depression spread out internationally. In the fall of 1920, financial markets crashed in India. The initial wave of financial panics was followed by a steep international depression.

In a full social and cultural history, one would add a number of other shocks to this list. Most conspicuous internationally were the effects of movements for *democracy*, *socialism* and *women's rights*. These were transformative shocks in the consciousness of new participants in these movements, as they were 'alarm' shocks to those invested in the authority structures these movements opposed. They thus had a dual character also, energising those sympathetic to them while also inducing a strong reactionary movement: here too, the biennium 1919–20 appears as a hinge in social time.

The remainder of this essay surveys how some of these shocks shot back and forth across the intercommunicating social and commercial space of flows of maritime Asia during this historically dense interval.

The export boom and the accumulation of debts

To comprehend the global economic process after Versailles, it is useful to envision a picture of nested economic cycles operating at different timescales but all turning on the pivot of 1919–20. At a long-term, centennial scale, there was a reframing of the international political order, as the Vienna system of 1815 was replaced by the ultimately unsuccessful Paris system, as discussed in Cemil Aydin's contribution to this volume. Not only politically minded observers but also economically minded ones were attentive to the historical parallels to what happened a century before. They focused on the problems associated with wartime paper-money inflation and the prospective restoration of 'hard money', meaning deflation.[2]

At a medium-term timescale of multiple decades, this was the turn of a global inflation–deflation macrocycle – an economic long wave – that had begun 24 years before, in 1895–6. After 1896, prices in the gold-standard countries had begun to trend upward, ending the long run of falling prices that had commenced in 1873. The inflationary 'A phase' of this macrocycle culminated in the speculative bubble of 1919. In the spring of 1920 the crisis broke, initiating the deflationary trend-period that culminated in the Great Depression of the 1930s.

At a year-to-year timescale, there was a globally synchronised cycle-within-a-cycle in 1919–20, composed of a phenomenal inflationary boom in the second half of 1919, followed in 1920–1 by the most extreme price deflation of the twentieth century. The focus of this chapter is here, on the temporal microstructure of this great turn.

Japan's experience takes on a special significance here, for its story frames this global process in time. Firstly, the postwar bubble rose to exceptionally great heights in Japan – greater, perhaps, than anywhere else in the world. Secondly, Japan was where the international postwar crash first began, in the spring of 1920. I have described Japan's experience and its articulation with this global process elsewhere,[3] so Japanese developments are sketched here only minimally, in order to direct attention to region-wide aspects of the crisis.

During the European war, factory industrialisation boomed in Japan, China and India. Not only did Asian factories produce goods to supply European wartime demand, but local production also substituted for many of the goods formerly imported from Europe. These effects were strongest in Japan, where factories also began to make manufactured consumer goods for export to markets in Asia and other regions that were no longer being supplied by Europe. Export agriculture boomed as well. Especially significant was the increase in intra-Asian trade. Between 1913 and 1920, the nominal value of trade between Asian countries increased by more than three times. This was substantially more than the increase in Asian countries' trade with Europe during the period.[4]

A salient feature of intra-Asian trade in the early twentieth century was the shipment of Indian raw cotton to Japanese mills. Japanese mills, in turn, produced for export to China and other markets. India's trade, however, tended to stagnate during the war, constrained by the shortage of shipping. This trade stagnation was exceptional among Asian countries. Japan, with its own booming shipbuilding industry, became more than ever the main engine in the expansion of intra-Asian trade. China's trade with other Asian countries also expanded remarkably, and much of it was handled by networks of overseas Chinese merchants. In line with the themes of this chapter, it is also significant that these overseas Chinese networks were a social matrix of China's anti-Qing national revolutionary movement before 1911, of the anti-Japanese national movement after 1915, and of the international Communist movement after 1919.

Despite the overall stagnation of India's trade, its trade with other Asian countries did grow during the war years, and this trade was facilitated by overseas Indian trading networks. Initially, Indian exports to Japan fell off greatly, as British colonial authorities restricted shipments of raw materials to places other than Britain. In 1915, India–Japan trade began to recover, and in 1916 it surged. In 1918, Japanese exports to India were seven times the prewar level; Japan had become India's number two source of imported goods after the UK.[5] Japanese companies also developed new markets in many other countries during the war. After the war they were forced to retreat from many of them, for a time. Asian countries in general ran large trade surpluses with the European allies during the war. But the trade surpluses of British colonies, managed by British authorities in the British interest, had a particularly unrequited nature.

In India, the war strongly encouraged import substitution, but exceptionally, it did not create a general industrial boom. This was prevented not only by the shortage of shipping but also by the shortage of capital (likewise diverted to Britain for the conduct of the war), and by the unavailability of imported machinery.[6]

In China, the 'economic miracle caused by the First World War' helped produce a 'golden age of Chinese capitalism' in the years 1917–23. (These are the words of Marie-Claire Bergère, writing in advance of China's great capitalist boom of the 1990s.)[7] Despite the political turbulence of the period, Chinese industry in the 1910s experienced higher growth rates than any seen until the First Five Year Plan of 1953–7. In China, as in Japan and India, Europe's wartime trade restrictions functioned like a de facto protective tariff for local industry. This effect was especially visible because British colonial authorities had denied tariff protection to Indian industry, allowing only a flat revenue tariff, while Chinese industry had been denied tariff protection under the semi-colonial system of treaties imposed by Britain and the other Western powers. The war also brought a boom in world demand for raw-material exports.

For China, the wartime increase in the price of silver also meant the appreciation of the Chinese silver currency relative to the Western and Japanese currencies. This made it easier for Chinese to repay foreign-currency debts.

The greater purchasing power of Chinese currency did not at this point induce a surge of imports because European goods were not to be had. Nor could machinery be imported from Europe. Chinese industry, like Indian industry, could therefore not grow as robustly as industry in Japan, where a nascent national machinery industry was already in place. In its point of development, Japanese industry was thus well poised to take full advantage of wartime opportunities. There were also major shifts in the composition of trade, as France and Britain, under wartime duress, stopped imports of Chinese silk and tea in 1917.

The provision of services also generated payments surpluses. For Japan, the provision of shipping services, and to an extent marine insurance, produced great profits. India and China supplied military and civilian labour services. Beginning in 1916 and then expanding after August 1917, with the Beijing government's policy of 'using labourers as soldiers', at least 140,000 Chinese went to France. About 40,000 of these men worked for the French as labourers and factory workers, while nearly 100,000 worked as labourers for the British army in France. Many of them dug trenches at the front lines. The British employed several thousand more Chinese as labourers in Iraq, Egypt and elsewhere. The British military often treated the Chinese labourers like prisoners. Several times, Chinese workers responded with protests and riots, met by massacres on the part of British 'overseers'. French treatment was less harsh and less racist; American attitudes were more like those of the British.[8] As late as October 1919, the British camps still employed 50,000 Chinese labourers, though by then they were being repatriated quickly. In his extensive study of the subject, Xu Guoqi does not mention how these workers, who worked ten hours a day, seven days a week, were paid. But the money they sent or brought home with them was surely a significant factor in the overall picture of China's international balance of payments at the time. These men also brought back influenza pathogens, though they evidently had much less severe effects in China than in India. They also brought 'contagious' ideas. Chow Tse-tsung reports that 28,000 of the Chinese in France were educated student-workers and would be considered intellectuals in the Chinese context of the time. Many took part in strikes at French factories, and many, on their return home, served as radicalising leadership elements. Although they both went to France as students rather than workers, Zhou Enlai and Deng Xiaoping were part of this current.[9]

For India, the number who served abroad was an order of magnitude greater. British imperial authorities dispatched more than 1 million Indian soldiers and labourers for campaigns in France and Iraq.[10] Close to 300,000 British officers and men maintained on the Indian government payrolls were also sent overseas. This was an astounding human and logistical undertaking. With these 1.3 million people went some 170,000 animals and 3.7 million tons of supplies. Many people were also recruited to substitute for and support this overseas personnel dispatch. Of the Indians dispatched abroad, about half were labourers and half soldiers. More than half of them went to Iraq; the others went to France, Egypt, East Africa, Aden and Gallipoli. Unlike the smaller dispatch of workers from China, this dispatch of men, animals and supplies overseas did not generate a corresponding flow of remittances because the British Parliament 'consented' (their term) that the government of India should be permitted to continue to pay the expenses of Indian forces sent overseas.[11]

The support of this great expeditionary force thus occasioned huge Indian expenditures without compensating remittances, which probably had economically depressing effects. The expenses paid by the British state were funded, as the British funded so much else, on Indian credit.[12] This meant a great build-up of British debts to India.

For Japan also, wartime specie embargoes meant that large gold balances owed to Japanese exporters remained blocked in London and New York. The Bank of Japan, Japan's central bank, and the Yokohama Specie Bank, the official foreign-exchange bank, funded the ongoing export boom by creating new credits, which stimulated an inflationary boom. There were comparable responses in other countries.

From the demand side, growing Asian trade surpluses put upward pressure on the price of silver, which was still the basis for the monetary and trading systems in much of the region. Wartime embargoes caused silver shortages. From the supply side, the United States restricted silver exports in September 1917, while revolution in Mexico, as in the 1810s, closed silver mines there. China was the world's largest sphere of silver circulation, with a silver-based monetary system that functioned on an open market basis with little state control. Overseas Chinese merchants continued to trade on the basis of silver dollars of various descriptions. Thailand, Indochina, Singapore and the Straits Settlement had gold-exchange standards that had been adapted from silver-dollar systems, and they too continued to rely on a large circulation of silver coins. The Indian rupee was likewise on a gold-exchange standard but in popular practice it retained substantial elements of a silver standard.

For India, there were two critical monetary consequences. Firstly, the rising price of silver caused British authorities repeatedly to raise the exchange rate of the rupee vis-à-vis the British pound. These upward valuations began in December 1916 and carried the rupee from the old rate of 1 shilling and 4 pence (1s. 4d.) to 2s. 2d. in November 1919. The British called this a 'revaluation of the rupee' but it was equally a devaluation of sterling. In fact, the British pound depreciated significantly against almost all Asian currencies during the wartime and immediate postwar periods.

A second consequence was that British authorities remodelled the Indian monetary system from a relatively silver-based to a relatively paper-based system. British authorities paid for large wartime shipments of Indian goods mainly with paper IOUs rather than with silver. In 1914, only about 20 per cent of the Indian government's reserve against the issue of paper rupee notes consisted of paper securities, mainly British Treasury bills. By the spring of 1917 the proportion had grown to 56 per cent.[13] On the issue side, there was a large production of rupee banknotes. As a rule, the Indian public preferred silver coins and did not like to hold paper banknotes, creating a large pent-up demand for conversion of the new paper notes into silver.

Significantly, however, there was no great inflation in India. The general price index rose moderately, pushed up by the increase in import prices owing to restricted imports from Britain, but the rupee's upward valuation limited price increases compared to other countries. Remarkably, grain prices in India actually fell from 1914 to 1917. There was a poor harvest in 1917–18 and substantial price increases came then. This was part of a regionally widespread livelihood shock, which coincided with the worldwide influenza pandemic.

Summer to autumn 1918: pandemic, livelihood crises, popular revolts

The influenza pandemic spread across the world in three waves in 1918 and 1919. It sickened more than a billion people – more than half of the world population. It took the lives of several tens of millions – perhaps as many as 50 million, perhaps even more.

The influenza seems to have first appeared as a relatively mild form of swine influenza that began spreading among people in the spring of 1918, at a mobilisation point for US soldiers in Fort Funston, Kansas. From there it propagated via railway lines across the United States.[14] American soldiers carried it to the Western front of the European war. It could therefore be called the 'American flu'. By May 1918 the new influenza had become combined in Europe with a virulent pneumonia and began to strike down healthy young adults. It spread rapidly in the crowded and unhygienic conditions of military encampments, hospitals and trains. As it spread across Europe, it was named the 'Spanish flu' because news of the pandemic was censored in the combatant countries under wartime emergency authority; in Spain, a neutral country, it was more fully reported. By the end of August 1918, the flu had spread back to Boston, USA, in its new, virulent form. At the same time it reached Freetown in Sierra Leone and began to spread in Africa.[15]

Japan was affected already by the first, milder wave of the influenza, in April 1918. The flu spread through the Japanese navy in May. The second wave of the much more virulent type began in August, simultaneously with the outbreak of nationwide rice riots and strikes. It affected about a third of the Japanese population between October and December 1918. Another wave followed in early 1919. A second flu epidemic, of another type, came to Japan in the winter of 1919–20. Altogether, some 300,000 people died.[16]

In India, the numbers indicate an immense human tragedy. Official reports estimated, conservatively, that 12–13 million people died in the 1918–19 pandemic. In a careful re-evaluation of the evidence, I. D. Mills proposes a number of 17–18 million.[17] These estimates suggest that India alone suffered at least a third of world influenza deaths and perhaps as many as two-thirds of them. As elsewhere, the disease struck down large numbers of people in their twenties and thirties, and affected women disproportionately more than men.

The milder first wave of the influenza became epidemic in India by June 1918. It apparently originated in the port area of Bombay, which was the great connecting point between India and points west, a place from which troops and military labourers shipped out and to which they returned from overseas. The epidemic spread from there along the railway lines, moving with returning troops and other infected people.

In September 1918 the second, virulent wave of the influenza became established in Bombay and, like the first wave, appears to have spread out from there. It peaked in the Bombay Presidency in October and elsewhere in November. The deaths were concentrated in western, central and northern India. In the Bombay Presidency alone, which had a population of 20 million, an estimated 10 million fell ill, of whom about 1 million died. With fuel prices already soaring, there was insufficient firewood to cremate the bodies of all the dead, and the rivers were clogged with corpses. Death rates differed greatly by social class. Official records indicate that more than 16 per cent of low-caste Hindus in the city of Bombay died in the single year of 1918, of all causes. Close to 40 per cent of these deaths were attributed to influenza. By contrast, the total mortality rate among local Europeans and Parsees in 1918 was under 3 per cent, with 30 per cent or fewer of those deaths attributed to influenza. Within the British-commanded Indian army, British soldiers were diagnosed with influenza at a substantially higher rate than were Indians, but Indian troops had a 70 per cent higher rate of death from the disease. Nursing care was one key variable. The Sanitary Commissioner for Bombay suggested that mortality among unnursed patients may have been eight times higher than among nursed patients.[18] Indian medical workers, of whom there were not too many to begin with, had been sent abroad to serve in the war, including some 3,000 doctors and nurses, and 30,000 medical support personnel.[19]

Malnutrition, intensified in many places by famine and near-famine conditions, was probably the greatest variable factor accounting for the epidemic's severe effects in India. It had been 28 years since the last major influenza epidemic in India, that of 1889–90, which likewise happened during an El Niño monsoon failure and famine.[20] Now, the failure of the southwest monsoon rains in June and July 1918 caused crops to wither across western and central India. The economic effects of the war greatly compounded the effects of the weather. Grain reserves were depleted during the war, as grain was shipped to Europe. Railway carriages to carry grain were often unavailable because they had been diverted to the war effort. The same was true of steamships to carry rice from Rangoon. The cotton boom brought about by the war caused demand for grain to surge in Bombay, raising grain prices there, pulling in supplies from elsewhere, and thus raising prices for everyone else, including for those who gained nothing by the boom. The same 'Dutch disease' effect was seen in other booming export zones.

By the end of the summer there was an influx into Bombay of 'thousands of refugees from famine stricken areas in a weakened and destitute condition'.[21]

Half of the working-age population was ill during the period of the harvest of the early crop and sowing of the late crop, so the epidemic in turn reduced agricultural production, worsening the food shortages. In the Bombay Presidency in 1918, despite the inducement of higher crop prices, this combination of factors led to a 19 per cent reduction in the area under cultivation for food crops and a 15 per cent reduction in the area cultivated for non-food crops (of which cotton was by far the most important). The epidemic wave passed through each area it affected in 2–3 months. It faded away in the Bombay Presidency in December and elsewhere by January 1919.

The impression from the existing historiography is that, notwithstanding high mortality, the global epidemic came and went with few lasting social effects. Individual families suffered, but the mortality was dispersed across the whole population, and it has not (so far) registered among historians as a historically significant event. But if we consider the pandemic (or the combined famine–pandemic) as an aspect of the World War, then we will have to say that in terms of the sheer number of deaths, *India was among the countries that suffered most by World War I.*

Food riots have been given some historiographical attention, and strikes have been given even more. Both were closely connected to the worldwide price inflation. Price inflation has a certain mechanistic aspect, captured in the idea that prices are determined by the ratio of money to goods: other things being equal, if the monetary numerator increases, prices go up; and if the goods denominator decreases, prices also go up. Now both things were happening. But people's expectations can also be determinative, and inflationary expectations now fed on themselves, leading to hoarding of goods, panic buying, and attempts by speculators to corner the market in various commodities. Wartime food shortages and locally severe price inflation also provoked an international wave of demonstrations, strikes and food riots.

In South India, the effects of the influenza epidemic were relatively moderate, but the El Niño drought caused a poor rice harvest there in 1918, as the monsoon came too early in the spring and then fizzled out. The impending rice shortage led to speculative hoarding, local market shortages and the sudden doubling of rice prices. The British colonial government intervened extensively in the markets in support of the war. When it came to the people's livelihood, however, the government practised a policy of laissez-faire. In practice, this meant that state authorities stood aside while speculators cornered the rice markets in many districts. The authorities considered imposing price controls, already in place in many countries, only after the crisis was over. Scarce food supplies were therefore rationed according to people's ability to pay. Authorities counselled 'economy of consumption', meaning malnutrition on the part of the poor, and this in turn contributed to influenza deaths.[22]

The conjunction of transport bottlenecks, shortages and profiteering affected other staples such as cloth, salt, kerosene, ghee, chillies and sugar. In India, several of these staple goods were imported – not only kerosene but even cloth, sugar and salt – meaning they were in short supply and going up in price. This is part of the context of Gandhi's *swadeshi* (self-sufficiency) campaign, which focused on import substitution.

Dearth thus coincided with huge merchant stockpiles, particularly in the railway yards from which goods were being shipped to other regions. Rioters therefore often targeted the railway yards. Beginning as early as mid-May of 1918, an 'epidemic' (as it was sometimes called) of grain riots swept Tamil Nadu. The grain riots peaked during the first part of September, simultaneously with the peak of the nationwide rice riots in Japan. Surveying the social and economic strains that had developed in India by the summer of 1918, and the increase in strikes and agrarian unrest, B. R. Tomlinson concluded that 'only the slowing down of the war effort as the [November 11] armistice approached kept the situation within bounds.'[23]

In Japan, privately owned factories increased their payrolls by some 650,000 workers from 1914 to 1919, adding up to a factory workforce of 1.6 million in 1919. Housing for these new urbanites was in short supply, poor in quality and expensive. After a period of stable and even falling prices early in the war, rice prices doubled in Japan between the beginning of 1917 and June 1918. In 1917, nearly 60,000 workers took part in nearly 400 strikes and lockouts. This was a record level. More than 60,000 workers were again involved in strikes and lockouts in 1918 and in 1919, when nearly 500 incidents of strikes and lockouts were recorded. Viewed more closely, this wave of militancy itself resolves into component waves. In 1918, roughly half of the strikes for the year came in August and September, coinciding with the rice riots.[24]

Japan's nationwide rice riots and protests began in late July of 1918. In August and early September, they grew to involve a million or more people in more than 500 locations, before they too subsided. The army was sent to suppress the protestors, and they opened fire on workers in several mining areas.[25] The shock of the rice riots caused a political course change, as the Japanese oligarchs asked the leader of the majority party in Japan's lower house of parliament, Hara Takashi, to form a new cabinet in September 1918, making Hara the first commoner to serve as prime minister. Mass riots and strikes thus pushed forward the democratic movement in politics, which, in a self-reinforcing movement, inspired further popular mobilisations demanding wider political and economic inclusion for propertyless workers, women and hereditary outcaste communities. As in other countries, these manifestations inspired a new generation of activists with a vision of the potential of mass mobilisation.

After the autumn 1918 harvest, rice prices in Japan stabilised for a few months. Again in the summer of 1919, rice prices surged, and again there was another wave of strikes in July and August of that year. In 1920, as prices crashed and the postwar depression set in, the level of strike activity subsided somewhat. In the strikes of 1920, there was also a significant shift in character, from demands for social recognition and higher wages to defensive resistance to wage cuts and layoffs. Although the level of strike activity remained below the 1918–19 peak through the 1920s, the great increase in labour militancy that happened then represented a lasting, stepwise increase in labour activism.[26] As in other countries, the strike wave coincided with a surge of union organising, which gave structure and duration to the new movement.

Japan's experience also clarifies a significant gendered dimension in the dynamics of inflation, deflation and consumption. In their public rhetoric, government officials and elite male commentators associated inflation and its disorders with women, and they presented deflation policies as a masculine restoration of hierarchy and discipline. This kind of rhetorical linkage has a long history and appears across cultures.[27] Women were also associated with consumption when it came to the daily responsibilities of household consumption. In this role as family providers, women frequently took the first steps in popular uprisings to protest against grain shortages and price inflation. These included the February 1917 revolution in Russia, which burgeoned out of a demonstration on International Women's Day. It was also a local 'wives uprising' (*nyōbo ikki*) that inaugurated the Japanese rice riots in July 1918.[28] At the same wartime and postwar moment – happening in the space of a little more than a year – women gained formally equal political rights in most of the Western industrialised countries. The postwar moment thus appears also as an international 'women's rights shock', visible in its overt political results as well as at the level of broader popular mobilisations.

Spring to summer 1919: national awakenings, the ongoing livelihood crisis

In the spring of 1919 came a great surge of mass-based national awakening movements in Korea, Egypt, India, Indonesia, China and elsewhere. It is at this point that we come to the Versailles moment itself and to the postwar political wave that has attracted historians' attention. The explosiveness of these developments was surprising to hundreds of thousands of people who suddenly discovered themselves to be part of a national *movement* – suddenly, for millions, a new vision of dignity, autonomy and membership seemed possible. These social explosions were also shocking to the colonial and other authorities against whom these movements were directed. National awakening movements happened within a context of antisystemic popular mobilisation that included a worldwide wave of strikes and factory occupations – the greatest temporal conjunction of such events that had yet happened. As we try to grasp the specificity and significance of the spring of 1919, it is especially the transnational *simultaneity* of these movements that ought to surprise us.

In Europe, the wave of strikes and factory seizures created an apparently revolutionary situation, and this moment has since then figured prominently in political and theoretical debates. Quantitative studies make the extraordinary surge of labour militancy around 1919 all the clearer.[29] There was a simultaneous strike wave in the Americas. As Elizabeth Perry has noted in reference to China, an 'arresting, yet relatively unexplored' feature of modern protest movements 'is their tendency to erupt with remarkable simultaneity in different countries'. In this, we can compare the international student revolts and strikes of 1968. Both historical moments were also conspicuous for the universalising sense of making history shared by many participants: 'Conscious that they were actors in a drama of global proportions, participants tended to downplay particularistic demands in favor of more universalistic claims,' as Perry put it.[30] She also describes a global 'popcorn' effect, a metaphor for an explosive change of state happening when a critical threshold is reached. Especially important here was the synchronicity of political, intellectual–cultural and economic movements. This was a time of numerous utopian 'news' (or rumour) bubbles concerning expectations of imminent national independence or of imminent world revolution. Following from the awakening of expectations there also came the inflation of expectations. Ideas too trace out a kind of social boom–bust process.

The Paris Peace Conference opened on 18 January 1919. Even before it opened, it had become a source of news shocks. Here it is worth reviewing some outlines of the contemporaneous Eurasian geopolitical situation, to highlight the deep, often catastrophic restructuration of political macrozones then under way. In Russia, the battle lines in the civil war were moving fast in early 1919, breaking in favour of the Communists along fronts that extended across European Russia and Siberia, through the Caucasus and the former Baltic provinces of the Russian Empire. These battle fronts were part of a region-wide 'system' of postwar wars, involving Poland, the Ukraine, Hungary and Anatolia (the latter discussed in Aydin's contribution to this volume). Further west in Europe, it was a matter of social battles and revolutions. Three days before the Peace Conference opened, German army and Freikorps troops crushed the Spartakist rising in Berlin. A revolutionary soviet still claimed government power in Bremen. The 'German Workers' Party' – the future Nazi party – had been founded two weeks before. Three days after the Paris Peace Conference opened, Sinn Féin declared a free Irish republic. The national movement in Ireland exemplified the anticolonial fault-lines that were now opening across the territories occupied by the European imperial powers. This too was a hemisphere-wide process. On 1 March, Korean nationalists declared independence. The nationalist revolt in Egypt began a week after that. A national revolt began in India two weeks after that. Hungary had both national war and Communist revolution. Italy was convulsed by industrial and agrarian battles. On 4 May, news from Paris of the selling out of Chinese national interests to Japan provoked student demonstrations in front of the Tiananmen Gate, signalling the outbreak of the mass-based national movement in China. Those who know the histories of these various countries realise how pivotal these events were in their own streams of national history. Altogether, Russia, Eastern and Central Europe, Anatolia, Syria, Iraq and Arabia thus formed a great zone of regional indeterminacy. China and Mongolia could be described in the same way. Most of these things were conditioned by the war to some degree; in any case, they were now happening synchronously.

Japan's experience has already been indicated, and in general, in countries where factory industrialisation was just getting under way, the wartime intensification and expansion of industrial production had major social effects. Masses of new industrial workers were recruited from the countryside and brought together hurriedly in makeshift living conditions. As consumers, they depended on food markets in which prices were rising very rapidly. Wages in general did not catch up to these cost-of-living increases until the 1920s. Political movements among the burgeoning urban working classes were also taken, on all sides, as signs of things to come and treated with a far greater seriousness than might be indicated by workers' actual demographic weight.

Thus there were waves of industrial strikes in India, Indonesia, China, Japan and elsewhere in Asia. This worldwide movement was felt acutely in numerous colonised countries. Egypt experienced a great wave of both rural and urban strikes, which took on a sharp political edge in March 1919 and were integrally a part of the nationalist movement. Other countries in Africa also experienced waves of strikes from 1918 to 1921, likewise provoked by the increase in prices, which caused real wages to fall by more than half. These included, for example, the first modern strike wave in the history of Zimbabwe (Southern Rhodesia), where privileged white workers and subordinated African workers both struck for higher wages.[31]

In China, the strikes in support of the May Fourth Movement included commercial and student strikes, and their political aspect was predominant.[32] Wartime price inflation in China was relatively moderate (approximately a 30 per cent price increase, in terms of silver, from 1914 to 1920). Here the connection to the political results of the war – the news from Versailles – was direct. The Shanghai general strike in support of the May Fourth Movement began with strikes against Japanese-owned mills and grew to involve 60,000 workers, students and businesspeople. Under this pressure, the Chinese government refused to sign the Versailles Treaty. This was the first time Chinese workers had participated en masse in a decisive moment in political history.[33]

In Punjab, which had been the great source of British military recruitment as well as the great source of wheat exports, people began to protest en masse against the postwar maintenance and intensification of wartime state-of-emergency powers. A series of large and sometimes violent protests in early April reached a climax at the Sikh New Year, 13 April 1919, at Amritsar, when British officers ordered troops to fire into the crowd. Like the May Fourth incident in China, the Amritsar massacre became an energising source of the burgeoning Indian national movement.

Southeast Asia had very little factory industry and no large class of factory-worker rice consumers at the time. But several regions did have extensive European-owned plantations, and plantation workers depended on regional or international rice imports. Malaya particularly, with its plantation and mining economy, depended on imports for two-thirds of its rice consumption.[34] This rice came mainly from Burma, Thailand and Vietnam. Owing to the heavy demand for Burmese rice in India, shipments to Malaya were sharply curtailed in the autumn of 1918. By end of 1918, Thai rice prices also tripled. There was also a poor Vietnamese rice harvest in 1918. Japanese buyers were simultaneously in the market buying Southeast Asian rice. Grain prices continued to increase in early 1919. In Singapore, market prices for rice from Bangkok and Saigon doubled between January and June 1919. In Thailand, rice prices by June of 1919 were five times previous normal levels.

There was a large monetary component to the inflation. In Thailand, the volume of silver coins in circulation grew moderately during the wartime boom period, but in 1917, with the rise of silver prices, the market value of the silver in the baht coins came to exceed their face value, and coins began to be melted down and smuggled out of the country. The silver circulation was now surpassed by the circulation of inconvertible paper money, which expanded by 3.6 times from 1915 to 1919. As monetary authorities saw it, high rice prices meant more money was needed to finance booming rice exports, which the Thai treasury accommodated by increasing the amount of money in circulation.[35] Whatever the logic of this response, it fed price inflation still further.

In the aftermath of the 1918 rice crisis, British colonial authorities imposed controls on rice production on Burma, but rice production and trade were difficult to control. Rice was produced by a mass of small-scale family producers, and the trade in rice was handled mainly by Chinese merchant networks. In Burma, British authorities began a programme of secret official purchasing of rice through a handful of British trading companies. They carefully excluded Chinese traders. Their rationale was the need to keep the news of their action from getting out and pushing up prices. It incidentally reserved the large profit to be had for British merchants. British authorities urged the Thai government to follow their example and commandeer rice for export to British-occupied Malaya. Thai authorities judiciously ignored the request.[36]

In these circumstances, another wave of food riots began. On 22 June 1919, in solidarity with the May Fourth Movement in China, Chinese workers in Penang staged an anti-Japanese demonstration. Livelihood grievances quickly came to the fore, as demonstrators turned their attention to local rice stores. This was the trigger that set off a wave of rice riots in mining and plantation camps across the country. As the British Governor, Young, saw it, the problem was with the Chinese workers. Tamil workers from British India were 'well acquainted with the idea of famine' and willing to accept substitutes for rice, but 'the Chinese labourer as compared with any labouring class in the world is extremely prosperous' and accordingly fastidious about food and accustomed to a plentiful supply of it.[37] The Governor's claims might be taken to suggest a lower threshold for social action among Chinese as opposed to Tamil workers, based on their respective group histories and conceptions of tolerable consumption standards. Or, they may point to the different social conditions of working on dispersed agricultural plantations, where most of the Tamils worked, versus mines, where Chinese workers were concentrated and which, as illustrated in

Japan the year before, are famous in most countries as centres of labour militancy. The rioters looted rice stores, and the colonial government declared martial law and mobilised local militia.

It was also at this point that Communist ideas first began to be taken in within the Chinese community of mainly younger male sojourning workers. In Kuala Lumpur, the anarcho-Communist Goh Tun-ban founded a daily newspaper in March 1919 and in July began to advocate an anti-Japanese boycott in support of the May Fourth Movement, while calling also for a revolutionary Soviet government for China (something that Sun Yat-sen himself was then moving much closer to).[38] British authorities forcibly suppressed the revolutionary Communist movement in the latter part of the year, but it would later grow as an anti-Japanese, anti-British armed movement.

After the June 1919 rice riots in Malaya, authorities fixed prices for all types of rice. On 1 July, notwithstanding the war's end, British colonial authorities used the new war-powers legislation to impose controls on rice distribution.[39] Under its terms, the government forced Burmese rice growers to sell at below-market rates and then profited by selling the rice at much higher prices. These colonial state profits from the sale of Burmese rice helped offset the losses British authorities incurred in subsidising sales in Malaya of expensive free-market rice from Vietnam and Thailand. Burmese farmers, subjected to a compulsory monopsony system, thus subsidised British control of Chinese labourers in Malaya. By August 1919, controlled prices in Rangoon were 64 per cent below free-market prices in Bangkok.[40] On 12 July 1919, the Thai government imposed its own controls on rice exports. In the autumn of 1919 there was a poor Thai harvest due to drought, and at the end of December the government placed an absolute ban on rice exports. In 1920 British authorities imposed controls on the rice trade throughout the British Empire in Asia.

In Indonesia too, the prices of basic consumption goods increased by twice or more between 1913 and 1920. Like Malaya, Java depended on imported rice and was directly affected by international rice shortages. Prices soared between 1918 and 1920, which was also 'the age of strikes' in Indonesia and a period of surging growth of labour unions. The Islamic nationalist movement, Sarekat Islam, grew from nothing in 1912 to 450,000 members in October 1918, and then grew explosively in 1919, to two and a half million members. In Dutch colonial policy, there was a moment of relative liberal tolerance toward the new workers' movement in 1918–19, in line with new concessions to the idea of partial self-government. The colonial state then cracked down in the autumn of 1919. Workers continued to succeed in negotiating demands for higher wages into the spring of 1920, but by the summer of 1920, as the international depression set in, an 'age of reaction' was under way and the movement began to falter.[41] The Communist Party of the Indies (PKI) was founded in May 1920 out of a fissioning of the nationalist movement.

In Japan, the government responded to the 1918 rice riots by taking policy measures to increase the production of rice and lower its cost. It strove particularly to increase rice procurements in Korea and Taiwan. This policy had notorious effects in Korea especially, as it enhanced Japanese urban consumption at the cost of rice consumption by Koreans, which actually declined (from a relatively low base) during the 1920s. These rice-supply policies also shaped the deflationary agrarian conjuncture of the 1920s in Japan, where falling crop prices squeezed farmers and increased the real burden of their debts. This squeeze was more intense in Korea. Throughout Southeast Asia, governments likewise responded to the postwar rice crisis by adopting measures to increase the production of rice and lower its cost. As Paul Kratoska has summarised it, the goal was 'to persuade a large number of small farmers to produce more and sell for less'. Rice riots, or the fear of them, thus provoked pro-consumer but effectively antiproducer policies across the region. Consider Burma's position as a major rice-exporting country, as described by Kratoska: 'Had Burmese rice producers been allowed to sell their crops in a free market, the high prices of 1919 and 1920 would have offered a reprieve from the growing threat of indebtedness and landlessness.'[42] The pressure on Burmese livelihoods was very great, as indicated ten years later when severe agrarian crisis led to open rebellion and bloody repression.[43] Thus, impoverished Burmese producers were denied one of the rare moments of beneficial terms of trade that could have kept them afloat through a difficult business cycle. We see parallel circumstances in India. As Balachandran wryly put it, 'British policy-makers felt the need to insulate the Indian economy from global upswings.'[44] It was a highly selective buffering process, which allowed much fuller participation in global depressions.[45]

Summer 1919 to spring 1920: the release of specie flows and the inflation of the postwar bubble

In its foreign trade, the United States had a large export surplus in most directions, but it had a large import surplus with Japan, owing mainly to heavy purchases of Japanese raw silk. For Japan, these large export surpluses with the United States normally balanced its import surpluses with India and other countries. Wartime embargoes on shipments of gold and silver created difficulties for the financing of the India–Japan trade particularly.[46] On June 1919, the US government lifted its embargo on specie exports. Thus commenced the 'dreaded' gold outflow to Japan (as British Treasury expert Ralph Hawtrey called it), as Japanese exchange banks began requesting payment for the dollar claims they had accumulated during the war.[47] The surge of shipments of gold and silver from the United States helped reinflate the international boom, which now entered its final phase.

In Japan, the boom turned into a bubble in the second half of 1919. In Bombay, as well, there was a boom in the flotation of joint-stock companies, which developed into the greatest bubble in the Bombay financial markets since 1865. But while expectations boomed, the actual growth of the export trade halted for most Asian countries, while their imports began to surge. This double movement presaged the beginning of severe financial difficulties. US financial authorities also became alarmed by the magnitude of the specie outflow after June 1919 and in the autumn of the year adopted a policy of deflation, which would be instrumental in bringing on the postwar panic and depression.

Against expectations, the increase in the international availability of silver after June 1919 did not immediately reduce the price of silver. Rather, pent-up demand for silver in China and India at first greatly accelerated the rise in silver prices. In the ten months after May 1919, the price of silver doubled (in terms of gold-based currencies); this level was almost four times the price at the beginning of 1915. Thus, by the end of 1919 and the beginning of 1920, silver prices had actually regained and slightly surpassed the previous high level of 1872.[48] The abrupt doubling of silver prices meant a doubling of the value of the Chinese silver tael against gold-standard currencies (including the Japanese yen) and stimulated an import boom in China too. Japanese exporters benefited most. The threat posed to Chinese manufacturers by suddenly cheaper Japanese imports also helped motivate the anti-Japanese boycotts embraced by Chinese industrialists during the May Fourth Movement.

At the same time, China's inflation was moderate compared to that in most other countries, but profits during the boom were very high. Wages increased much less. In Shanghai, there was a boom in the formation of new companies.[49] Growth was especially conspicuous in cotton spinning, flour milling, cigarette manufacture and other consumer-goods industries. Banks, both Western-style and Chinese-style, developed conspicuously. Despite the appreciation of silver, Chinese exports also boomed in 1919.

Bubble phenomena thus appeared in many places in late 1919 and early 1920. International commodity prices reached high levels not seen since the 1860s and early 1870s, further stimulating an increase in commodity production for international markets. The conditions for the post-1920 phase of 'over-production' (as it was widely perceived) were thus also being put into place.

Spring to summer 1920: the postwar crash

As the inflation was international, so too was the movement for deflation. In fact, the English word *deflation*, in its economic sense, was coined at this time. The first actual steps to bring deflation about were taken in Japan, when the Bank of Japan raised interest rates on 4 October 1919. This measure was in step with the subsequent interest-rate hikes by the Bank of England and the Federal Reserve Bank of New York. By late November, the Japanese central bank had raised its prime lending rate to more than 8 per cent. It maintained this high rate for more than five years, right through the collapse of the Japanese bubble after March 1920. Here again we see Japan's role as an international pacesetter in this bubble-and-bust cycle, something that has yet to be properly appreciated and considered.[50]

Another global movement insufficiently appreciated by most historians also got under way at this point. A basic motive for the US central bank to raise interest rates in late 1919 and early 1920 was the desire to stem large gold outflows, especially to Japan, in order to defend the US gold standard, restored as of 26 June 1919. In this respect, the international depression of 1920–1 was more than simply the postwar depression that necessarily followed the postwar boom. It was also America's own *gold-restoration depression*. As such, it was the first of a series of gold-restoration depressions that affected country after country over the course of the 1920s. This movement culminated in Japan's own gold-restoration depression in 1929–31.[51]

Following the lifting of the US embargo on gold and silver exports in June, British financial authorities reopened the London gold market on 12 September 1919, although gold shipments in and out of the UK were still controlled by a government licence system. British financial authorities also feared they could not restore London's former central place in world gold trading if Indians were allowed to purchase gold freely. Before the World War, Indians regularly purchased the equivalent of about one-quarter of annual world gold production. Most of this gold was fashioned into jewellery and kept as a store of wealth.[52] These flows of gold to India displeased London financiers, who wanted to keep it in London. Two decades before, such considerations had shaped the colonial gold-exchange standard that British policymakers devised for India, which pegged the value of the Indian rupee to the British pound and effectively substituted sterling debt instruments for actual gold in India's 'gold-standard' reserve.[53] Thus, the official British report on India's gold-standard reserve, as of 31 December 1919, indicates that the balance of the reserve held in India was 'nil'. The balance held in cash, at the Bank of England was less than £1,000. The balance held in British government securities, also in London, was £36,800,000. This was a big number: the Bank of England's own gold reserve against note issue stood at £93 million in early January 1920.[54] The report thus reveals two things: that the Indian gold-standard reserve was not really India's; and that it was not really gold. In this way, poor India systematically extended credit to rich England, and these credit operations were greatly extended during the war, when British authorities used gold only as necessary, to pay for the import of supplies from those foreign countries whose monetary systems they could not directly manipulate. India's persistent export surpluses with Britain grew even larger immediately after the war, but imports of gold into India during 1919–21 were restricted to only one-quarter of their prewar levels. When the US government lifted its gold embargo in June 1919, British authorities also made informal arrangements with the Americans in order to limit Indian access.[55]

The dollar price of gold was legally fixed under the revived US gold standard but the prices of everything else gyrated. As noted already, world silver markets were particularly volatile. On 11 February 1920, silver prices reached a final peak at 89½ pence per ounce on the London exchange. They then began to collapse.

Great shifts in rupee exchange rates accompanied these price movements.

The December 1919 report of a committee of British financiers to British state authorities, published 2 February 1920, focused on the problem of high prices and recommended a high exchange rate for the rupee. This exchange rate handicapped Indian exports and encouraged imports. The strong rupee, combined with India's backlogged demand for imports, caused India's balance of trade to shift suddenly from surplus to deficit.[56] The trade balances of Japan and of most other Asian countries were swinging into deficit at the same time.

The spike in international silver prices had itself been based on speculative purchases, usually on credit. Traders in Shanghai especially had built up very large stocks of silver. The final surge and subsequent collapse of silver prices in early 1920 was intensified by a seasonal effect, as the Chinese New Year was the time for settling debts, meaning an extra demand for silver with which to make payments. Even in ordinary years, this effect was sufficient to affect world silver prices, which typically tended to rise before the lunar New Year and fall thereafter.

This is when the generalised price collapse began in Japan. Japan, a gold-standard country since 1897, divided its trade about equally between the mainly Western gold-standard macrozone and the mainly Asian silver-standard zone. Japanese trade was thus highly sensitive to movements in gold:silver rates. The wartime and postwar rise of silver prices buoyed demand for Japanese products in silver-using countries. The collapse of silver prices then triggered panic selling in Japanese commodity and financial markets. Commodities and stock markets in Japan reached their peak price levels in early March, a month after silver prices peaked. Japanese share prices fell sharply on 11 March, as did rice prices. The Japanese army, accompanied by various business adventurers, was engaged in its own speculative adventure in eastern Siberia, to which troops had been dispatched in 1918. This operation too was now unravelling, as signalled by the massacre by Russian partisans of Japanese at Nikolayevsk on the Amur. This news, on 12 March, gave speculators in Tokyo new cause for perceiving the impending collapse of the inflated structures in which they had invested. Panic selling on the Tokyo stock exchange caused authorities to suspend trading on 15 March. On 27 March, panic selling spread to the rice wholesale markets. The prices of other commodities also began to fall. On 7 April, a major bank failed in Osaka, and panic swept the Osaka markets. Japanese financial and commodities exchanges were shuttered through much of April and May. The Bank of Japan organised an extraordinary bank bailout. On 1 May, silk prices collapsed in Yokohama, and company bankruptcies and bank failures mounted. Thus began the era of stagnation and deflation that dominated national business conditions until 1932.[57] By the middle of June, silver prices were down more than 50 per cent from their peak levels of four months earlier. Overleveraged speculators faced losses and bankruptcy, and the effects rippled out through both the credit system and the real economy. World silver prices continued to fall for the next ten years, to reach a new historic low against gold during the next great round of global monetary crisis in 1931.

The collapse of the postwar bubble was felt across Japan's formal and informal empires. Manchuria had its own bubble, exemplified in an extraordinary real-estate bubble in Dalian (Dairen) and a speculative Japanese commercial advance into the former Russian sphere of influence in North Manchuria, backed by the Bank of Chosen as a semicommercial agency of the Japanese state. These bubbles now collapsed too. Commodity prices in the London markets also peaked at the end of March. The commodity-export boom ended simultaneously in Malaya and elsewhere.

The fall in silver prices caused the Japanese yen to gain value relative to the Chinese currency, hurting the price-competitiveness of Japanese exports and (again) providing de facto protection to Chinese businesses, which none the less faced growing competition from Japanese-owned factories located in China. Falling demand for Japanese cotton goods in turn suppressed Japanese demand for Indian raw cotton, depressing India's export trade too. China's exports also fell off substantially in 1920 because of the international downturn, but domestic demand largely filled the gap.

Simultaneously, European exports again began to supply customers in China, India and Southeast Asia. Japan's great wartime trade surplus was thus converted to a trade deficit in early 1920. India's trade surplus also turned into a trade deficit in early 1920. By June of 1920, the initial wave of panic had calmed in Japan, but economic collapses commenced at this point in other countries, including the United States, Britain and countries connected to them. Japanese exports continued to decline, commercial bankruptcies spread and more bank runs followed later in 1920, as the recession began to settle in.

The boom in Malaya, stimulated by the great increase in tin and rubber prices, also ended in March 1920, and falling commodity prices led to a severe slump in 1921. Malaya experienced an economic recovery in the mid-1920s, followed by renewed depression after 1927.[58] This chronology reminds us that in many commodity-exporting countries, the second great wave of interwar depression began not in 1929 but already in 1927.

In Thailand, the monetary crisis interacted with the rice crisis discussed above, as the prohibition of rice exports at the beginning of 1920 contributed to a major exchange crisis. There was a severe deflation of the currency in circulation, as the national money supply contracted 49 per cent from its July 1919 peak to March 1921.[59]

The Philippines also experienced a great export boom during World War I. The newly established Philippine National Bank was temporarily able to get possession of the colonial currency reserves, which US authorities had formerly required to be held in New York banks. They were thus enabled to leverage the proceeds of the boom to create more credit locally, further stimulating the inflationary boom.[60] At the same time, however, in a fashion parallel to British conduct in India, US dollar funds were pulled out of the Philippines for investment in US war bonds. Philippine trade, like that of other Asian countries, fell into a deficit position after the war, creating the conditions for a credit crisis.

The crisis was temporarily covered by a record-breaking export boom in late 1919 and early 1920. Prices for Philippine export goods peaked at record highs in June 1920, three months after the peak of the commodity bubble in Japan. Prices then collapsed, while interest rates spiked. US colonial authorities thereafter followed a severe deflation policy, reducing the money supply by some 40 per cent and provoking a severe 'liquidation', characterised by 'widespread failures, strikes, unemployment, and, in general, though perhaps in an exaggerated degree, all the concomitants of the post-war reaction and deflation suffered by many other countries at this time'.[61] The terms of trade shifted severely against the agricultural exporting country; by 1921, the Philippines was delivering a substantially increased physical volume of goods (mainly to the United States) and getting 40 per cent less in exchange for it. Banks were bailed out locally and US creditors were protected, so the burdens of adjustment were carried further down the social–economic hierarchy.

Table 1.1 gives a region-wide picture of the expansion and subsequent fallback of the export trade of Asian countries.

As shown in the table, the effects of this boom–bust cycle were very great in a highly trade-dependent economy such as that of Malaya. For China, foreign trade counted for a much smaller share of the national economy, and the decline was also less severe. Nor was 1920 in China the great turning point in the inflation process, as it was elsewhere. Rather, moderate inflation continued through the 1920s, in tandem with the depreciation of silver prices. Indochina likewise experienced a great expansion of trade during the wartime and postwar boom period but, being tied to the French economy, which was also still undergoing a phase of postwar inflation, it appears to have been little affected by the international trade crisis of 1920. Burmese rice also continued to be in demand, buoying Burmese trade during a time of general decline.

The depression in Western markets fed back into Asian economies. For the

Table 1.1 Export boom and bust. Exports of selected Asian countries from the World War boom to the postwar depression (in millions of local-currency units).

	1913 level	Peak level (*year*)	*% increase*	Trough level (*year*)	*% decline*
Thailand	115	175 (*1919*)	52%	65 (*1920*)	63%
Malaya	389	1,077 (*1920*)	177%	434 (*1921*)	60%
Indonesia	614	2,225 (*1920*)	262%	1,136 (*1922*)	50%
Japan	715	2,374 (*1919*)	232%	1,503 (*1921*)	37%
India	2,290	3,038 (*1919*)	33%	2,145 (*1921*)	29%
China	403	631 (*1919*)	57%	542 (*1920*)	14%
Indochina	285	1,284 (*1921*)	351%	1,112 (*1922*)	13%
Burma	389	572 (*1919*)	47%	545 (*1920*)	5%

Note: Countries are ranked in order of severity of the fall of exports from 1919–20 peak levels to 1920-2 troughs. Data: Sugihara, *Ajia-kan bōeki*.

United States, the depression of 1920–1 has been overshadowed in memory by the greater depression that began in 1929. In fact, the fall of US prices in 1920–1 – more than 40 per cent – was steeper than anything that has happened in the century since. To find comparably steep price declines in the US historical record, one must go back to the postwar depressions that followed the 1812 war with Britain and the Civil War of 1861–5.[62] Some 4 million US workers lost their jobs in the depression of 1920–1. The formerly booming US demand for raw silk and other commodities suddenly dropped off.

In India, a British-mandated 'stabilisation' programme in 1920 resulted in 'deflationary overkill', as Balachandran has put it.[63] The same phrase could be applied to monetary policy in Japan, the United States, and domestically in Britain as well. In India, the peak of the boom in most branches of industry came in April 1920.[64] In Bombay, the speculative boom in company promotion continued relatively late, until October 1920. Authorised company capital there more than doubled in 1919–20 over that of 1918–19, but the amount of this projected capital actually paid in was only a fraction of this, about 16 per cent.[65] Bombay's general share price index increased by some 3.7 times between January 1915 and October 1920, when the market peaked. Recession in late 1920 was followed by depression and big liquidations in 1921–2, with a 'drastic weeding out of many of the mushroom companies'.[66] Despite Britain's large wartime debt to India, India actually became a net exporter of gold during the international depression of 1920–2. These gold outflows marked the appearance of a new process that would go to an extreme during the next phase of world depression, in the 1930s, when India again exported a large amount of gold to Britain. The effect was to ease British adjustment to the depression, and to intensify deflation and depression in India – a relationship of displacement that was then the rule in British–Indian economic relations.[67]

In China, against the movement elsewhere, local industries benefited from the depreciation of silver and the de facto protection against imports that it provided. The financial boom there thus continued later than elsewhere, yielding an extremely bifurcated social picture against the backdrop of the severe famine in northern China in the winter of 1920–1, which followed upon widespread drought in the spring and summer of 1920. Flooding in the summer of 1921 then spread famine in central China in 1921–2. In 1922, share prices crashed on the newly established Shanghai Stock and Produce Exchange, ending the phase of 'mushroom growth'.[68] China's urban boom and the liberal moment that accompanied it thus ended after 1923, even as Western imperialist pressure returned, Japanese economic advances continued and the national revolutionary movement surged.

In general, the concern of people doing business around the world shifted abruptly from fear of shortages in early 1920 to fear of 'over-production'. This tendency would continue through the deflationary period of the 1920s and early 1930s. World tea production, for example, was now estimated to be 25 per cent above consumption. This brought about moves to restrict production in India and Ceylon.[69] Similar stories can be told about many other goods. While agrarian difficulties deepened internationally, urban consumers tended to benefit from the falling prices of the early 1920s. In Japan, for example, the ratio of wages to prices rose in the first part of the 1920s and urban consumption levels appear to have improved.[70]

The great boom–bust cycle of 1919–20 echoed through the decade that followed. In Japan, fiscal and monetary policies oscillated between expansionary and contractionary modes, culminating in the extreme deflation policy of 1929–31. This was Japan's version of the Brüning deflation in Germany (1930–2), the Hoover deflation in the United States, and parallel deflation policies in India, Indonesia and many other places.[71] An important task for historians is to correlate and connect the chronology of these policy cycles and to understand their transnational interconnections.

A globally synchronous microcycle

The world had never experienced a boom–bust cycle synchronised across so many countries as that of 1919–20. In the view presented here, the World War of 1914–18 was something like a storm of globalisation, involving a violent acceleration of numerous globalising forces, both economic and non-economic. Economic movements are only part of the story. Social processes of many kinds underwent self-reinforcing phases of sudden exponential growth in 1918 and 1919. In 1920 and 1921, these expansive, often bubble-like, movements collapsed.

The global boom–bust cycle of 1919–20 also marked the crest of a much longer and slower movement. The international depression of 1920–1, steep but also relatively brief in most places, was the beginning of an extended phase of deflation in the 1920s. This was the first lurch in a process that led to a second, more catastrophic world depression in 1929, and to a third in 1937. The place of the 1929 depression cannot be properly understood without grasping this wider time-context. The US-centred historiography of the depression is particularly apt to mislead on this point because it often treats the crisis of 1929 as a geographically and temporally local, US-created crisis, which had unfathomably outsized international consequences. To consider 1920 and 1929 as moments in a common deflationary process will step us up a scale level, both temporally and geographically, to a view that takes in the whole 'Great War, Great Depression' process at the level of the whole world economy. If we consider a still wider temporal span, it will bring into view the long macrocycle that ran from the world depression of the 1890s to the world depression of the 1930s. This long-wave movement was already discerned and analysed in the mid-1920s by the Russian econometrician N. D. Kondratiev, followed by J. A. Schumpeter and others, who understood the price collapses of 1920 as the beginning of a multidecadal deflation comparable to the two long phases of deflation that had followed the inflations of the Napoleonic Wars and the mid-century wars of national integration.[72]

International monetary flows and credit/debt dynamics were at the heart of the deflationary movement, and Asia was more integral to the whole movement than has so far been understood in European-centred histories. To repeat, it was in Japan, at the interface between the gold and silver zones of the world economy, that the international inflationary boom first broke in March 1920. Running along the boundary of the mainly Western gold zone and the mainly Asian silver zone, one sees something like a frontal system along which a series of social–economic storms developed, extending from the Japanese Empire in northeast Asia through Southeast Asia and the Indian Ocean world. The year 1920 was not universally the turning point from inflation to deflation. China's experience was different, as we have seen. In the defeated countries of Central Europe, postwar inflation and then hyperinflation continued into the early 1920s; thereafter, deflation set in there too. By about 1926, the international deflation that began in 1920 was nearly universal. The turn to deflation did not just happen of itself but was triggered by the putting in place of a postwar monetary 'restoration', directed by public and private financial authorities in the major victorious countries, including Japan, where the first actual steps were taken. The postwar monetary settlement was closely coordinated with the postwar political settlement, though the connections have been overlooked by historians who view the 'political' and the 'economic' as separate domains.[73]

If we take an integrative view, the synchronous timing of systemic breaks in these two domains will immediately attract our attention. Thus, for instance, the decade-long movement to restore the international gold standard began with the lifting of the US embargo on gold exports on 26 June 1919; this happened two days before the signing of the Treaty of Versailles on 28 June. The organic connection between the projects of political 'stabilisation' and monetary 'stabilisation' (as it was called) is visible again in the second systemic breakpoint, when both projects failed together. The canonical date for the collapse of the restored international gold-standard system is 21 September 1931, when the British government announced the resuspension of the British gold standard and allowed the British pound to plummet in value against other currencies. On the same weekend, the Japanese Guandong army executed its invasion–coup in Manchuria, which began the undoing of the Versailles/League of Nations system. In early 1933, the Versailles system openly failed. It was in February 1933 that the Japanese delegation walked out of the League of Nations; simultaneously, Hitler was establishing a dictatorship in Germany. At the same time, bank runs were spreading across the United States, which finally abandoned the gold standard in April 1933. Essays in the present volume reveal several other social and intellectual dimensions in which 1931 or 1933 stand out as the end of the 'Versailles era'. By professional training and specialisation, political and intellectual historians treat one side of this movement while monetary and economic historians treat the other. But both were aspects of a combined movement within which mutual influences ran back and forth without respecting the jurisdictional boundaries erected by government bureaucracies and academic specialisations.

The questions raised by this synchronisation are many and deep. Historians recently have written many microhistories in which the microlevel is conceived in social and spatial terms. The present sketch, although confined mainly (and artificially) to the region from Japan to India, suggests that we need a microhistory in a temporal sense of the biennium 1919–20, written with the broadest possible geographical focus. Only a close attention to chronology can clarify the densely transnational interconnection of events in this transformative interval. Needless to say, numerous systemic structures and legacies that were created then remain operative today, a long lifetime later.

Questions of nations and nationalism were manifestly at the centre of the World War and its all-too-temporary settlement. In the historiography of nationalism, however, one often encounters an implicit model of history as an ideologically driven and media-driven process. From reading much of the literature on the national revolutions at the end of World War I, one would not learn of the simultaneous inflationary groundswell, the livelihood crisis, and the social explosions that accompanied it. In some histories, the exclusion of economic material is so complete as to mislead. Issues of daily livelihood, including critical fluctuations in the income/expenditure balances of households, condition many other things. So too do critical fluctuations in the income/expenditure balances of business firms and states. Monetary zones, pressures and flows were structured by national and imperial territorialities, but they created effects that were as difficult to contain as those of disease pathogens.

In several domains, the work of correlation is proceeding. By now, several generations of historians have examined the political and national aspects of the post-World War I settlement. This formerly European-focused work has more recently extended to take in Asia as well.[74] Aydin's work, in this volume and in his 2007 book, offers a sweeping 'pan-Asian' view that integrates movements in the East Asian and Islamic civilisational worlds into a single picture. Manela's 2007 study of the 'Wilsonian Moment' – one could call it the Wilson bubble – correlates national political stories around the ideational bubble generated in the spring of 1919 by Woodrow Wilson's call for national self-determination, as diffused via international news networks. This happened simultaneously with a Leninist moment – a millenarian 'world revolution' bubble, for Wilsonianism existed in tension with Leninism and reacted to it as an antipole. While stories of war, revolution, national self-determination and a new world order captured headlines, international specie flows invisibly – and, in a way, automatically – transmitted shocks in another dimensionality through the monetary space of flows.

Moments of general, systemic crisis thus present us with a synchronisation of crisis across social domains that are often kept separate in our understanding. Moments of systemic crisis are also *personally* critical; for countless people, including many of the cultural innovators and thought-leaders of their generation, these crises were also moments of personal conversion and changes of life-course. Such historical moments are thus vital points for integrating in our understanding macrolevel moments with the level of personal biography, bringing together the 'structural–conjunctural' and the 'event' levels of history. In the intellectual and cultural fields, as well in the economic field, the inflationary 'upside' of 1919 thus gave us a new spring tide of nations, of liberation, of world revolution. The deflationary 'downside' of 1920–1 had an abruptly different and more conservative tone. This economic–conjunctural turn meshed with shifts in political atmosphere and mass consciousness, as expectations of imminent possibilities of transcendence seemed suddenly to turn into dreams downsized or deferred to a more distant future.

Notes

1. In the time since I first drafted this chapter, Tooze, *The Deluge*, has gone a long way to remedy this.
2. E.g. Cannan, *The Paper Pound*, Preface.
3. Metzler, *Lever of Empire*, chs 5–7; Bytheway and Metzler, *Central Banks and Gold*, chs 4–7.
4. Sugihara, *Ajia-kan bōeki*, pp. 95, 130, 146–7.
5. Saini, 'Economic aspects', pp. 167–8.
6. Tomlinson, 'India and the British Empire', p. 351; Saini, 'Economic aspects', p. 166.
7. Bergère, 'Chinese bourgeoisie', p. 745; Bergère, *Golden Age*, pp. 63–83.
8. Xu, *China and the Great War*, pp. 126–37.
9. Chow, *May Fourth Movement*, pp. 37–40.
10. Pradhan, 'Indian army', p. 55; Saini, 'Economic aspects', pp. 143–5.
11. Saini, 'Economic aspects', pp. 141–6; Singha, 'Finding labor', p. 412.
12. See Balachandran, 'Britain's liquidity crisis', and Balachandran, 'Towards a "Hindoo marriage"'.
13. Balachandran, 'Britain's liquidity crisis', p. 577.
14. Hollenbeck, '1918–1919 influenza pandemic'; Crosby, *America's Forgotten Pandemic*.
15. Tomkins, 'Colonial administration', p. 68.
16. Rice and Palmer, 'Pandemic influenza', p. 393.
17. Mills, '1918–1919 influenza pandemic', pp. 1–2; Arnold, 'Looting, grain riots and government policy', p. 111.
18. Mills, '1918–1919 influenza pandemic', pp. 33–5.
19. Saini, 'Economic aspects', p. 146.
20. Mills, '1918–1919 influenza pandemic', p. 20; Davis, *Late Victorian Holocausts*.
21. Bombay Health Officer's Report for the third quarter of 1918, quoted in Mills, '1918–1919 influenza pandemic', p. 35.
22. Arnold, 'Looting, grain riots and government policy', pp. 111–19, 140–1.
23. Cited in Saini, 'Economic aspects', p. 162.
24. Garon, *State and Labor*, pp. 40–1, 249.
25. Lewis, *Rioters and Citizens*.
26. Garon, *State and Labor*, p. 249.
27. Metzler, 'Woman's place'.

28. Kaplan, 'Women and communal strikes'; Lewis, *Rioters and Citizens*, pp. 45–55.
29. See, e.g., Screpanti, 'Long economic cycles'.
30. Perry, 'From Paris to the Paris of the East', p. 348.
31. Yoshikuni, 'Strike action'.
32. Chow, *May Fourth Movement*, pp. 145–58.
33. Perry, 'From Paris to the Paris of the East', pp. 349–52.
34. Kratoska, 'British Empire', p. 115, whose account forms a starting point for analysis.
35. Ingram, *Economic Change*, pp. 154–8; Kratoska, 'British Empire', pp. 127, 131.
36. Kratoska, 'British Empire', p. 127; Ingram, *Economic Change*, p. 156.
37. Kratoska, 'British Empire', p. 130.
38. Yong, 'Origins and development', pp. 626–8.
39. Kratoska, 'British Empire', p. 130.
40. Kratoska, 'British Empire', p. 125.
41. Shiraishi, *An Age in Motion*, pp. 109–14, 216–17, 224; Ingleson, 'Life and work', p. 462; Kahin, *Nationalism and Revolution*, pp. 73–5.
42. Kratoska, 'British Empire', p. 144.
43. Scott, *Moral Economy*, pp. 149–56.
44. Balachandran, 'Towards a "Hindoo marriage"', p. 618n.
45. See Rothermund, *Global Impact*, pp. 89–96.
46. Metzler, *Lever of Empire*, pp. 104–5.
47. Hawtrey, 'Federal Reserve system', p. 237; Bytheway and Metzler, *Central Banks and Gold*, ch. 5.
48. King, *Hongkong Bank*, p. 70.
49. Bergère, 'Chinese bourgeoisie', pp. 746–7.
50. Bytheway and Metzler, *Central Banks and Gold*, ch. 5.
51. Metzler, *Lever of Empire*, ch. 8. The term 'gold-restoration' depression (*kinkaikin fukyō*, 金解禁不況) was used as a generic expression for this type of recession by Takahashi Kamekichi.
52. See Balachandran ('Liquidity crisis', 'Towards a "Hindoo marriage"'), from which much of the following background information is drawn.
53. Keynes, *Indian Currency*; Kemmerer, *Modern Currency Reforms*; Matsuoka, *Kin kawase hon'isei*.
54. 'Billion', *The Economist*, 17 January 1920, p. 119.
55. Balachandran, 'Liquidity crisis', p. 580.
56. Pillai, 'Financing of Indian industry'; Vakil, 'Indian financial statistics', pp. 93–4.
57. Further details are given in Metzler, *Lever of Empire* (pp. 133–6 for the 1920 crash).
58. King, *Hongkong Bank*, p. 21.
59. Ingram, *Economic Change*, pp. 156–8.
60. This and the following information are drawn from Luthringer, *Gold-Exchange Standard*, pp. 127–9.
61. Luthringer, *Gold-Exchange Standard*, pp. 138, 160.
62. Friedman and Schwartz, *Monetary History*, pp. 231–4.
63. Balachandran, 'Liquidity crisis'.
64. Gadgil, *Industrial Evolution*, p. 254.

65. Pillai, 'Financing of Indian industry', pp. 248–9.
66. Kaul, 'Some indices of prices'.
67. Balachandran, 'Liquidity crisis', pp. 575–6; Bytheway and Metzler, ch. 9.
68. Bergère, 'Une crise de subsistance'; Fuller, 'North China famine'; Bergère, 'Chinese bourgeoisie', pp. 748–9.
69. *Economist*, 'Commercial history and review of 1920', 21 February 1921, p. 356.
70. Metzler, 'Woman's place'.
71. Metzler, 'Partisan policy swings'; Metzler, *Lever of Empire*; Patrick, 'Economic muddle'; Hara, '1920 nendai'.
72. Kondratiev, 'Die langen Wellen der Konjunktur'; Schumpeter, *Business Cycles*.
73. Eichengreen, *Golden Fetters*, offers a good European-centred account.
74. See Ellinwood and Pradhan, *India and World War I*, for an early volume on India, which now needs revisiting; Dickinson (*War and National Reinvention*; *World War I and the Triumph of a New Japan*) for excellent studies of Japan; Xu, *China and the Great War*, for China; and Manela, *Wilsonian Moment*, on the reception of Wilson's call for national self-determination in Asia. In the Japanese-language historiography, Asia's inclusion is well established.

References

Arnold, David, 'Looting, grain riots and government policy in South India 1918', *Past & Present*, 84 (August 1979), pp. 111–45.
Balachandran, G., 'Britain's liquidity crisis and India, 1919–1920', *Economic History Review*, 46:3 (1993), pp. 575–91.
Balachandran, G., 'Towards a "Hindoo marriage": Anglo-Indian monetary relations in interwar India, 1917–35', *Modern Asian Studies*, 28:3 (1994), pp. 615–47.
Bergère, Marie-Claire, 'Une crise de subsistance en Chine (1920–1922)', *Annales. Histoire, Sciences Sociales*, 28:6 (November–December 1973), pp. 1361–402.
Bergère, Marie-Claire, 'The Chinese bourgeoisie, 1911–37', in John K. Fairbank and Denis Twitchett (eds), *The Cambridge History of China, Volume 12, Republican China 1912–1949* (Cambridge: Cambridge University Press, 1983), pp. 722–825.
Bergère, Marie-Claire, *The Golden Age of the Chinese Bourgeoisie 1911–1937*, transl. Janet Lloyd (Cambridge: Cambridge University Press, 1986).
Bytheway, Simon and Mark Metzler, *Central Banks and Gold: How Tokyo, London, and New York Shaped the Modern World* (Ithaca, NY: Cornell University Press, 2016).
Cain, P. J. and A. G. Hopkins, *British Imperialism, 1688–2000*, 2nd edn (London: Longman, 2001).
Cannan, Edwin (ed.), *The Paper Pound of 1797–1821. The Bullion Report, 8th June 1810*, 2nd edn (London: P. S. King & Son, 1925).
Chow, Tse-tsung, *The May Fourth Movement: Intellectual Revolution in Modern China* (Stanford: Stanford University Press, 1960).
Crosby, Alfred, *America's Forgotten Pandemic: The Influenza of 1918* (New York: Cambridge University Press, 1989).

Davis, Mike, *Late Victorian Holocausts: El Niño Famines and the Making of the Third World* (London: Verso, 2001).

De Cecco, Marcello, *Money and Empire, The International Gold Standard, 1890–1914* (Oxford: Basil Blackwell, 1974).

Deole, C. S., 'Stability of exchange', *Indian Journal of Economics*, vol. 2 (1920–1), pp. 537–41.

Dickinson, Frederick R., *War and National Reinvention: Japan in the Great War, 1914–1919* (Cambridge, MA: Harvard University Press, 1999).

Dickinson, Frederick R., *World War I and the Triumph of a New Japan, 1919–1930* (Cambridge: Cambridge University Press, 2013).

Eichengreen, Barry, *Golden Fetters, The Gold Standard and the Great Depression, 1919–1939* (New York: Oxford University Press, 1992).

Ellinwood, DeWitt C. and S. D. Pradhan (eds), *India and World War I* (New Delhi: Manohar, 1978).

Friedman, Milton and Anna Jacobson Schwartz, *A Monetary History of the United States, 1867–1960* (Princeton: Princeton University Press, 1963).

Fuller, Pierre, 'North China famine revisited: Unsung native relief in the warlord era, 1920–1921', *Modern Asian Studies*, 47:3 (May 2013), pp. 820–50.

Gadgil, D. R., *The Industrial Evolution of India in Recent Times, 1860–1939*, 5th edn (Bombay: Oxford University Press, 1971).

Garon, Sheldon, *The State and Labor in Modern Japan* (Berkeley: University of California Press, 1987).

Hara, Akira, '1920 nendai no zaisei shishutsu to sekkyoku, shōkyoku ryō seisaku rosen' [Government spending in the 1920s and the positive and negative policy lines], in Takafusa Nakamura (ed.), *Senkan-ki no Nihon keizai bunseki* [Analysis of the Japanese Economy in the Interwar Period] (Tokyo: Yamakawa Shuppansha, 1981), pp. 77–109.

Hawtrey, R. G., 'The Federal Reserve system of the United States', *Journal of the Royal Statistical Society*, 85:2 (March 1922), pp. 224–69.

Hollenbeck, James E., 'The 1918–1919 influenza pandemic: A pale horse rides home from war', *Bios*, 73:1 (March 2002), pp. 19–27.

Ingleson, John, 'Life and work in colonial cities: Harbour workers in Java in the 1910s and 1920s', *Modern Asian Studies*, 17:3 (1983), pp. 455–476.

Ingram, James C., *Economic Change in Thailand, 1850–1970* (Stanford: Stanford University Press 1971).

Kahin, George McTurnan, *Nationalism and Revolution in Indonesia* (Ithaca, NY: Cornell University Press, 1952).

Kaplan, Temma, 'Women and communal strikes in the crisis of 1917–1922', in Renate Bridenthal, Claudia Koonz and Susan Stuard (eds), *Becoming Visible: Women in European History*, 2nd edn (Boston: Houghton Mifflin, 1987), pp. 429–49.

Kaul, B. N., 'Some indices of prices of securities and their relation to money market', *Indian Journal of Economics*, vol. 5 (1924–5), pp. 255–84.

Kemmerer, Edwin Walter, *Modern Currency Reforms, A History and Discussion of Recent Currency Reforms in India, Porto Rico, Philippine Islands, Straits Settlements and Mexico* (New York: Macmillan, 1916).

Keynes, John Maynard, *Indian Currency and Finance*, vol. 1 of *The Collected Writings of John Maynard Keynes* (London: Macmillan, 1971 [1913]).

King, Frank H. H., *The Hongkong Bank between the Wars and the Bank Interned, 1919–1945*, vol. III of *The History of the Hongkong and Shanghai Banking Corporation* (Cambridge: Cambridge University Press, 1988).

Kondratjew [Kondratiev], N. D., 'Die langen Wellen der Konjunktur', *Archiv für Sozialwissenschaft und Sozialpolitik*, 56:3 (1926), pp. 573–609. Partially transl. by W. F. Stolper as 'The long waves in economic life', *Review of Economics and Statistics*, 17:6 (November 1935), pp. 105–15.

Kratoska, Paul H., 'The British Empire and the Southeast Asian rice crisis of 1919–1921', *Modern Asian Studies*, 24:1 (1990), pp. 115–46.

Lewis, Michael, *Rioters and Citizens, Mass Protest in Imperial Japan* (Berkeley: University of California Press, 1990).

Luthringer, George F., *The Gold-Exchange Standard in the Philippines* (Princeton: Princeton University Press, 1934).

Manela, Erez, *The Wilsonian Moment: Self-Determination and the International Origins of Anticolonial Nationalism* (Oxford: Oxford University Press, 2007).

Matsuoka, Kōji, *Kin kawase hon'isei no kenkyū* [Research on the Gold-Exchange Standard] (Tokyo: Nihon Hyōronsha, 1936).

Maxon, R. M., 'The Kenya currency crisis, 1919–1921, and the imperial dilemma', *Journal of Imperial and Commonwealth History*, 17 (1989), pp. 323–48.

Metzler, Mark, 'Woman's place in Japan's Great Depression: Reflections on the moral economy of deflation', *Journal of Japanese Studies*, 30:2 (Summer 2004), pp. 315–52.

Metzler, Mark, *Lever of Empire: The International Gold Standard and the Crisis of Liberalism in Prewar Japan* (Berkeley: University of California Press, 2006).

Metzler, Mark, 'The cosmopolitanism of national economics: Friedrich List in a Japanese mirror', in A. G. Hopkins (ed.), *Global History: Interactions between the Universal and the Local* (London: Palgrave Macmillan, 2006), pp. 98–130.

Metzler, Mark, 'Partisan policy swings in Japan, 1913–1932', *Asiatische Studien – Études Asiatiques* 69:2 (May 2015), pp. 477–510.

Mills, I. D., 'The 1918–1919 influenza pandemic – The Indian experience', *Indian Economic and Social History Review*, 23:1 (January–March 1986), pp. 1–40.

Mwangi, Wambui, 'Of coins and conquest: The East African Currency Board, the rupee crisis, and the problem of colonialism in the East African protectorate', *Comparative Studies in Society and History*, 43:4 (2001), pp. 763–87.

Patrick, Hugh T., 'The economic muddle of the 1920s', in James W. Morley (ed.), *Dilemmas of Growth in Prewar Japan* (Princeton: Princeton University Press, 1971), pp. 211–66.

Perry, Elizabeth J., 'From Paris to the Paris of the East and back: Workers as citizens in modern Shanghai', *Comparative Studies in Society and History*, 41:2 (April 1999), pp. 348–73.

Pillai, P. P., 'The financing of Indian industry', *Indian Journal of Economics*, vol. 4 (1923-4), pp. 225–67.

Pradhan, S. D., 'Indian army and the First World War', in DeWitt C. Ellinwood and S. D. Pradhan (eds), *India and World War I* (New Delhi: Manohar, 1978), pp. 49–67.

Rice, Geoffrey W. and Edwina Palmer, 'Pandemic influenza in Japan, 1918–19: Mortality patterns and official responses', *Journal of Japanese Studies*, 19:2 (Summer 1993), pp. 389–420.

Rothermund, Dietmar, *The Global Impact of the Great Depression, 1929–1939* (London: Routledge, 1996).

Saini, Krishan G., 'The economic aspects of India's participation in the First World War', in DeWitt C. Ellinwood and S. D. Pradhan (eds), *India and World War I* (New Delhi: Manohar, 1978), pp. 141–76.

Schiltz, Michael, *The Money Doctors from Japan: Finance, Imperialism, and the Building of the Yen Bloc, 1895–1937* (Cambridge, MA: Harvard East Asian Monographs, 2012).

Schumpeter, J. A., *Business Cycles: A Theoretical, Historical, and Statistical Analysis of the Capitalist Process*, 2 vols (New York: McGraw–Hill, 1939).

Scott, James C., *The Moral Economy of the Peasant: Rebellion and Subsistence in Southeast Asia* (New Haven: Yale University Press, 1976).

Screpanti, Ernesto, 'Long economic cycles and recurring proletarian insurgencies', *Review (Fernand Braudel Center)*, 7:3 (Winter 1984), pp. 509–48.

Shiraishi, Takashi, *An Age in Motion: Popular Radicalism in Java, 1912–1926* (Ithaca, NY: Cornell University Press, 1990).

Singha, Radhika, 'Finding labor from India for the war in Iraq: The jail porter and labor corps, 1916–1920', *Comparative Studies in Society and History*, 49:2 (2007), pp. 412–45.

Sugihara, Kaoru, *Ajia-kan bōeki no keisei to kōzō* [Formation and Structure of Intra-Asian Trade] (Kyoto: Minerva Shobō, 1996).

Suh, Sang-Chul, *Growth and Structural Changes in the Korean Economy, 1910–1940* (Cambridge, MA: Harvard University Press, 1978).

Tomkins, Sandra M., 'Colonial administration in British Africa during the influenza epidemic of 1918–19', *Canadian Journal of African Studies*, 28:1 (1994), pp. 60–83.

Tomlinson, B. R., 'India and the British Empire, 1880–1935', *Indian Economic and Social History Review*, vol. 12 (1975), pp. 337–80.

Tooze, Adam, *The Deluge: The Great War, America, and the Remaking of the Global Order, 1916–1931* (New York: Viking, 2014).

Vakil, C. N., 'Indian financial statistics', *Indian Journal of Economics*, vol. 5 (1924–5), pp. 87–99.

Xu, Guoqi, *China and the Great War: China's Pursuit of a New National Identity and Internationalization* (Cambridge: Cambridge University Press, 2005).

Yamasaki, Kakujiro and Gotaro Ogawa, *The Effect of the World War upon the Commerce and Industry of Japan* (New Haven: Yale University Press, 1929).

Yong, C. F., 'Origins and development of the Malayan Communist movement, 1919–1930', *Modern Asian Studies*, 25:4 (October 1991), pp. 625–48.

Yoshikuni, Tsuneo, 'Strike action and self-help associations: Zimbabwean worker protest and culture after World War I', *Journal of Southern African History*, 15:3 (April 1989), pp. 440–68.

Chapter 2

Muslim Asia after Versailles

CEMIL AYDIN

According to dominant narratives about the transition from the world of empires in the mid-nineteenth century to the world of nation states in the mid-twentieth century, the Great War in Europe was the key turning point, with the double impact of Wilson and Lenin. The Bolshevik challenge to the imperial world order and the Wilsonian call for self-determination culminated in global expectations at the Paris Peace Conference and created a qualitative rupture in the international legality of the call for national self-determination of various anticolonial movements. In more recent histories, non-Western and subaltern actors are attributed agency in the triumph of the idea of national self-determination and sovereignty, although almost all of these international norms were traced back to Western Europe.[1] It appears as if it was the subaltern and non-Western actors who fulfilled the promises of Western universalism and Western-originated values during their struggles against Western hegemony and colonialism. On the surface and in many retrospective accounts, this transition looks very straightforward. Empires were illiberal and oppressive of national rights, and nationalism was inevitable. Western and Japanese colonialism delayed this inevitable process, causing much suffering in their colonies and beyond. Yet, with the triumph of nationalism in Asia and the completion of decolonisation (which took up until the 1960s), the ideals of freedom from foreign hegemony, and natural rights to national sovereignty won over.

Many historical processes and events complicate and challenge this linear decolonisation narrative of transition from empires to nation states. During this transition, for example, pan-nationalist ideals were crucial. We cannot understand the nature of decolonisation without looking at the significant role played by pan-Islamic, pan-Asian and pan-African visions of world order. For example, pan-Islamism among Indian Muslims and their growing ties to the Ottoman Empire from the 1880s to the 1920s contradict a narrative of nationalism. In this process, the religious and political legitimacy of the caliphate institution as a symbol of global Muslim solidarity increased. The Ottoman Empire, perceived as the sick man of Europe, was increasingly seen as the leader and symbolic focus of unity for colonised Asian Muslims.

Thus, future visions of Asian Muslims after Versailles were closely tied to the destiny of the Ottoman Empire. In that context, it would be simplistic to assume that the defeat of the Ottoman Empire in World War I ended Ottoman influence in the imagined Muslim world, or terminated pan-Islamic visions related to the Ottomans. Instead of seeing Versailles and 1919 as a turning point, we need to look at crucial developments from the Paris Peace Conference and the Treaty of Sèvres to the Turkish War of Independence, the Khilafat Movement, the Lausanne Treaty and the abolition of the Caliphate in 1924. It is the cumulative impact of these developments over a period of five years that helps us better understand the ambivalence and complexity of global trends for the historical actors who transformed the nature of pan-Islamic visions and encouraged a secular nationalist path after 1924. Only on the basis of such historical contextualisation – that is, one that seriously acknowledges the impact of the Lausanne Treaty and the Caliphate Question on various Muslim anticolonial projects – can we fully understand the transition from the world of empires to the era of nationalism in Asia.

The impact of World War I and the Versailles Treaty was as crucial for Muslims in Asia as it was for Europe.[2] Most of the Muslim populations in the 1910s lived in Asia, and an overwhelming majority of them were ruled by a European empire at the time of the Versailles Treaty. The wartime mobilisation of Muslim subjects of empires all over the world demonstrated the power of various imperial state structures, be they British, French, Austrian, Russian or Ottoman.[3] The fact that millions of Muslim men could be brought together in uniform and made to fight against each other shows the organising capacity and legitimacy of those empires in the lives of the Muslim populations of Asia. Yet, throughout World War I, imperial policymakers perceived the Muslims of Asia through geopolitical and civilisational lenses, with exaggerated fears or hopes regarding Muslim solidarity. Thus, the impact of the Great War and of the Treaty of Versailles was also regionally differentiated. We should not assume that World War I had the same impact in all the different regions of the world, despite the global synchronicity of the many key events and political developments of the time. When Eastern Europe received a Wilsonian deal with the emergence of ten or so new nations, even more areas of Muslim societies were being colonised in a new mandate system that looked like the extension of the Scramble for Africa and the Middle East. Despite the dramatic impact of the Bolshevik Revolution and the emergence of a Bolshevik government, pan-national regionalism in Asia, Africa and the Muslim world continued to be politically relevant. After World War I, a revival of the Russian, German, Austro-Hungarian and Ottoman Empires, which had disintegrated at the end of the war, no longer seemed probable. The victorious British, French, Japanese and Italian Empires did not, however, take this as the occasion to end their own imperial projects in Asia, Africa and the Middle East. Thus, even though the idea of national self-determination gained a new international legitimacy, its destiny was shaped by confrontations with imperial realities, as well as pan-national regionalist solidarity projects.

Overall, we have to see the impact of the Versailles moment for the Muslim societies of Asia from the perspective of a long transformation from 1911 to 1924 that altered the balance between imperial, national and regional political imaginations through new compromises and bargains, without terminating the relevance of any of them. Attention to the regional, religious and civilisational specificity of the impact of World War I and the Versailles Treaty would complement the existing historiography, which often emphasises the global impact of nationalism and the decolonisation process of the war without paying sufficient attention to differentiation according to a particular region.

In this essay, I will focus on the impact that thirteen long years of war, between 1911 and 1924, had on the Muslim societies of Asia. This attention to specific historical turning points for the Muslims of Asia, which partly differ from those in Europe, is necessary because we need to recognise the disparate, albeit connected, narratives of the impact of World War I in each geopolitical region. Thus, the Wilsonian moment of the post-World War I period was also a peak of pan-Africanism and pan-Asianism, while the pan-Islamic Khilafat Movement reached its mass mobilisation between 1920 and 1923. Moreover, it was only in Central and Eastern Europe that the end of Austria–Hungary, Germany and Russia signalled a new era of independent nations. This process had been almost complete as early as 1913 for the Ottoman-ruled southeast of Europe. As late as 1924, however, there were still only four independent countries with a Muslim majority anywhere in the world (Turkey, Iran, Afghanistan and Albania), and only two independent African polities (Ethiopia and Liberia). Though nationalism became the most legitimate form of political imagination available for Muslim groups challenging colonial rule after 1919, this nationalism was still tied to discourses of transnational Muslim solidarity and identity, and suppressed by a new wave of empire-building in the form of post-World War I mandates. Pan-Islamic debates on the political meaning of the caliphate were as important as nationalism for many Muslim elites. Likewise, ideas of pan-African solidarity continued to be significant throughout the interwar period. The decolonisation of the large populations of Africa and of Muslim-majority populations in Asia through the formation of nationalist movements would take another half-century and is beyond the timeframe of this chapter. In other words, the impact of Versailles for the Muslim populations of Asia should not be constructed as a singular narrative of the rise of nationalism against the Eurocentric imperial world order, but rather as a multistranded, regionally and chronologically differentiated development.

The multiplicity of Muslim wartime identities

On the eve of World War I, a pan-Islamic regional identity, often synonymous with the term 'the Muslim world', coexisted in a symbiotic relationship with the reality of multiple empires, created by their infrastructure as well as rivalries. Throughout the war, imperial confrontations utilised or managed the emotions, identities and networks of Muslim world regionalism. Within a decade of the start of World War I, however, the centuries-old rule of the Muslim Ottoman dynasty over the Arab populations of the Middle East had terminated. The holy cities of Mecca and Medina came under the rule of Arab kings, and the third most sacred city of Islam, Jerusalem, was promised as a Jewish homeland under a British mandate.

In order to evaluate the impact of World War I on Muslim societies better, we must consider several crucial events preceding the Great War and their implications for broader Muslim networks, political projects and identity: the Italian invasion of Libya in 1911 and the Balkan Wars of 1912–13, occasions that led to pan-Islamic mobilisations stretching from Africa to South Asia and Indonesia. One can view the Italian invasion of Ottoman territories in Libya from the perspective of an inter-imperial conflict within the broader European region. Yet it soon transformed into a larger pan-Islamic campaign with calls to boycott Italian products on the part of Muslims in countries stretching from India to Indonesia. The Balkan Wars of 1912–13 had similar regional–civilisational implications, especially agitating Muslim public opinion in the British-ruled Indian Ocean zone, where the British Empire was asked to intervene on behalf of the Ottoman side. The fact that Muslim soldiers in the Indian army would collect donations to send to victims of the Balkan Wars, or boycott Italian products while simultaneously asking the British government to help the Caliph, indicates the complexity of the relationship between pan-Islamism in British–Ottoman visions of cooperation.

Despite, and yet because of, the Ottoman Empire's loss of territory in the Balkan Wars, the global manifestations of the emotional, humanitarian and economic mobilisation of Muslim public opinion in Asia and Africa in support of the Ottoman Empire were striking. This was a process that convinced German officers that there was a 'Muslim world' and that the German Empire could benefit from this world if there were an imperial war with its rivals. It was also striking that, on the eve of World War I, transnational Muslim identity had its peak in modern world history, sustained by dense networks of Muslim press and journalism, and religious and political identity links to the Ottoman Caliphate.

The Balkan Wars did seem like a new Crusader attack on Muslims, although the reality was much more complex. From the Tanzimat period to the 1910s, realist Ottoman bureaucrats insisted on the primacy of their imperial interests and valued the loyalty of their Christian subjects over their pan-Islamic image. Pan-nationalist identities existed, and were well formulated as a grand strategy for the Ottoman Empire by a Russian Muslim intellectual, Yusuf Akçura, in his treatise *Three Methods of Grand Politics* (that is, Ottomanism, pan-Islamism and pan-Turkism), published in British-controlled Cairo in 1904. In this book, Akçura argued that cosmopolitan, imperial Ottomanism had failed because of the disloyalty of its Christian subjects, and that pan-Islamism, though emerging as a strong vision, was impractical, as it threatened the most powerful empire in the world, the British Empire. Akçura was aware of the fact that the British

Empire controlled, and seemed to have the loyalty of, the majority of the world's Muslims. He argued that it would be more feasible if the Ottoman Empire could pursue a pan-Turkic regionalism in cooperation with the British Empire, as this would threaten only the Russian Empire.[4] Yet, eventually, he suggested that the Ottoman Empire could still utilise both pan-Islamic and pan-Turkic policies in world politics, even though both of these policies seemed unrealistic, due to the need to challenge two powerful empires. Other Ottoman bureaucrats and intellectuals criticised this merger of imperial foreign policy with regionalist identity. After all, as one Ottoman critic of this book noted, 'while dreaming of saving India from British rule, the Ottoman State could lose Western Thrace just fifty miles away from its capital city.'[5] In fact, using the same imperial logic, the Ottoman Sultan did not endorse the 1907 Pan-Islamic Congress in Cairo: for Abdulhamid II, pan-Islamism should be a basis of British–Ottoman cooperation. The Cairo conference on pan-Islamism was organised by a modernist Russian intellectual, Ismail Gaspirali, in cooperation with Egyptian pan-Islamists such as Rashid Rida.[6] The Ottoman Empire's cautious policy, as reflected in its carefully distancing itself from the Cairo conference, was derived from avoiding direct challenges to the European empires and instead focusing on the security and territorial integrity of the Ottoman Empire. This reflects the legacy of Ottoman inter-imperial diplomacy until the 1910s, partly based on the realisation that overt pan-Islamism would contradict attempts to gain the loyalty of Armenian and Greek Ottoman subjects.

However, once the Balkan Wars had resulted in the complete loss of Ottoman territories in Europe, and other European empires approved these border changes that had come about by force, the Ottoman Muslim elite became convinced that there was a new modern Crusade against the last Muslim empire and that they should utilise pan-Islamic networks and public opinion as leverage to protect their empire. They also foresaw population politics, confirmed in their eyes by the expulsion of Muslims from the Balkans by Christian armies, as the future of international affairs – a diagnosis that would shape the ethnic cleansing policies directed at the Armenian populations in 1915.[7] During the Balkan Wars, a pan-Islamic humanitarianism expressed itself in the extraordinary levels of donations to the Red Crescent Society in countries from Central Asia to India and Southeast Asia, and the volunteering of Muslim medical doctors from India for service. Donations to the Society from different corners of the world reached a peak as the Red Crescent charity became a symbol of a new pan-Islamic region divided into multiple empires.

Once the Ottoman government entered World War I, it immediately began to utilise pan-Islamism as a propaganda tool. The Ottoman political elite did not fully abandon the legacy of inter-imperial cooperative diplomacy, as their pan-Islamic policy was planned in cooperation and alliance with the German and Austro-Hungarian Empires. The influence of pan-Islamic ideas, especially the diagnosis of international relations as a modern Crusade by the West against the Muslim world, became crucial for gathering Ottoman public support for entering World War I on the side of Germany.⁸ Popular notions of pan-Islamic solidarity provided Ottoman policymakers with the vision that, upon entering the war, they would be able to exploit the contradictions and weak points in the legitimacy of the imperial world order by encouraging Muslim disobedience and (if possible) open revolt against it. German imperial policymakers shared these assumptions about the existence of a Muslim world region and its anticolonial emotions, as well as the Ottoman Sultan's religious position as caliph of all Muslims. Thus, the German Empire could contemplate using an inter-regional vision of conflict between Islamic and European–Western regions for pursuing its own imperial interests against its rivals in Europe.⁹

Pan-nationalist World War I propaganda soon demonstrated that an appeal to religions, civilisations or geopolitical identities was an unsuitable basis for mobilising armies, and thus Ottoman and German intelligence agents could not provoke any large-scale Muslim revolt against Western colonialism. More importantly, pan-Islamist propaganda contradicted the fact that the Ottoman Empire was still recruiting its non-Muslims citizens, such as Armenians, Greeks and Jews. Yet, as Michael Reynolds aptly describes, the Ottoman and Russian perception of their insecurities and their vision of solving their problems through war eventually led to the 'shattering' of their own empires in World War I. As a result, the lives of millions of people within those empires, as well as in their borderlands, were also shattered.¹⁰

When the Ottoman and German governments announced the liberation of colonised Muslim lands as one of the aims of the war and asked Muslims in India to rebel against British rule, they soon realised that their jihad proclamation was based on a serious miscalculation of the nature of pan-Islamism. There was clearly a symbiotic relationship between British imperial infrastructure and Muslim connectivity that created pan-Islamism, and asking Muslims to rebel against the British Empire also missed one of the main concerns about Muslim-minority status in a Hindu-majority continent. Thus, the Ottoman–German jihad demonstrated those countries' illusions about the nature of the imagined global community of the Muslim world, divided into multiple empires.

This battle around the soul and spirit of the illusionary Muslim world during World War I soon came to focus on the legitimacy of the Ottoman Caliphate. There was no doubt that the Muslim world existed. But was the Ottoman Caliph its true representative? Was he even a legitimate caliph? Thus, World War I-era military conflicts occurred against the background of an intellectual battle about the meaning of the Ottoman Caliphate and pan-Islamic solidarity. Some of the pro-Ottoman books that claimed the Ottoman Caliphate's legitimate leadership over the Muslims living under British rule included Hindli Abdülmecid, *İngiltere ve Alem-i Islam* [England and the Muslim World], published in 1910; Hamdi Paşa's *İslam Dünyası ve İngiliz Misyoneri: İngiliz Misyoneri Nasıl Yetiştiriliyor?* [The Muslim World and the British Missionary: How Do they Train British Missionaries?] of 1916; and Şehbenderzade Ahmed Hilmi's *Senusiler ve Sultan Abdulhamid* [Sanusi Order of Africa and Sultan

Abdulhamid II]. Responses from European imperial centres likewise included academic refutations of the Ottoman claim to caliphate with reference to classical texts of Islam, such as that by Russian Orientalist Vasili V. Barthold, who wrote 'Caliph and the Sultan' in the journal *Mir Islama* in 1912, or the Italian Carlo Alfonso Nallino (1872–1938), who published *Appunti sulla natura del 'Califfato' in genere e sul presunto 'Califfato Ottomano'* (1917) in Rome as a report presented to the Italian Foreign Ministry. Due to its importance, this Italian report was translated into both English and French as part of a joint war propaganda effort.[11] George Samne (1877–1938), most probably an Arab–Christian, wrote *Le Khalifat et le panislamisme* (Paris, 1919) in French. Last, but not least, Arnold J. Toynbee joined the discussion with a similar set of arguments in his 'The question of the Caliphate' (1920). There was even an American scholarly intervention on the topic: namely, Albert T. Olmstead's *The New Arab Kingdom and the Fate of the Muslim World*, published in 1919, the year of the Paris Peace Conference.

There were clearly pro-Ottoman expressions in different parts of the colonial world when Istanbul declared jihad, enough to raise special concern among colonial officers and necessitating a counter-propaganda effort. Expressions of sympathy with the Ottoman Caliphate were even seen in places beyond India, Malaya, Russia and the Dutch East Indies, such as Australia, South Africa, Singapore and Madagascar. However, German and Ottoman governments soon recognised that having sympathisers to their cause among Muslim public opinion in different European colonies was not enough to coordinate and create a revolt against these empires. In areas that Ottoman–German agents could reach with their military and financial aid, such as Libya or Afghanistan, they could find allies who would potentially support them. For example, the 1915 Mutiny in Singapore clearly had something to do with Muslim soldiers influenced by the Caliph's call for jihad, as well as the Ghadar Party's connections to Indian soldiers.[12] Developments disappointed German and Ottoman expectations of a Muslim revolt in India, however. There were soon various proclamations by Russian Muslim clerics or Indian or Malay Muslim notables and princes expressing their loyalty and solidarity to the British, Russian and Dutch empires. Many Muslims in India did not find it contradictory to express loyalty to the Raj, while at the same time stressing the importance of the institution of the Ottoman Caliphate for Muslims. Thus, to make their case stronger, special British propaganda directed at the Muslims of India and Malaya emphasised that the Ottoman government was under the control of infidel Germans, while the British would honour the sanctity of the Muslim holy cities, the institution of the caliphate and the pilgrimage routes.[13]

Instead of rebelling against their rulers, Indian Muslims renewed their loyalty to the British Empire with an implicit contract: they would serve the Empire and sacrifice their lives in return for London's respect for Muslim religious sensibilities, including respect for the Caliph who issued the call to jihad, as well as the continuation of Muslim rule over the holy cities of Arabia. From the very beginning of Ottoman participation in the war, the British government in India showed an awareness of Istanbul's link with Indian Muslims (as well as with Muslims in Egypt and Sudan) and emphasised that the war against the Ottoman Empire was of a defensive nature and did not mean a war against the Caliph. Indian Muslims were repeatedly told that the British Empire would not get involved in any military operation that would offend the sensitivity of Muslims and would respect all the sacred places in Arabia, as well as the institution of the caliphate. These imperial promises then constituted an implicit contract for Muslim loyalty and sacrifices for the British Empire.

Ottoman–German war propaganda clearly misdiagnosed the relationship between the European empires and the emergence of global Muslim public opinion, as these two were not necessarily antagonistic. It was European imperialism that united Muslim societies across Asia and Africa in terms of their identities. British imperial rule in the Indian Ocean from Singapore to Jeddah was especially adept at fostering pan-Islamic networks of connectivity. The majority of Muslim subjects of the British Empire preferred to keep multiple loyalties to the British king or queen, to a newly defined Muslim *ummah* and to the Ottoman caliph. Asking Indian, Nigerian or Tunisian Muslims to rebel against their Christian imperial rulers was to simplify and misinterpret a complex imperial pan-Islamic identity. If European colonial officers misinterpreted every act of pan-Islamic connections as a sign of potential threat, the Ottoman and German elites were equally misled in thinking that the global connectivity of Muslims living under colonial rule could be exploited to create rebellion against their Christian rulers. For example, Arnold Toynbee, working as an intelligence officer during World War I, identified the Ottoman Empire with the Muslim world, while Abdullah Yusuf Ali, a prominent Indian Muslim also working for British intelligence and war propaganda, was trying to define a Muslim world identity loyal to the British Empire.[14] Indian Muslims' discontent with Islamophobic white and Christian discourses coming from colonial officers, as well as metropolitan public opinion, did not equate to a total rejection of the British Empire.

Muslim–Christian regional identities became a sensitive issue for all the empires during World War I, and one that needed careful monitoring. When Edmund Allenby entered the Old City of Jerusalem as victorious British general in December 1917, the British papers referred to it as the successful completion of the Crusades (with a Christian victory). In truth, however, Allenby had respectfully entered the Old City on foot through the Jaffa Gate instead of riding on a horse or in a vehicle, to show respect for the holy site. He was the first Christian military commander since the Crusaders to control Jerusalem. Yet, the Prime Minister of the United Kingdom, David Lloyd George, described the capture of this holy city as 'a Christmas present for the British people'.[15] Mustafa Kemal Ataturk, who was in Berlin on the day that Jerusalem was lost in the winter of 1917, repeatedly spoke to an Arab–Ottomanist intellectual, Shakib Arslan, of his desire to take Jerusalem back.[16]

One other major event of the war was the rebellion of Sharif Hussein, in cooperation with British agents, against Ottoman rule. This was the first instance of a Muslim revolt against a Muslim monarch since the rebellion of Muhammad Mahdi in Sudan during the 1880s. Since Sharif Hussein soon gained control of the holy cities of Mecca and Medina, this development was highly disorienting for the world's Muslim populations. When Sharif Hussein's son, Faisal, in cooperation with British agents such as Lawrence of Arabia, attacked the Ottoman Hejaz Railway connecting Damascus to Medina, itself a symbol of pan-Islamic modernism, he was asserting the power of British-controlled steamship routes to Mecca over Ottoman–German-controlled railway routes. During World War I, the British Empire was still the greatest 'Mohammedan power', with many Muslim princely states and kings under its protection. Sharif Hussein was joining the side of Muslims allied with the British Empire, with grand promises of becoming ruler of a larger Arab kingdom in the Levant. Observing these dramatic events in Mecca, the Begum (queen) of the Indian princely state of Bhopal noted that Mecca was still ruled by a Muslim notable and that it would be acceptable for Muslims if, one day, an Arab took the position as leader of the Ottoman dynasty and Caliphate. Yet, she noted, Muslims of the world would want to see a caliph with temporal powers in Istanbul as their representative to the club of European imperial powers:

> Islam looks on the Sultan of Turkey as a sort of *vakil* (representative) to the court of Europe, and would be gravely hurt if that *vakil* were removed from Europe. But Islam would not care a button if the Sultan were removed to be replaced in Istanbul by the Arab.[17]

Thus, even at the peak of the war, Indian Muslims could express complex multiple loyalties when their holy cities came under the indirect control of the British Empire through the agency of an Arab notable.

In the same way that Indian Muslims remained loyal to the British Empire, Arab populations declared their loyalty to the Ottoman Empire at the beginning of the Great War. It was clear that the Ottoman Empire during World War I pursued a non-ethnic Muslim nationalism in the Arab territories of the Empire, and Sharif Hussein's revolt did not signify a broader Arab nationalist trend. This 'Muslim interpretation of Ottomanism' was very different from post-1923 Turkish and Arab nationalism, as it included a vision of the continuation of Ottoman rule as an empire of Arab, Kurdish, Turkish and other ethnic Muslims within a revised Ottoman commonwealth.[18] Only after the realisation that the Ottoman Empire was defeated and that its Arab-majority provinces were now occupied by the British or French Empire can we observe the emergence of Arab nationalist claims. Even during the post-World War I era of Arab nationalism, the Arab nationalists maintained close ties with the nationalist movement in Ankara and saw post-Ottoman Turkey as an ally and potential big brother in the region. It is in this context that the new League of Nations needed a legally more justifiable and subtle form of colonisation for the Arab lands (and former German colonies in Africa and Asia), in harmony with the new principles of self-determination. For this, they coined the term 'mandate system'. Muslim intellectuals across Asia immediately recognised that this was merely a new name for the old colonial practices of the British and French Empires.

Solving the postwar puzzle

It is from the perspective gained from examining this long-term pan-Islamic background to the World War I conflict between the British and the Ottoman Empires that we can make sense of the postwar puzzle. Despite the Ottoman defeat, there was extraordinary activism surrounding pan-Islamism in the postwar period. When World War I ended, some British officers believed that their policies had permanently damaged pan-Islamism and the Caliphate. However, they soon faced a new wave of rebellions that seemed ambiguously linked to each other: a Wilsonian–nationalist revolt in Egypt; another rebellion in Iraq exhibiting unity among Kurds, Sunnis and Shia; a caliphate movement in India; Bolshevik-supported Muslim activism in Afghanistan or the Near East; and a network of former Ottoman leaders from Switzerland to Moscow and beyond. A Bolshevism–pan-Islamism alliance became colonial officers' new nightmare. There were, in fact, pan-Islamist Indian migrants to Afghanistan, following the call to jihad by the Ottoman Empire, who found themselves in a position to cooperate with the Bolshevik government in Moscow against the common enemy, the British Empire. In particular, Panjabi *muhajirs*, some of whom had parents serving in the British army, became disillusioned by the treatment they received from both the Afghan King and Turkmen tribes during their long journey from North India to Central Asia. This disillusionment with Muslim unity prepared them to take the universalist and anti-imperialist message of the Bolshevik Revolutionaries more seriously. In return, the Bolsheviks and their Indian allies, such as M. N. Roy, hoped to cooperate with Indian pan-Islamism to create revolt in India against the British Empire, which was supporting the White Army against the Bolsheviks. Thus, there was a significant group of pan-Islamist *muhajirs* who ended up becoming either Communists or Muslim allies of Communists in the turbulent period between 1918 and 1922.[19] It was in this context that Turkish nationalists under the leadership of Mustafa Kemal could receive support from both pan-Islamists in India and the Bolshevik government in Moscow. At a certain point, British intelligence became alarmed as it watched Mustafa Kemal's Turkish nationalists coordinate different anti-European forces, from Bolshevism to pan-Islamism, for their own struggle.

Between 1920 and 1925, the British intelligence services produced a set of reports that illustrate the confusion about the new political forces of Bolshevism and nationalism, and in relation to earlier threats of pan-Islamism combined with German and Ottoman imperial strategies. After relying on a plan to encourage various Arab nationalist-kingdom projects against the Ottoman Empire, the British Empire struggled to understand the surprising alliance of German, Turkish nationalist, Bolshevik and pan-Islamic forces. Among these, Mustafa Kemal seemed to be the most threatening force from the Muslim world, as he could make an alliance with the Bolsheviks while calling for Muslim solidarity in his appeal to Arab nationalists and Indian Muslims. Despite Sharif Hussein's revolt against the Ottomans during World War I, the nationalist government in Ankara well knew that Hussein did not represent Arab public opinion, and kept in touch with various Arab leaders in Palestine, Syria, Iraq and the Hejaz region. The British were concerned that, under the new circumstances, their former wartime ally might even cooperate with Ankara.

The Allied Powers used the promise of national autonomy for Arab Muslims to weaken the appeal of pan-Islamism during World War I. These promises of nationality were ambiguous in scope and content, and did not yield much success initially. As in the case of Indian Muslims remaining loyal to the British Empire, Arab populations sided with the Ottoman Empire at the beginning of the Great War. It was clear that the Ottoman Empire during World War I pursued a non-ethnic Muslim nationalism in the Arab territories of the Empire, and Sharif Hussein's revolt remained an exception that did not signify a broader Arab nationalist trend. This 'Muslim interpretation of Ottomanism' was very different from post-1923 Turkish and Arab nationalism because it included a vision of the continuation of Ottoman rule as the empire of Arab, Kurdish, Turkish and other ethnic Muslims.[20] Only after the realisation that the Ottoman Empire was defeated and that its Arab-majority provinces were occupied by the British or French Empires do we observe the emergence of realist Arab nationalist claims in the wider public, including Arab intellectuals formerly loyal to the Ottoman Empire. As mentioned above, it is in this context that the new League of Nations adopted the term 'mandate system' (attributed to South African statesmen Jan Smuts) as a more legally justifiable and subtle form of colonisation of Arab lands (and former German colonies in Africa and Asia), in harmony with the new principle of self-determination.[21] However, Arab nationalists in former Ottoman territories understood that this was but a new name for the old British and French imperial colonial practices. From their perspective, the mandate system did not signal the end of the era of empires, but rather placed Arabs under the rule of empires governed by Christian elites, with discriminatory patterns of discourse and practices against Muslims.

Yet 1919 was too late to revive the claims of Europe's 'civilising mission' and the 'white man's burden', especially for Arab populations that had gone through almost a century of Ottoman imperial public schooling and understood Muslim modernist debates on history, civilisation and world order. Nevertheless, some Arab and even Turkish parties thought that the United States could act as a decent mandatory power. Contrary to the wishful thinking of the Turkish or Arab nationalists, however, the United States' Christian identity meant that the Americans were more interested in a mandate over a future Armenia in Eastern

Anatolia. Since the US Senate did not approve the outcome of the Paris Peace Conference, only the British and French Empires were given the new mandates, and the League of Nations created a Permanent Mandates Commission to monitor the progress and implementation of this system. Similar to the Minorities Committee, the Permanent Mandates Commission of the League of Nations claimed to be moving away from the old imperial system, but remained ineffective when confronted with the realities of empire. Both the British and French Empires had had to use military force and brutal methods to establish their control of the region. In some sense, the Ottoman soldiers of Arab descent continued to fight against the British and French forces under a different name right up until the Second World War.

Meanwhile, the Muslim elite of the Ottoman Empire rejected the terms of the Sèvres Treaty, which divided the remaining Ottoman lands into various mandate zones, due to their Wilsonian demands that they be given a national home in Anatolia, where Muslims were in the majority. The Sèvres Treaty divided Anatolia into Greek, Armenian, Italian, French, British, Kurdish and Turkish zones. The Armenians made an argument for a historic homeland and referred to their recent experience of ethnic cleansing. The Greeks similarly made a historic argument, supported by strong minority populations in Western Anatolia. Even before the signing of the Sèvres Treaty, the Greek armies began their invasion of Anatolia, triggering a more organised Muslim resistance movement under the leadership of Mustafa Kemal, still referencing the values of a Wilsonian compromise.

It is in the context of rejection of a Wilsonian deal for the Ottoman Empire at the Paris Peace Conference, and ambiguity surrounding the future of the Ottoman Empire, that a pan-Islamic Khilafat Movement emerged in India, reaching the peak of its activism between 1920 and 1923. While supporting the Ottoman–Turkish struggle for sovereignty and independence, against the terms of the Sèvres Treaty, Khilafat turned into the biggest social–political movement in British India, winning support from Hindu-origin nationalists such as Mahatma Gandhi.[22] Hindu nationalist support for the Muslim claims of the Khilafat Movement was focused on reminding British imperial rulers of the wartime promises they had made to Muslims about the holy places of Islam and the institution of a caliphate. Reneging on these promises, the British Empire occupied Istanbul, assigned Jerusalem as a Jewish homeland, and provoked a revolt against the Caliphate in the holy cities. Roughly sixty years after the Indian Rebellion of 1857, the British Empire was facing another mass Hindu–Muslim solidarity movement. Yet, Khilafat was also asking the British Empire to be truly cosmopolitan and represent the needs and demands of its Muslim subjects. In some sense, the Khilafat Movement, with this trans-imperial demand for justice for Muslim Turkey and the Caliphate, was reiterating Muslim interest in equal imperial citizenship. Thus, the Aga Khan, one of the strongest British loyalists and imam of the Isma'ili sect of Islam, could also support the Khilafat Movement.

Beyond practical material and moral support for the Turkish War of Independence, the Khilafat Movement symbolised a desire to have a 'collective deal' for the Muslim-majority areas of Asia and Africa, defined as the 'Muslim world': that is, to call for justice and dignity for the world's Muslim populations in an imperial context. This was not simply about empowering Indian Muslims but rather linking this empowerment to the destiny of the imagined 'Muslim world' globally. Influential Indian pan-Islamist Syed Ameer Ali raised this question in his address at the time of the Paris Peace Conference, formulating the general neglect and subjugation of the Muslim populations of the world during the debates on the new League.[23] These demands were formulated in hybrid language during the pan-Islamic campaigns, utilising the Wilsonian arguments for giving Ottoman sovereignty to Muslim-majority areas in Anatolia, while warning that the Muslim populations of other empires were behind Ottoman Turkey's struggle and that it would be dangerous for the British Empire, with its large Muslim populations, to punish Turkey and divide it. Loyalty to the British Empire, pan-Islamism, internationalism and Wilsonianism were all present in the eclectic language of the Khilafat Movement.[24] In that context, many observers writing on world events, such as Lothrop Stoddard, noted the *revival* of Muslim regionalism and unity after World War I, not its fragmentation into nationalism.[25] The Arabic translation of Lothrop Stoddard's book, *The World of Islam* (1921), contains long, dissenting commentaries by leading pan-Islamist Shakib Arslan on issues of detail, but agrees on the basic framework of interpreting world affairs as a conflict between the Muslim world and the West, despite the reality of Muslim loyalty to various European empires.[26]

During the Turkish War of Independence, the Muslim nationalist government, based in Ankara, benefited greatly from pan-Islamic aid campaigns in South Asia and from the moral support of Arab populations of the Middle East, although the movement's goal was to keep the Caliphate in Istanbul, which was under British-led Allied occupation. Muslim nationalists won military victories against the Greek armies and utilised their diplomatic successes by signing treaties with the Bolshevik government and then with the French Republic. Their military victories eventually compelled the British Empire to agree to a revision of the peace terms in the Sèvres Treaty at a peace conference held in Lausanne. The final conclusion of the Treaty of Lausanne (1923) ensured full sovereignty of the Ankara government in the remaining Ottoman territories, in return for the Turkish government renouncing all of its rights, claims and privileges in former Ottoman territories from Iraq and Syria to Egypt.[27] The Lausanne Treaty symbolised a trade-off between the British Empire and the Muslim elites of the new Turkey. The British Empire had to recognise Turkish sovereignty over Muslim-majority boundaries in Anatolia. In return, it implicitly asked Turkey to renounce its Ottoman and pan-Islamic credentials and influence over the Muslims of British India.

Various geopolitical writers considered the Lausanne Treaty to be another step in the awakening of 'coloured races' against white supremacy. As the

American missionary writer Basil Mathews noted, in his 1924 book *The Clash of Color*, 'The Treaty of Lausanne was discussed in every bazaar in India, by the night fires of Arab sheiks, and in student debates from Cairo to Delhi, Peking and Tokyo.'[28] Sun Yat-Sen's 1924 speech in Kobe on Greater Asianism started with references to the inspiration he received from the success of the Turkish nationalists.[29]

The nationalist government in Ankara kept the Caliphate in Istanbul for about five months after declaring the Republic and abolishing the Ottoman dynasty in October 1923, as the Caliphate had an immense prestige and respect among Muslims in Africa, Asia and Central Asia. It retained a member of the Ottoman dynasty as caliph with spiritual powers residing in Yıldız Palace. Yet, in the aftermath of the Lausanne Treaty, Muslim leaders of the new Turkish Republic decided to withdraw from their key position in pan-Islamic networks and began to espouse an idea of national sovereignty that did not directly challenge European colonial rule in other Muslim-majority areas. The abolition of the Ottoman Caliphate by the Turkish National Assembly on 3 March 1924 came as a shock to many pan-Islamic supporters of Turkey and shaped the destiny of the Muslim political imagination during the interwar era.[30] There was a *Realpolitik* calculation on the part of the Ankara government as to whether keeping the Caliphate would be a burden or an opportunity in terms of both challenging British colonialism and asserting Turkey's transnational power and influence. It should not be forgotten that there were strong voices among the Muslim Turkish elite for keeping the institution, from both religious and secular perspectives, in order to gain prestige and influence in Muslim societies and leverage in their relations with the European powers. Yet, the new state sovereignty compromise reached in the Lausanne Treaty already indicated problems with any transnational claim of the Caliphate in an age of reasserted European imperialism and rising nationalism. As Mustafa Kemal later noted, the paradoxical fact was that British-controlled Egypt and India had a larger Muslim population than Turkey. He commented on how unreasonable it was for the 8 million Muslims of Turkey to host an internationally significant caliphate that was capable of interfering in the affairs of British colonial domains for the sake and protection of the more than 100 million Muslims living there.[31] The Turkish Republic's implicit message was that it represented the 'Muslim liberation' in *one* state of a recently homogenised Muslim population, with full sovereignty and without extraterritoriality.[32]

Mustafa Kemal's reforms and the emergence of a Turkish nation state out of the Ottoman Empire shaped the political imagination in other Muslim societies. For example, Indonesian Muslim elites followed developments in Turkey very closely, with leaders such as Sukarno advocating a secular Muslim nation modelled on post-1924 Turkey. It may seem paradoxical that, even after the abolishment of the Caliphate in Istanbul, the Republic of Turkey continued to play a key role in the political imagination of other Muslim societies, thus illustrating the persistence of a pan-Islamic network of ideas and international visions.[33]

Conclusion: After the abolition of the Caliphate

The abolition of the Caliphate in 1924 ended a two-decade-long period of Ottoman–British confrontation over the leadership and destiny of the imagined Muslim world, and could have been a great relief for British imperial visions. After all, British policymakers blamed Istanbul and the Ottoman Caliph for being instigators of anti-British Muslim discontent and tried to sever the link between Britain's 'loyal Muslim subjects' in Asia and the Young Turk government in Istanbul. The British Empire's control over Muslim societies became even deeper and wider with mandates over Iraq and Palestine, as well as allies in Arabia. Yet British officials were puzzled to see that the link between Indian Muslims and Ottoman Turkey became even stronger with the post-World War I Khilafat Movement. Moreover, Indian Muslims perceived both the British occupation of Istanbul and the Balfour Declaration (1917) regarding the creation of a Jewish homeland in Palestine as betrayals of their implicit contract with London at the beginning of World War I, in which London promised to respect pan-Islamic symbolic claims over Istanbul and the holy cities of Arabia in return for the loyalty and sacrifice of Muslims to aid British war efforts. When the Khilafat Movement, in its support for the Turkish War of Independence, became a powerful sign of mass mobilisation in India, British officers asked both the Istanbul and Ankara governments to use their influence over Indian Muslims to encourage Muslim loyalty to the British Empire.[34] Thus, the Khilafat Movement of Indian Muslims formed part of the background for British–Turkish negotiations towards the Lausanne Treaty of 1923, and clearly empowered the claims of Turkish nationalists, partly leading to the interpretation of the latter's diplomatic achievements at Lausanne as a victory for the Muslim world. The Turkish government's abolition of the Caliphate in March 1924 thus looked like a blessing for the British Empire. They no longer had to worry about a caliph in Istanbul intervening on religious grounds in their sovereign rule over their Muslim subjects. Yet 1924 was too late for the British Empire to return to its celebrated status as 'greatest Muhammedan power' in the world.[35] Developments in World War I irreparably damaged British imperial legitimacy in the eyes of its Muslim subjects and yet the Muslim political imagination of the interwar period lacked any dominant unitary pattern.

In the aftermath of the abolition of the Caliphate, various Muslim leaders tried to resurrect that institution as an imaginary centre of a trans-imperial Muslim commonwealth. Muslim leaders from India to Egypt and from Mecca to Berlin protested against the decision and immediately attempted to convene an international gathering to establish a new caliphate. The destiny of the alternatives to the abolished Ottoman Caliphate demonstrated the problems of pan-Islamic solidarity in the ambivalent imperial era of the interwar years. Just two days after the Turkish National Assembly's decision, on 5 March 1924, Sharif Hussein of Mecca proclaimed his status as the new Caliph but did not receive much support among other Muslims, given his background of collaboration with the British armies against the Ottoman Empire. Egypt's religious scholars, on 10 March, declared that there needed to be a congress to discuss the issue of the Caliphate. The deposed Caliph, Abdülmecid Efendi, also supported this idea of a congress and even suggested a democratic mechanism of election.[36] Although Sharif Hussein was planning another caliphate congress in Mecca, coinciding with the pilgrimage season of 1925, Mecca came under the control of the Wahhabi State of the Saudis. Meanwhile, Egypt's King Fuad sponsored a different caliphate congress in Cairo in May 1926, ending in similar failure to forge an agreement. In the same year, the Saudi family, which had recently gained control of the holy cities of Arabia, organised a Muslim congress in Mecca; as Wahhabis, however, they were not even interested in the idea of a caliphate, and they had very little widespread transnational Muslim support. The very fact that the organisers of these caliphate conferences could write invitations to hundreds of delegates in different and distant parts of the world indicates the existence of a trans-imperial Muslim public sphere. The actual capability of each invitee to come to Cairo, Jerusalem or Mecca then illustrated the real imperial restrictions on the mobility of these delegates.

At the end of World War I, some former pro-Ottoman pan-Islamists such as Rashid Rida first put their hopes in the Arab Kingdom of Faisal in Damascus, whose independence, however, was soon abolished due to secret agreements among the Allied Powers that allocated the area to the French Empire. Rashid Rida then transferred his hopes to the Saudi King in Riyadh as the potential head of Arab unity. Similarly, a famous late-Ottoman-era pan-Islamist, Shakib Arslan, tried to create a new Arab royal federation by forming an alliance among the Kings of Iraq, Saudi Arabia and Yemen during the mid-1920s.[37] Meanwhile, the Arab nationalism of Iraq's British-appointed King Faisal entertained a vision of a Hashemite Arab kingdom under the umbrella of the British imperial world order. The very fact that these attempts were focused on Arab kingdoms without any input from South Asian Muslims, who were wealthier and more numerous, illustrates a key contradiction: it would have made sense if the new caliph was from the Muslims of the British Empire. This idea was entertained by the Nizam of the Hyderabad Princely State, who arranged the marriage of his son with the daughter of the last Ottoman caliph during the interwar period so that his descendants could inherit this title from their maternal grandparent. Yet, not having full sovereignty under the protection of the British Empire, whose reputation was damaged in the eyes of Muslim populations, the Nizam of Hyderabad never had any opportunity at all to make a serious claim to this title.

One of the most surprising repercussions ensuing from the abolition of the Caliphate occurred in Shia-majority Iran, which also followed developments in Turkey very closely. Muhammad Riza, the military general who deposed the Qajar dynasty, entertained the idea of creating a republic like Turkey, following the achievements of the Turkish nationalist movement under the leadership of Mustafa Kemal and its diplomatic victory in Lausanne. He was prime minister at that time and, according to this plan, would become president of a Persian Republic. Yet, when the Turkish National Assembly abolished the Caliphate in March 1924, certain segments of Iranian public opinion, especially the clergy, worried about the secularising impact of the Turkish model. In that context, more Iranians became supportive of crowning Muhammad Riza as shah and the new monarch of Persia, rather than having a secular republic.[38]

Just as important as the abolition of the Caliphate and Turkey's retreat from the imagined 'Muslim world' was the control of Mecca and Medina by the new Saudi state in the Najd area of Arabia in 1924. Despite almost a century of anti-Wahhabi discourse among British colonial officers, who would always attribute any Muslim rebellion in its dominions in Asia and Africa to that sect's influence, colonial officers in Egypt and India arrived at an understanding with the Saudi state against their former collaborator, the Hashemite Kingdom of Sharif Hussein. Sharif Hussein continued to serve as a new intermediary of British indirect mandate rule in Jordan and Iraq, but the vision of a great Arab kingdom and caliphate based on Hashemite leadership in the whole region had already been abandoned when the Saudi state took over the two holy cities.[39] Control of Mecca and Medina by the new Saudi state was traumatic for Muslims of the Indian Ocean area and Africa, as this change threatened the existence of many sufi orders, charities and madrasahs in Mecca and Medina that were funded by Muslims in different parts of the world. Wahhabi control of the holy lands curtailed important networks of the Muslim commonwealth, as it restricted the diversity of Muslim practices in their holy lands and even at some point decreased the number of pilgrims to Arabia due to concerns about puritanical Saudi punishments. It took about a decade for the Saudi Kingdom to establish its own credentials as protector of two holy cities, and reshaped the Muslim networks crisscrossing Mecca.

In short, the cumulative impact of the 1914–24 period for the Muslim political imagination was full of paradoxes and unexpected twists. Muslim regionalist imagination continued without the Caliphate and the Ottoman Empire's symbolic leadership. Yet, the end of the Empire, coupled with the model of territorial nationalism furnished by the Turkish Republic, encouraged a nationalist version of Muslim regionalism. The end of the Ottoman Empire also revealed the symbiotic relationship among rival empires, in the sense that the demise of the Caliphate strengthened the Muslim nationalist counter-imagination against the British and Dutch Empires. In Indonesia, for example, it was the end of the Ottoman Caliphate that strengthened secular nationalist visions over pan-Islamic ones.[40] The era of nationalism was as damaging to Muslim regional networks of mobility as it was to the imperial world order, even though there were new ways of reconfiguring a regional solidarity with nationalism. When Nasser and Sukarno met at the Bandung Conference of 1955, during the peak of decolonisation of the Muslim societies, they would represent nationalised visions of Muslim solidarity in ways very different from the imperial-era pan-Islamism associated with caliphate. It was very difficult to speak on behalf of all Muslims after the end of Caliphate, though many felt that *somebody* should speak on their behalf. Thus, a focus on the impact of World War I on Muslim-majority regions shows that, even though World War I had strengthened the political legality of demands made in the name of national self-determination, Muslim claims to rights in the name of a broader racial and civilisational community ended up being suppressed and curtailed.

Notes

1. See, inter alia, Manela, *The Wilsonian Moment*.
2. Afflerbach (ed.), *An Improbable War?*
3. Aksakal, '"Holy War Made in Germany"', pp. 184–99; see also Aydin, *The Politics of Anti-Westernism in Asia*.
4. Akçura, *Üç Tarzı Siyaset*, pp. 39–40.
5. See also İleri, *İttihad-i İslam*, pp. 10–11.
6. Kırımlı and Türkoğlu, *İsmail Bey Gaspıralı*.
7. Bloxham, *The Great Game of Genocide*.
8. Aksakal, '"Holy War Made in Germany"', pp. 184–99.
9. Manjapra, 'The illusions of encounter', pp. 363–82.
10. Cf. Reynolds, *Shattering Empires*.
11. See *Caliphate* (Cairo, 1918) and, for French, see *Notes sur la nature du 'Califat' en général et sur le prétendu 'Califat Ottoman'* (Rome, 1919).
12. Ramnath, *Haj to Utopia*, pp. 189–93.
13. van Dijk, 'Religion and the undermining of British rule', pp. 109–33.
14. Sherif, *Searching for Solace*.
15. Mortlock, *The Egyptian Expeditionary Force*, p. 149.
16. Adal, 'Constructing transnational Islam', p. 180.
17. Alavi, *Muslim Cosmopolitanism*, pp. 325–6.
18. Kayalı, *Arabs and Young Turks*.
19. Ansari, 'Pan-Islam and the making of the early Indian Muslim socialists', pp. 509–37.
20. Kayalı, *Arabs and Young Turks*.
21. On Smuts's role and the 'imperial internationalism' of the League, see Mazower, *No Enchanted Palace*, pp. 28–65. Article 22 of the League of Nations Covenant includes the Mandate principle: 'To those colonies and territories which as a consequence of the late war have ceased to be under the sovereignty of the States which formerly governed them and which are inhabited by peoples not yet able to stand by themselves under the strenuous conditions of the modern world, there should be applied the principle that the well-being and development of such peoples form a sacred trust of civilization [. . .].' See also Weitz, 'From the Vienna to the Paris system', pp. 1313–43.
22. Kidwai, *The Future of the Muslim Empire*; Kidwai, *The Sword Against Islam*.
23. Ali, 'Address by the Right Hon. Syed Ameer Ali', pp. 126–44.
24. Willis, 'Debating the Caliphate', pp. 711–32.

25. Stoddard, *The New World of Islam*.
26. For the 1924 Arabic translation, see Lûthrub Stûdard [Lothrop Stoddard], *Hadir al-Alam al-Islami*; for the 1922 Ottoman translation, see Stoddard, *Yeni Alem-i Islam*.
27. Allied and Associated Powers (1914–20), *Treaty of Peace with Turkey*.
28. Matthew, *The Clash of Color*, p. 23.
29. See Brown, 'Sun Yat-sen', pp. 75–85, with a full translation of Sun's Kobe speech.
30. Ardıç, *Islam and the Politics of Secularism*.
31. Öke, *Mustafa Kemal Paşa ve İslam dünyası*.
32. Sadiq, *The Turkish Revolution and the Indian Freedom Movement*.
33. Formichi, 'Mustafa Kemal's abrogation of the Ottoman Caliphate', pp. 95–115.
34. Japanese diplomatic correspondence from occupied Istanbul documents these negotiations, cf. Esenbel, 'Friends in opposite camps', pp. 257–78.
35. Counter-intuitively, the presence of a caliph in Istanbul, who also doubled as monarchic ruler of another empire, strengthened British imperial credibility among its Muslim subjects rather than weakening it, as colonial paranoia always assumed.
36. Hassan, *Loss of Caliphate*. See also Bruinessen, 'Muslims of the Dutch East Indies', pp. 115–40; Milner, 'The impact of the Turkish Revolution on Malaya', pp. 117–30.
37. Cleveland, *Islam Against the West*.
38. Katouzian, *State and Society in Iran*.
39. Teitelbaum, *Rise and Fall of the Hashimite Kingdom*.
40. Laffan, *Islamic Nationhood and Colonial Indonesia*.

References

Abdülmecid, Hindli, *İngiltere ve Alem-i Islam* [England and the Muslim World] (Istanbul: Matbaa-i Amire, 1910).

Adal, Raja, 'Constructing transnational Islam: The East–West network of Shakib Arslan', in Stephane A. Dudoignon, Komatsu Hisao and Kosugi Yasushi (eds), *Intellectuals in the Modern Islamic World: Transmission, Transformation, Communication* (London: Routledge, 2006), pp. 176–210.

Afflerbach, Holger (ed.), *An Improbable War? The Outbreak of World War I and European Political Culture Before 1914* (New York: Berghahn, 2007).

Akçura, Yusuf, *Üç Tarzı Siyaset* [Three Methods of Politics] (Ankara: Türk Tarih Kurumu Basımevi, 1987).

Aksakal, Mustafa, ' "Holy War Made in Germany"? Ottoman Origins of the 1914 Jihad', *War in History*, 18.2 (2011), pp. 184–99.

Alavi, Seema, *Muslim Cosmopolitanism in the Age of Empire* (Cambridge, MA: Harvard University Press, 2015).

Ali, Syed Ameer, 'Address by the Right Hon. Syed Ameer Ali on Islam in the League of Nations', *Transactions of the Grotius Society*, vol. 5: *Problems of Peace and War, Papers Read before the Society in the Year 1919* (1919), pp. 126–44.

Allied and Associated Powers (1914–20), *Treaty of Peace with Turkey: And Other Instruments Signed at Lausanne on July 24, 1923, Together with Agreements Between*

Greece and Turkey Signed on January 30, 1923, and Subsidiary Documents Forming Part of the Turkish Peace Settlement (London: H.M. Stationery Office, 1923).

Ansari, Humayun, 'Pan-Islam and the making of the early Indian Muslim socialists', *Modern Asian Studies*, 20:3 (1986), pp. 509–37.

Ardıç, Nurullah, *Islam and the Politics of Secularism: The Caliphate and Middle Eastern Modernization in the Early 20th Century* (London: Routledge, 2012).

Aydin, Cemil, *The Politics of Anti-Westernism in Asia: Visions of World Order in Pan-Islamic and Pan-Asian Thought* (New York: Columbia University Press, 2007).

Barthold, Vasili V., 'Caliph and the Sultan', *Mir Islama* (St Petersburg), 1:2–3 (1912).

Bloxham, Donald, *The Great Game of Genocide: Imperialism, Nationalism and the Destruction of the Ottoman Armenians* (Oxford: Oxford University Press, 2005).

Brown, Roger H., 'Sun Yat-sen: "Pan-Asianism," 1924', in Sven Saaler and Christopher W. A. Szpilman (eds), *Pan-Asianism: A Documentary History*, vol. 2: *1920–Present* (Lanham: Rowman & Littlefield, 2011), pp. 75–85.

Bruinessen, Martin van, 'Muslims of the Dutch East Indies and the Caliphate Question', *Studia Islamika*, 2:3 (1995), pp. 115–40.

Cleveland, William, *Islam Against the West: Shakib Arslan and the Campaign for Islamic Nationalism* (Austin: University of Texas Press, 1985).

Esenbel, Selçuk, 'Friends in opposite camps or enemies from afar: Japanese and Ottoman Turkish relations in the Great War', in Toshihiro Minohara, Tze-ki Hon and Evan Dawley (eds), *The Decade of the Great War: Japan and the Wider World in the 1910s* (Boston: Brill, 2014), pp. 257–78.

Formichi, Chiara, 'Mustafa Kemal's abrogation of the Ottoman Caliphate and its impact on the Indonesian national movement', in Madawi al-Rasheed, Carool Kersten and Marat Shterin (eds), *Demystifying the Caliphate: Historical Memory and Contemporary Contexts* (New York: Columbia University Press, 2013), pp. 95–115.

Hassan, Mona F., *Loss of Caliphate: The Trauma and Aftermath of 1258 and 1924*, unpubl. PhD thesis (Princeton University, 2009).

Hilmi, Şehbenderzade Ahmed, *Senusiler ve Sultan Abdulhamid* [Sanusi Order of Africa and Sultan Abdulhamid II] (Istanbul: Ses Yayınları, 1992).

İleri, Celal Nuri, *İttihad-i İslam: İslamin Mazisi, Hali, İstikbali* [Pan-Islamism: The Past, Present and Future of Muslims] (Istanbul: Yeni Osmanli Matbaasi, 1913).

Katouzian, Homa, *State and Society in Iran: The Eclipse of the Qajars and the Emergence of the Pahlavis* (London: I. B. Tauris, 2006).

Kayalı, Hasan, *Arabs and Young Turks: Ottomanism, Arabism, and Islamism in the Ottoman Empire, 1908–1918* (University of California Press, 1997).

Kidwai, S. Mushir Hosain, *The Future of the Muslim Empire: Turkey* (London: Central Islamic Society, 1919).

Kidwai, S. Mushir Hosain, *The Sword Against Islam; or, A Defence of Islam's Standard-Bearers* (London: Central Islamic Society, 1919).

Kırımlı, Hakan and İsmail Türkoğlu, *İsmail Bey Gaspıralı ve Dünya Müslümanları Kongresi* [Ismail Gasprinsky and Muslim World Congress] Islamic Area Studies Project: Central Asian Research Series, no. 4 (Tokyo: Tokyo University, 2002).

Laffan, Michael Francis, *Islamic Nationhood and Colonial Indonesia: The Umma Below the Winds* (New York: RoutledgeCurzon, 2003).

Manela, Erez, *The Wilsonian Moment: Self-determination and the International Origins of Anticolonial Nationalism* (Oxford: Oxford University Press, 2009).

Manjapra, Kris, 'The illusions of encounter: Muslim "minds" and Hindu revolutionaries in First World War Germany and after', *Journal of Global History*, 1 (2006), pp. 363–82.

Mathews, Basil, *The Clash of Color: A Study in the Problem of Race* (New York: Missionary Education Movement of the United States and Canada, 1924).

Mazower, Mark, *No Enchanted Palace: The End of Empire and the Ideological Origins of the United Nations* (Princeton: Princeton University Press, 2009).

Milner, Anthony, 'The impact of the Turkish Revolution on Malaya', *Archipel*, 31 (1986), pp. 117–30.

Mortlock, Michael J., *The Egyptian Expeditionary Force in World War I: A History of the British-led Campaigns in Egypt, Palestine, and Syria* (Jefferson, NC: McFarland, 2011).

Nallino, Carlo Alfonso, *Appunti sulla natura del 'Califfato' in genere e sul presunto 'Califfato Ottomano'* (Rome: Tip. del Ministero degli affari esteri, 1917).

Öke, Mim Kemal, *Mustafa Kemal Paşa ve İslam dünyası: hilafet hareketi* [Mustafa Kemal Ataturk and the Muslim World: The Caliphate Movement] (Istanbul: Aksoy Yayıncılık, 1999).

Olmstead, Albert T., *The New Arab Kingdom and the Fate of the Muslim World* (Urbana: War Committee of the University of Illinois, 1919).

Paşa, Hamdi, *İslam Dünyası ve İngiliz Misyoneri: İngiliz Misyoneri Nasıl Yetiştiriliyor?* [The Muslim World and the British Missionary: How Do they Train British Missionaries?] (İzmir: Tibyan Yayıncılık ve Matbaacılık, 2006 – reprint of the 1916 pamphlet).

Ramnath, Maia, *Haj to Utopia: How the Ghadar Movement Charted Global Radicalism and Attempted to Overthrow the British Empire* (Berkeley: University of California Press, 2011).

Reynolds, Michael A., *Shattering Empires: The Clash and Collapse of the Ottoman and Russian Empires, 1908–1918* (Cambridge: Cambridge University Press, 2011).

Sadiq, Mohammad, *The Turkish Revolution and the Indian Freedom Movement* (Delhi: Macmillan India, 1983).

Samne, George, *Le Khalifat et le panislamisme* (Paris: Dubois et Bauer, 1919).

Sherif, M. A., *Searching for Solace: A Biography of Abdullah Yusuf Ali, Interpreter of the Qur'an* (Kuala Lumpur: Islamic Book Trust, 1994).

Stoddard, Lothrop, *The New World of Islam* (New York: Scribner's, 1921).

Stoddard, Lothrop, *Yeni Alem-i Islam* [The World of Islam], transl. Ali Riza Seyfi (Istanbul: Ali Şükrü Matbaasi, 1922).

Stoddard, Lothrop [Lûthrub Stûdard], *Hadir al-Alam al-Islami* [The World of Islam], transl. Ajjâj Nuwayhid, ed. al-Amîr Shakîb Arslân (Cairo: Matbaa-i Salafiyah, 1924).

Teitelbaum, Joshua, *The Rise and Fall of the Hashimite Kingdom of Arabia* (London: Hurst, 2001).

Toynbee, Arnold J., 'The question of the Caliphate', *The Contemporary Review* (February 1920), pp. 192–6.
van Bruinessen, Martin, 'Muslims of the Dutch East Indies and the Caliphate Question', *Studia Islamika*, 2:3 (1995), pp. 115–40.
van Dijk, Kees, 'Religion and the undermining of British rule in South and Southeast Asia during the Great War', in R. Michael Feener and Terenjit Sevea (eds), *Islamic Connections: Muslim Societies in South and Southeast Asia* (Singapore: ISEAS, 2009), pp. 109–33.
Weitz, Eric D., 'From the Vienna to the Paris system: International politics and the Entangled histories of human rights, forced deportations, and civilizing missions', *The American Historical Review*, 113:5 (2008), pp. 1313–43.
Willis, John, 'Debating the Caliphate: Islam and nation in the work of Rashid Rida and Abul Kalam Azad', *The International History Review*, 32:4 (2010), pp. 711–32.

Chapter 3

From Versailles to Shanghai: Pan-Asianist Legacies of the Paris Peace Conference and the Failure of Asianism from Below

TORSTEN WEBER

In the past decade, the focus of the debate on 'Asia'[1] as a political concept has shifted from examining *what* 'Asia' means to *how* 'Asia' means.[2] The major inspiration for this new Asia discourse is derived from the writings of the Japanese Sinologist and critic Takeuchi Yoshimi (1910–77). In 'Asia as method' (1961), Takeuchi had distinguished between 'Asia as an object' (*taishō*) and 'Asia as a method' (*hōhō*). Advancing the latter, Takeuchi provided relief from the search for Asia's distinctive substance (*jittai*), which almost inevitably leads to the conclusion that, historically Asia is a heterogeneous and eventually empty, foreign-imposed category, nothing but the West's 'backward' Other. Instead, Takeuchi proposed grasping Asia primarily as a *method* to criticise defects of Western modernity. This critique, according to Takeuchi, could consecutively generate a process of Asia's self-formation. In addition, by applying 'Asia as a method' to the West, Asia could transform the West itself 'in order to raise to a higher level the universal values that were themselves engendered by the West'.[3] In the present-day politico-intellectual discourse, which links the critique of capitalism and globalisation to the debate of Asia in general and to visions of an East Asian community in particular, public intellectuals throughout East Asia have arduously been promoting this Takeuchian understanding of Asia.[4]

Historically, the First World War constitutes one of the first instances during which the concept of Asia was linked by people from different parts of Asia to criticism of the assumed superiority of Western modernity and of globalisation along Western standards. Encouraged by the self-destructive Great War and incited by continuous racial discrimination, numerous Asian thinkers embarked on a full-scale attack on European civilisation as the emblem of Western materialistic modernity. Simultaneously, the hitherto neglected concept of Asia was re-evaluated.[5] Constrained by the legacies of the traditional Sinocentric order, in the case of China, and of the pursuit of 'Europeanisationism' (Japanese *Ōkashugi*), in the case of Japan, this embrace of Asia occurred only in a hesitant and piecemeal fashion. Asia's 'Asia' itself, both in its imagination and reality, needed to be transformed before Asians could speak affirmatively on behalf of 'Asia' to Asians and to the West. Before applying 'Asia as a method' to the West, therefore, Asians needed to review their own understanding of Asia. It is in this context that the concept of Asianism (Japanese *Ajiashugi*, Chinese *Yaxiya zhuyi*

/ *Yazhou zhuyi*) emerged in mainstream political discourse during the First World War as a key political concept[6] throughout East Asia and inspired pro-Asian thought and activity in the interwar period. Often without defining Asia itself, Asianism offered a political alternative to both nationalist and internationalist ('world-ist') blueprints for the postwar order. Ranging from regionalist–pragmatic and social–Utopian to racialist–culturalist and imperialist–hegemonic notions, initially most Asianist conceptions remained divorced from and largely oppositional to official government rhetoric and policy. Borrowing Maruyama Masao's distinction of different stages of Japanese fascism,[7] this article draws attention to the existence of various manifestations of Asianism from below[8] – Asianist thought and action initiated and driven by low-key non-government actors – between the Paris Peace Conference and the second Pan-Asian Conference in Shanghai (1927). Eventually, transnational networks of civil society actors in the interwar period failed to instantiate their Asianist aims, most prominently the creation of an Asian League as a counter-organisation to the League of Nations. Ironically, the Asianist rationale and rhetoric established by these networks between the Paris and Shanghai Conferences facilitated the smooth appropriation of Asianism from above and its utilisation for state propaganda and government policy in Japan as well as by collaborationist regimes throughout Asia during the so-called Fifteen Years War (1931–45).

Asianism and the significance of Versailles

Although Asianist proposals for the postwar order displayed a remarkable diversity regarding their contents, their envisioned new order commonly rested on two key demands: firstly, the creation of an Asian League or Asian Union and, secondly, racial equality between the 'Yellow People' and the 'White People'. Sometimes the former was seen as a potential instrument to achieve the latter. Although similar Asianist visions had been proposed by several thinkers and activists from the late nineteenth century onwards, they had hardly had any impact on political discourse and even less on political reality.[9] After the war, however, the imminent realisation of the much grander-scale League of Nations equipped plans for an Asian League of Nations – previously dismissed as illusionary and Utopian – with new credibility and a sense of realism. Similarly, the rejection of the racial equality clause at Versailles[10] added a unique momentum to the smouldering political debate throughout Asia that critiqued the continuous and legalised racial discrimination against Asians, in particular in the United States, and the accompanying anti-Asian discourse in the West. Asianist rhetoric built on the assumption, and increasingly on the fact, that Asians were not only physically oppressed by 'the Whites of Euro-America' but also rhetorically demonised by Yellow Peril discourse.[11] In reality, of course, the dividing line between imperialist oppression and anti-Asian rhetoric on the one side and the oppressed and demonised on the other side did not run neatly through the East–West divide. From the late nineteenth century onwards, Japan itself had become a colonial power with the acquisition of Taiwan and Korea. Moreover, subsuming the Japanese under the category of yellow people had not been a popular idea in Japan historically.[12] In the realm of diplomacy, Japan had, in particular during and after the Russo-Japanese War of 1904/5, carefully avoided employing Asianist rhetoric and had vehemently rejected any plans for leading Asia against the West. Still in 1913, in the context of the first Californian land law, which restricted Japanese land possession, Japanese mainstream media and an assembly of public figures, including politicians, journalists, scholars and entrepreneurs, unanimously rejected any Japanese affiliation with 'the other Asians', the 'pariah', whose company Japan tried to avoid. 'Not even in its dreams would [Japan] think of planning such a disadvantageous and risky thing as to lead other Asians under the banner of pan-Asianism [*han-Ajiashugi*] into a fight against the White countries of Euro-America,' an editorial in the *Tokyo Nichi Nichi* newspaper read.[13] In a similar vein, former (and future) premier Ōkuma Shigenobu (1838–1922) emphasised that the Japanese, unlike other Asians, possessed a character of worldliness and adaptability. In contrast to China, which still pursued 'narrow provincialism', Japan had already become part of the civilised world. It was 'a bigotry', therefore, to judge the Japanese as inferior simply because of the colour of their skin.[14] Before World War I, racial discrimination had been a sensitive issue in Japan, not because Japan spoke on behalf of Asia but exactly because it viewed itself as different from, meaning superior to, the rest of Asia.

During the First World War and even more notably in its aftermath, Japan's hitherto relatively uniform official and mainstream public Asia discourse gradually drifted in opposite directions. After a few unenthusiastic and short-lived moves into a more proactive Asianist direction, the Japanese government remained principally anti-Asianist and pro-Western until the early 1930s. Public discourse, however, as expressed in newspaper editorials and journal articles, shifted towards an embrace of Asianist positions. From the mid-1910s onwards, these positions became popularised under the slogan 'Asia for the Asians'. Importantly, its appeal was by no means limited to Japan.[15] Chinese Republicans, most prominently Sun Yat-sen (1866–1925) and his disciple Dai Jitao (1890–1949), as well as the Marxist thinker Li Dazhao (1889–1927), at least temporarily embraced – China-centred – conceptions of Asianism as useful supplements to their political agendas in the late 1910s and 1920s.[16] Similarly, a number of Indians, including the Bengali and Hindu revolutionaries Taraknath Das (1884–1958), Rash Bihari Bose (1886–1945) and Mahendra Pratap (1886–1979), found value in the political programme of Asianism for Indian independence and for recruiting Japanese help to this end.[17] As a result, on the eve of the Paris Peace Conference, Asianism had become a widespread political concept in public discourse throughout many parts of Asia, particularly in East Asia and India. Interestingly, around the same time too in Europe and the United States, a large number of works appeared that discussed Asian unity and Asian commonality, partly in a derogatory tone reminiscent of Yellow Peril literature, but sometimes also as research into world and Asian affairs.[18] Asianism had developed into an issue of global political concern.

The Asianist moment at Versailles

The Paris Peace Conference is usually perceived as having promoted, both theoretically and practically, nationalism and internationalism.[19] In fact, the second half of the 1910s in East Asia illustrates particularly well the impact of competing nationalist agendas. During the war, Japan had issued the infamous Twenty-One Demands (1915) to the Chinese government, and amidst the Peace Conference in Versailles the anti-Japanese March First Movement for independence in Korea emerged. Just a few weeks later, anti-Japanese demonstrations triggered the May Fourth Movement in China, the origin of popular Chinese nationalism. None the less, as historian Akira Iriye has noted, as a result of China's decision to enter the war on the side of the Allies, at Versailles 'for the first time, China and Japan sat on the side of the victors'[20] together and, in spite of bitter rivalry, the Chinese delegation supported Japan's proposal for the inclusion of a racial equality clause in the Covenant of the League of Nations. According to Iriye, this was 'as striking an example of Asian self-consciousness as any, for it was the first time in modern history that non-European states got together to insist on equal treatment'.[21] However, neither the two countries' participation on the same side at Versailles nor Chinese support for Japan's racial equality proposal was intended as Asianist behaviour. In fact, neither side linked its actions to the cause of Asia. Revealingly, apart from the racial equality proposal, there was little else that the representatives of the Chinese and Japanese governments at Versailles could agree on. Not even the Japanese delegation, which had proposed the racial equality clause in the first place, had intended to speak or act on behalf of Asia. The proposal itself, as presented to the League of Nations Commission by the Japanese delegation in February 1919, did not contain a single reference to the cause of Asia, 'the East' or the coloured peoples. As has been argued, it is probably best understood as a rather symbolic expression of Japan's claim to world power status and as a bargaining chip.[22] Indeed, the racial equality proposal was all about Japan and its pursued aim of entrance into the exclusive club of Western powers. In the realm of diplomacy, Japan remained committed as ever to a policy that sought conciliation, not confrontation, with the West. Therefore, when the proposal was officially rejected in Paris, the Japanese delegation only protested half-heartedly and the Japanese government none the less decided to join the League of Nations as a founding member.

The Asianist twist to the proposal was rather given 'from below' – by the popular outcry that accompanied its fate at Versailles. On 5 February 1919, several hundred people had assembled in Tokyo's Ueno Park to adopt a resolution that urged the Japanese delegation to fight for inclusion of the clause into the Covenant of the League of Nations. 'The Japanese People', it read, 'resolve that at the Peace Conference the racially discriminatory treatment up to now practised internationally be abolished.'[23] To support and coordinate its activities, the assembly decided to found a League for the Promotion of the Abolishment of Racial Discrimination (*Jinshu-teki Sabetsu Teppai Kisei Taikai*). It claimed to support 'wholeheartedly' the creation of a future League of Nations, if only the proposal to abolish racial discrimination be adopted. In the following months, under the leadership of the liberal politician Sugita Teiichi (1851–1929), the *Taikai* organised public gatherings, gave interviews, and distributed articles and speeches. Its aims were to influence Japan's public opinion in the direction of a positive attitude towards the proposal in general and, eventually, towards an outspoken pro-Asianist attitude. Sugita had been among the first to re-embark on the Asianist project during the First World War. In the midst of the war, he renewed his earlier call for the creation of an Asian League (*Ajia Renmei*) based on a Sino-Japanese alliance that would ultimately link the Buddhist countries of East Asia with the Muslims of Central and Western Asia. Although Sugita considered Japan's alliance with Great Britain as disadvantageous, he emphasised that his conception of Asianism would neither run counter to any of Japan's existing alliances nor promote any exclusionist thought based on racialist notions.[24]

From February to April 1919, the *Taikai* convened three major assemblies that were attended by several hundred members and sympathisers. With a few exceptions, such as Sugita and the future ministers of law Ōki Enkichi (1871–1926) and Ogawa Heikichi (1870–1942), all participants were activists, academics, journalists of relatively little prominence or mid- and low-ranking politicians and military staff.[25] Interestingly, the *Taikai* also welcomed non-Asian members, and the French journalist–researcher Paul Richard (1874–1967) soon became its most fervent spokesman. Richard was an illustrious writer and traveller in Asia having personal contacts with a number of well-known Asian-minded thinkers, including Okakura Tenshin, Ōkawa Shūmei and Miyazaki Tōten. In fact, it was Richard who most explicitly linked the debate about racial equality to 'the revival of Asia'. In particular, Richard called on the Japanese to embark on the task of 'awakening Asia' and of forming an Asian League:

> Awaken Asia by organising her, by uniting her. And to that end, be not masters, but allies of her peoples. Cease you also to cherish against them prejudices of race. Treat them as brothers, not as slaves. Those who are slaves liberate that they may become your brothers. Form with them all one single family. Organise the League of Nations of Asia – the United States of Asia.[26]

The anticolonial notion in Richard's conception of an Asian League of Nations formed the crux in any proposal for a united Asia. From a Chinese and Indian perspective, 'Asia for the Asians' always contained the precondition of national liberation: 'India for the Indians' and 'China for the Chinese'. In other words, an Asian League had to consist of free and decolonised nations. While

Japan's assistance and even leadership towards this end was warmly welcomed, any Japanese ambitions to replace 'White' rule by Japanese rule was strongly rejected. Richard's speech directly confronted the Japanese with this ambivalence. On the one hand, he ascribed to the Japanese the role of organiser and 'saviour' of Asia. On the other hand, however, he criticised the Japanese for their racial prejudice against other Asians.

It is important to remember here that while mainstream contemporary publications reveal a remarkable shift and pro-Asianist trend in Japanese public opinion, Asianist discourse was accompanied by scepticism and rejections in Japan too. Was it in Japan's national interest to support the independence of India and China? Were efforts towards Asia's decolonisation, however morally justified they appeared, worth risking Japan's status quo? Was Asianism not merely a selfish trick played on Japan by the weak of Asia? While leftists such as Yoshino Sakuzō and Miyazaki Tōten dismissed Japanese Asianists' claims in the context of racial equality as hypocritical,[27] others merely saw Japan's own fate at stake if it pursued Asianist policies. The pacifist and social activist Ōyama Ikuo denounced Asianism as the 'gospel of the weak'[28] that would put Japan's achievements and reputation at risk, while Nanigawa Arata, a nationalist scholar of international law, rejected Asianism as the 'dream of a madman' that would inevitably cause Europeans to view the Japanese as instigators and outlaws, and turn all Western powers as enemies against Japan.[29]

In the midst of this heated and controversial political debate, the *Taikai* – probably owing to Sugita's prominent participation – managed to receive extensive media coverage in Japan. Representatives of the Japanese government, however, avoided the *Taikai* and the only prominent politician who agreed to support it, Ōkuma Shigenobu, preferred to send a letter rather than appearing in person. Contrary to the *Taikai*'s resolution, Ōkuma refused to link the racial equality proposal to Japan's participation in the League of Nations. Instead, he limited his criticism to the Australian Prime Minister Hughes's 'extreme racial prejudice' and the Powers' lack of support at Versailles for Japan's efforts at establishing 'common happiness and peace for all mankind' and 'eternal peace in the world'.[30]

Ōkuma's commitment to the *Taikai*'s cause was as half-hearted as the Japanese delegation's stance in Versailles regarding the racial equality clause. Although the proposal received the majority of votes in April 1919, upon Wilson's intervention the clause was eventually dropped and the case at Paris was closed. The case was not closed, however, for Asianists in Japan and elsewhere in Asia. While there is no evidence that the *Taikai* institutionally continued its campaigns after the rejection of the racial equality clause in Versailles, its rhetoric and political rationale survived the whole interwar period and blended rather well with Japan's later official wartime propaganda.

The persistence of racial discrimination and Asianist action 'from below'

Despite the *Taikai*'s short-lived fate, the topic of racial discrimination remained on the agenda of mainstream political discourse throughout the 1920s. As a consequence of the Johnston–Reed Act (1924), land lease by Asians was prohibited and Asians were virtually excluded from new immigration to the United States. In Japan, where the law became known as the so-called 'anti-Japanese immigration law', the reaction to the Act was stronger than ever as it confronted even the most apologetic and pro-Western Japanese with the foreign-imposed relegation of the Japanese to the category of Asians. The 1924 Act, therefore, appeared to prove that Asianists had been right from the beginning in criticising the hypocrisy of 'the Whites' who had coined justice and righteousness, peace and equality as key phrases at Versailles but refused to extend these values to non-Whites. The first day of July, the day the law went into effect, was declared the 'Day of National Humiliation' in Japan. But the humiliation was shared, to some degree at least, by other Asians. Japanese newspapers quoted non-Japanese Asians of no lesser prominence than Sun Yat-sen and Nobel laureate Rabindranath Tagore (1861–1941), who made statements of sympathy. Sun renewed his call for a 'Great Alliance of the Asian Peoples' in reaction to the 'tyrannical behaviour of the Whites' and encouraged the Japanese to abandon their pro-Western stance to fight for the liberation of oppressed peoples.[31] Tagore criticised the Act as the 'beastly behaviour of barbarians' and the 'humiliation of all Asian peoples'.[32] He demanded that any exchange between East and West should follow the ideals of humanism, virtue and civilisation. These statements clearly reveal that the values and political demands formulated at Versailles and traditionally seen as belonging to the canon of 'Western ideals' also appealed to Asian-minded Asians. Therefore, Asianist anti-Westernism based on an irreconcilable East-versus-West dichotomy was but one facet of Asianism and must be examined within its concrete historical context. Rather than assuming or even promoting a strict and eternal West–East dichotomy, many Asianists in the interwar period attempted to overcome this polarity by taking a self-affirmative stance as Asians. It was 'Asia', however defined, that had to remind the 'West' of the universality of its own values; irrespective of its substantive or regional definition, 'Asia' now mattered as a concept representing the righteous demand for equality, freedom and peace. According to Asianist logic, the task of improving the general conditions in the world, put on the agenda under Wilson's leadership at Versailles, had now fallen to the Asians – as Asian peoples, not governments.

Against the given political background, there was little need to agitate public opinion any further and Asianists found it easier than ever to channel public outrage into Asianist straits. As their argumentation had increasingly become self-explanatory in the light of continuous racial discrimination, Asianists now turned from theoretical and propagandistic work to more practical steps towards the creation of a common forum for discussing and implementing Asianist policies with the eventual aim of creating an Asian League of Nations. In 1924, at the height of public anger over the US racial exclusion legislation, the All Asia Association (*Zen-Ajia Kyōkai*) was founded in Tokyo. Its self-declared aim was 'to strive for the development of freedom based on the equality of all human beings'.[33] It not only saw itself as a platform for the awakening of Asians but also aimed at reconciling East and West to establish 'a new global civilisation'. Similar to Takeuchi's 'Asia as method', the mission statement skipped elaborations of the substance of Asia in favour of its potential functions for the improvement of the contemporary world in toto. It criticised the gap between universal values created in the West and hailed in Paris on the one hand, and the exclusion of non-Whites from them on the other hand. The Association did not reject modernity as such but rather aimed at replacing its corruptness by a 'new global civilisation'. According to Asianist logic, this task fell to Asia because of the civilisational achievements of Asians in the past and the deficiency of Western civilisation in the present, which the First World War and racial exclusionism had brought to light. Different from earlier (and again later) conceptions of Asianism that displayed more aggressive and revanchist stances,[34] the Asia as envisioned by the Association was not to conquer and colonise the West by force in revenge but to improve the general conditions of the entire world within a framework of decolonisation and decentralisation. To this end, naturally, the tone of its founding manifesto was not outspokenly anti-Western. Although anticolonial Asianist rhetoric generally drew much on anti-Westernism,[35] the Association, as well as its transnational activities, put the emphasis on reconciliation and harmony between East and West rather than on confrontation. The difference between their and the Japanese government's conciliatory position towards the West, however, lay in the Association's affirmative and inclusive view of Asia; it affirmed Asia's existence and significance, and, according to their conception of Asia, Japan was part of Asia.

Similar to the *Taikai*, the Association's membership consisted of politicians, entrepreneurs, academics and writers of limited prominence. Some members of the defunct *Taikai*, in fact, later became members of the All Asia Association.[36] Initially, it was led by Iwasaki Isao (1878–1927), a lawyer and member of the Lower House since 1912, who later became the secretary-general of the centre-right Seiyūkai party. Imazato Juntarō,[37] a minor political figure from the same party and member of the Lower House from 1924 to 1928, functioned as the Association's main spokesman and managing director. Both in parliament and in the press, Imazato was known as a pro-Chinese Asianist who was highly critical of Japanese government policies towards China. Despite the notably pro-Asianist shift in published opinion, Imazato was faced with persistent nationalist and pro-Western opposition, which dismissed his Asianist activities and writings as 'empty theory' or 'extremely dangerous'.[38]

Different from the somewhat Japan-centred *Taikai* and contrary to later pan-Asian organisations active in the 1930s,[39] the Association actively sought cooperation with existing Asianist groups and activists outside of Japan. To this end, it sent Imazato to Beijing, where a Great Alliance of Asian Peoples (*Yaxiya Minzu Da Tongmeng*) had been established in August 1925.[40] Under the leadership of some low-ranking officials[41] of the Nationalist Party (*Guomindang*), academics, journalists and entrepreneurs from China, Japan, Korea and India had organised a transnational organisation 'to resist the countries that practise imperialism in Asia and to attain the aim of freedom and equality of all peoples'.[42] The Japanese members gave a special declaration in which they explained their motivation for participating. 'The Japanese government', it read, 'is imperialist but we oppose imperialists and completely agree with the aims of this organisation.'[43] The declaration and the transnational character of the organisation obviously aimed at breaking off the national(ist) paradigm, which ran counter to the Asianist and anti-imperialist agenda of the Alliance.

After several meetings in China and Japan, the Japanese Association and the Chinese Alliance joined hands to prepare an All Asian Peoples' Congress, also known as the Pan-Asiatic Conference, to be held in Shanghai or Tokyo in the spring of 1926. Its aims were to establish 'true international everlasting peace based on equality and righteousness', the 'promotion of freedom and happiness by abolishing class, racial and religious discrimination', and the 'organisation of an All Asian League [*Zen-Ajia Renmei*]'.[44] Despite the Association's moderate and reconciliatory tone, which was not too dissimilar from the official Japanese diplomatic rhetoric of 'international accommodationism',[45] the Japanese Interior Ministry, as well as several diplomatic missions of Japan abroad, closely watched the activities of the Association and the preparations for the Congress.[46] Out of fear that the assembly might be dissolved prematurely by the authorities, the original locations of Shanghai and Tokyo were abandoned and replaced by Nagasaki, a port city far off-centre in southern Japan. The delegates for the largest pan-Asian political gathering in history thus far had been recruited through the Japanese and Chinese host organisations and included fifteen Japanese, eleven Chinese, four Indians, four Filipinos, three Koreans,[47] one Afghani and one Vietnamese. The most prominent of them, the Indian revolutionary Rash Bihari Bose, who had lived in exile in Japan for more than a decade, was to play a significant role as mediator between conflicting interests, above all between Japanese and Chinese participants. In his opening address, Bose explained why the assembly was aiming at the creation of an Asian League.

> Some people may ask why we should create an Asian League as there already is an International League [of Nations]. But those two differ profoundly. The League of Nations was created for 500 million people; however, the Asian League will be made for 1500 million coloured people. [. . .] We must unite not only to give birth to a new Asian civilisation but also to give birth to a new civilisation. Eventually, this is not only for the good of the Asian peoples but to save the unfortunate human race globally.[48]

Both points raised by Bose reveal the lasting impact of 1919 on Asianist political discourse. While agreeing to the organisation of an international league

– as established in Versailles – in principle, it criticised the negligence of Asian concerns. Similarly, it agreed to the high-flying ideals of eternal peace and the happiness of the human race enunciated at Paris but attributed the task of their realisation to Asia, not the West. The legacy of Versailles was also prominently reflected in the Provisional Constitution adopted by the Congress. Article One defined the object of the proposed Asian League as bringing 'permanent peace to the world, based on the principle of equality and justice, eliminating all discrimination, whether social, religious or racial, and thus to assure liberty and happiness to all the races of the world.'[49] In other words, the Asian League was to accomplish more or less the same goals as the League of Nations in Geneva. Of course, in the case of the former this included rather prominently the abolition of racial discrimination, the demand that the Japanese and Chinese government delegations at Versailles had failed to insist on.[50]

On the whole, the practical implications of assumed Asian commonality that underlay each of the individual proposals, as well as the general framework of the Congress, proved rather difficult. The language question was a case in point. By the mid-1920s, Chinese was no longer, if it ever was, the *lingua franca* for most Asians and certainly not for those assembled in Nagasaki. Refugees from British- and French-colonised countries were usually Japanophiles and had a better command of Japanese than of Chinese. Nevertheless, the Chinese were suspicious of Japanese as the official language since Japan was the only Asian country that itself had become an imperialist power. Japanese, therefore was regarded as a rather unfitting representative of the Asianist cause. But English, perceived as the main language of the imperialist West, of course, was not acceptable either. Esperanto as an alternative was briefly discussed but likewise rejected as a language originating from the West. According to contemporary sources, communication during the sessions at the Congress was mainly conducted in Japanese, Chinese and English – with translations provided. As a future goal, however, the Congress decided to undertake research into the invention of an Asian version of Esperanto as a neutral language.[51]

The language problem was a good reflection of the artificial and forced character of the concept of Asia in general. Where it implied cultural homogeneity (Confucian legacy, Chinese characters), it excluded vast areas such as India and Western parts of Asia. Where it openly embraced its diversity, Asia became void of any definable contents – it needed to reinvent itself artificially. The assumed common history and heritage that so many Asianists appealed to paled in the face of practical implementation. However, as the Congress also symbolised rather well, by the mid-1920s Asians did not leave this definitional task to others, especially the West. 'Asia' increasingly became a self-defined concept with positive connotations. Within this process, the self-affirmative embrace of Asia joined hands with the inherent and unavoidable Othering of the West. Importantly, as opposed to Asianism discourse that was limited to the relatively homogenous Sino-Japanese sphere, Asianist discourse that included wider parts of South and West Asia acknowledged the diversity of Asia and avoided falling into the trap of extreme forms of culturalist self-essentialisation. Instead, it embarked on the project of reviving Asia as a modern and, if necessary, consciously artificial concept that could appeal to Asians and, potentially, also to the wider world.

The failure of Asianism from below

Despite the rather limited success of the Nagasaki Conference, the pan-Asian Congress reconvened in November 1927 in Shanghai for its second annual meeting. With only eleven delegates, the conference was much smaller than the preceding one. However, continuity regarding participants testifies to the significance attributed to the Asianist undertaking by the Chinese Alliance, led by Huang Gongsu, the Japanese Association, led by Imazato, and other returning delegates, including Bose and Pratap. Yet, against the background of China's national unification process under General Chiang Kai-shek (Jiang Jieshi) from 1926 onwards ('Northern Expedition'), and attempts by the new Japanese government under the new Prime Minister, Tanaka Giichi, to secure what it defined as Japanese interests in China ('Tanaka Memorandum'), delegates at the Shanghai Conference found it ever more difficult to see in their counterparts more than representatives of national or even governmental interests. Again, the conference almost failed before its opening. Only after Pratap's mediation did the Chinese and Japanese agree to alter their respective proposals so that they did not offend each other. Instead of the original Chinese demand to end the 'Japanese invasion' of Manchuria and Mongolia, the final version of the resolution merely urged Japan to 'strive towards a reform of its policy in Manchuria and Mongolia in full acknowledgement that the current Japanese policy towards China hurts the feeling of the Chinese people'.[52] In turn, the Japanese dropped their plans for an Asian Central Monetary Institution and the inter-Asian railway project, which had both caused too much suspicion on the Chinese side. While these examples may serve as proof of the difficulties of any practical joint Asian enterprise beyond Asianist rhetoric, it also demonstrates the possibilities of inter-Asian – and more specifically, Sino-Japanese – dialogue and compromise at a time of fierce nationalist agitation within both countries.

The Shanghai Conference had been watched with suspicion by both Chiang's ruling Guomindang (GMD) party and the foreign authorities.[53] The premature end to the official part of the Conference after only one day, however, was caused by the GMD itself. It had forbidden any political gatherings on the tenth anniversary of the Russian Revolution, which coincided with the day the Conference opened.[54] The assembly hurriedly adopted a ten-point 'common proposal', including the desire to 'help China by a sincere cooperation with Japan', elected a standing executive committee consisting of Huang, Imazato, Bose, Pratap and four others, and departed for Nanking to continue informally as a private gathering.[55] At Pratap's suggestion, a third pan-Asian Conference was announced for the following year in Kabul but historians have been unable to uncover any proof of its actual convention.⁵⁶ Similarly little is known about the host organisations after 1927.

Asianism as a political concept, however, remained prominent both in China and in Japan, although it now served less as an alternative to nationalist and internationalist ideas than as an eclectic ingredient of otherwise defined political agendas or ideologies. Where it stressed anti-imperialist notions, Asianism frequently appealed to Communist internationalists. Anti-Communist nationalists and imperialists also found some value in the concept of Asian uniqueness and unity, which was, in their views, best represented or achieved by national tradition or the expansion of a single nation. As a consequence, in the early 1930s, nationalists in China and Japan competed for the prerogative of the rightful interpretation of Asianist concepts. Even within China's Nationalist Party itself, where Asianism had become an important part of Sun Yat-sen's politico-intellectual legacy, various Asianist conceptions were employed in the internal power struggle among Sun Yat-sen's followers.⁵⁷

While Asia consciousness among Asians had, without doubt, increased tremendously in the interwar period, the concept of 'Asia' had already failed to appeal to the solidarity and common aims of Asians by the time Asianist rhetoric and rationale became gradually appropriated by the Japanese military and government after the Manchurian Incident (1931), the founding of Manchukuo as a Japanese quasi-puppet state (1932), and Japan's departure from the League of Nations (1933). Also, against this background of intra-Asian dispute and expanding Japanese imperialism, 'Asia' had lost its credibility as a critique of Western hypocrisy, injustice and immorality. By the late 1920s, the Asianist momentum of Versailles, which had driven much of the Asianist civil society activities during the 1920s, had waned and the transnational project of pan-Asia had collapsed in the face of nationalist aspirations, suspicions, and government policies that displayed little interest in pan-Asian dialogue and compromise. Against these constraints, transnational activists and thinkers throughout Asia had failed to turn the 'decline of the West' into the revival of Asia – and much less 'the improvement of global conditions' or the creation of a 'new global civilisation'. Instead, and somewhat ironically, the combination of regionalist and racialist claims inherent in most conceptions of Asianism supplied the Japanese military and government with the rhetorical ammunition it then started to fire at its own population, at the Chinese, at other Asians, and subsequently at the West in the name of 'Greater Asia' during the 1930s and early 1940s.

As a consequence, the more pan-Asian idealism served as window dressing for Japanese colonialism (and justification of collaborationist regimes), the more Asianist affirmations disappeared from political agendas elsewhere in Asia in favour of nationalistic ideals. Asianism from below, much like Japan's fascist movement 'from below', in Maruyama's words, had 'remained to the end a movement of a small number of patriots (*shishi*) – extremely idealist, Utopian and lacking in plan'.⁵⁸ Importantly, however, interwar Asianists did not – unlike fascists – resort to intimidation, assassinations and the plotting of coups d'état, although, subsequently, even greater bloodshed was caused in the name of 'Greater Asia'.

Why had Asianism from below failed? To refer solely to the social explanation used by Maruyama to explain the case of fascism – lack of mass energy as a main force in political change, i.e. the non-existence of a functional civil society – would fall short of important politico-ideological reasons. In the age of nationalism and Empire – Japan's empire had been a fait accompli by the time the transnational networks of Asianism came into existence, both the appeal of and trust in decentred transnational political formations were limited. In addition, the disparity between Japan and other Asian countries in economic and military terms, had hindered the development in Japan of a consciousness that rendered an Asiaphile policy necessary or desirable while, in other parts of Asia, Japanese Asianism caused constant suspicion over its 'real', assumedly nationalistic and imperial, intentions.

Conclusion

'Asia' after Versailles was not the same as before. Through heated debate rather than consensus, and often as an expedient or a mere tool of rhetoric rather than a principle, Asia had become a key concept in political discourse in Japan, China, other parts of Asia and, indeed, in the world. Change in this direction had already started in the late nineteenth century; however, it was only during and after the epoch-making First World War that Asians increasingly started to embrace Asia as a potentially positive concept that would allow them self-affirmatively to confront their Other, 'the Whites of Euro-America', who had dominated vast parts of Asia politically, economically, militarily and discursively for decades and indeed centuries. After the First World War had revealed the deficiencies of the self-declared superior Western civilisation – a model that many Japanese in particular had followed and believed in – the Paris Peace Conference once more brought to light the rhetorical contradictions of peace, equality and righteousness on the one side and the power-based and interest-led *Realpolitik* on the other. The rejection of the racial equality proposal at Versailles therefore functioned as a catalyst for the smouldering dissatisfaction with the new, yet in many ways old, status quo that continued to relegate 'non-Whites' in general to an inferior position. To the same degree that the First World War and the Paris Peace Conference had, in the eyes of many Asians, failed to mark a new beginning in world affairs, it nourished visions of alternative world and regional orders. 'Asia for the Asians', the key Asianist slogan, combined the two major political ideas of the postwar era – self-determination and internationalism – in an Asianist inflection, with the abolition of racial discrimination and the formation of an Asian League as its pursued instantiations. To the visionaries of Asian commonality and unity, it mattered less what Asia included and how it was defined than what it meant to speak and act on behalf of 'Asia', above all, to the West. Asianism as a political concept facilitated this discourse particularly well because it elevated Asia, at least rhetorically, to the rank of a principle and yet was vague enough to be incorporated into a variety of political agendas – imperialist, anti-imperialist, socialist, nationalist, internationalist and others. As a consequence, it never developed into a fully-fledged political doctrine and never had to. As the case studies of two Pan-Asian Conferences demonstrate, political reality, combined with nationalist aspirations and suspicion, impeded transnational dialogue among Asians and Asianist action from below, despite the existence of a wide range of common interests and common goals. Although Japan, as the main perpetrator during the Second World War in Asia, could have taken a number of different roads between 1919 and 1931 (and even thereafter), it is difficult not to include the establishment of Asianist rhetoric and rationale from below in the interwar years, and its subsequent appropriation from above during the 1930s and 1940s, as two of the manifold legacies of Versailles. Transnational networks of pro-Asian critical thinkers and activists in Asia today are faced not only with the challenges of globalisation and the persistence of nationalisms but also with this dual legacy of their historical precedents.

Notes

1. Following the terminology used by the debaters under study, 'Asia' and 'the East' in this article are mostly identified with East Asia (China/Taiwan, Japan, Korea), which also constitutes the spatial focus of this study.
2. See Sun, 'How does Asia mean?', pp. 13–47; Koyasu, *'Ajia' wa dō katараretekitaka*; Chen, *Asia as Method*; Yan and Vukovich, 'Introduction: What's left of Asia', pp. 211–24; Spivak, *Other Asias*. To a certain degree, this focus resembles Edward Said's famous critique of Western 'Orientalist' scholarship or, rather, to be chronologically correct, Said's work contains arguments that Takeuchi had discussed in Japan some decades earlier. The most important difference between Said's 'Orientalism' on the one side and historical and contemporary Asianist discourse on the other side is that, in the latter case, 'Asia' is affirmatively employed by Asians themselves to denote a positive meaning and function of the concept. In addition, Said's 'Orient' was mainly the Middle East and largely excluded East Asia.
3. See Takeuchi, 'Hōhō toshite no Ajia', p. 469.
4. See, especially, Sun et al. (eds), *Posuto 'Higashi Ajia'*; Dushu (ed.), *Dushu jingxuan 1996–2005: Yazhou de bingli*; and Chen and Chua (eds), *The Inter-Asia Cultural Studies Reader*. Importantly, this understanding of 'Asia' is not only directed against capitalism-driven globalisation but also opposes essentialist conceptions of Asia as advanced in the so-called Asian Values debate of the mid-1990s.
5. Alternatively, the Japanese victory over Russia in 1905 has been identified as the starting point of a re-evaluation of the concept of 'Asia' and of the affirmative embrace of Asia by Asians. See Fischer-Tiné, 'Indian nationalism and the "world forces"', pp. 325–44 and Esenbel, 'Japan's global claim to Asia and the world of Islam', pp. 1140–70 for the impact the Russo-Japanese War had on Asian thinkers and activists in India and Western Asia. However, in Japan, the concept of 'Asia'

remained marginalised and was largely rejected as disadvantageous until the late 1910s; see Weber '"Unter dem Banner des Asianismus"', pp. 34–52.
6. Due to constraints of space, a discussion of the functions of key concepts in political discourse has to be omitted here. See Ball, 'Conceptual history and the history of political thought', pp. 75–86.
7. See Maruyama, 'Nihon Fashizumu no shisō to undō', pp. 259–322 and, for an English translation, 'The ideology and dynamics of Japanese fascism', pp. 25–83.
8. Here, 'from below' does not refer to the so-called grassroots level of society, which appears to be a less appropriate category in the study of political thought than in other fields, such as social history. In Maruyama's study of fascism, 'from below' particularly refers to low-key members of the military and other activists, as opposed to elite military circles and government authorities. This study adopts a similar understanding of 'from below', including thinkers and activists who, however, had no or very limited influence on political decision-making and did not normally hold any leading positions in government or the military, as opposed to those who later advocated and implemented Asianist policies 'from above'.
9. For early Asianist proposals, see Matsuda, '"Ajia" no "tashō"sei. Ajiashugi izen no Ajiaron', pp. 33–53 and Katsurajima, 'Ajiashugi. Doko kara, doko e', pp. 267–304.
10. See Shimazu, *Japan, Race and Equality*.
11. This double frustration with the West is particularly well captured in Kodera Kenkichi's *Dai-Ajiashugi Ron*, p. 1; see also Saaler, 'The construction of regionalism in modern Japan', pp. 1261–94.
12. See Matsuda, '"Ajia" no "tashō"sei', pp. 33–53.
13. See Anonymous, 'Nihonjin to hoka no Ajiajin'.
14. See Ōkuma, 'Our national mission', p. 4.
15. None the less, Japan played a crucial role both as a cradle for ever-new Asianist visions and activities, and as a hub for the exchange of ideas among Asian-minded Asians. Most of the non-Japanese Asians mentioned in this article had lived in Japan for some time as students or refugees and formulated their own Asianist visions in relation to different Japanese conceptions of Asianism. See, in particular, Li Dazhao's 'New Asianism' as a rejection of, among others, Kodera Kenkichi's and Tokutomi Sohō's 'Greater Asianism' and as a modification of Ukita Kazutami's own 'New Asianism' (see Weber, '"Unter dem Banner des Asianismus"').
16. On the appropriation of Asianism by Chinese thinkers in the 1920s and 1930s, see Kawashima, 'Kindai Chūgoku no Ajia kan to Nihon', pp. 415–41.
17. See Taraknath Das, *Is Japan a Menace to Asia?* and for Bose and Pratap below.
18. Lothrop Stoddard's *The Rising Tide of Color Against White World-Supremacy* (1920) and his *The Revolt Against Civilization: The Menace of the Under Man* (1922) belong to the most notorious books of the former category, while H. M. Hyndman's *The Awakening of Asia* (1919) and Stanley Rice's *The Challenge of Asia* (1925) are examples of the latter. Whereas only a few Western writers displayed an awareness of the diversity of Asia discourse in Asia, Japanese and Chinese Asianists frequently formulated their own conceptions of Asian unity in explicit affirmation or rejection

of Western notions of Asian commonality: for example, as expressed in the works mentioned above.

19. See Stegewerns, 'The dilemma of nationalism and internationalism in modern Japan', pp. 3–15.
20. Iriye, 'East Asia and the emergence of Japan, 1900–1945', p. 143.
21. Iriye, 'East Asia', p. 143.
22. See Shimazu, *Japan, Race and Equality*, pp. 115–16 and Burkman, *Japan and the League of Nations*, pp. 80–6.
23. Anonymous, 'Sabetsu teppai sengen', p. 3.
24. See Sugita, 'Wa Gaikō to Tōa Renmei'.
25. They included, among others, Soejima Giichi (1866–1947), Ōtake Kan'ichi (1860–1944), Okabe Jirō (1864–1925), Shiba Teikichi (1869–1939), Tanaka Zenryū (1874–1955), Shimada Saburō (1852–1923), Nishimura Tanjirō (1866–1937), Itō Tomoya (1873–1921) and Andō Masazumi (1876–1955).
26. Paul Richard's speech to the assembly on 22 March 1919, quoted after his 'The unity of Asia', p. 6. On Paul Richard and his Asianist views, see Szpilman, 'Paul Richard', pp. 287–95.
27. See Yoshino, 'Jinshu teki sabetsu teppai undōsha ni atau' and Yabuta, 'Kenkyū nōto', pp. 277–377.
28. Ōyama, 'Dai Ajiashugi no unmei ikan', p. 22.
29. See Ninagawa, 'Monrō Shugi no mohō', pp. 16–20.
30. Anonymous, 'Hai sabetsu ron'.
31. Sun quoted after Anonymous, 'Ajia minzoku no daitō tanketsu o hakare', p. 2.
32. Tagore quoted after Anonymous, 'Jūteki na ban kōi', p. 2.
33. Zen Ajia Kyōkai, 'Zen Ajia Kyōkai setsuritsu shushi', p. 1.
34. See Kodera Kenkichi's *Dai-Ajiashugi Ron* [On Greater Asianism], which called for Asian revenge on 'the Whites'.
35. See Aydin, *The Politics of Anti-Westernism in Asia*.
36. Members of both organisations include Ogawa Heikichi, Tanaka Zenryū (1874–1955), Gokubo Kishichi (1865–1939) and Furuhata Mototarō (1864–1931).
37. Imazato originates from Nagasaki prefecture and was a graduate of Tokyo's Waseda University. He became a member of parliament in May 1924, when the debate over racial discrimination and pan-Asian solidarity in the context of the US immigration law reached its climax in Japan.
38. See Ninagawa, 'Ajia Renmei no kūron', pp. 12–17 and his 'Kiken naru jinshu byōdō no seikō', pp. 20–2. Ninagawa had criticised emerging Asianist conceptions since the First World War (see above).
39. The Greater Asia Association (Dai Ajia Kyōkai), founded in 1933, was the major Asianist organisation during the Fifteen Years War and, often via members of the military, set up branches throughout Japanese-occupied Asia. For the Association's thought and activities, see Weber, 'The Greater Asia Association and Matsui Iwane, 1933', pp. 137–47.
40. On the Alliance's origins, see Huang, *Yaxiya Minzu di yici Dahui shimo ji*, pp. 3–4 and Zhou, 'Yaxiya Minzu Huiyi', pp. 128–59.

41. For details on the participants, see Zhou, 'Yaxiya Minzu Huiyi', pp. 129–33. The leading initiators were Huang Gongsu and Li Zhaofu (1887–1950), both members of the dissolved parliament of the Chinese Republic.
42. Quoted after Zhou Bin, 'Yaxiya Minzu Huiyi', p. 130.
43. Quoted after Zhou Bin, 'Yaxiya Minzu Huiyi', p. 130.
44. Zen Ajia Kyōkai, 'Zen Ajia Kyōkai setsuritsu shushi', pp. 2–3.
45. Burkman, 'Nitobe Inazō', p. 196.
46. An impressive collection of official reports on the host organisations and the Nagasaki Conference is available online via the Japan Center for Asian Historical Records (http://www.jacar.go.jp/), including reports by the Japanese consular representations from China, Australia, France and Argentina, by Japanese prefectural authorities on foreigners planning to enter Japan as participants of the Conference, and by the Asia Department of Japan's foreign office on the meetings of the All Asia Association in Japan. See Naimushō Keihokyoku Hoan Ka (Home Ministry, Special Observation Office, Public Security Division), *Zen Ajia Minzoku Kaigi tenmatsu* (Details of the All Asian Peoples Conference), October 1926.
47. Not surprisingly, the Korean 'delegates' were denounced as collaborators in the Korean media, where the hypocritical character of the assembly was condemned. See Anonymous, 'A Korean denunciation', p. 157.
48. Anonymous, 'Imazato Juntarō o gichō ni kaigi hajimaru' and Anonymous, 'Ajia Minzoku Taikai'.
49. Anonymous, 'Ajia Minzoku Taikai'.
50. See Anonymous, 'Ajia Minzoku Taikai'.
51. On the language problem, see Asada Hajime, 'Ajia minzoku kaigi ni nan kokugo o tsukau ka' and Anonymous, 'Ajia Minzoku Taikai'.
52. Zhou, 'Yaxiya Minzu Huiyi', pp. 151–2.
53. See Zhou, 'Yaxiya Minzu Huiyi', pp. 150–3 and Anonymous, 'Asiatic congress', p. 497.
54. See Zhou, 'Yaxiya Minzu Huiyi', p. 152.
55. See Zhou, 'Yaxiya Minzu Huiyi', p. 152.
56. Still in August and September 1928, newspapers reported that, at the invitation of King Amanullah, a Pan-Asian Conference was scheduled to be held in Kabul in November that year and that T. E. Lawrence ('Lawrence of Arabia') was returning to Arabia to persuade Arabs not to participate in such a gathering. See Anonymous, 'Lawrence goes back to Arabia', p. 8 and Anonymous, 'Pan-Asiatic Congress', p. 12.
57. See Weber, 'Nanjing's Greater Asianism', pp. 209–20.
58. See Maruyama, 'Nihon Fashizumu', pp. 295–6.

References

Anonymous, 'Nihonjin to hoka no Ajiajin' [Japanese and other Asians], *Tokyo Nichi Nichi* (26 June 1913).

Anonymous, 'Sabetsu Teppai Sengen' [Declaration of the abolishment of discrimination], *Yomiuri Shinbun* (6 February 1919), p. 3.

Anonymous, 'Hai sabetsu ron. Shubetsu teppai taikai ni okeru ryō ensetsu' [On anti-discrimination. Two speeches at the assembly for the abolition of racial discrimination], *Tokyo Nichi Nichi* (26 April 1919).

Anonymous, 'Ajia minzoku no Daitō tanketsu o hakare' [Let's plan a great union of Asian peoples], *Tokyo Asahi* (25 April 1924), p. 2.

Anonymous, 'Jūteki na ban kōi' [Beastly behaviour of barbarians], *Tokyo Asahi* (26 April 1924), p. 2.

Anonymous, 'Ajia Minzoku Taikai' [Asian Peoples' Conference], *Osaka Asahi* (1 August 1926).

Anonymous, 'Imazato Juntarō o gichō ni kaigi hajimaru' [The conference starts with Imazato as chairman], *Osaka Mainichi* (2 August 1926).

Anonymous, 'A Korean denunciation', *Japan Weekly Chronicle* (5 August 1926), p. 157.

Anonymous, 'Asiatic congress', *Japan Weekly Chronicle* (10 November 1927), p. 497.

Anonymous, 'Lawrence goes back to Arabia', *Atlanta Constitution* (26 August 1928), p. 8.

Anonymous, 'Pan-Asiatic Congress', *Manchester Guardian* (27 September 1928), p. 12.

Asada, Hajime, 'Ajia minzoku kaigi ni nan kokugo o tsukau ka' [What language will the Asian Peoples' Conference use?], *Osaka Asahi* (29–30 July 1926).

Aydin, Cemil, *The Politics of Anti-Westernism in Asia: Visions of World Order in Pan-Islamic and Pan-Asian Thought* (New York and Chichester: Columbia University Press, 2007).

Ball, Terence, 'Conceptual history and the history of political thought', in Iain Hampsher-Monk, Karin Tilmans and Frank van Vree (eds), *History of Concepts: Comparative Perspectives* (Amsterdam: Amsterdam University Press, 1998), pp. 75–86.

Burkman, Thomas W., 'Nitobe Inazō: From world order to regional order', in Thomas J. Rimer (ed.), *Culture and Identity: Japanese Intellectuals During the Interwar Years* (Princeton: Princeton University Press, 1990), pp. 191–216.

Burkman, Thomas W., *Japan and the League of Nations: Empire and World Order, 1914–1938* (Honolulu: University of Hawaii Press, 2008).

Chen, Kuan-hsing, *Asia as Method: Toward Deimperialization* (Durham, NC: Duke University Press, 2010).

Chen, Kuan-hsing and Beng Huat Chua (eds), *The Inter-Asia Cultural Studies Reader* (London and New York: Routledge, 2007).

Das, Taraknath, *Is Japan a Menace to Asia?* (Shanghai: published by the author, 1917).

Dushu (ed.), *Dushu jingxuan 1996–2005: Yazhou de bingli* [A Selection from *Dushu*, 1996–2005: The Ills of Asia] (Beijing: Sanlian Shudian, 2007).

Esenbel, Selçuk, 'Japan's global claim to Asia and the world of Islam: Transnational nationalism and world power, 1900–1945', *American Historical Review*, 109:4 (October 2004), pp. 1140–70.

Fischer-Tiné, Harald, 'Indian nationalism and the "world forces": transnational and diasporic dimensions of the Indian freedom movement on the eve of the First World War', *Journal of Global History*, 2:3 (2007), pp. 325–44.

Huang, Gongsu, *Yaxiya Minzu di yici Dahui shimo ji* [Complete Record of the First Conference of the Asian Peoples] (Beijing: Yaxiya Minzu Datongmeng, 1926).

Hyndman, H. M., *The Awakening of Asia* (London: Cassell, 1919).

Iriye, Akira, 'East Asia and the emergence of Japan, 1900–1945', in Michael Howard and Wm. Roger Louis (eds), *The Oxford History of the Twentieth Century* (Oxford: Oxford University Press), pp. 139–50.

Katsurajima, Nobuhiro, 'Ajiashugi. Doko kara, doko e' [Asianism: From where to where?], in *Iwanami Kōza Gendai Shisō 14: Kindai/Han kindai* (Iwanami Course Contemporary Thought: Modernity/Anti-modernity) (Tokyo: Iwanami, 1994), pp. 267–304.

Kawashima, Shin, 'Kindai Chūgoku no Ajia kan to Nihon. "Dentō-teki" taigai kankei to no kanren de' [Japan and Modern Chinese views on Asia. With reference to the 'traditional' foreign relations], in Akio Takahara, Tamura Keiko and Satō Yukihito (eds), *Gendai Ajia Kenkyū 1: Ekkyō* [Contemporary Asia Research 1: Transcending Borders] (Tokyo: Keiō Gijuku Daigaku Shuppan kai, 2008), pp. 415–41.

Kodera, Kenkichi, *Dai-Ajiashugi Ron* [On Greater Asianism] (Tokyo: Hōbunkan 1916).

Koyasu, Nobukuni, *'Ajia' wa dō katararetekitaka: Kindai Nihon no Orientarizumu* [How has 'Asia' been narrated? Modern Japan's Orientalism] (Tokyo: Fujiwara Shoten, 2003).

Maruyama, Masao, 'The ideology and dynamics of Japanese fascism', in *Thought and Behavior in Modern Japanese Politics*, ed. Ivan Morris (Oxford: Oxford University Press, 1969), pp. 25–83.

Maruyama, Masao, 'Nihon Fashizumu no shisō to undō' [Thought and movement of Japanese fascism], *Maruyama Masao Shū* [Collected Writings of Maruyama Masao], vol. 3 (Tokyo: Iwanami, 1995 [1948]), pp. 259–322.

Matsuda, Kōichirō, '"Ajia" no "tashō"sei. Ajiashugi izen no Ajiaron' [The foreign-imposed character of 'Asia'. Asia discourse before Asianism], in Nihon Seiji Gakkai (ed.), *Nihon Gaikō ni okeru Ajiashugi* (Asianism in Japan's Foreign Policy) (Tokyo: Iwanami, 1999), pp. 33–53.

Naimushō Keihokyoku Hoan Ka [Home Ministry, Special Observation Office, Public Security Division], *Zen Ajia Minzoku Kaigi tenmatsu* [Details of the All Asian Peoples Conference] (October 1926).

Ninagawa, Arata, 'Monrō Shugi no mohō' [An imitation of the Monroe Doctrine], *Gaikō Jihō*, 267 (December 1915), pp. 16–20.

Ninagawa, Arata, 'Ajia Renmei no kūron' [Empty theory of an Asian League], *Tōhō Kōron* [Eastern Review] (February 1926), pp. 12–17.

Ninagawa, Arata, 'Kiken naru jinshu byōdō no seikō' [Dangerous political plan of racial equality], *Tōhō Kōron* [Eastern Review] (July 1927), pp. 20–2.

Ōkuma, Shigenobu, 'Our national mission', in Naoichi Masaoka (ed.), *Japan's Message to America*: A symposium by representative Japanese on Japan and American–Japanese relations (Tokyo, 1914), pp. 1–5.

Ōyama, Ikuo, 'Dai Ajiashugi no unmei ikan' [What will be the fate of Greater Asianism?], *Shin Nihon*, 6:3 (March 1916).

Rice, Stanley, *The Challenge of Asia* (London: John Murray, 1925).

Richard, Paul, 'The unity of Asia', in Aurobindo Ghose (transl.), *The Dawn over Asia* (Madras: Ganesh, 1920), pp. 1–10.

Saaler, Sven, 'The construction of regionalism in modern Japan: Kodera Kenkichi and his "Treatise on Greater Asianism" (1916)', *Modern Asian Studies*, 41 (2007), pp. 1261–94.

Shimazu, Naoko, *Japan, Race and Equality: The Racial Equality Proposal of 1919* (London and New York: Routledge, 1998).

Spivak, Gayatri Chakravorty, *Other Asias* (Oxford: Blackwell, 2008).

Stegewerns, Dick, 'The dilemma of nationalism and internationalism in modern Japan: National interest, Asian brotherhood, international cooperation or world citizenship?', in Dick Stegewerns (ed.), *Nationalism and Internationalism in Imperial Japan: Autonomy, Asian Brotherhood, or World Citizenship?* (London and New York: RoutledgeCurzon, 2003), pp. 3–15.

Stoddard, Lothrop, *The Rising Tide of Color Against White World-Supremacy* (New York: Scribner, 1920).

Stoddard, Lothrop, *The Revolt Against Civilization: The Menace of the Under Man* (New York: Scribner, 1922).

Sugita, Teiichi, 'Wa Gaikō to Tōa Renmei' [Our foreign policy and an East Asian League], *Nihon oyobi Nihonjin* [Japan and the Japanese], 674 (February 1916).

Sun, Ge, 'How does Asia mean?', *Inter-Asia Cultural Studies*, 1:1 (2000), pp. 13–47.

Sun, Ge, Baik Young-seo and Chen Kuan-Hsing (eds), *Posuto 'Higashi Ajia'* [Post-'East Asia'] (Tokyo: Sakuhinsha, 2006).

Szpilman, Christopher W. A., 'Paul Richard: *To Japan*, 1917, and *The Dawn over Asia*, 1920', in Sven Saaler and C. W. A. Szpilman (eds), *Pan-Asianism: A Documentary History 1860–2010* (Boulder: Rowman & Littlefield, 2011), vol. 1, pp. 287–95.

Takeuchi, Yoshimi, 'Hōhō toshite no Ajia' [Asia as method], *Nihon to Ajia* [Japan and Asia] (Tokyo: Chikuma Shobō, 1993 [1961]), pp. 442–70.

Weber, Torsten, '"Unter dem Banner des Asianismus": Transnationale Dimensionen des japanischen Asianismus-Diskurses der Taishō-Zeit (1912–1926)' ['Under the banner of Asianism': Transnational dimensions of Japanese Asianism discourse during the Taishō period], *Comparativ*, 6 (2008), pp. 34–52.

Weber, Torsten, 'The Greater Asia Association and Matsui Iwane, 1933', in Sven Saaler and C. W. A. Szpilman (eds), *Pan-Asianism: A Documentary History 1860–2010* (Boulder: Rowman & Littlefield, 2011), vol. 2, pp. 137–47.

Weber, Torsten, 'Nanjing's Greater Asianism: Wang Jingwei and Zhou Huaren, 1940', in Sven Saaler and C. W. A. Szpilman (eds), *Pan-Asianism: A Documentary History 1860–2010* (Boulder: Rowman & Littlefield, 2011), vol. 2, pp. 209–20.

Yabuta, Ken'ichirō, 'Kenkyū nōto: Miyazaki Tōten no "Ajiashugi" to dai Ichiji Sekai Taisen go no Sekai shichō' [Research note: Miyazaki Toten's 'Asianism' and ideas of a new world order after the First World War], *Dōshisha hōgaku*, 48:1 (1996), pp. 277–377.

Yan, Hairong and Daniel F. Vukovich, 'Introduction: What's left of Asia', *Positions: East Asia Cultures Critique*, 15:2 (2007), pp. 211–24.

Yoshino, Sakuzō, 'Jinshu teki sabetsu teppai undōsha ni atau' [To the activists for the abolition of racial discrimination], *Chūō Kōron* (March 1919).

Zen Ajia Kyōkai, 'Zen Ajia Kyōkai setsuritsu shushi' [Purpose for the establishment of the All Asia Association], *Zen Ajia Kyōkai Kaihō* [Bulletin of the All Asia Association] (April 1926), 1–3.

Zhou, Bin, 'Yaxiya Minzu Huiyi yu Zhongguo de fandui yundong' [The Asian Peoples' Congress and the Chinese opposition movement], *Kang-Ri Zhanzheng Yanjiu* [Studies of China's War of Resistance against Japan], 3 (2006), pp. 128–59.

Part II

Chapter 4

A Cultural History of Diplomacy: Reassessing the Japanese 'Performance' at the Paris Peace Conference

NAOKO SHIMAZU

On 16 December 1918, the American journalist Walter Duranty wrote for *The New York Times*:

> 'It is far worse than when the Czar of Russia visited Paris – you would think every Parisian had determined not to rest happy until he had a close personal view of President Wilson.' The speaker was a veteran gendarme attached to the force guarding the entrances of the Rue de Monceau where Prince Murat's house is situated, from the overcurious crowds. . . . Somehow the news had spread yesterday . . . that the president had been to church and would return at about noon. The result was an enthusiastic gathering before the police barriers – hundreds of people, quiet and well-behaved, in their Sunday clothes, but resolved not to leave the spot before the President had passed. . . . Suddenly, the boy on the outskirts of the crowd cried: 'Le voila!' as a limousine turned a corner. Hats came off, flags and handkerchiefs were waved, and the air rang with shouts of 'Vive Wilson! Vive le President!' Smiling with unaffected pleasure the Presidential party passed through the hedge of spectators down the street. . . . Not the least striking feature of the President's popularity is Parisians have learnt how to cheer in order to greet him properly. . . . There has been another change in the city during the last few weeks. Paris is recovering its old gayety. . . . Now with illuminations in Wilson's honor, confetti have reappeared on the boulevards, until the pavements are covered with the bright-hued jetsam.[1]

The above reporting tells us many things: the symbolic linking of Wilson with the French aristocracy, the heroic stature of Wilson amongst Parisians, and added to this the evident smugness that even the French have had to change their old ways and learn to do things in an American way in order to please the President. Indeed, the media covered Wilson's activities with a paparazzi-like zealousness – such as reporting on Wilson being seen at the races, Wilson seen on his daily round of motoring in the Bois de Boulogne, and so on and so forth. The amount of media attention that Wilson attracted was a reflection, at one level, of how the world was changing and how Wilson was seen to symbolise the new configuration of power in international relations that placed the United States at its helm.[2] Most of all, the piece is an excellent example of how effectively the American propaganda machine was working at Paris – in presenting

Wilson and the influence of the United States in Europe, by appealing to the popular penchant for heroic figures. Arguably, the Paris Peace Conference represented the climax of the American war propaganda campaign, as the First World War was fought in the media as well as in the trenches.[3]

What this study attempts to do is to suggest the importance of the symbolic in diplomacy; or, more precisely, how images of diplomacy, as constructed largely by the media during the Paris Peace Conference, tended to inform contemporary perceptions of the success of peace conference diplomacy in Paris.[4] Looking from this perspective, I will argue that the Japanese 'performance' at Paris suffered a serious setback because the Japanese leadership, both in Tokyo and at the peace conference, had failed to grasp the importance of 'public diplomacy' as an integral aspect of peace conference diplomacy. For our purpose, 'public diplomacy' is defined as 'the ways in which both government and private individuals and groups influence directly or indirectly those public attitudes and opinions which bear directly on other governments' foreign policy decisions.'[5] Therefore, in spite of having made two principal gains from the peace terms, Shandong and the Micronesian Islands, the failure over the racial equality proposal came to symbolise the failure of Japanese diplomacy at Paris, as far as Japanese public opinion was concerned.

President Wilson's public performance at Paris

Before we delve into the Japanese 'performance' at Paris, a brief analysis of the American delegation will provide us with helpful insights into how the most powerful state in the world saw the workings of symbolic power. Americans were very aware of the symbolic importance of their representation at the peace conference, and this can be seen in many details of the American presence. Paris was being 'liberated' by the Americans, as the American Mission to Negotiate Peace, with a vast entourage of well over 1,000 staff, occupied the geographical centre of Paris, taking the Hôtel Crillon, which faced Place de la Concorde, as its headquarters. And the above-mentioned mansion of Prince Murat – that is, Wilson's temporary 'home' – became known as the 'Paris White House'.[6] The positioning of the Americans in the centre of Paris is significant because it reveals much about their self-perception. What it is important to emphasise here is that even the physical positioning of the American headquarters can project its sense of national power. Moreover, the fact that Wilson was hosted at the mansion of a French aristocrat was doubly significant, if not ironic.

It was reported that the arrival of Wilson as a 'saviour' of war-ravaged Europe was symbolic not only for Americans and Europeans but also for the many oppressed peoples of the world.[7] The Italian foreign minister, Francesco Saverio Nitti, later wrote of Wilson: 'I have seen Wilson come to Europe in 1918 acclaimed as the apostle of the new civilisation and the liberator of the peoples. . . .'[8] Figure 4.1, showing an American press photograph of Rue Royale immediately after the passing of Wilson's cavalcade, captures the fervour that gripped

Figure 4.1 'Vive Wilson', an illuminated sign across Rue Royale, Paris, in front of Maxim's, December 1918 (Princeton University Library, Woodrow Wilson Coll., box 42, folder 5).

Paris on his arrival, and acts as a visual testimony to the press write-up. Even the choice of location in the photograph, which includes Maxim's sign (on the left) with 'Vive Wilson' blazoned across the image, is significant, as the restaurant is synonymous with Parisian high life. Moreover, the entire composition suggests not only the victor's entry into the city but also, allegorically, even a moral victory of the New World over the Old World. The frequent biblical allegory used to capture the popular enthusiasm for Wilson implied that the American President was represented as an embodiment of the 'sacred' political values of contemporary times. One could even argue that traditional notions of monarchical sanctity were being put into use to legitimise Wilson's political authority. In some sense, it was ironic that the Old World had to rely on the idioms of traditional, monarchical absolutism to privilege the political leader from the New World.

The decision taken by Wilson to attend the peace conference was not without its problems. Wilson was personally very keen to come to Paris, as he believed that he alone commanded the moral authority necessary to create the League of Nations. There were those like Secretary of State Robert Lansing, however, who argued strongly against it on the grounds that his personal presence would diminish the near-mythical quality of Wilsonian idealism.[9] As the main part of

Figure 4.2 Diplomats and the Shadow on the Blind: The Problems of Peace – 'President Wilson arrives in Paris', *The Herald*, 21 December 1918.

the Peace Conference lasted for the first six months of 1919, there was also the problem of dual-track diplomacy, which began to evolve at Paris: the last two months of the peace conference were characterised by the summit diplomacy of the Big Four, via which the major political decisions were made (more on this later), and in parallel, 'Peace Conference diplomacy', through bureaucrats and diplomats who laboriously planned out the details in special commissions. Not surprisingly, the Big Four's lack of knowledge as to how to conduct international diplomacy 'properly' led to behind-the-scene criticisms of the bosses by their diplomats.[10] Figure 4.2 epitomises the sense of bureaucratic jealousies felt by diplomats, who must have resented being marginalised by the presence of their top statesmen, who would invariably turn the Peace Conference into political pageantry and monopolise the limelight. The diplomat on the left is seen carrying a manual on 'Diplomacy: Its Art and Practice', which might have been a reference to the publication *A Guide to Diplomatic Practice* by Sir Ernest Satow in 1917.[11] Strikingly, it is Wilson himself (depicted in the silhouette) who was portrayed as a 'problem of peace' by diplomats.

What becomes evident is that the role of the media in the new age of public diplomacy was of paramount importance, requiring state actors either to create their own news agencies and/or to cultivate good working relations with commercial presses. To this end, the US government was well ahead of the game, having created the Committee on Public Information (CPI henceforth) in April 1917, with George Creel at its head. As the work of CPI has been covered in the existing literature, it will suffice here to emphasise that the successful 'packaging' of Wilson underlined the success of the CPI's propaganda activities.[12] Wilson even had his own press secretary at the peace conference in Ray Stannard Baker. Excessive reliance on press campaigns was not altogether without its own problems either. The fact that the American delegation was divided internally resulted from time to time in the dispatching of separate and ill-coordinated messages between the offices of Wilson, Colonel Edward House (special advisor to the President) and Robert Lansing.[13] As Der Derian points out, the technological revolution of the twentieth century has allowed for the development of an increasingly globalised audience, leading to the emergence of 'techno-diplomacy'.[14] Visual images of Wilson in press photographs and newsreels distributed globally came to assume great importance, often becoming the key reference point of the event for the public at large. Indeed, it is not an overstatement to say that 'the power of images [worked] as substitutes for reality.'[15] The over-exposure of Wilson resulted in over-expectations – and this meant that his downfall was so much greater when he failed to deliver the 'goods' – national self-determination – to the colonised world.

For one thing, the rising importance of public diplomacy at Paris can be accounted for by the change in the political environment of the states represented there. One of the most important characteristics of the Paris Peace Conference, which marked it out from previous peace conferences such as the Congress of Vienna, was that it was predominantly a gathering of the top *elected* representatives of the newly emerging liberal democratic world. In Woodrow Wilson's very own words, Vienna was 'a Congress of "bosses"' whereas 'Versailles ... must be a meeting of the servants of the peoples represented by the delegates'.[16] By 1919, all the great powers apart from Japan had universal male suffrage, the first being France in 1792 (re-enacted in 1848), followed by the United States in 1869, Britain and Italy in 1918, and Japan in 1925. Added to the fact that the First World War had mobilised so many and resulted in such an enormous number of casualties, a sense of crisis pervaded many Western societies, aggravated by the threat of Communism in the Bolshevik Revolution. As the first total war, the First World War was a paradigm-shifting experience in so far as political accountability was concerned, as popular expectations placed on political leaders were much greater than at any other time. Greater media scrutiny of their political leaders in 1919 was a reflection of the changing nature of the relationship between the political elite and the ever-expanding electoral body.

All the statesmen at Paris were therefore, to varying degrees, 'performing' for the benefit of their domestic audience back home. In lieu of monarchical pageantry, the public became interested in a new diplomatic pageantry of the grandest kind as it unfolded at Paris, and climaxed symbolically in the Hall of Mirrors of the Palace of Versailles, now filled with politicians and bureaucrats who were the new 'royalties' in the age of popular democracy.[17]

The Japanese 'stage' at Paris

Let us now revisit the Japanese 'performance' at Paris through the angle of diplomacy as a 'public performance'.[18] In doing so, I will attempt to reframe peace conference diplomacy as a theatre of power.[19] It is important to recognise that 'performance' can only take place when there is a performer who performs and a spectator who observes the performance. Because performance is a two-way process, this approach enables us to consider peace conference diplomacy as 'public performance', where peacemakers play out their assigned roles in front of multiple audiences – be they their fellow peacemakers, the international public or the domestic public. This approach seems doubly appropriate in the age of public diplomacy, as it presents us with a more interactive model of understanding the nature of diplomatic power, which traditionally has been largely consigned to the realm of high politics, excluding the public and especially the popular audience. What will be revealed in the following analysis is that the general lack of understanding of the importance of the 'performative' nature of diplomacy in the Japanese leadership had weakened the overall image of their diplomatic 'performance' as actors on stage at Paris. This had serious implications not only for international public opinion but also, more importantly, for Japanese public opinion. I will attempt to illustrate this through three examples: firstly, the selection of the plenipotentiaries, which reflected the mentality of the Japanese political elite towards the peace conference; secondly, Japan's exclusion from the Big Four; and thirdly, the Japanese public response to the racial equality proposal.

First and foremost, the Japanese leadership spoke and understood only one 'language' of diplomacy in 1919 – the language of the *Realpolitik* of the Old World. This meant, for instance, that the Japanese government had no idea that there would have to operate in parallel at Paris a new type of diplomacy: that is, public diplomacy for which the states had to be prepared to face and win multiple audiences through the manipulation of the media. This inability to grasp the changing times (*jisei*) meant that their general attitude towards the Peace Conference was out of tune with the other great powers. Structurally, the Japanese Foreign Ministry was too small to operate effectively as a great power. The Japanese delegation, with its sixty-four members (compared with approximately 1,000 in the American delegation), was far too small to deal with the vast range of peace issues that were discussed and decided at Paris. Whilst the plenipotentiaries based themselves in the Hôtel Meurice, the delegation's headquarters was based at the Hôtel Bristol (Figure 4.3).

Baron Makino criticised his diplomats' lack of linguistic ability, as there were too few who were fluent enough in English to represent Japanese interests in the commissions set up at the Peace Conference; in some cases, they even had to recruit Japanese expatriates living in Paris to help out.[20] Another senior Japanese diplomat noted the three key weaknesses of Japanese diplomacy at Paris as being linguistic ability, negotiating skills and oratorical skills.[21] To this, I would add the lack of publicity skills. The problem was that the weakness of the Japanese representation, which underlined the general lack of awareness of the importance of the Peace Conference, had repercussions in many different areas that affected the overall political performance of Japan.[22] Even if we consider the question of the seating of the Japanese delegation at the Plenary Session of the Peace Conference, as shown in Figure 4.4, the Japanese delegation was the fifth great power in name only: they were seated on the outer fringe, at the bottom end of the long conference table, after the British Dominions and the Government of India, opposite Hedjaz, Guatemala, Ecuador and China.

Figure 4.3 The Japanese delegation photographed at the Hôtel Bristol, Paris, 1919 (Diplomatic Archives of the Ministry of Foreign Affairs of Japan).

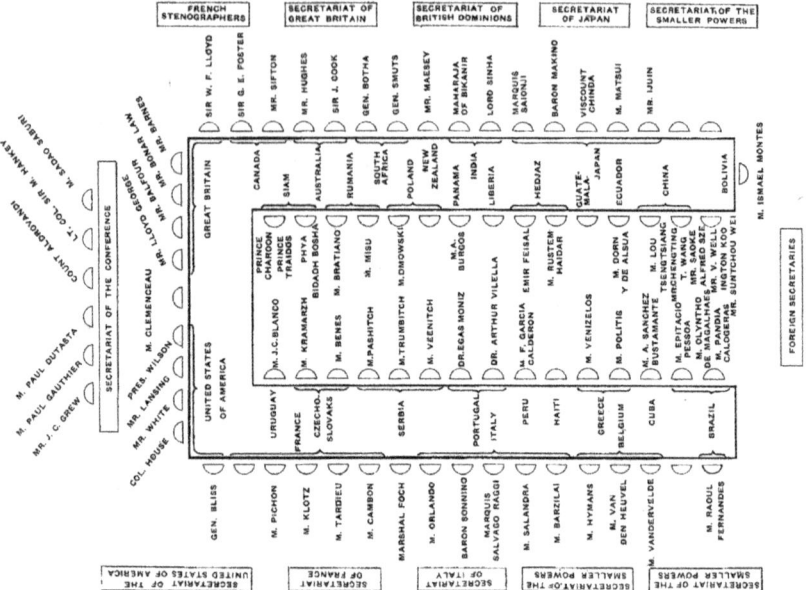

Figure 4.4 Seating at the Plenary Session of the Peace Conference (Charles T. Thompson, *The Paris Peace Conference Day by Day*, New York: Brentano's, 1920, after p. 118).

A tiny press office was established at the headquarters of the Japanese delegation in the Hôtel Bristol, with Matsuoka Yōsuke at its head. In addition, a special Peace Conference service from Paris was established by the semi-official Kokusai Press Service.[23] Apart from the *Tokyo Nichi-Nichi Shinbun*, which had sent its own correspondent to Paris to cover the Peace Conference, other newspapers had to rely on the Kokusai Press Service and on Associated Press for coverage. According to Nakano Seigō, then a young journalist who accompanied the delegation to Paris, the fundamental problem with the Japanese official attitude was that it had no idea or understanding that peace conference diplomacy ought to incorporate a substantial propaganda activity, involving a sustained public relations campaign via the media to disseminate Japanese policy.[24] Instead, journalists were kept at bay and given only an insubstantial official 'statement' drafted by Mr Kennedy, an Irish employee of the Japanese government. Even this Mr Kennedy was hard pressed to write anything substantive, given the lack of direction offered by his employer. This was all due to the fact that there was only very cursory preparation undertaken for peace by the Japanese Foreign Ministry, as the basic assumption remained, throughout the four years, that it was a 'European war' in which Japan had limited interests.

Although fostering a good relationship with the media should have played an important part in the activities of the Japanese delegation, the latter was secretive and distrustful of the media.[25] Therefore, the media did not warm to the Japanese delegation and this resulted in negative coverage of the Peace Conference; the coverage was particularly critical of the 'performance' of the Japanese delegates. On this point, the Japanese press was much more unforgiving than the international press, so much so that Saionji and Makino felt the necessity to explain why this was so in their report to Prime Minister Hara on their return from Paris, reasoning that the delegation had simply been too short-staffed to pay adequate attention to the media.[26] In any case, it seems that Matsuoka did not put any emphasis on disseminating visual images of the Japanese plenipotentiaries 'in action': for example, a photograph of Makino in conversation with Lord Robert Cecil or, indeed, a shot of Saionji with Clemenceau, which would have been highly prized. There was very little visual material to suggest that the Japanese were 'communing' with others as a great power. The lack of visual representation (in other words, the physicality of the Japanese presence at the peace conference) could well have been interpreted as marginalisation and alienation of the Japanese delegation at Paris. The power of appealing to an international audience through courting international opinion was a sine qua non of peace conference diplomacy. Not only were delegates expected to wrestle with the practical day-to-day negotiations but also they were required to play up to the invisible 'audience' in the age of technological advancement, as newsreels were sent off around the world to disseminate relatively up-to-date information about the proceedings at the 'court' in Paris. In this, the Japanese delegation 'performed' very poorly.

A poisoned chalice

To the illustrious, star-studded line-up of leaders headed by Woodrow Wilson, Georges Clemenceau, David Lloyd George and Vittorio Emmanuele Orlando, but also including Dmowski of Poland, Venizelos of Greece, Prince Feisal (not to mention Lawrence of Arabia) and Queen Marie of Romania, the Japanese government sent a delegation headed by Marquis Saionji Kinmochi, deputised by Baron Makino Nobuaki (acting chief plenipotentiary), Viscount Chinda Sutemi (ambassador to London), Viscount Matsui Keishirō (ambassador to Paris) and Ijūin Hikokichi (ambassador to Rome). Not a single member of the Japanese delegation was an acting top-ranking statesman. Japan therefore did not have a 'face' to represent itself, and this placed the delegation at a great disadvantage.

From London, Ambassador Chinda Sutemi sent a desperate telegram on 21 November 1918 to Foreign Minister Uchida Yasuya, asking for the Prime Minister and the Foreign Minister himself to be present at Paris; on the same day, back in Tokyo, the issue was being discussed amongst some members of the Diplomatic Advisory Council.[27] It was a case where those who were keen to go – namely, Katō Takaaki (Leader of the Opposition, Kenseikai) and Itō Miyoji (Privy Councillor and member of the Diplomatic Advisory Council) – were considered to be too enthusiastic and not trustworthy for different reasons. Makino seemed wary of being appointed, only agreeing to serve if Saionji were the delegation chief.²⁸ He was most concerned that the chief plenipotentiary was someone who commanded immense respect domestically, in case Japanese peace conference diplomacy did not produce positive results. Intriguingly, Makino, as an important member of the Diplomatic Advisory Council, was worried about the possibility of failure before he had even set off for Paris, even when there were very little grounds for suspecting that Japanese diplomacy would fail to secure what really mattered at the forthcoming peace conference: namely, the two territorial demands.

Makino knew that he was no world statesman, and his conduct shows that he simply did not possess the acumen to make the most of the politics of the circumstances, and use it to maximise the Japanese bargaining position at Paris.²⁹ As British Ambassador to Japan, Sir Conyngham Greene summarised:

> Baron Makino is a well bred, agreeable and straight forward gentleman, and my relations with him have always been most friendly and even cordial. He is also a friend of my wife and daughter and so we know him fairly intimately. He speaks and writes English, and is well read and up to date in passing events. On the other hand he is not brilliant, and he is slow in conversation and rather retiring in manner.³⁰

Even though a Japanese diplomat tried to offer the justification that Makino and Chinda were held in high esteem internationally and that they were popular amongst foreign dignitaries for their 'gentlemanliness', this did not muster any public confidence either domestically or internationally at Paris.³¹ According to Harold Nicolson, Baron Makino was 'inscrutable and inarticulate, observes, observes, observes'.³² Indeed, one Japanese pundit opined that Japan needed more world-level politicians and diplomats as 'Makino was left to tussle a comeuppance like V. K. Wellington Koo' – a scene too pathetic for words.³³ The Chinese delegation had a star performer in V. K. Wellington Koo, a Columbia University-educated lawyer who possessed oratorical power – an important element of 'stage performance' that appealed to Western audiences, as already remarked on by Clemenceau:

> Wellington Koo, like a young Chinese cat, Parisian of speech and dress, absorbed in the pleasure of patting and pawing the mouse, even if it was reserved for the Japanese. His inexhaustible flow of eloquence used to irritate Baron Matsui, a massive chunk of Japanese mentality, who spoke little, but did not shrink from speaking out.³⁴

In fact, 'silence' became a hallmark of the tactical behaviour of the Japanese plenipotentiaries at international conferences during the Meiji and Taisho periods: Komura Jutarō, chief plenipotentiary for the Portsmouth peace negotiations in 1905, was also known for his 'silence'.³⁵ Seemingly, Komura was outwitted by his Russian counterpart, Count Sergei Witte, who understood the importance of fostering friendly relations with the American media. Ironically, Plenipotentiaries Chinda, Matsui and Ijūin were all acting diplomats at the time of the appointment, and even Makino was a one-time diplomat. Therefore, they were simply acting out of their professional role-expectations as top bureaucrats. They might even have secretly shared a sense of being 'shown up' by the world leaders, as superbly caricatured in Figure 4.2 above. Moreover, the lack of executive power meant that the Japanese plenipotentiaries were emasculated in the eyes of the great powers, as they could only act as Tokyo's messengers.

It was Genrō Yamagata who finally managed to persuade Saionji to go to Paris, as the Foreign Minister had also refused to go, and the Prime Minister was not keen on the Leader of the Opposition representing Japan.[36] In Japanese political circles, the selection of the Marquis – the liberal aristocratic 'elder statesmen' (*genrō*), who had twice served as prime minister and who was, most importantly, a Francophile, having studied law in Paris and being an old acquaintance of Clemenceau[37] – to act as a distinguished figurehead no doubt appeared to be appropriate. It was reported in the broadsheet *Yomiuri Shinbun* that 'only the marquis would be able to compete with the American president Wilson and Britain's Lloyd George . . . as the first-class politician of our country, whilst at the same time, an intimate friend of Clemenceau, fluent in French . . . .'[38] Clemenceau, too, noted in his memoir, 'Amiable Prince Saionji, impetuous once, today quietly ironical, an old comrade of mine at the lectures of our law professor, Émile Accollas.'[39]

Evidently, the Japanese government had not intended to make the ageing and ailing Marquis do any serious work at Paris either, as he arrived in Marseilles at a leisurely pace on 28 February 1919 (more than one month after the start of the conference), with a mistress in tow. Ambassador Greene viewed the marquis as 'The Patrician Liberal' who 'passes . . . in official circles as being somewhat indolent and a bad head of a Department in consequence, and he is moreover somewhat handicapped by advancing age and indifferent health'.[40] Yet *The Times* gave a full endorsement of the Marquis as 'the only statesman who is trusted by all classes and all parties for his great intelligence and tried patriotism'.[41] The Americans concluded that the composition of the Japanese delegation was 'modestly liberal' and sympathetic to the status quo as far as international order was concerned.[42] Needless to say, the French press was the most favourably disposed to Saionji, *Le Temps*, *Le Matin* and *Le Figaro* all reporting his arrival in Paris, and dedicating their front page to Saionji's much-delayed peace policy pronouncements.[43]

If Japan had any inkling of the importance of political representation at Paris, then, the delegation should have consisted of at least Prime Minister Hara Kei and Foreign Minister Uchida Yasuya, and preferably also Minister of the Army Tanaka Giichi, Finance Minister Takahashi Korekiyo, and Makino lastly as a safe senior member of the Diplomatic Advisory Council. Instead, the peace delegation was regarded as a poisoned chalice by the Japanese leadership. Why was this so? Most likely, it was the traumatic memory of the Hibiya Riot of September 1905 at the conclusion of the Russo-Japanese War of 1904–5 that explains the extreme reluctance of top politicians to attend the Paris Peace

Conference. At the time, the personal safety of the chief plenipotentiary, Foreign Minister Komura, was in jeopardy, and the Hibiya Riot that started in Tokyo in September 1905, as a result of the signing of the Treaty of Portsmouth, quickly spread throughout every major city in Japan. Consequently, Tokyo was placed under martial law for nearly two months. One of the most striking features was the rampant and sustained attack on the plenipotentiaries by the Japanese media, almost all of which suffered a publication ban imposed by the government during the period of martial law.[44] Although fourteen years had elapsed since the Hibiya Riot, the top political and military leadership in 1919 must still have harboured raw memories of the event, and feared that such a nightmare scenario could recur.[45] It certainly haunted Makino enough that he would only serve as a deputy under Saionji at Paris.

The lack of concern about strong political participation at Paris can be explained by the weak espousal of popular representation in Japanese politics, which still smacked of transcendentalism. The government did not understand that part of the grand strategy of peace diplomacy ought to have included political 'stage-acting' at Paris, where the Japanese delegates visibly 'performed' great power diplomacy for the benefit of the domestic as well as international audience. Clearly, Japan's political leaders had considered it more important to set their own house in order, as the Rice Riots of 1918 had overturned the Terauchi cabinet and led to the emergence of Prime Minister Hara as the first commoner to lead the Japanese government.[46] They had therefore failed to grasp the world historical significance of the Peace Conference, mainly because their interests were orientated entirely domestically. As the preparatory work for the Peace Conference has revealed, the inability to 'read' the political and intellectual trends of the time, such as the emerging importance of a league of nations as the basis for a new postwar international order, was symptomatic of Japanese official attitudes towards the Peace Conference. This was a major weakness of Prime Minister Hara (and the wartime governments): his inability to appreciate international politics beyond the narrow confines of the domestic political agenda. Little did he know that his general neglect of peace conference diplomacy was to have a devastating long-term effect on domestic politics, by weakening the hands of the foreign ministry in the eyes of the public and also in the eyes of the army and the navy. From the Japanese point of view, the Paris Peace Conference remained a Western gathering, in which Japan's limited interests had already been de facto secured through a series of secret treaties signed in 1917.

The Big Four fiasco

A major blow to the Japanese government came in late March 1919, when it was excluded from the Council of Four, which became known as the Big Four (also as 'the Olympians' as in Figure 4.5).[47] This was when the Council of Ten, which had been the original top-level committee at Paris, was disbanded, in order to increase efficiency and prevent leakage.[48]

Figure 4.5 The 'Big Four' or the 'Olympians' (Courtesy of the Woodrow Wilson Presidential Library, Staunton, Virginia).

Effectively, what this signalled was that Japan had been de facto demoted to the status of a power with special interests (that is, lesser powers) from its previous status of a great power with general interests.[49] According to Stephen Bonsal, the reason for the Japanese exclusion was the absence of the head of the state or prime minister.[50] In all, the Japanese approach to the Peace Conference had demonstrated to the Big Four that the Japanese government operated on a different system of decision-making from the dominant system of executive decision-making shared by the Big Four. The lack of executive power on the part of the plenipotentiaries meant that every decision had to be referred back to Tokyo, as painfully demonstrated in the case of the racial equality negotiations. The Japanese government had not realised that Japan's status as a great power, in the presence of Wilson, Clemenceau, Lloyd George and Orlando, necessitated the granting of executive power to its plenipotentiaries. Hence, it was hardly surprising that the Japanese were marginalised in the key decision-making issues at Paris.

Moreover, the Big Four effectively operated like a small, intimate clique, as shown in Figure 4.6. In it, Wilson, Lloyd George, Clemenceau and Orlando sit cosily together in a library, attended to by Paul Mantoux (though not at all times). In this kind of atmosphere, it is not at all surprising that the Japanese were excluded because the Big Four operated like a highly exclusive Western

Figure 4.6 The 'Big Four' in situ (Author unattributed).

club where there was an implicit understanding of the shared culture of the Western elite, and a collective awareness of the significance of their mission.[51] How could someone like Makino have felt comfortable enough to role-play amongst the Big Four, even if he had been included? This underlines the importance of shared sociality, based on the shared social practices of the cosmopolitan Western political elite. In this way, contemporary international diplomacy was inherently disadvantageous to a non-Western newcomer state like Japan, as being a great power required the acquired cultural sensibility of sociality in the dominant group.[52]

In any case, Plenipotentiary Chinda's thinly veiled excuse for the apparent exclusion of Japan – that these four leaders had 'private negotiations' to conduct – fell on deaf ears back home in Japan.[53] Katō Takaaki, for one, expressed strong criticism that 'as a result of this detachment on the part of Baron Makino and his colleagues, Japan is seemingly lumped with the minor Powers' and warned ominously that such a degrading of Japan in the eyes of the world was to have 'an important bearing on Japan's future'.[54] According to one British Foreign Office source, 'Japanese dissatisfaction is quite intelligible. Japan is not playing a very distinguished part at the Peace Conference, where her representative is not [one of?] the "big Four," nor did she play a very brilliant part in the war.'[55]

In sum, Alston was not too far off the mark when he opined in the report to Lord Curzon, 'Abroad the opportunity of a thousand years offered by the Peace Conference has, speaking broadly, been lost, and we have succeeded neither in advancing Japan's position nor yet her reputation.'[56] The emergence of the Big Four had sealed the fate of Japan as an honorary great power at Paris – a great power in name only.

Public relations disaster over the racial equality proposal

As I have explained elsewhere the intricacies of the negotiations behind the racial equality proposal, I will simply emphasise here the significance of the failure of this particular proposal from the point of view of the Japanese 'public performance' at the Peace Conference.[57] It would not be an over-statement to claim that the racial equality negotiations were nothing short of a public relations disaster from the point of view of the Hara government. In spite of the proposal being the least politically important demand amongst the three principal Japanese peace terms, the protracted and tortuous negotiations surrounding it became the most highly publicised 'performance' of the Japanese delegates at Paris in the Japanese domestic newspapers. Much to the chagrin of Makino and Chinda, it became a *cause célèbre* for the domestic public, and exposed the antagonistic nature of the relationship between the delegation and the media.

Notwithstanding the problem of not having executive power, the plenipotentiaries' 'silence' over the racial equality negotiations was interpreted in the domestic media as being symptomatic of the demonstrably inept diplomacy. Domestically, a number of cross-partisan pressure groups, the most notable of which was the League to Abolish Racial Discrimination (*Jinshuteki sabetsu teppai kisei taikai*), had emerged in January 1919, and campaigned in the media against the Hara government's weak-kneed diplomacy (*nanjaku gaikō*). Therefore, in February 1919, even the usually placid Foreign Minister was forced to instruct Makino in Paris to make public statements about the Japanese government's aims and policies as often as possible, with the chief aim of quelling public 'noises' made by such pressure groups.[58] In spite of the urgency of the racial equality issue (seeing that it was connected with the establishment of the League of Nations), the Japanese government continued to rely on a circuitous route to learn about the outcomes of the negotiations at Paris; it waited patiently for an official telegram, usually written as a report a week or two after the event by Plenipotentiary Matsui, whilst the Japanese broadsheets often reported the Paris proceedings within twenty-four hours. The huge gulf between the snail-paced official channels of communication and the immediacy of private sector reporting on the Paris proceedings glaringly pointed up the huge gap in their outlooks and became a source of public ridicule. How could the leadership in Tokyo seemingly remain unperturbed about the unacceptably long time lag in decision-making on peace issues, which threatened to jeopardise the authority and legitimacy of the plenipotentiaries in Paris in front of a world audience?

The tragedy is that records of negotiations from the British and American delegations show the tireless efforts made by Makino and Chinda on the racial equality proposal. Instead of keeping mum on the issue, the Japanese headquarters in the Hôtel Bristol should have launched a full media campaign and taken a two-pronged approach: one targeted to influence international opinion in Paris, and the other to appease domestic opinion in Japan. Instead, the official silence only fuelled anger and frustration in Japan by alienating the media still further. The sad truth was that the symbolic value of the racial equality proposal meant that its defeat also became symbolic of the failure of Japanese diplomacy. A barrage of press criticisms of the racial equality negotiations,[59] though not on the same scale as media criticisms of the Treaty of Portsmouth in September 1905,[60] none the less had the ring of historical familiarity. The major difference was that, in 1919, the Japanese government did nothing to rectify its damaged reputation in the media.

Conclusion

The Paris Peace Conference left many young delegates with a sense of disillusionment with the old order. John Maynard Keynes was one such delegate, who vented his spleen in the well-known *Economic Consequences of Peace*. The aforementioned Nakano Seigō, the young, impetuous journalist, had left the Peace Conference in mid-February 1919, already feeling totally disillusioned by the ineffective diplomacy conducted by the Japanese team led by Makino. Younger Japanese diplomats Arita Hachirō, Shigemitsu Mamoru, Horiuchi Kensuke and Saitō Hiroshi started a reform movement within the Foreign Ministry, calling themselves the Society of Reformists of the Foreign Ministry (*Gaimushō kakushin dōshikai*), with the objective of expanding the organisational structure, training the personnel, practising 'Open Door' and so on.[61] It was not only Foreign Ministry officials who had misgivings about the performance at Paris; the lacklustre performance had also left Colonel Satō to report back to the Chief of Staff of the Imperial Army that the Japanese delegation had a serious problem with organisation due to a lack of top-level representation, coupled with the reduced staff, who could not deal adequately with the number of issues to be addressed. In the end, he recommended that Foreign Ministry bureaucrats might not be the most suitable 'types' to be sent out to major peace conferences.[62] Although Vice-Admiral Takeshita had already raised the points in February 1919 that the Japanese delegation was not aggressive or forward-thinking enough, and that the Foreign Ministry clearly needed some organisational restructuring, he none the less expressed his readiness to cooperate with the ministry at the Peace Conference.[63]

A new breed of diplomatic revisionists thus emerged in Japan from the ashes of Paris, and this was to have a profound effect on the course of Japanese foreign policy in the interwar period. What the cultural approach to understanding diplomacy emphasises is the importance of the 'perception' that the lacklustre Japanese 'performance' at Paris had created. We can conclude that the apparent weakness of Japanese diplomacy, as it was 'performed' at Paris, had devastating consequences in two areas. First and foremost, the greatest damage had been done to the reputation of the new Hara government and the Foreign Ministry, in their lack of capacity to conduct diplomacy commensurate with Japan's newly found status as one of the five great powers of the world. There was acute awareness in Japanese public opinion of the country's lack of dignity as a great power, and Opposition Leader Katō Takaaki was quick to deride the government on this score.[64] Gotō Shinpei apparently lamented to the British that

> Japan, though ranking among the five Great Powers, unfortunately compared but poorly with them in actual fact. He considered that both at the Paris Conference and elsewhere Japanese journalists, scholars, politicians and officials all failed to reach the average level of capacity.[65]

Kanokogi Kazunobu, an ultra-nationalist philosopher and naval officer, lambasted the plenipotentiaries in *Ajia Jiron*: 'The Japanese people ought to die of shame in face of the fact that they sent to the Peace Conference such ineffective and disgraceful representatives.'[66] These criticisms had a genuine impact on Japanese domestic opinion, and contributed to the weakening of the Foreign Ministry's standing in Japanese politics over the next decade.

Secondly, the inability of the Japanese to 'read' the political climate of the time accurately meant that Japan had not realised that the new game was public diplomacy; hence, 'performative' aspects of diplomacy, including posturing and pageantry, and 'behaving' like a great power in a manner that the Western powers would understand, should have been an integral part of their peace diplomacy. For the Hara government, it was doubly unfortunate that the double 'winning' of the class 'C' mandates (former colonies that had been transferred to the trusteeship of the League of Nations under the Covenant of the League of Nations) and of the Shandong Settlement could not dispel the sense of disillusionment caused by the failure of the racial equality proposal, which became an emblematic cause at the Peace Conference. This illustrates the workings of the public imagination – controversy courts popular interest and galvanises the media into action. This can turn the tide of public opinion in unexpected directions.

Finally, the overall Japanese 'performance' at the Paris Peace Conference should also be understood from the point of view of the weight of historical memory, and how it might have affected the mentality of the plenipotentiaries. Successive Japanese governments did not have fond memories of the peace conferences from the first two major international wars of 1894–5 and 1904–5, as the Triple Intervention of 1895 and the Hibiya Riot of 1905 continued to mar

Japanese diplomatic efforts vis-à-vis the great powers. The hesitance and reluctance of the Japanese plenipotentiaries to act more decisively and confidently in 1919 can be partly explained by fear of the recurrence of a historical nightmare, particularly of the 1905 experience, should their efforts fail. Such a memory might have been particularly acute for the leadership, as the country had just emerged out of the rubble of the Rice Riots of 1918, another major civil disturbance that came only thirteen years after the Hibiya Riot.

Notes

1. Walter Duranty, 'Paris has learned how to cheer', *The New York Times*, 16 December 1918.
2. Gardner, *Safe for Democracy*, p. 6.
3. For an interesting account of American war propaganda, cf. Mock and Larson, *Words that Won the War*.
4. For a fuller treatment of the idea of 'performance' in diplomacy, cf. Shimazu, 'Diplomacy as theatre', pp. 231–4.
5. Hoffman (ed.), *International Communication*, p. 3, quoted in Der Derian, *On Diplomacy*, p. 202, fn. 2.
6. 'Interview with President Wilson', *The Times*, 21 December 1918.
7. Manela, *The Wilsonian Moment*.
8. Francesco Saverio Nitti, *La Pace* (Turin: Piero Gobetti, 1925), p. 11, quoted in Osiander, 'Peacemaking and international legitimacy', p. 460.
9. Lansing, *The Peace Negotiations*, p. 14; Floto, *Colonel House in Paris*, p. 70.
10. Curzon to Derby, 2 April and 7 April 1919, FO 608/124, f 6445, National Archives, London.
11. For an insightful discussion on Satow's manual, cf. Otte, '"A Manual of Diplomacy", pp. 229–43.
12. Creel, *Complete Report of the Chairman of the Committee on Public Information*; Creel, *How We Advertised America*; Manela, *The Wilsonian Moment*, pp. 48–52.
13. I discuss the American delegation and its internal division in my *Japan, Race and Equality*, especially Ch. 6.
14. Der Derian, *On Diplomacy*, p. 202.
15. Elwall, *Building with Light*, p. 9.
16. 'Interview with President Wilson', *The Times*, 21 December 1918.
17. Ursula Stark Urrestarazu, '"Theatrum Europaeum" or: the Presentation of International Identity Relations at Peace Congresses', working paper presented at the workshop, 'Anthropology meets IR: potentials, prospects and pitfalls', 29–30 November 2012, Peace Research Institute Frankfurt, pp. 25–32. These pages contain a particularly interesting analysis of the German delegation in the Hall of the Mirrors at Versailles for the signing. I thank the author for sharing this paper.
18. For my earlier work on Japanese participation in the Peace Conference, see *Japan, Race and Equality*.

19. The notion of 'cultural performance', often used in theatre and performance studies, is a useful and important one because it allows us to understand the underlying normative system of social relations. MacAloon, 'Introduction', in his *Rite, Drama, Festival, Spectacle*, pp. 4, 7–8.
20. Makino, *Kaikoroku*, vol. 2, pp. 34–5, 187.
21. Ishii, *Gaikō yoroku*, p. 436.
22. For such an opinion, see, for instance, [no author] 'Teikoku no shudōteki kōwa jōken', *Kaizō*.
23. MacMurray in Tokyo to the Secretary of State, 26 February 1919, Reel 394, SDR 763.72119/3904, National Archives Microfilm Publication M367, Records of the Department of State relating to World War I and its termination, 1914–1929.
24. Nakano, *Kōwa kaigi*, pp. 12–15.
25. For instance, see Takaishi Masagoro to Makino, 24 March 1919, *Makino Shinken monjo*, National Diet Library, Tokyo.
26. Hara (ed.), *Hara Kei Nikki*, vol. 8, pp. 133, 142.
27. Chinda to Uchida, 21 November 1918, *Nihon gaikō monjo*, vol. 3 (1918), Ministry of Foreign Affairs, Japan; Kobayashi (ed.), *Suiusō nikki*, pp. 97–9.
28. Makino, *Kaikoroku*, vol. 2, pp. 172–3.
29. Nakano, *Kōwa kaigi*, pp. 16–19.
30. Conyngham Greene to Balfour, 2 December 1918, FO 608/211, f 475, National Archives, London.
31. Kikuchi, *Hakushaku*, pp. 218–24.
32. Nicolson, *Peacemaking 1919*, p. 329.
33. [no author] 'Pari kōwa kaigi no antō'.
34. Clemenceau, *Grandeur and Misery of Victory*, p. 140.
35. Schattenberg, 'The diplomat as "an actor"?', pp. 167–94.
36. Koizumi, *Saionji Kinmochi jiden*, pp. 168–9.
37. 27 February 1919, *Le Temps*, Paris.
38. 'Kōwa tokushi kettei', *Yomiuri Shinbun*, 28 November 1918.
39. Clemenceau, *Grandeur*, p. 140.
40. Conyngham Greene to Balfour, 2 December 1918, FO 608/211, f 475, National Archives, London.
41. 15 March 1919, *The Times*, London.
42. Telegram from Morris to Secretary of State, 29 November 1918, Reel 388, SDR 763.72119/2830, National Archives Microfilm Publication M367, Records of the Department of State relating to World War I and its termination, 1914–1929.
43. 28 February, 3 and 5 March 1919, *Le Matin*, Paris; 4 March 1919, *Le Figaro*, Paris. The article featured in *Le Figaro* had been written by Auguste Gérard, who was the French ambassador to Tokyo and held Saionji in the highest regard. See also Gérard, *Ma mission au Japon*, p. 400.
44. See Shimazu, *Japanese Society at War*, Ch. 1; cf. also Gordon, *Labour and Imperial Democracy in Prewar Japan*.
45. Reinhart Koselleck's concepts of 'space of experience' and 'horizon of expectation' are helpful in understanding this phenomenon. See his '"Space of Experience" and

"Horizon of Expectation": Two Historical Categories', in *Futures Past*, Ch. 14. I would like to thank Tino Schölz (Halle) for bringing this work to my attention.
46. Hara, *Hara Kei Nikki*, vol. 8, pp. 31–59.
47. Lansing, *Peace*, p. 198.
48. Mantoux, *Paris Peace Conference 1919*, p. xvi.
49. Shimazu, *Japan, Race and Equality*, p. 90; Diary of Grayson, 24 March 1919, in Wilson, *The Papers*, vol. 56, p. 205.
50. Diary, 16 March 1919, Container 18 (Typescript–Peace Conference), Stephen Bonsal Papers, Library of Congress.
51. Cf. Wight, *Power Politics*; Bull, *The Anarchical Society*; Bull and Watson (eds), *The Expansion of International Society*.
52. Hannah Pakula's recent biography (*The Last Empress*, 2009) of Soong Meiling, the wife of Chiang Kai-shek, states that Meiling played a seminal role in diplomacy during the Second World War years, being the mouth of the generalissimo. Chiang hardly spoke English and did not feel as comfortable with the Western leaders as did his wife, who had been brought up in the United States. This underlines the importance of shared cultural sociability.
53. 'Jogai saretaru nippon', *Tokyo Nichi-Nichi Shinbun*, 3 April 1919.
54. Alston to Curzon, 17 July 1919, Confidential Print 11580, no. 17, FO 410/67, National Archives, London.
55. This is a comment made on the report submitted by Conyngham Greene in Tokyo to the Foreign Office, on 26 March 1919, FO 371/3820, f 49481, National Archives, London.
56. Alston to Curzon, 17 July 1919, Confidential Print 11580, no. 17, FO 410/67, National Archives, London.
57. Cf. my earlier work, *Japan, Race and Equality*, for details of the racial equality negotiations.
58. Uchida to Matsui, 4 February 1919, no. 104, *Nihon gaikō monjo*, part 1, vol. 3 (1919) Ministry of Foreign Affairs, Japan.
59. For instance, 22 February, 6 May 1919, *Tokyo Nichi-Nichi Shinbun*; 13, 16, 17 April 1919, *Kokumin Shinbun*; 9 April 1919, *Yamato Shinbun*; 16, 30 March 1919, 2, 20 April 1919, 23 May 1919, *Yomiuri Shinbun*.
60. See Shimazu, *Japanese Society at War*, Ch. 1.
61. Arita, *Bakahachi to hito wa iu*, pp. 28–9.
62. Colonel Satō to Chief of Staff, 19 April 1919, no. 541.5, Teikoku (Japan), 2.3.1./ 1–4, *Pari heiwa jōyaku: rekkoku no taido oyobi seikyō*, Diplomatic Record Office, Tokyo.
63. Takeshita to Navy Vice-Minister, 7 February 1919, telegram no. 9, Bessatsu Takeshita Kaigun Chujō hōkokushū, 2.3.1./17–1, (January 1919–), *Pari heiwa kaigi*, Diplomatic Record Office, Tokyo.
64. 'Dai yonjū-ikkai gikai hōkokusho', *Kensei*, 2:3 (1919): 5–6; 'Katō sōsai no enzetsu', *Kensei*, 2:6 (1919): 13. Katō also expressed a similar view to Alston, who was at the British Embassy in Tokyo, in Alston to Curzon, 20 June 1919, Confidential Print 11580, no. 14, FO 410/67, National Archives, London.

65. Most secret memo, 22 October 1919, FO 371/3816, f 148769, National Archives, London.
66. Despatch no. 298, Alston to Curzon, 9 July 1919, FO 608/241, file 1643/2/1, National Archives, London.

References

Primary sources

National Diet Library, Tokyo:
Makino Shinken monjo [The Makino Shinken Papers].

Diplomatic Archives, Ministry of Foreign Affairs, Tokyo:
Nihon gaikō monjo [Documents on Japanese Foreign Policy], vol. 3, 1918; part 1, vol. 3, 1919.
Teikoku (Japan), 2.3.1./1–4, *Pari heiwa jōyaku: rekkoku no taido oyobi seikyō* [The Paris Peace Treaty: Attitudes of States and Political Situations].
Bessatsu Takeshita Kaigun Chujō hōkokushū, 2.3.1./17–1, (January 1919–), *Pari heiwa kaigi* [The Paris Peace Conference].

National Archives, London, UK:
FO 371/3816.
FO 410/67.
FO 608/124.
FO 608/211.
FO 608/241.

Library of Congress, Washington D.C., United States:
Stephen Bonsal Papers.

National Archives, Washington D.C., United States:
National Archives Microfilm Publication M367, Records of the Department of State relating to World War I and its termination, 1914–1929.

Periodicals:
Le Figaro, Paris.
Kaizō, Tokyo.
Kensei, Tokyo.
Kokumin Shinbun, Tokyo.
Le Matin, Paris.
New York Times, New York.
Le Temps, Paris.
The Times, London.
Tokyo Nichi-Nichi Shinbun, Tokyo.

Yamato Shinbun, Tokyo.
Yomiuri Shinbun, Tokyo.

Secondary sources

Arita, Hachirō, *Bakahachi to hito wa iu: Gaikōkan no kaisō* [People Call Me the Stupid Hachi: A Memoir of a Diplomat] (Tokyo: Kōwadō, 1959).
Bull, Hedley, *The Anarchical Society: A Study of Order in World Politics* (Basingstoke: Macmillan, 1977).
Bull, Hedley and Adam Watson (eds), *The Expansion of International Society* (Oxford: Oxford University Press, 1984).
Clemenceau, Georges, *Grandeur and Misery of Victory* (London: George G. Harrap, 1930).
Creel, George, *Complete Report of the Chairman of the Committee on Public Information* (Washington, D.C.: U.S. Government Printing Office, 1920).
Creel, George, *How We Advertised America* (New York: Harper and Brothers, 1920).
Der Derian, James, *On Diplomacy: A Genealogy of Western Estrangement* (Oxford: Basil Blackwell, 1987).
Elwall, Robert, *Building with Light: The International History of Architectural Photography* (London: Merrell, 2004).
Floto, Inga, *Colonel House in Paris: A Study of American Policy at the Paris Peace Conference* (Princeton: Princeton University Press, 1980).
Gardner, Lloyd C., *Safe for Democracy: The Anglo-American Response to Revolutions, 1913–1923* (New York: Oxford University Press, 1984).
Gérard, Auguste, *Ma mission au Japon: 1907–1914* (Paris: Librairie Plon, 1919).
Gordon, Andrew, *Labour and Imperial Democracy in Prewar Japan* (Berkeley: University of California Press, 1991).
Hara, Keiichirō (ed.), *Hara Kei Nikki* [Diary of Hara Kei], vol. 8 (Tokyo: Kengensha, 1950).
Ishii, Kikujirō, *Gaikō yoroku* [Diplomatic Jottings] (Tokyo: Iwanami, 1930).
Kikuchi, Takenori, *Hakushaku Chinda Sutemi den* [Biography of Viscount Chinda Sutemi] (Tokyo: Kyōmeikaku, 1938).
Kobayashi, Tatsuo (ed.), *Suiusō nikki: Itō ke bunsho* [Diaries of Suiusō: The Itō Family Papers] (Tokyo: Hara shobō, 1966).
Koizumi, Sakutarō, *Saionji Kinmochi jiden* [Autobiography of Saionji Kinmochi] (Tokyo: Kōdansha, 1949).
Koselleck, Reinhart, *Futures Past: On the Semantics of Historical Time* (New York: Columbia University Press, 2004).
Lansing, Robert, *The Peace Negotiations: A Personal Narrative* (London: Constable, 1921).
MacAloon, John J., *Rite, Drama, Festival, Spectacle: Rehearsals Toward a Theory of Cultural Performance* (Philadelphia: Institute for the Study of Human Issues, 1984).
Makino, Nobuaki, *Kaikoroku* [Reminiscences], vol. 2 (Tokyo: Chūōkoronsha, 1978).

Manela, Erez, *The Wilsonian Moment: Self-Determination and the International Origins of Anticolonial Nationalism* (Oxford: Oxford University Press, 2007).
Mantoux, Paul, *Paris Peace Conference 1919: Proceedings of the Council of Four (March 24–April 18)* (Geneva: Librairie Droz, 1964).
Mock, James and Cedric Larson, *Words that Won the War: The Story of the Committee on Public Information 1917–1919* (Princeton: Princeton University Press, 1939).
[no author] 'Teikoku no shudōteki kōwa jōken', *Kaizō* 1:1 (April 1919), p. 14.
[no author] 'Pari kōwa kaigi no antō', *Kaizō* 1:1 (April 1919), pp. 56–60
Nakano, Seigō, *Kōwa kaigi o mokugeki shite* [Witnessing the Peace Conference] (Tokyo: Tōhō jironsha, 1919).
Nicolson, Harold, *Peacemaking 1919* (London: Methuen, 1933).
Osiander, Andreas, 'Peacemaking and international legitimacy: Stability and consensus in the States System of Europe 1644–1920', unpubl. DPhil thesis (University of Oxford, Trinity, 1991).
Otte, T. G., '"A manual of diplomacy": The genesis of Satow's *Guide to Diplomatic Practice*', *Diplomacy and Statecraft*, 13:2 (June 2002), pp. 229–43.
Pakula, Hannah, *The Last Empress: Madame Chiang Kai-shek and the Birth of Modern China* (New York: Simon & Schuster, 2009).
Schattenberg, Susanna, 'The diplomat as "an actor on a great stage before all the people"? A cultural history of diplomacy and the Portsmouth peace negotiations of 1905', in Markus Mösslang and Torsten Riotte (eds), *The Diplomat's World: A Cultural History of Diplomacy 1815–1914* (Oxford: Oxford University Press, 2008), pp. 167–94.
Shimazu, Naoko, *Japan, Race and Equality: The Racial Equality Proposal of 1919* (London: Routledge, 1998).
Shimazu, Naoko, *Japanese Society at War: Death, Memory and the Russo-Japanese War* (Cambridge: Cambridge University Press, 2009).
Shimazu, Naoko, 'Diplomacy as theatre: Staging the Bandung Conference of 1955', *Modern Asian Studies*, 48:1 (January 2014), pp. 231–4.
Wight, Martin, *Power Politics* (Leicester: Leicester University Press, 1978).
Wilson, Woodrow, *The Papers of Woodrow Wilson*, vol. 56 (Princeton: Princeton University Press, 1986).

Chapter 5

India's Freedom and the League of Nations: Public Debates 1919–33

MARIA FRAMKE

The aftermath of the First World War constituted a turning point in the history of India and its national independence movement.[1] From 1919 until the mid-1930s, the subcontinent faced two mass campaigns that were directed against British rule and more specifically against the different constitutional reforms suggested or implemented by the British. Most Indian nationalists rejected those suggestions as not extensive enough and demanded either dominion status or *swaraj* (self-rule). While the two mass protest campaigns, known as the non-cooperation and civil disobedience movements, respectively, constituted one way of putting forward Indian demands, other nationalists rather looked for a more conciliatory policy in dealing with the British 'masters'. One of these moderate approaches was to suggest arbitration through the League of Nations.

This organisation, of which India was a founding member, had always held a particular position within Indian public opinion. The present chapter examines the perception of the League of Nations in Indian newspapers and journals,[2] as well as by Indian nationalists. The main focus is on the question of how the League was seen and approached by Indian nationalists and the newspapers to make a case for India's independence.

Attempts to define public opinion entail a number of methodological problems, not least because there is no commonly acknowledged definition. In this paper, the term public opinion is used to describe 'firmly settled convictions of a group and . . . the process of developing opinions'.[3] Thereby, public opinion is understood to be expressed either by the Indian press or by public associations and nationalist movements. It is important to keep in mind that there was not just one public opinion; rather, one has to acknowledge that the views held by the Indian press and public associations were highly diversified.

India in the League of Nations – public perceptions of its status and representation

India, owing to its contribution to the First World War, and also because of public opinion within British India, was allowed not only to participate in the Paris Peace Conference in 1919, but also to sign the peace treaties along with the representatives of other sovereign states on the basis of legal equality of status.⁴ During the Peace Conference negotiations, it was also determined to set up an international organisation that would preserve peace in the future.⁵ After long discussions, India was admitted to the League of Nations.⁶ What is striking about this fact is that India was the only non-sovereign state – the only non-self-governing member of the League of Nations.⁷ This anomaly – the fact that India enjoyed official sovereign rights in external matters in the League of Nations, while neither being autonomous nor having any power in internal affairs – became one of the major themes of public debate in India.

However, India's anomalous status was not the only aspect that was widely written and argued about in Indian newspapers and journals; the issue of representation and the precise status of India – commonly depicted in the domestic press as dependent – evoked further discussion. Many suspected a British conspiracy behind India's improbable membership of the newly created club. For example, the Marathi newspaper *Rajakaran*, published in Pune (Poona), reported in November 1919 that 'England secured a vote for India on the League of Nations in order to be able to command a larger number of votes.'⁸ It added that 'India's representation on the League will not benefit her [India] in any way.'⁹ In 1923, the *Bombay Chronicle*, an English daily, went even further by describing India's position as that of a 'lackey of Great Britain'.¹⁰ Distrust of the British government, naturally refracted through the optic of colonialism in India, left Indian public opinion in a state of discontent. Hence, the one argument that was repeated time and again in the domestic press until the early 1930s was that, although India was represented in the League of Nations, it had no voice of its own.¹¹

When it came to the issue of Indian representation in the League of Nations, one aspect that was widely questioned in India was the nature and mode of selecting the delegates who went to the annual assembly meetings in Geneva.¹² The Indian delegation consisted of three people, who were neither elected nor nominated by the Indian public but were appointed by the Secretary of State for India in consultation with the government in India.¹³ This procedure, together with the fact that, until 1928, it was usually a Briton who led the delegation,¹⁴ was resented by both the majority of Indian nationalist politicians and the wider public. Critics felt that the selected delegates, British as well as Indian, would rather work along the prescribed official lines of the British government and would therefore not represent India's real wishes and ambitions.¹⁵ This fear gained wide publicity in 1925 when the nomination of Viscount Willingdon, former Governor of the Presidencies of Bombay and Madras, as leader of the delegation to Geneva caused discomfort and anger in the Indian press. The *Swarajya*, published in Madras, remarked against this background that the representatives 'are selected by the Government of India and [that] they are capable only of repeating the lessons taught by the Government of India'.¹⁶ On the same issue, the *Sampad Abhyudaya*, published in Mysore, stated:

> It is generally thought that this year's selection of the Indian delegation to the League of Nations is as unrepresentative of Indian public opinion as it is derogatory to India.

> ... The selection of these extinct volcanoes [the delegates] to represent India in the League of Nations not only humiliates India, but also leads to the unjust conclusion that suitable Indian representatives are not available. It makes the political thraldom of India not only more explicit, but also more emphatic.[17]

Such views none the less also make it clear that the anger was directed not only towards the leader, Lord Willingdon, but also towards other nominees: for example, the High Commissioner for India, Atul Chandra Chatterjee, and the Maharajadhiraj of Patiala. Both of these Indian members were also seen as unsuitable for representing India's concerns.[18]

After intense protest and nationalist agitation, the government of India agreed that, from 1929 onwards, an Indian would usually assume leadership of the delegation.[19] However, the Indian government did not revise the policy of nomination that remained a cause of great grievance within Indian public opinion.

The above-cited feeling that India had been humiliated in the eyes of the world by this forced choice was widespread. Still, there was a more deep-rooted reason for the fierce reactions in the press. It was feared that the delegates propagated an image in Geneva that India was not worthy of attaining freedom. The *Swarajya* expressed this suspicion in the following manner:

> As usual, the representatives of other countries will be told that the Indians do not desire freedom and that they have not proved themselves fit for it. By making this show, it will be proclaimed that India has been given a high status in the Empire. But, in fact, it is only harm that will result to India from this, as it gives room to screen the real situation of the country and to carry on a mischievous propaganda. It must be demonstrated to the world that India is kept in chains of slavery.[20]

Widespread Indian rejection of the existing procedure regarding representation in the League was thus due to the convergence of several factors: the feeling of humiliation stemming from being a colonised country, the belief that the British nominees could not represent India according to its real ambitions and wishes in Geneva, and the fear that India would be displayed as unfit for freedom and self-determination in the eyes of the world. All three reasons, however, connect to the larger point: that is, the aspiration expressed in the Indian press regarding India becoming independent and self-governing. The question of India's independence itself thus formed an important topic that was discussed in connection with its role in the League of Nations.

The League of Nations, Tilak and India's fight for freedom until 1926

After the country's substantial contribution to the British war effort, Indian nationalists expected – and general public opinion shared this expectation – some favourable gestures from Great Britain in matters of political participation. The idea of attaining home rule – that is, self-government in internal affairs, as well as approval of India's dominion status within the British Empire, was encouraged in August 1917 by the announcement of the Secretary of State for India, Edwin Montagu, that the British government would adopt a policy to promote 'the gradual development of self-governing institutions with a view to the progressive realisation of responsible government in India as an integral part of the British Empire'.[21] The hopes and ambitions of Indian nationalists were further strengthened by the policy adopted by US President Woodrow Wilson, who declared his support for national self-determination of the peoples in wartime. Although not speaking about India and not mentioning the word self-determination explicitly in his fourteen-point programme,[22] Wilson's engagement was most favourably received in India. Consequently, political organisations like the Indian National Congress (INC), the Home Rule League of Annie Besant and the Muslim League adopted resolutions calling for the application of the principle of self-determination in India. Furthermore, it encouraged Indian nationalist leaders to appeal directly to Wilson for his help in securing this position.[23]

One person who became eminently engaged in this matter, and whose activities were widely discussed in the Indian press, was Bal Gangadhar Tilak. Tilak, the erstwhile leader of the extremist wing of the national movement from Maharashtra, was elected by the INC as one of its representatives to the Peace Conference in France in December 1918. Already in London since October 1918, he became wholeheartedly involved in this issue. The idea of bringing India's case to the League of Nations seemed a promising way to promote India's independence. The League, during this time, had a crucial role in the formation of the political ideas not only of Tilak but also of other Indian nationalists. It also played an important part in shaping some of the other related concerns of the domestic press in India, especially regarding issues that dealt with the future preservation of world peace and the establishment of what today would probably be called global governance. This, of course, as pointed out above, was accompanied by a belief that the League would also have a greater say in matters of national self-determination.[24] This expectation, however, which was fuelled by the statements made by President Wilson during the war and the anomalous grounds on which India was admitted into the League, proved to be illusory. The Covenant of the League did not include any article about the self-determination of colonised countries and did not clarify the anomaly of the Indian case.[25] In spite of this obvious misinterpretation of the League's tasks and abilities, Tilak pursued his mission. Denied permission by the British government to go to Paris from London, Tilak still managed to propagate the idea of India's self-determination, by, for example, distributing pamphlets on 'Self-determination for India', published by the India Home Rule League's Office in London in 1918,[26] and by organising a petition campaign,[27] as well as by writing two famous letters. The first letter was sent to the President of the Peace Conference, Georges Clemenceau;[28] the other was addressed to President Wilson, asking him to ensure that the Peace Conference would apply Wilson's principle of right and justice to India.[29] Tilak did receive a reply, written by Wilson's private secretary, assuring him that India's case 'will be taken up in due time by the proper authorities'.[30] However, the issue was not even discussed at the Peace Conference and Tilak's efforts turned out to be completely futile. This failure did not stop him working towards having India's claims represented in the League. On his return to India in November 1919, Tilak propagated his views in his English newspaper, *Mahratta*, which was published in Pune (Poona). His work, however, did not prove successful, and he soon died, somewhat disillusioned, in August 1920.[31]

Initially, the Indian press's reaction was supportive of Tilak's efforts, but on seeing no positive outcome, the tone of the writings soon changed to disappointment. For example, the *Indian Emigrant*, published in Madras, expressed appreciation of his efforts in May 1919,[32] while the Marathi newspaper, *Sāndesh*, published in Bombay, stated after his return in November 1919 that 'Tilak's mission to Europe has proved a failure.'[33] These judgements have to be understood against a background of the general perceptions of the League and its perceived commitment to Indian self-determination. As shown above, a rather misleading notion about the League's tasks and goals had persisted in India. This was not reflective of a lack of understanding on the part of the Indian intelligentsia and politicians – there did exist a section that was aware of this misinterpretation. Their critique of the League was thus based not on fulfilling the perceived task (which actually, constitutionally speaking, did not exist), but rather on a more serious account. It was based on a realisation that the League was not interested in issues of self-determination for colonial countries.[34] An article in the Anglo-Gujarati newspaper *Praja Bandhu*, published in Ahmedabad, brought this issue to the fore:

> President Wilson's intention of having peace for the whole world in future by the establishment of a League of Nations, is not likely to be fulfilled as can be seen from the articles of the covenant of the League of Nations. . . . Thus the principle of self-determination has almost disappeared. That no reference is made with regard to the self-determination of countries like India, Ireland and Egypt is its greatest defect. In short, there is no prospect of improvement in the present state of things by the establishment of this League of Nations.[35]

This pessimistic view regarding the question of whether or not any help for India's case could be expected from the League of Nations was often connected with suggestions to change its current policy by taking up 'full power to apply the principle of self-determination'.[36]

Parallel to this debate were the efforts made by the colonial state in India. A Government of India Act was promulgated in 1919. The Act, also popularly known as the Montagu–Chelmsford Reforms, basically represented India's 'reward' from Britain for its war efforts. The Act was also the first step towards self-governance, however. It introduced an indigenous constitutional system called diarchy, which encompassed a central government that was almost completely under British control, and provincial governments, responsible to provincial legislatures, in which Indian ministers were allowed to take charge of certain areas.[37] The reform scheme did not satisfy Indian nationalistic ambitions because the concessions granted fell short of the original demands for home rule or self-determination. The *Andra Patrika*, published in Madras, took a clear nationalist stance by declaring in May 1919 that

> the Montagu–Chelmsford scheme is against the principle of self-determination and that a free and self-governing India would be a source of strength to the British Empire and the peace of the world, while a weak and dependent India would defeat the objects of the Peace Conference by being a cause of constant jealousy and war among the bigger powers . . . and that the Reform Scheme should be improved in accordance with the principle of self-determination . . . which the League of Nations proposes to apply to the colonies of the enemy powers.[38]

The arguments in the press were presented at two levels. At the international level, it was argued that a colonised India would contradict the goals of the League. On the domestic front, it was demanded that the act should be improved by incorporating the principle of self-determination. Nothing seemed to have changed, though; the implementation of the Montagu–Chelmsford Reforms made it plain to the Indian nationalists and the Indian press that their demands for self-determination would, for the present, not be fulfilled.

Amongst other factors, this disillusionment was also responsible for the beginning of a new phase of political action in British India, with M. K. Gandhi emerging as the national leader under whose aegis the first nationwide mass protest campaign, called the non-cooperation movement, took place.[39] The emergence of new forms of political resistance also entailed a change in perceptions of the League and its importance with regard to India's freedom over the following years. While, in 1919, the League was seen either as an organisation that could help India gain self-determination or one that could at least mediate or even change its policy to include self-determination in its constitution, by now, the early 1920s, a general disappointment persisted in public opinion.[40] An article in the *Modern Review* in 1927, for example, came to the caustic conclusion that 'India can never expect the least help or sympathy from the League in their fight for freedom.'[41]

None the less, there were still a few who believed that the League could act as an arbitrator in times of conflict between Great Britain and India. One of these people was the Indian revolutionary and international scholar, Taraknath Das.[42] Despite his disbelief in the current form of this organisation, Das appealed to his fellow countrymen and Indian nationalists, in an article published in the *Modern Review* in 1924, in particular to 'utilise the League of Nations and present India's case before the members of the League collectively and individually, officially and unofficially'.[43] He recommended that India should take advantage of

British sensibilities regarding international public opinion by bringing its issues before the tribunal and hence making them better known to the wider public. He believed that, even if India's efforts to secure justice through the League would be unsuccessful, the people of India would gain internationally and would come to know which countries would side with Britain's policy and which powers would support India.[44]

Seemingly, Das's ideas did not gain currency. The non-cooperation movement was called off by Gandhi by early 1922, without even achieving clarity amongst the Indian nationalists on the question of the meaning and implications of *swaraj*. The INC took up rather a quiescent stance in political matters that concerned international deliberations. Neither did it show much enthusiasm and belief in the League and its powers of arbitration. Mahatma Gandhi, by then one of the most important figures in the INC, considered the League to be an imperialist agent equivalent to Great Britain and France. He did not expect any help from it for colonised peoples.[45] Gandhi's was not the only critical, or even dismissive, voice; he was merely one among many Indian leaders like Jawaharlal Nehru or Subhas Chandra Bose, who held similar views.[46] To a large extent, their attitude was derived from a perception that the League was created to uphold the international status quo.[47] Thus, rather than effecting changes, particularly for colonial societies, they saw the League as a body that remained indifferent, if not hostile, to the ideas of self-governance. A similar assessment was made in the Indian press in the 1920s.[48] Those Indians struggling for a change in their status and for their freedom were naturally opposed to the maintenance of the existing world order and to the League of Nations as its perceived preserver.

Critical statements regarding the League's role in world politics, especially as to the self-determination of colonised countries, not only appeared in written form in the Indian press, but were also voiced through satirical sketches. We see one such illustration in an album of satirical representations called *Vyanga Chitravali: Caricature Album, A Collection of Political and Social Caricatures* published in Kanpur (Cawnpore) in 1925. In the 'Funeral procession of Wilson's 14 Points', one can see France, President Wilson and England (from left to right) having a conversation, while fourteen stone slabs symbolising Wilson's Fourteen Points are carried away to the sea (Figure 5.1).[49] The dialogue reads:

> Wilson (weeping): 'Alas! My fourteen children!'
> France: 'Being wise, why do you mourn? One who is born is doomed to die. See, the daughters of God (the hopes) also did not survive.'
> England: 'And if "League of Nations" remains alive, we will have many more children!'

The sketch deals with the perceived decline of the Wilsonian ideas, and also with the positions of the two great powers, France and Britain, regarding this development. While France was seen as adopting a rather practical approach to the decline of the high hopes – the Fourteen Points – envisioned by the US

Figure 5.1 'Funeral Procession of Wilson's 14 Points' (*Vyanga Chitravali: Caricature Album, A Collection of Political and Social Caricatures*, Cawnpore, 1925; in the collection of the British Library).

President, Great Britain was depicted as imperialistic, pointing to the opportunities a surviving League of Nations would give to the big powers: that is, through the mandate system.[50]

In connection with the question of maintenance of the existing world order, one also can find voices in the newspapers that were critical of India's own role. The *Aj*, published in the United Provinces, remarked in 1926:

> This venomous reptile [the League of Nations] is also nourished by India. We become beside ourselves with rage and shame when we see that this institution despite its black deeds of omission and commission is maintained with the blood of our hearts. By becoming its member we are destroying ourselves and bringing calamities on Asia. We are prolonging the subjection of subject peoples and depriving independent nations of their liberty. We wish India to protest against the contribution made by the Government of India towards the maintenance of the League of Nations and to tell the world that she is not willingly nourishing this cobra. . . . We have no place in the League of Nations. We want to be in the company of those who are dependent, who are oppressed and who are struggling for their life.[51]

Critical assessments like this often led to the demand that India should leave the League of Nations and should rather concentrate on its struggle for independence. It also made visible the fact that the financial contribution of India to the League was very much resented.[52]

A new phase of political resistance in India and the role of the League of Nations, 1927–33

In 1927, the British government had sent the so-called Simon Commission to India to examine the political situation and render recommendations for future constitutional reforms. The commission faced strong protests in India because all its members were British – not a single Indian had been selected. In the following months, politicians from different organisations tried to develop their own scheme for an Indian constitution with a demand for the introduction of dominion status. Although the outcome of this attempt, the Nehru Report, was not unanimously accepted by every important political organisation, the demand for dominion status was made to Great Britain at the annual meeting of the INC in December 1928. The INC further determined that, if this concession was not granted by the end of 1929, it would launch a new mass protest campaign – civil disobedience. This time, the intensity was exemplified by adding the word *purna* (complete) to the word *swaraj* that had already been in place in the earlier phase of deliberations and protest.[53]

The tactic of presenting the demand in terms of an ultimatum to the British rulers was not unanimously well received, neither amongst politicians nor in the press. Some people favoured other ways to help India's case; one such way was to have recourse to the League. A typical example of this stance was Chakravarti Vijiaraghavachariar, a South Indian lawyer and prominent member of the INC, of which he had been president in 1920.[54] He came up with the idea of going to the League in his pamphlet 'League of Nations and India's case of emancipation', written in 1929. This pamphlet contained an interview with him that had appeared in the newspaper *The Hindu* on 2 March 1929. It also included some introductory remarks written by him.[55] In the pamphlet, he argued that India's 'political and economic salvation lay with the League of Nations'.[56] He described the League as the fairest arbitrator between nations.[57] Vijiaraghavachariar, although generally believing in the concept of Indian mass protest movements like the non-cooperation or civil disobedience ones, held that it would take too long and would involve a lot of organisational effort to gain self-rule through this method. The League of Nations appeared to him to be the only viable alternative.[58] Regarding the actual course of bringing this question before the League, Vijiaraghavachariar argued that there were different alternatives. Firstly, the governments of Great Britain and India could submit the matter to the Council of the League under Article XV of the Covenant. Secondly, any other member state of the League could use its 'friendly rights' under clause (2) of Article XI and pay attention to the issue.[59] Thirdly, 'the Assembly or the Council of

League ... [could] set the whole process of the Covenant in motion for the purpose of the investigation of the dispute and taking all such actions as the Covenant commands and warrants.'[60] He was convinced that the League would take up the issue due to its obligation to keep world peace and also because of India's anomalous status within the League.[61]

Vijiaraghavachariar's proposal was discussed in the English language weekly, *The Servant of India*, and later republished in *The Hindu* on 17 August 1929. The author of this article conceded that there was a need to use every possible way of attracting international attention to India's demand for *swaraj*, but he also found Vijiaraghavachariar too optimistic in his assessment of the League if he thought that the League would help, and in the event that it did help, that it would lead to successful mediation. The main reason for this doubt was the conviction that both the given articles of the Covenant would not apply.[62] The League would not interfere in domestic questions by applying Article XV (8),[63] due to the fact that India's case could be understood as a domestic affair of Great Britain's. Neither would it, in the opinion of the author, treat the denial of immediate self-rule for India as a threat to world peace, as required under Article XI.[64] For these reasons, a successful mediation by the League seemed rather unlikely.

The idea of dispensing propaganda on India's behalf was taken up by the Geneva correspondent of *The Hindu*, who found the suggestion that 'any such propaganda should be extended to all large centres of political activity in the world ... worthy [of] serious and immediate consideration'.[65] Thereby, debates to establish foreign contacts and to stimulate international interest in India's plight were by no means completely new. Indian nationalists had been campaigning for the sympathy and support of other countries since the late nineteenth century.[66] The 1920s, however, witnessed a new wave of more extensive activities[67] that included, according to T. A. Keenleyside, four major components: (1) the setting up of the Foreign Congress Department (1928 and again in 1936), (2) the establishment of different Indian nationalist bureaus overseas (in Great Britain and the United States in particular), (3) the participation in non-governmental conferences, and (4) personal diplomatic initiatives.[68]

The speculative discussion regarding whether India's case should be brought before the League and whether it would prove successful continued over the next few years. While the majority held the view that the League was not the right arbitrator for India's demands because it had no right to interfere in the internal affairs of its members,[69] a very few still wanted to appeal to the League for help.[70] By the end of 1929, it also became clear that Great Britain would not grant dominion status to India. This resulted in the INC launching its civil disobedience movement. Over the course of the next few years, this movement influenced debates about constitutional reforms, but in the end the British enacted the Government of India Act of 1935, which introduced further reforms but failed to meet the INC's demand for self-rule.[71]

Conclusion

The above account clearly shows that Indian public opinion had engaged widely with the League of Nations. Its foundation, India's place within this organisation, the question of the Indian representatives, and the limitations of the League in contrast with the aspirations of Indian nationalists were some of the issues that were discussed extensively in the domestic press. While, initially, there were a few positive assessments of issues like India's status and representation in the League, and especially its demand for self-determination, most voices soon emerged as rather critical. It would certainly not be an exaggeration to say that, by the mid-1920s, a negative view of the League prevailed in the Indian public sphere with regard to its political work.[72] The debate did not die out completely thereafter, as from time to time one can find journalists, as well as Indian nationalists, launching appeals to approach the League. The dominant view, however, remained extremely critical of the idea. The same holds true for the INC, which, after 1919, did not try to bring its demands directly before the League. Although no further institutional action was taken, individual members of the organisation still viewed the League as a helpful tool to enforce their demands and took appropriate measures.

Elements of the criticism issuing from the Indian public on the missing arbitration were less connected with the League itself, but rather were associated with the perception of Great Britain as ruler of India. The Indian government – that is, the prevalent official line – could not act independently because it was subordinate to the British government. It was precisely because of this asymmetrical distribution of power that India could not 'ask the League of Nations to arbitrate between itself and its master the Government of Britain'.[73] The sober conclusion drawn by many was that 'the people of India must, therefore, rely mainly on their own efforts for success in their nonviolent fight for freedom.'[74]

Notes

1. The author would like to thank Harald Fischer-Tiné, Nitin Sinha and Nikolay Kamenov for their helpful comments. In this chapter, the term 'India' is used as a description of the political–administrative unit of British India and not as a concept of any 'imagined' community. However, since the 1870s, intellectuals and politicians in India had vividly discussed the question of nationality and nationhood that fused the twin concepts of the nation state as a territorial unit and nationalism as a binding ideology of the imagined community. In the first three decades of the twentieth century, competing ideas on these themes existed and gave rise to the presence of different nationalisms in India. India in this essay, therefore, functions as a territorial unit, which in turn was itself undergoing a process of formation, as defined through these competing frameworks. The use of the term 'Indian nationalists' here refers to the mainstream nationalism of the Indian national movement. The relevant

literature on this theme includes: Goswami, *Producing India*; Six, *Hindi–Hindu–Hindustan*; Chatterjee, *Nationalist Thought*; and Anderson, *Imagined Communities*. Furthermore, by applying the word 'Indian', the author follows the standard terminology used in the contemporary sources.

2. The Indian press – that is, newspapers and journals in Indian ownership – emerged and consolidated itself in the second half of the nineteenth century. Being initially a product of Indian reform movements, the press became highly influenced by and was closely connected to the anticolonial movement in the first decades of the twentieth century. Due to its specific history of origin, the Indian press is perceived as a 'national medium'. Thereby 'national', according to Schneider, relates not only to its geographical area of circulation, but particularly to its major role with regard to the emergence of anticolonial nationalism and the liberal–classical public in India (Schneider, *Zur Darstellung von 'Kultur'*, pp. 82 and 89–93; Sonwalkar, '"Murdochization" of the Indian press', pp. 823–4).

3. Veerathappa, 'Growth of public opinion', p. 228.

4. Verma, *India and the League of Nations*, pp. 1–13. For India's participation in the First World War, see, amongst others: Ellinwood and Pradhan, *India and Word War I*; Roy, Liebau and Ahuja, *When the War Began*; Singh, *The Testimonies of Indian Soldiers*; Das, 'Imperialism, nationalism and the First World War', pp. 67–85; and Singha, 'Finding labour from India', pp. 412–45.

5. For the establishment of the League of Nations, see Wertheim, 'The League of Nations', pp. 210–32 and MacMillan, *Paris 1919*. For a discussion of recent research trends with regard to the League of Nations, see Pedersen, 'Back to the League of Nations', pp. 1091–117.

6. For a discussion of opposition of the United States to India's admittance to the League of Nations, see Anand, 'The formation of international organizations', pp. 10–12.

7. Anand, 'The formation of international organizations', pp. 8–10; Verma, *India and the League of Nations*, pp. 14–24; Coyajee, *India and the League of Nations*, pp. 20–3. India's admission to the League of Nations was due to the fact that India was an original member of the League. Because of this, it automatically acquired membership of the League under Article I, paragraph I of the Covenant.

8. *Rajakāran*, 2 November 1919, *Report on Newspapers published in the Bombay Presidency* [hereafter cited as *INR Bombay*], no. 45 of 1919, p. 8.

9. *Rajakāran*, 2 November 1919, *INR Bombay*, no. 45 of 1919, p. 8.

10. *Bombay Chronicle*, 2 October 1923, *INR Bombay*, no. 40 of 1923, p. 953.

11. See, amongst others, *Andra Patrika*, 14 July 1923, *Report on English Papers Examined by the Criminal Investigation Department, Madras, and on Vernacular Papers Examined by the Translators to the Government of Madras* [hereafter cited as *INR Madras*], no. 29 of 1923, p. 864; Anonymous, 'Editorial', p. 6; Gupta, 'India and the League of Nations', p. 161.

12. It has to be stated that there were a lot of other grievances regarding India's membership of the League of Nations. Public opinion, for instance, was critical about the money India had to pay as a membership contribution, about the small numbers

of Indians employed in the League and about the marginal representation in the League Council.
13. Verma, *India and the League of Nations*, p. 46.
14. The British leader was normally joined by two Indian representatives, one of whom was a public figure in British India and the other a ruling prince of an Indian state.
15. Verma, *India and the League of Nations*, pp. 58–9; *Paisa Akhbar*, 30 October 1920, *Punjab Press Abstracts* [hereafter cited as *INR Punjab*, the name for the *Punjab Press Abstracts* changed in the 1920s to *Note on the Punjab Press*], vol. 33, no. 45, p. 443; *Andra Patrika*, 16 July 1924, *INR Madras*, no. 30 of 1924, p. 957; *Swarajya*, 30 November 1929, *INR Madras*, no. 49 of 1929, p. 1675; Anonymous, 'Inadequate representation', p. 221. See also Keenleyside, 'The Indian nationalist movement', p. 283.
16. *Swarajya*, 15 July 1925, *INR Madras*, no. 30 of 1925, p. 925.
17. *Sampad Abhyudaya*, 21 July 1925, *INR Madras*, no. 30 of 1925, p. 926.
18. In connection with the nomination of Indians, one also could find critical voices regarding the motives of the delegates themselves. The Indian nationalist Shyamji Krishnavarma, while writing about the case of the nominee Srinivasa Sastri, pointed to the supposed selfishness in his journal, *The Indian Sociologist*, in August 1922: 'rather than being a representative of his countrymen he may be regarded as a self seeking unjust agent of a tyrannical alien government which is always ready to buy hireling by offering service, honours and emoluments to its victims.' Krishnavarma, 'India and the League of Nations', p. 2. For Krishnavarma's perception of the League of Nations, see also Fischer-Tiné, *Shyamji Krishnavarma*.
19. Verma, *India and the League of Nations*, pp. 51 and 65–75; Anonymous, 'Leader of Indian delegation', p. 530; *Tribune*, 19 July 1924, *INR Punjab*, no. 29 of 1924, p. 243; *Bombay Samāchār*, 10 May 1928, *INR Bombay*, no. 19 of 1928, p. 508. The question of the leadership of the delegation troubled politically minded Indians in such a way that they tried persistently to convince the government to appoint an Indian. P. C. Sethna in particular addressed this matter intensively and moved several resolutions in the Council of State demanding that an Indian lead the delegation. The agitation and efforts of P. C. Sethna and his nationalist colleagues, which were largely supported by the press, were finally crowned with success in 1929.
20. *Swarajya*, 15 July 1925, p. 925.
21. Manela, *The Wilsonian Moment*, p. 83.
22. Wilson announced his so-called Fourteen Points in an address given to a joint session of Congress on 8 January 1918. His ideas for a new world order included such concrete steps as the restoration of Alsace and Lorraine to France, territorial adjustments in Central and Eastern Europe, the Balkans and Asia Minor on the basis of nationality, and fair adjustment of colonial claims. On general issues, Wilson proposed freedom of navigation upon the seas, removal of trade barriers, reduction of armaments, open covenants of peace and finally the foundation of a general association of nations that would guarantee political independence and territorial integrity to great and small states. He did not mention in this speech the word self-determination, which was actually used three days earlier by the British Prime

Minister, David Lloyd George. See Cooper, *Breaking the Heart of the World*, p. 24. For a discussion on Wilson's political ideas with regard to self-government, see T. Throntveit, 'The fable of the Fourteen Points', pp. 445–481. For a discussion of the concept of self-determination and its history, see Weitz, 'Self-determination', pp. 462–96.

23. Manela, *The Wilsonian Moment*, pp. 77–97.
24. Verma, *India and the League of Nations*, pp. 27 and 270; Manela, *The Wilsonian Moment*, pp. 166–8; *Andra Patrika*, 6 May 1919, *INR Madras*, no. 20 of 1919, p. 743.
25. Ostrower, *The League of Nations*, pp. 19–25.
26. Manela, *The Wilsonian Moment*, pp. 163–6.
27. Manela, *The Wilsonian Moment*, p. 167. Tilak organised a petition campaign to secure the League's help for India. Over its course, dozens of Indian organisations sent messages to the Peace Conference and its leaders, asking for self-determination in India.
28. Manela, *The Wilsonian Moment*, p.163.
29. Tilak to Wilson, 02.01.1919, LOC, WWP, series 5f, reel 446, cited in Manela, *The Wilsonian Moment*, p. 163.
30. Close to Tilak, 14.01.1919, quoted in *Mahratta*, 19.10.1919, cited in Manela, *The Wilsonian Moment*, p. 166.
31. Manela, *The Wilsonian Moment*, pp. 173–4.
32. *Indian Emigrant*, 15 May 1919, *INR Madras*, no. 22 of 1919, p. 812.
33. *Sāndesh*, 4 November 1919, *INR Bombay*, no. 45 of 1919, p. 8.
34. Anand argues that the League was seen by many Indians as an 'instrument of imperialism', 'a organization of white people', primarily interested in preserving the existing status quo (Anand, 'The formation of international organizations', p. 14; for this discussion, see also Keenleyside, 'The Indian nationalist movement', p. 284). Critical Indian perceptions of the newly established mandate system under the League of Nations might also have contributed to these views. For more information on this theme, see Grant and Trivedi, 'A question of trust', pp. 21–43.
35. *Praja Bandhu*, 23 February 1919, *INR Bombay*, no. 9 of 1919, pp. 18–19.
36. *Andra Patrika*, 2 April 1919, *INR Madras*, no. 15 of 1919, p. 568.
37. Metcalf and Metcalf, *A Concise History*, p. 166. The areas that came under the responsibility of Indian ministers, such as agriculture and education, carried less political weight and attracted few funds.
38. *Andra Patrika*, 6 May 1919, no. 20 of 1919, p. 743.
39. Metcalf and Metcalf, *A Concise History*, pp. 166–7 and 179–81. Disillusionment with the Montagu-Chelmsford Reforms was not the only reason for launching the non-cooperation campaign. The government of India also introduced the Rowlatt Acts in 1919, which contained provisions for the continuance of many wartime powers of detention and trial without jury. This measure was bitterly resented by Indians and, in the course of their protest against it, martial law was applied in different provinces and the massacre of Jallianwala Bagh, causing the deaths of hundreds of people, took place.
40. *Tamil Nadu*, 18 July 1920, *INR Madras*, no. 31 of 1920, pp. 851–2; *Saiphul Islam*,

17 October 1923, *INR Madras*, no. 43 of 1923, pp. 1316–17; *Aj*, February 1926, *Note on the Press, United Provinces of Agra and Oudh* [hereafter cited as *INR United Provinces*], no. 6 of 1926, p. 1; Anonymous, 'The League of Nations and "weaker nations"', pp. 606–7.

41. Anonymous, 'India and the League of Nations', p. 257.
42. *Siyasat*, 3 February 1921, *INR Punjab*, vol. 34, no. 7, p. 69; Das, 'India and the League of Nations', pp. 163–7. Throughout his life, Taraknath Das (1884–1958) was a staunch nationalist who worked for India's freedom first as revolutionary, and later as scholar and educationalist. Das was an active member not only of the Anusilan Samity, a secret revolutionary organisation in Bengal, but also of the US-based Ghadar Party, which tried to free India militarily during the First World War with German help. In 1918, in the course of the Hindu German Conspiracy Case, he was sentenced to 22 months' imprisonment in the United States. Afterwards, although distancing himself from any violent struggle, Das worked constantly for India's independence by pursuing his academic carrier. He wrote numerous books and articles on the subject of international politics and India. See Günther, *Taraknath Das*, pp. 3–34.
43. Das, 'India and the League of Nations', p. 166.
44. Das, 'India and the League of Nations', p. 166.
45. Gandhi, *The Collected Works of Mahatma Gandhi*, p. 441.
46. Nehru, *Glimpses of World History*, pp. 681 ff.; Bose, *The Indian Struggle*, p. 365. Initially, Subhas Chandra Bose had not been critical of the League of Nations. During a stay in Europe, he went to Geneva in 1933 to explore 'the possibilities of utilizing the League of Nations for advancing the cause of India's freedom'. While he was there, Bose realised that 'the machinery of the League of Nations was controlled fully by Britain and France and that it was impossible to utilise the League for India's liberty.' He became a forceful critic of the League and of India's membership of the organisation.
47. Verma, *India and the League of Nations*, pp. 273–4.
48. *Roznāma-e-Khilafat*, 6 September 1922, *INR Bombay*, no. 36 of 1922, p. 900; *Aj*, January 1926, *INR United Provinces*, no. 3 of 1926, p. 1; *Mathrubhumi*, 2 October 1925, *INR Madras*, no. 42 of 1925, p. 1300.
49. Anonymous, *Vyanga Chitravali*.
50. For the mandate system of the League of Nations, see Pedersen, *The Guardians*.
51. *Aj*, 23 January 1926, *INR United Provinces*, no. 3 of 1926, p. 1.
52. Verma, *India and the League of Nations*, p. 330. India contributed yearly from 1921 onwards to the expenses of the League of Nations. Its share went up from 4.90 per cent in 1921 to 6.97 per cent in 1924. After this high point, the Indian contribution went slowly down to 5.44 per cent in 1935 and levelled off at 5.25 per cent between 1937 and 1939.
53. Metcalf and Metcalf, *A Concise History*, pp. 187–9.
54. Parthasarathy, *Dawn and Achievement of Indian Freedom*, p. 105.
55. Vijiaraghavachariar, *League of Nations*.
56. Vijiaraghavachariar, *League of Nations*, p. 3.

57. Vijiaraghavachariar, *League of Nations*, p. 6.
58. Vijiaraghavachariar, *League of Nations*, pp. 3–4.
59. Vijiaraghavachariar, *League of Nations*, pp. 15–16. Article XV (1) states, 'If there should arise between Members of the League any dispute likely to lead to a rupture, which is not submitted to arbitration in accordance with Article 13, the Members of the League agree that they will submit the matter to the Council. Any party to the dispute may effect such submission by giving notice of the existence of the dispute to the Secretary-General, who will make all necessary arrangements for a full investigation and consideration thereof.' Article XI (2) states, 'It is also declared to be the friendly right of each Member of the League to bring to the attention of the Assembly or of the Council any circumstance whatever affecting international relations which threatens to disturb international peace or the good understanding between nations upon which peace depends.' See Ostrower, *The League of Nations*, pp. 21–2.
60. Vijiaraghavachariar, *League of Nations*, p. 16.
61. Vijiaraghavachariar, *League of Nations*, p. 5.
62. Anonymous, 'India and the League of Nations: Mr. Achariar's proposal examined', p. 20.
63. Ostrower, *The League of Nations*, p. 22. Article XV (8) states, 'If the dispute between the parties is claimed by one of them, and is found by the Council, to arise out of a matter which by international law is solely within the domestic jurisdiction of that party, the Council shall so report, and shall make no recommendation as to its settlement.'
64. Anonymous, 'India and the League of Nations: Mr. Achariar's proposal examined', p. 20.
65. Anonymous, 'Our Geneva letter', p. 19.
66. Keenleyside, 'Diplomatic apprenticeship', pp. 97–8.
67. For the involvement of Indians with multiple forms of internationalism and their work towards establishing global support networks for India, see, amongst others: Stolte, 'Enough of the Great Napoleons!', pp. 403–23; Fischer-Tiné, *Shyamji Krishnavarma*; Manjapra, 'Knowledgeable internationalism', pp. 53–62; Raza, Roy and Zachariah, *The Internationalist Moment*.
68. Keenleyside, 'Diplomatic apprenticeship', pp. 99–106. The idea of pursuing all possible means to achieve India's independence also became visible in the setting up of the Foreign Department by the INC in 1936. This was done 'with a view to create and maintain contacts with Indians overseas, and with international, national, labour and other organisations abroad with whom co-operation is possible and is likely to help in the case of Indian freedom' (Anonymous, *The Indian National Congress, 1934–36*, p. 75).
69. Ram and Sharma, *India & the League of Nations*, pp. 139–40; Hanumantharao, 'League of Nations and India', p. 19; Gandhi, 11.01.1933, *INR Madras*, no. 1 of 1933, p. 14.
70. *Andra Patrika*, 2 November 1931, *INR Madras*, no. 46 of 1931, p. 1508. Keenleyside points out that the only national Indian political organisation that upheld its support

for the League of Nations was the National Liberal Federation. Although the Federation was aware of the political shortcomings of the League, it felt that, since the Genevan body 'provided an opportunity for Indians to participate in international affairs with delegates of independent countries, their participation would enhance the achievement of dominion status by India' (Keenleyside, 'The Indian nationalist movement', pp. 286–7).
71. Sarkar, *Modern India*, pp. 284–6 and 308–42.
72. The assessment of the League of Nations' non-political work in Indian nationalist circles tended to be rather ambivalent. Karl Schmidt and T. A. Keenleyside show that parts of India's intelligentsia, as well as nationalist politicians, felt satisfied with the League's activities in fields such as the traffic in drugs and women, health issues and intellectual cooperation. However, criticism in these circles also existed with regard to the extent, implementation and outcomes of the respective measures decided by the League and its bodies (Schmidt, 'India's role in the League of Nations', pp. 191–246; Keenleyside, 'The Indian nationalist movement', pp. 288–9; Framke, 'Internationalizing the Indian war on opium', pp. 155–71).
73. Anonymous, 'The League of Nations and the Indian situation', p. 661.
74. Anonymous, 'The League of Nations and the Indian situation', p. 661.

References

Native newspaper reports

Note on the Press, United Provinces of Agra and Oudh.
Punjab Press Abstracts [later *Note on the Punjab Press*].
Report on English Papers Examined by the Criminal Investigation Department, Madras, and on Vernacular Papers examined by the Translators to the Government of Madras.
Report on Newspapers published in the Bombay Presidency.

Other primary sources

Anonymous, *Vyanga Chitrawali: Caricature Album, A Collection of Political and Social Caricatures*, Cawnpore, 1925.
Anonymous, 'Inadequate representation of India at Geneva', *Modern Review*, 40:2 (1926), p. 221.
Anonymous, 'India and the League of Nations', *Modern Review*, 41:2 (1927), pp. 257–8.
Anonymous, 'The League of Nations and "weaker nations"', *Modern Review*, 42:5 (1927), pp. 606–7.
Anonymous, 'Editorial', *The Hindu*, 5 October 1929, p. 6.
Anonymous, 'India and the League of Nations: Mr. Achariar's proposal examined', *The Hindu*, 17 August 1929, reprinted from *The Servant of India*, 9 August 1929, p. 20.
Anonymous, 'Leader of Indian delegation to League of Nations', *Modern Review*, 45:4 (1929), p. 530.
Anonymous, 'Our Geneva letter', *The Hindu*, 11 October 1929, p. 19.

Anonymous, 'The League of Nations and the Indian situation', *Modern Review*, 47:5 (1930), pp. 661–2.
Anonymous, *The Indian National Congress, 1934–36: Being the Resolutions Passed by the Congress, the All India Congress Committee and the Working Committee during the Period Between May, 1934 and April, 1936* (Allahabad: Allahabad Law Journal Press, 1936).
Bose, S. C., *The Indian Struggle, 1920–1942*, ed. by S. K. Bose and S. Bose (New Delhi: Oxford University Press, 2007).
Coyajee, J. C., *India and the League of Nations* (Madras: Waltair, 1932).
Das, T., 'India and the League of Nations', *Modern Review*, 35:2 (1924), pp. 163–7.
Gandhi, M. K., *The Collected Works of Mahatma Gandhi: Vol. 28* (Ahmedabad: Publications Division, Ministry of Information and Broadcasting, Government of India, 1968).
Gupta, J. S., 'India and the League of Nations', *Modern Review*, 40:2 (1926), pp. 161–4.
Hanumantharao, C. V., 'League of Nations and India: Some suggestions', *Hindustan Review*, 57:326–8 (1932), pp. 17–21.
Krishnavarma S., 'India and the League of Nations: Indian delegates mere tools of Indian despotism', *The Indian Sociologist*, 13:1 (1922), pp. 1–2.
Nehru, J., *Glimpses of World History* (London: Lindsay Drummond, 1949).
Ram, S. V. and B. M. Sharma, *India & the League of Nations* (Lucknow: Upper India Publishing House, 1932).
Vijiaraghavachariar of Salem, C., *League of Nations and India's Emancipation* (Madras: National Press, 1929).

Secondary sources

Anand, R. P., 'The formation of international organizations and India: A historical study', *Leiden Journal of International Law*, 23:1 (2010), pp. 5–21.
Anderson, B., *Imagined Communities: Reflections on the Origin and Spread of Nationalism*, rev. edn (London: Verso, 2006).
Chatterjee, P., *Nationalist Thought and the Colonial World: A Derivative Discourse?* (London: Zed Books, 1986).
Cooper, J. M., *Breaking the Heart of the World: Woodrow Wilson and the Fight for the League of Nations* (Cambridge: Cambridge University Press, 2001).
Das, S., 'Imperialism, nationalism and the First World War in India', in J. D. Keene and M. S. Neiberg (eds), *Finding Common Ground: New Directions in First World War Studies* (Leiden: Brill, 2011), pp. 67–85.
Ellinwood, D. C. and S. D. Pradhan (eds), *India and Word War I* (New Delhi: Manohar, 1978).
Fischer-Tiné, H., *Shyamji Krishnavarma: Sanskrit, Sociology and Anti-Imperialism* (London and New Delhi: Routledge India, 2014).
Framke, M., 'Internationalizing the Indian war on opium: Colonial policy, the nationalist movement and the League of Nations', in H. Fischer-Tiné and J. Tschurenev (eds), *A History of Alcohol and Drugs in Modern South Asia* (London: Routledge, 2013), pp. 155–71.

Goswami, M., *Producing India: From Colonial Economy to National Space* (Chicago: University of Chicago Press, 2004).

Grant, K. and L. Trivedi, 'A question of trust: The Government of India, the League of Nations, and Mohandas Gandhi', in R. M. Douglas, M. D. Callahan and E. Bishop (eds), *Imperialism on Trial: The International Oversight of Colonial Rule in Historical Perspective* (Oxford: Lexington Books, 2006), pp. 21–43.

Günther, L., *Taraknath Das – Ein Lebensbild* (Berlin: Taraknath-Das-Stiftung, 1996).

Keenleyside, T. A., 'The Indian nationalist movement and the League of Nations: Prologue to the United Nations', *India Quarterly: A Journal of International Affairs*, 39 (1983), pp. 281–98.

Keenleyside, T. A., 'Diplomatic apprenticeship: Pre-independence origins of Indian diplomacy and its relevance for the post-independence foreign policy', *India Quarterly: A Journal of International Affairs*, 43:2 (1987), pp. 97–120.

MacMillan, M., *Paris 1919: Six Months that Changed the World* (New York: Random House, 2003).

Manela, E., *The Wilsonian Moment: Self-Determination and the International Origins of Anticolonial Nationalism* (Oxford: Oxford University Press, 2007).

Manjapra, K., 'Knowledgeable internationalism and the Swadeshi Movement, 1903–1921', *Economic & Political Weekly*, 47:42 (2012), pp. 53–62.

Metcalf, B. D. and T. R. Metcalf, *A Concise History of India* (Cambridge: Cambridge University Press, 2002).

Ostrower, G. B., *The League of Nations, From 1919 to 1929* (New York: Avery Publishing Group, 1996).

Parthasarathy, R. T., *Dawn and Achievement of Indian Freedom: Being the Life and Times of Dr. C. Vijiaraghavachariar – Patriot and Thinker* (Salem: Court Press, 1953).

Pedersen, S., 'Back to the League of Nations', *The American Historical Review*, 112:4 (2007), pp. 1091–117.

Pedersen, S., *The Guardians: The League of Nations and the Crisis of Empire* (Oxford: Oxford University Press, 2015).

Raza, A., F. Roy and B. Zachariah (eds), *The Internationalist Moment: South Asia, Worlds and World Views, 1917–39* (Los Angeles: Sage, 2015).

Roy, F., H. Liebau and R. Ahuja (eds), *When the War Began We Heard of Several Kings: South Asian Prisoners in World War I Germany* (New Delhi: Social Science Press, 2011).

Sarkar, S., *Modern India: 1885–1947* (New Delhi: Macmillan, 1983).

Schmidt, K. J., *India's Role in the League of Nations, 1919–1939*, unpubl. PhD thesis (Florida State University, 1994).

Schneider, N.-C., *Zur Darstellung von 'Kultur' und 'kultureller Differenz' im indischen Mediensystem: Die indische Presse und die Repräsentation des Islams im Rahmen der Zivilrechtsdebatte, 1985–87 und 2003* (Berlin: Logos, 2005).

Singh, G., *The Testimonies of Indian Soldiers and the Two World Wars: Between Self and Sepoy* (London: Bloomsbury, 2014).

Singha, R., 'Finding labour from India for the war in Iraq: The Jail Porter and Labour Corps, 1916–1920', *Comparative Studies in Society and History*, 49:2 (2007), pp. 412–45.

Six, C., *Hindi–Hindu–Hindustan: Politik und Religion im modernen Indien* (Vienna: Mandelbaum, 2006).

Sonwalkar, P., '"Murdochization" of the Indian Press: From by-line to bottom-line', *Media, Culture & Society*, 24:6 (2002), pp. 821–34.

Stolte, C., '"Enough of the Great Napoleons!" Raja Mahendra Pratap's pan-Asian projects (1929–1939)', *Modern Asian Studies*, 46:2 (2012), pp. 403–23.

Throntveit, T., 'The fable of the Fourteen Points: Woodrow Wilson and national self-determination', *Diplomatic History*, 35:3 (2011), pp. 445–81.

Veerathappa, K., 'Growth of public opinion in administration in princely Mysore', in N. R. Ray (ed.), *Growth of Public Opinion in India: 19th and Early 20th Centuries (1800–1914)* (Calcutta: Naya Prokash, 1989), pp. 228–35.

Verma, D. N., *India and the League of Nations* (Patna: Bharati Bhawan, 1968).

Weitz, E. D., 'Self-determination: How a German Enlightenment idea became the slogan of national liberation and a human right', *American Historical Review*, 120:2 (2015), pp. 462–96.

Wertheim, S., 'The League of Nations: a retreat from international law?', *Journal of Global History*, 7:2 (2012), pp. 210–32.

Chapter 6

Dashed Hopes: Japanese Buddhist Perspectives on the Paris Peace Conference

JOHN LOBREGLIO

> If we are to carry out a truly critical examination of Japan's colonial discourse, the tension and anxiety over the dominant West, which were constitutive of Japanese identity, must be taken into consideration.
>
> (Rumi Sakamoto, 'Race-ing Japan', 2004)

The Japanese 'tension and anxiety over the dominant West', referred to in the epigraph above, have roots deep in the nineteenth century, and thus predate anything that did, or did not, happen at the Paris Peace Conference in 1919. In the weeks leading up to, and the months of, the Peace Conference, though, there opened a window of widespread optimism – cautious, to be sure – grounded in the belief that the modus operandi of international imperialism had run its course. Many Japanese Buddhist intellectuals and leaders, both lay and priestly, joined in the global intoxication with Wilsonian idealism and held out hope that the Peace Conference would be the venue in which delegates drafted the blueprint for a new international order no longer based upon the acute economic and political competition, and fragile balance of powers, that culminated in the First World War. Their opinions on the conference, including two formal manifestos, were published in the leading Buddhist newspaper, *Chūgai nippō*, and exhibit a similar type of idealism, founded upon universal principles, to that which not only was prevalent in much of the Japanese press,[1] but which was also, indeed, a worldwide phenomenon.

We know that this window of optimism closed all too quickly. The reasons it did so for many Japanese Buddhists are detailed below and demonstrate at least three things. Firstly, unlike the simplistic, and predominantly negative, portrayal of early twentieth-century Japanese Buddhism as 'conservative' and supportive of Japanese imperialism, many of its leading figures supported an internationalism undergirded by universal principles. Secondly, far from being peripheral to the Japanese experience, the decisions taken at the Peace Conference were carefully monitored and had profound repercussions in the years following the conference. Lastly, perspectives on the Peace Conference from outside the Anglo-American arena, such as that of Japanese Buddhists, provide fodder for a re-evaluation of one of the great and on-going debates of the twentieth century: namely, whether, or to what extent, the decisions made in Paris in 1919 gave rise to the ensuing international troubles of the 1920s and 1930s, and led ultimately to the Second World War.

There is a conspicuous dearth of scholarship in Western languages on interwar Japanese Buddhism, and the little that does exist indicates that it was predominantly 'conservative' and supportive of Japanese imperialism.[2] The very few exceptions, such as Sen'ō Girō (1889–1961) and the Shinkō Bukkyō Seinen Domei to which he belonged, are presented as isolated and anomalous examples that serve to accentuate the sclerosis of institutional Buddhism and its complicity in the rise of Japanese militarism. Descriptions such as 'conservative' and 'supportive of Japanese imperialism', though, are imprecise markers and do not necessarily entail a rejection of internationalism or universalist principles. Goto-Shibata writes that the predominant historiographical trend, at least until the 1990s, has been to bifurcate interwar Japanese organisations and thinkers into two groups, 'extreme nationalists and others', with internationalists situated clearly on the 'other' side of the fence.[3] Such an overly simplistic explanation overlooks, as Shibasaki Atsushi has argued, the fact that 'inter-war internationalism in Japan essentially coincided with nationalism'.[4] An awareness of this is necessary to understand and contextualise not only the position of most interwar Buddhists, but that of most interwar Japanese intellectuals as well.

It is precisely such an awareness that is lacking in Brian Victoria's *Zen at War* and its follow-up, *Zen War Stories*[5] – the most widely read treatments of early twentieth-century Japanese Buddhism. Regrettably, both volumes reproduce the simplistic binary paradigm that Goto-Shibata identifies. The first volume was ground-breaking and had an enormous impact not only on contemporary Japanese Buddhist institutions but also on American and European Zen lineages descended from the Zen masters he treats therein.[6] According to Victoria's own account, the book sent 'shock waves' through the latter communities because 'it demonstrated that wartime Japanese Zen masters, almost to a man, had been fervent supporters of Japanese militarism.'[7] His volumes provide a wealth of primary source documents in translation that show this conclusively to be the case, and for this reason they deserve the praise that has been heaped upon them. Nevertheless, both works are highly problematic, ironically enough, for failing to engage with their stated goal of 'understanding the *reasons* behind the slavish subservience of Zen leaders to Japanese militarism' (emphasis mine).[8] The censorious tone of this sentence is characteristic of both volumes, which do not at all consider the 'reasons' why virtually all Zen masters (as well as many others in Japanese society) might have supported Japanese militarism in the way they did. There is no attempt to consider the effects that the global context of the 'new imperialism' of the preceding decades – that is, 'the tension and anxiety over the dominant West' – might have had on the psyches of contemporary Japanese. Rather, in one of the few places in either book that Victoria mentions this wider context, he cursorily dismisses Japanese Buddhist claims to defend 'the "Mongolian race" from the hands of Western, white, and Christian imperialists' as 'jingoistic' and 'shrill'.[9]

There is a further and related problem with Victoria's historical understanding in that he sees the imperial-way Buddhism (*kōdō Bukkyō*) of the 1930s as part of a continuum that reaches 'at least as far back as the Russo-Japanese War' (1904–5).[10] There is, however, a significant lacuna in this continuum, as he sums up Taishō-period developments in a six-page discussion of four Buddhist leaders.[11] Despite such scant treatment, he is able to conclude: 'By the end of the 1920s institutional Buddhism had firmly locked itself into ideological support for Japan's ongoing military efforts, wherever and whenever they might occur.'[12] Victoria cites 'one notable voice of dissent' against imperial-way Buddhism at this time, Ōtani Sonyū (1886–1939), though even he 'would later abandon his critical stance' and in 1937 join 'the first cabinet of Prince Konoe Fumimaro as the Minister for Colonial Affairs, a position giving him direct responsibility for running Japan's constantly expanding empire'.[13] Such an abridged account of the Taishō-period Buddhist world elides the widespread presence of moderate, internationalist-minded Buddhists – both institutional and independent – to be discussed below, and it fails, again, to ask the highly relevant question of *why* voices once critical of the state, such as that of Ōtani Sonyū, might soon become its avid supporters. The sober reactions of Japanese Buddhists to the unfolding events at the Paris Peace Conference dispel the caricature found in Victoria's portrayal and begin to provide the context, and the *reasons*, that he omits.

The *Chūgai nippō* newspaper

The *Chūgai nippō* newspaper is the primary source of information concerning Taishō-period (1912–26) Buddhism, and all of the Buddhist reflections presented below are drawn from its pages. It was founded by Matani Ruikotsu (1869–1956)[14] in 1897 as the *Kyōgaku hōchi*, a tabloid for disseminating Buddhist teachings, and became the *Chūgai nippō* in 1902. While there were numerous Buddhist newspapers in the Meiji period (1868–1912), the *Chūgai nippō* was the only one that published daily (six times per week). At its height, it had an average circulation of between 20,000 and 30,000 copies, with some issues rising to 60,000 or 70,000. By 1919, when dire economic conditions forced all of its competitors out of business, not only was it the sole vehicle for Buddhist priests and intellectuals to express their opinions, but also, because it was much cheaper and more convenient than mass mailings, it became an important means for head temples to communicate with their thousands of branch temples. Its centrality to the lives of Buddhist priests and institutions at the time of the Paris Peace Conference, thus, cannot be overstated.

The newspaper has been in nearly continuous publication since its founding and is still today considered to be Japan's leading newspaper dealing with religious affairs. While its original focus was on issues concerning the traditional Buddhist lineages, not only did its scope broaden to include religious issues in Japan and internationally, but also it came to address a wide array of cultural and political issues. Many leading Buddhist thinkers of the Meiji and Taishō periods were regular contributors, as were influential academics, public intellectuals and literary figures. Its founder and owner, Ruikotsu, functioned as the newspaper's publisher and chief editor for nearly sixty years and contributed editorials for virtually every issue. He was born into a Jōdo Shinshū (True Pure Land) temple household of the Nishi Honganji denomination and became a priest in this lineage. Despite this affiliation, his overriding concern was for the editorial stance of the newspaper to remain impartial and non-partisan (*fuhen futō*), and the range of contributors and opinions found in its pages reflects this ideal.

Two Buddhist manifestos on the upcoming Peace Conference

On 13 November 1918, just two days after the armistice was signed in Compiègne, the board of trustees of the Japan Buddhist Union (Nihon Bukkyō Rengōkai) convened in Kyoto and passed a unanimous motion to issue a statement concerning the upcoming peace conference. This was the largest pan-denominational Buddhist organisation of the day, representing the fifty-six established lineages, and is a precursor to the largest Buddhist umbrella organisation in Japan today.[15] It was decided at this meeting that all fifty-six lineages would submit their views to the Union's secretary general by 7 December and that he would then draft a statement based upon these opinions. Nine days later, the scholar–priest Watanabe Kaigyoku (1872–1933) had his own manifesto on this matter published on the front page of the *Chūgai nippō*.[16] Now in the public domain, this document seems to have served as a point of reference for all of the lineages as they formulated their own opinions over the next two and a half weeks. After receiving the submissions from each of the head temples and composing the Japan Buddhist Union's declaration in light of these, the secretary general then circulated his draft to the leaders of each denomination for further comment. This document, the 'Japanese Buddhist Declaration on the Issue of Peace', was then completed and translated into French by the end of December. On 3 January, the headquarters of the Japan Buddhist Union entrusted copies for the participating delegates of each country to a Mr Kondo, head of the Japan Mail Steamship Company, to hand-deliver in Paris. They also sent copies directly to the governments of thirty-four countries.[17] These manifestos, translated and presented below, constitute two major public pronouncements concerning what leading Buddhist figures hoped to see achieved at the Paris Peace Conference.

Watanabe Kaigyoku was a high-ranking official of the Jōdo (Pure Land) sect and one of the most active Buddhist leaders of the Taishō period. He was also an influential Buddhologist, probably best known among scholars for his supervision, along with Takakusu Junjirō (1866–1945), of the compilation of the colossal *Taishō Shinshū Daizōkyō* canon of Chinese Buddhist scriptures.[18] In addition to his scholarly pursuits, Kaigyoku was an educator and well-known social activist, concerned, among other things, with the welfare of impoverished workers.[19] He spent the years from 1900 to 1910 studying Buddhist canonical languages such as Sanskrit, Pali and Tibetan, as well as comparative religion, at Kaiser Wilhelm University in Strasbourg, then part of the German Empire. This extended first-hand encounter with European culture informs many of his scholarly writings on the role of Buddhism and Buddhist studies in the modern world, as well as the following manifesto. Entitled 'The Hopes of Buddhists for the Peace Conference',[20] it was published just eleven days after the signing of the armistice ending the First World War. It is thus one of the earliest, perhaps even *the* earliest, of such systematic petitions circulated in Japan.

The Hopes of Buddhists for the Peace Conference

by Watanabe Kaigyoku

One: May the Peace Conference proceed according to a merciful and charitable humanitarianism based upon the fundamental Buddhist doctrine of great compassion. It is not possible to establish the basis for world peace if one preaches humanitarianism while in actual fact one's actions are inhumane.

Two: Based upon the teaching that all beings have Buddha-nature innately (*shitsu-u busshō*), we hope that [the delegates] will guarantee an equal measure of human rights and freedom. The concepts of freedom and equality that arise from the Buddhist doctrine of all beings innately having Buddha-nature are the source of mutual love and mutual respect among humanity and the foundation of international amity. The solution to the matter at hand – the issue of peace – can most reliably be guaranteed according to this doctrine. If, because of racial (*jinshu no*) and religious differences, human rights and freedom are not accorded equally, it cannot but result in a fragile peace.

Three: As one of the most potent and necessary conditions for the establishment of peace, we hope that [the delegates] may take as the basis of the Peace Conference the entirely impartial and selfless justice found in the Buddhist truths of non-attachment and no-self (*mushū muga*).

Four: Out of a sense of love for humanity and egalitarianism we would like to urge [the delegates] to eradicate intolerant and narrow-minded prejudices concerning race and religion and to respect and value equally races and religions. The recent warfare was caused by Germany's holding of biased views such as that of the 'yellow peril', which transgresses against humanity via its racial and religious prejudices.

Five: We would like [the delegates] to respect, value and hold in high esteem the culture and history of every ethnicity (*minzoku*); to share with each other the virtues and accomplishments of these [cultures and histories]; and, to promote the welfare of the peoples of all nations (*kokumin*). Along with racial and religious prejudices, [the delegates] must abolish [attitudes] such as that which holds only the culture of white peoples and the history of Europe as praiseworthy, and which derides the cultures and histories of other ethnicities (*minzoku*). As each country differs in its respective history and culture, it is mistaken to regard only the history and culture of one's own country as good and beautiful, to force this upon the peoples of other nations (*kokumin*), and to do such things as attempt to alter their history and culture. Such is not the way to guarantee a permanent peace.

Six: According to the doctrine of 'repaying kindness' (*hōon*), we hope that all countries will operate according to the principle of mutual assistance and that they will engage in mutual economic and cultural support to repay the debts that they owe to each other. If this is put into practice, we will be able to mitigate to a certain extent an economic war following the Great War.

Seven: On the freedom to engage in missionary work. While all religion must be free to engage in propagation and missionary work in every country, it is not right that, depending on the country, the same rights for engaging in missionary work are not recognised. We would like the freedom to engage in missionary work, grounded in the great principle of the freedom of religious belief, to be guaranteed at the upcoming Peace Conference.

Eight: On the kind treatment of enemies. In regard to our enemy, Germany, we hope that [the delegates] will not repay violence with violence and, without cruelly going into detail about past crimes, will generate the so-called attitude of 'hating the crime but not the person'. Once the enemy's swords have been shattered, their arrows spent, and they have surrendered, it is the spirit of Japanese *bushido* and the spirit of Buddhist tolerance to pursue the matter no further. Thus, [the delegates] should not consider this solely as a political matter, but with spiritual concern should take the path of loving one's enemy.

Nine: We hope that concerning work for world peace, or [concerning] movements to get rid of vice and corruption and to promote culture, all religions will join together in a spirit of tolerance and freedom and engage in actions of united cooperation [concerning] the prohibition of alcohol, the abolition of prostitution, the prohibition of opium, the banning of scandalous literature and the elimination of other evils of the world. [We also hope that] all religions will be determined to act with united cooperation in regard to movements that could promote the wellbeing of humanity. Even though each religion differs in its respective doctrines and history, as each agrees in its objective of trying to promote the wellbeing of humanity, we are convinced that [religions] can unite and join together to a certain degree if they go about this in the right way.

Ten: We hope that all religions work together with like-minded spirit, and based on the authority of their beliefs, become pillars for the maintenance of peace, and that they may become the vehicles of a worldwide alliance that could prevent once and for all the devastations of war. If, from the standpoint of humanity, equality and justice, all religions keep in mind the safeguarding of world peace by means of a spirit of tolerance and freedom, we are convinced that we will avoid the mistakes and prejudices of the past, and that the enactment of like-minded cooperation is not at all impossible.

Kaigyoku's document is an expression of a widely and deeply held conviction among Japanese Buddhist intellectuals, from at least the middle of the Meiji period, that their teachings were the pre-eminent articulation of the human religious mind. Inoue Enryō (1858–1919), perhaps the best-known Buddhist thinker of the time, was instrumental in formulating this sentiment, and in 1887 captured it thus:

> Buddhism is now our so-called strong point. . . . Material commodities are an advantage of the West; scholarship is also one of their strong points. The only advantage we have is religion. This fine product of ours excels those of other countries; the fact that its good strain died out in India and China may be considered an unexpected blessing for our country. If we continue to nurture it in Japan and disseminate it some day in foreign countries, we will not only add to the honour of our nation but will also infuse the spirit of our land into the hearts and minds of foreigners. I am convinced that the consequences will be considerable.[21]

Kaigyoku too held these convictions and he sought to implement Inoue's call to disseminate Buddhism abroad by first raising the standards of Buddhist scholarship in Japan. At this he was highly successful, with the publication of the *Taishō* canon mentioned above serving as one glowing example. In the 1924 foreword to this collection, Kaigyoku writes that these scriptures thoroughly expound nothing less than 'the true reality of the universe' and that they are truly 'the fountainhead of wisdom and virtue for humanity and the great treasury of the world'. He continues:

> Yet apart from us, the Buddhist scholars of Japan, who can clarify and spread its teachings? The responsibility of propagation rests on our shoulders. All the more so, after the great world war, when the need to seek the truth presses most urgently upon us.[22]

This sense of responsibility and urgency pervades Kaigyoku's 1918 manifesto and is a reflection of the profound reversal of world historical destiny that Buddhists perceived the First World War to usher in. Jacqueline Stone acutely sums this up: 'Japan, recipient of Western enlightenment in the Meiji period, becomes the country that shall bring enlightenment to the world.'[23]

Kaigyoku's 'Hopes' is at once an indictment of the Western powers, an introduction to Buddhist doctrines for their leaders, and a set of prescriptions to bring about a lasting world peace. According to Goto-Shibata, the Japanese press at this time was often overtly critical of the West and employed terms such as 'justice' (*seigi*) and 'humanity' (*jindō*) 'to denote their moral high ground'.[24] Kaigyoku, too, seizes this moral high ground in article 1, by first grounding humanitarianism (*jindōshugi*), a putative Western ideal, in a *Buddhist* doctrine – that of 'great compassion' (*daijihi*), and then by warning against the hypocrisy of not practising what one preaches. It is an ironic and barely concealed barb requesting that Western leaders live up to their own ideals and suggesting that previously they have not. Although Kaigyoku does not use the term, he criticises aspects of 'imperialist' behaviour explicitly in five of the articles (1, 2, 4, 5 and 7) and implicitly in another (6). The indictments range from the hypocrisy mentioned above, to inhumane behaviour (article 1), racial and religious discrimination (articles 2, 4 and 7), cultural imperialism in the form of the denigration of the cultures and histories of non-European ethnic groups (article 5), and exploitative economic practices (article 6). The remedy for these 'mistakes and prejudices of the past', mentioned in article 10, lies in the implementation of universal principles, all of which find expression in traditional Buddhist doctrines.

It was a conscious concern of leading Buddhists to demonstrate to Western leaders that while, on the surface, some of their teachings might appear to contradict those of other religions and Western principles, in fact, at the most fundamental level there was profound agreement.[25] Kaigyoku seeks to demonstrate the congruity between Enlightenment ideals and Buddhist doctrine. As we saw, for him, humanitarianism flows from Buddhist compassion. Most importantly, perhaps, Kaigyoku, as well as numerous other contributors to the *Chūgai nippō* during the months of the Peace Conference, saw in the doctrine of *shitsu-u busshō* – all beings are innately endowed with Buddha-nature – a kind of Buddhist natural law upon which the ideals of freedom, equality and human rights are founded. Kaigyoku sees the racial (*jinshu no*) and religious prejudices of the past as the primary obstacles to achieving a future peace, and it is precisely for this reason that a foundational principle stressing human metaphysical equality is so crucial. As, in fact, racial and religious differences did *not* underlie the fraternal carnage of the recent European conflict, we see here a particularly Asian concern for a fundamental change in the Western powers' treatment of non-white peoples. In article 4, Kaigyoku decries the rhetoric of 'yellow peril' while untenably citing this as the cause of the 'recent warfare'. The lack of accuracy concerning historical causation, though, seems to be a clever means of obliquely chastising *all* of the Western powers while seemingly holding Germany alone accountable for such 'yellow peril' racism. Although Kaiser Wilhem may well have coined the phrase, the extensive legal implementation of such racism by white nations, especially in the Anglo-American world, is too well known to require discussion here.

The second major prescription that Kaigyoku declares necessary for the establishment of peace is leniency towards Germany. In article 3 he urges delegates to engage in 'entirely impartial and selfless justice', ideals that also proceed from Buddhist doctrines – those of non-attachment and no-self (*mushū muga*). In article 8, he extends this generalised condition to the specific case of Germany and makes an impassioned appeal for 'kind treatment' that draws not only upon Buddhist tolerance, but also upon Japanese martial virtues as found in *bushido*. By invoking 'the path of loving one's enemies' as further rationale for such leniency, he seems to be trying again to draw attention to parallels between Buddhist, and Japanese, teachings and the values underlying Western civilisation: in this case, a Christian one.

Another major concern of Kaigyoku's is the fate of religion in the postwar world (articles 2, 4, 7, 9 and 10). It is not surprising that discussions of the issues he raises in this regard fill the pages of the *Chūgai nippō* during 1919, and space does not permit a detailed examination of these here. It is worth highlighting, though, the widespread Buddhist hope that he articulates for a resolution concerning the freedom of missionary activity 'grounded in the great principle of the freedom of religious belief, to be guaranteed at the upcoming Peace Conference' (article 7). This hope, along with the two detailed above – the overcoming of racial prejudice and leniency toward Germany, comprise the paramount concerns of this manifesto.

The Japan Buddhist Union's manifesto was made public on the front page of the *Chūgai nippō* on 26 January 1919.[26] Unlike Watanabe's piece, which never seems to have reached its intended international audience, this 'Declaration' was, as mentioned above, translated into French and hand-delivered to the delegates in Paris.[27]

Japanese Buddhist Declaration on the Issue of Peace

The great World War has finally come to an end, and on the occasion of the Peace Conference that is about to begin, we the undersigned secretaries of the Imperial Japan Buddhist Union, on behalf of Japanese Buddhists, herein have the honour of respectfully presenting to you Gentlemen, representatives of the great powers, our hopes for a lasting world peace and a statement of our profound desire to plan for the everlasting well-being of humanity based on the teachings bequeathed by our founder the Buddha.

When the Conference of World Buddhists was held in San Francisco in the United States of America in August of 1915, we sent our Japanese Buddhist representatives Heki Mokusen and Uchida Kōyū, among others, to Washington. They had an audience with Mr President Wilson and ardently requested that he act as a mediator in the European War and that he devise a way to bring about world peace. As the President was in agreement with this objective, he consented. Since then, although some time has passed and there have been changes in the war situation, the first steps toward reconciliation will now be initiated by Mr Wilson. As for you gentlemen who are the authorities for the warring nations and who together are about to engage in this [reconciliation], for the sake of humanity, from the bottom of our hearts, we deeply rejoice over this fact and cannot restrain our hopes that you will succeed. It goes without saying that the basis of world peace exists in merciful and charitable humanitarianism, and as for putting this principle into practice, we celebrate and rejoice the fact that from remote antiquity this is precisely the fundamental objective of the Buddha's compassion. We firmly believe that when this infinite and profound benevolence is not taken as its basis, a lasting world peace cannot be maintained.

Buddhism maintains the doctrine that all living things have Buddha-nature innately and that this is constant and unchanging. It proposes that human beings are entitled to an equal measure of sober freedom and [their] just rights. From this perspective,

[Buddhism] does away with the distinctions as to whether a nation (*kokka*) is large or small, powerful or weak, civilised or primitive. It also does away with prejudices concerning race (*jinshu*) and religion. We hope that you will employ fair and honourable measures. If there is even one instance where they are lacking, the source of human mutual respect and mutual love will dry up then and there. At the core of international amity as well, there will be an anxiety that will surely call forth insecurity.

Because in Buddhism all beings bestow benevolences upon each other, it maintains the doctrine that the self is identical in essence with all others and that that which benefits oneself also benefits all others. Based on this perspective, it is our earnest wish that the world powers will repay their indebtedness, give mutual support to each other, conduct economic matters amicably, have an exchange of culture, abolish futile competition and devise a plan for [giving] benevolent aid. We believe, after all, that replenishing the shortages [caused by] the ravages of war and maintaining a lasting peace must be based upon this course of action. We hope that in the future politicians, religious figures, educators, businessmen and others will diligently, and without confusing their [respective] roles, conduct joint research and discussion for world peace, the elimination of vice and corruption, the improvement of public morals, as well as many other endeavours. We hope that they will unite both in spirit and in actual fact, and will devise a plan to engage in harmonious cooperation. If they decide upon this plan and are able to actualise it, we believe that it will certainly not only be of the greatest benefit to the world, but also that the mutual purposes of the great powers will naturally become in accordance, and that this will become an important means for cultivating the basis for peace. We Japanese Buddhists, together with the Buddhists of the world, declare our readiness to devote all of our spiritual energies toward this end.

Most of all, we do not ask for you to heed anything more than what is based upon Buddhist doctrines. In general, good causes produce good effects and bad causes invite bad effects. Moreover, appropriate retribution based on cause and effect (*inga ōhō*) is invariable: effects follow their causes in exactly the same way as a shadow follows its form. All of world history is the holy scripture [containing the doctrine of] appropriate retribution based on cause and effect; and the present state of worldly affairs is its proof. For this reason, the key to planning a lasting world peace and permanent well-being for humanity is nothing other than to make the world's great powers, as well as all mankind, eradicate the causes of their evil deeds and strive to promote good actions. Ultimately, it is our ardent wish that you understand that this doctrine of appropriate retribution based on cause and effect expresses a natural law (*tennen no hōritsu*) that permeates the universe for eternity.

Gentlemen, representatives of the great powers, truly nothing would fulfil the long-cherished hopes of we Buddhists more than if, by good fortune, you regard the details of each item described above as reference material and are able to further the welfare of the human beings of the world. Herein we once again expressly show our respect.

Similarities in turns of phrase, vocabulary and overall tenor suggest that this 'Declaration' was composed with some familiarity with Kaigyoku's 'Hopes'. Despite the general agreement of the documents, there is, nevertheless, one interesting difference that suggests that the Buddhist lineages were somewhat more restrained in their proposals than Kaigyoku. The 'Declaration' does not raise the issue of cultural imperialism – that is, the elevation of 'the culture of white peoples and the history of Europe' while deriding 'the cultures and histories of other ethnicities (*minzoku*)' – as Kaigyoku does in article 5. It also does not ask the delegates in Paris 'to respect, value and hold in high esteem the culture and history of every ethnicity (*minzoku*)' in the way that Kaigyoku does. The reason for this may lie in the established lineages' unease with the term '*minzoku*' ('ethnicity' or 'ethnic nation'), which does not at all appear in their manifesto. To call attention to the distinct cultures and histories of such social units could have raised awkward questions concerning institutional Buddhism's considerable role in the colonisation of Taiwan, Korea and China, and its own approaches to the cultures and histories of the ethnic groups therein. Rather, the Japan Buddhist Union's 'Declaration' uses the term '*kokka*', or 'the state' (a term not found in Kaigyoku's manifesto), to represent the fundamental constituent of social and political reality when it discusses the equality of all human beings based on their inherent Buddha-nature. It is only at the meta-level of the state, and not at the level of ethnic groupings, that this ontological equality is invoked to 'do away with' worldly distinctions such as 'large or small, powerful or weak, civilised or primitive' (paragraph three).

Such concern with the tension between ethnic groupings and the state was, as we shall see, soon to become a major source of dispute and self-questioning among leading Buddhist intellectuals.

Both manifestos ultimately, though, concur in two fundamental ways: each declares that the world's powers must institute fundamental changes to their international modes of engagement, and each expresses a cautious optimism that such changes are possible. As we have seen, both documents ground the possibility for change in universal Buddhist truths. The Japan Buddhist Union's 'Declaration' at first appears less incriminating of the Western powers than Kaigyoku's piece, which expresses either censure or concern in virtually every one of its articles. The penultimate paragraph of the 'Declaration', however, delivers a barely concealed chastisement of 'the world's great powers' based upon a Buddhist 'natural law' – that of 'appropriate retribution based on cause and effect'. The powers are called upon to 'eradicate the causes of their evil deeds and strive to promote good actions'. With some 15 million dead and another 20 million wounded, this historical moment was an unprecedented nadir in terms of the moral authority of Western civilisation, and Japanese Buddhists were not shy to point this out.

The documents also agree in their prescriptions concerning the two areas that the delegates to the Peace Conference most needed to effect if a lasting peace were to be achieved: leniency toward Germany and the eradication of racial discrimination. Failure in either of these regards, the manifestos warn, can only result in a 'fragile peace'[28] riddled with international 'anxiety' and 'insecurity'.[29] Despite clear reservations as to whether or not the great powers would indeed be able to break from their self-serving policies of the past, Japanese Buddhists could not help but 'deeply rejoice'[30] over the promise that the Peace Conference offered for success in this regard. Discussions in the *Chūgai nippō* during the course of the conference concerning the issues of the treaty terms for Germany and the eradication of racial equality trace the trajectory of how these hopes evolved.

Benevolence toward Germany

The benevolence towards Germany prescribed in both manifestos was given more concrete expression in an opinion piece of 29 January 1919, in which the author argues for an unconditional (*mujōken*) peace: 'If [the delegates] take even the slightest of reparations or a piece of territory the size of a bean, it will be completely counterproductive.'[31] The author views any such ambitions as sinister and calls for Japan itself to resist any notions of so benefitting from the war. Such benefit, he warns, would amount to a stain upon the noble virtues of Eastern countries. Rather, for a lasting world peace truly to be achieved, he urges Japan to take the lead in this regard and to request the Allied Powers neither to demand reparation payments from Germany nor to annex any of its territories.

The editorial stance of the *Chūgai nippō* during the Peace Conference likewise advocated leniency in the terms to be given to Germany. The main editorial writer during these months went by the pseudonym of 'Ume'. Though I have been unable to ascertain his identity, a number of factors suggest that he was most likely Matani Ruikotsu himself.[32] We know that Ruikotsu was the chief editor and contributed editorials almost daily. In addition, Ruikotsu was keen to preserve the anonymity of both his and other staff members' identities, as he felt this would help preserve the impartiality of their writing. For this reason he was often called 'master ninja' and 'nickname master'.[33] The fact that the editorials written by Ume almost always have prominence as the leading articles situated at the top of page one suggests their centrality to editorial concerns. Thus, whether or not Ume was in fact Ruikotsu, it is certain that Ruikotsu would have endorsed these editorials.

In the first *Chūgai nippō* commentary on the peace conference itself, Ume expresses both his profound excitement, and his unease concerning the type of 'justice' that will govern the proceedings. In a front-page editorial of 24 January, Ume gives a report of the opening ceremony that took place six days previously on the 18th. Based on a telegraphed account, he describes the line-up of dignitaries as French President Raymond Poincaré prepared to give his speech. 'Just in visualising [this spectacle]', he writes, 'one cannot stop one's heart from leaping.'[34] He then isolates, and comments upon, three short passages from Poincaré's lengthy opening address that express the newspaper's concerns regarding the fundamental principles underlying the conference. In the first passage Ume quotes Poincaré as stating, 'The recent victory is a complete victory. The delegates of the Peace Conference must now reap the full fruits from this complete victory.' Secondly, he relates Poincaré's statement that 'You delegates must not for a moment let your thoughts stray from the spirit of justice during these deliberations.' And lastly, he quotes from Poincaré's concluding statement: 'The future of the world is in your hands. I turn over to you the grave deliberations.'[35]

Ume comments on the last passage first. While agreeing on the profound repercussions that the conference would have on the rest of the world, he felt that to say the future of the world was in the delegates' hands was 'a slight exaggeration'.[36] It is possible to see in this passing remark an oblique criticism of a Euro-American centrism that, with an over-inflated sense of its own importance, blithely engulfs the entire world.

He then ironically criticises the first two passages by employing Poincaré's own words, albeit with a twist of his own. He writes that if the delegates are to 'really make this victory complete' and really 'reap the full fruits of this victory', then they must '*at every moment work toward actualising the spirit of justice uniformly and equally both for enemy and ally, one's own country and other countries*' (original emphasis).[37] It is necessary, he insists, for the delegates to search their consciences and exert self-restraint in order not to fall into the trap of getting carried away by their emotions and implementing unfair measures.

Some familiarity with the entirety of Poincaré's speech and its understanding of 'justice' is necessary to appreciate Ume's criticism. After imploring the delegates to seek justice, Poincaré went on to say,

> What [justice] demands first, when it has been violated, are restitution and reparation for the peoples and individuals who have been despoiled or maltreated. ... What justice also demands ... is the punishment of the guilty and effective guarantees against an active return of the spirit by which they were tempted.[38]

Clearly, this sense of punitive justice differs profoundly from the impartial justice and compassion advocated in both Kaigyoku's and the Japan Buddhist Union's manifestos. Poincaré's sense of justice was concerned not at all with Germany's well-being but rather with Allied, and predominantly French, strategic concerns. In fact, throughout his speech he studiously makes stark distinctions between ally and enemy, and between victim and aggressor, that leave no room for an inclusive Buddhist vision based upon notions such as the essential identity and the mutual indebtedness of all beings.

It was not long before Ume's suspicions concerning Poincaré's rhetoric became manifest in actual decisions made by the Supreme Council of the Peace Conference. The council first brought up the issue of the German colonies on 27 January, and Ume, who relates that he carefully observed the telegraph wires from Paris each day, published a two-part editorial entitled 'The dark side of the Peace Conference' on 8 and 9 February, commenting on the previous week's proceedings. In these he argues that, while the Peace Conference may be genuinely attempting to find a way to prevent the recurrence of the horrors just witnessed in the war, there is another, darker side to the proceedings: namely, that the strong – the Allied Powers – are exerting their influence over the weak – the German–Austrian alliance – and are dividing up the spoils of war among themselves. He likens the gathering of the victorious Allied delegates in one place to a multitude of ants swarming upon a lump of rotting flesh.

In the first instalment, Ume criticises the council's decision not to return to Germany any of its colonies that were seized during the war. He also rejects as mere pretext the Allied Powers' rationale for this: namely, that German rule in these territories was 'cruel' and that Germany might well in the future use some of these territories as submarine bases. Rather, he sees this decision as clearly motivated by aggrandising impulses (*shinryakuteki shōdō*) and self-interest. In the second part of this editorial, he argues that the proposal to place former German colonies under the authority of competent nations within the League of Nations mandate system could be justified only if Germany too were included in the League of Nations.

The fact that the Allied Powers were not even able to agree to this, for Ume, was a disturbing sign of their hypocrisy. He saw their decision to occupy German colonies as sending a contradictory message to the world. The heart of the contradiction lay in the fact that the Allied Powers, while professing to seek an end to future wars, were, in fact, engaging in the very behaviour – the above-mentioned 'aggrandising impulses' – that caused the war in the first place. He condemned such hypocrisy in scathing terms and likened the Allied Powers to 'looters at the scene of a fire nauseatingly allowing these territories to become open to plunder'.[39]

Ume predicted that this contradictory message would have subversive repercussions for the deliberations to come:

> Just as the peace conference is prepared in this instance to contradict itself, so too it is not difficult to imagine the profusion of contradictions that will surely emerge as a consequence in regards to all of the issues that will arise in the assembly hall from here on.[40]

The ultimate consequence, he argued, would be an eviscerated peace treaty in which 'international relations will herein revert to pre-war conditions. This can only guarantee the result of a world maintained by an armed peace based upon a so-called balance of powers.'[41] It is precisely this 'so-called balance of powers' approach to international relations that the Japanese Buddhist groups saw as an obstacle to genuine world peace and which, as presented in their 'Declaration', they hoped to replace with a compassionate humanitarianism based on Buddhist principles.

From the editorial perspective of the *Chūgai nippō* newspaper, the Paris Peace Conference did not get off to an auspicious start. Again, Ume's judgement was severe:

Each day when I carefully observe the news that reaches me from the telegraph wires from abroad and I imagine the goings-on in Paris, a spectacle presents itself of the foreign delegates of each country outwardly exchanging smiles and laughs and professing as if with evident delight the prospects of peace, while in their hearts they are biting at each other just like jackals and wolves. Or else, I am presented with a spectacle resembling that of mountain bandits scuffling with each other.[42]

Nevertheless, he ends the editorial by refusing to be disheartened and by maintaining hope that true peace could yet be achieved.

In early May, however, Ume still saw the Allied Powers' treatment of Germany as 'animal-like' and once again resorted to the metaphor of 'mountain bandits' to describe their demands concerning the payment of reparations. He envisioned the Allied leaders 'with veins bulging in their faces and fists clenched', and judged them to be 'just like mountain bandits in their caves starting to brawl over the sharing out of the loot'. Ume could not understand the justification for what he saw as an increasingly severe posture on the part of the Allied Powers toward Germany. Germany had, after all, acquiesced completely in the Allied Powers' demands and had renounced its prior militarism and imperialism. It was now the Allied Powers that he saw as aggressors: 'During the war, the Allied Powers were proclaiming a fight for peace against militarism, yet today have not friend and foe thoroughly reversed positions? Are the Allied Powers themselves not brandishing imperialism and challenging the pacifist Austro-German countries to fight?' Despite his dismay, Ume again refused to be disheartened by such a 'disgraceful spectacle' and was convinced that, in the end, man's nobility would win out over the more base, greed-driven impulses that he was witnessing.[43]

Two weeks later, though, the Allied peace terms were fixed and the German leaders were agonising over how to respond to them. Ume could not help but sympathise with what he viewed as Germany's impossible predicament and likened their position to standing at a crossroads, where each of the possible paths leads to certain death. He agreed with the German Chancellor Philipp Scheidemann's judgement that the peace terms were a death sentence and a humiliation. Yet, if the Germans did not agree to them, they were faced with the likelihood that more hawkish elements, such as the French Marshal Ferdinand Foch, would happily use this as the excuse to accomplish their objective of invading Germany.[44] Ume, a seemingly inveterate optimist, now no longer knew what to expect, and waited with bated breath, along with the rest of the world, to see how Germany would respond.

Japanese Buddhist prescriptions for benevolence towards Germany were, of course, not heeded. Contributors to the *Chūgai nippō* saw the Allied Powers as exercising punitive, not impartial, justice, and as still treating Germany as an enemy rather than a partner whose welfare was also crucial to the newly emerging world order. They perceived the seizing of German colonies and the demands for reparation payments as a sign that the Allied Powers were intent on perpetuating prewar patterns of international engagement based on greed, self-interest and aggression, and they viewed such behaviour as a hypocritical betrayal of Allied pre-conference rhetoric, largely encapsulated in Woodrow Wilson's Fourteen Points. The cautious hopes of Japanese Buddhists for a genuinely new approach to world diplomacy were, regarding the treatment of Germany, bitterly disappointed.

The abolition of racial prejudice

As with the issue of the German colonies, Japanese Buddhists were closely monitoring the fate of the so-called racial equality proposal submitted to the League of Nations Commission by the Japanese plenipotentiaries Makino Nobuaki and Chinda Sutemi. They presented the initial proposal on 13 February, and before news of its rejection could reach Tokyo, Ume, in an editorial of the 18th, wrote of his extreme incomprehension concerning Wilson and Lloyd George's failure to utter even a word about the equal treatment of races, considering that they were now engaged in establishing such a putatively enlightened institution as the League of Nations.[45] This sort of reaction highlights the irony that Naoko Shimazu has so convincingly demonstrated: despite the fact that the Japanese government did not intend their proposal as a statement of universal principle concerning racial equality, this is none the less precisely how it was perceived by the Japanese public. The final draft of the government's proposal no longer demanded the 'equality of races' but rather the more modest demand of an 'equality of nations'.[46] Ume relates in this editorial that *all* Japanese from *all* levels of society support the movement to abolish the racially prejudiced treatment of people, and that he himself has been arguing for this for a very long time. Ume, as well as numerous other *Chūgai nippō* contributors, shared this keen interest in the racial equality issue, which 'dominated the national editorials of the leading newspapers'[47] during the first few months of the conference. Ume saw the labelling of people as 'aliens' (*ijinshu*) and the discriminatory treatment that followed from this as major obstacles to world peace.[48] And, in line with nascent Japanese pan-Asianist stances, he argued that the Japanese 'have become the representatives of all the coloured races (*yūshoku jinshu*) of the world and are resolved to do their utmost to bring about the realisation of this principle'.[49]

The *Chūgai nippō*'s editorial stance on the issue of racial equality was significantly more progressive than that of the Buddhist temples themselves in that it squarely confronted issues of racial prejudice *within* Japan and drew attention to the hypocrisy such prejudice revealed concerning the Japanese clamour for international racial equality. Ume spoke out vehemently for the liberation of the Japanese *burakumin* underclass, taking bold stances such as supporting their rights to intermarriage and integrated dwelling with other Japanese.[50] He urged all Japanese Buddhist, Christian and Shinto followers to work together for religious freedom and racial equality within Japan,[51] and he did not hesitate to criticise leading Buddhist institutions for their discrimination against *burakumin*.[52] The so-called Machida Affair within the Sōtō Zen lineage in the 1980s revealed the extent to which such discrimination continued unabated for decades.[53] In this light, the *Chūgai nippō* position was indeed considerably ahead of its time.

Situated below Ume's editorials dealing with *burakumin* liberation on 27 and 28 February are two instalments by Takashima Beihō (1875–1949) entitled 'What shall we do about discriminatory prejudice toward our fellow countrymen?'.[54] Takashima was a leading voice in the 'New Buddhism' movement, which was highly critical of the established lineages.[55] In the first instalment, Takashima, like Ume, forcefully points out the contradiction between the clamour among many Japanese for the abolition of international racial prejudice (*jinshuteki sabetsu*) – via the racial equality clause – and the fact that such prejudice still exists in Japan. He finds it incredible that such designations as 'commoner', 'samurai family' and 'noble' not only still continue to play a role in society, but also, most of all, that the designation 'new commoner' (*shin heimin*) is used to isolate *burakumin* as a distinct social class with whom most Japanese are ashamed to interact. He raises the issue of Japanese hypocrisy in this regard in no uncertain terms: 'It is absolutely impossible to maintain as legitimate our demand that the international community abolish racial prejudice while Japanese citizens are practising such discriminatory prejudice toward their fellow countrymen.' In fact, he writes, it is shameful to do so.[56]

Events on the ground in Korea, though, were to reveal the limits of such Buddhist progressivism. On the day following the *Chūgai nippō* contributions in support of *burakumin* rights, the March First Independence Movement erupted across the Japanese-controlled territory of Korea. The first, very short, report of these events in the *Chūgai nippō* appeared on 5 March. While the article accurately describes these as 'major disturbances occurring throughout Korea', its grossly underestimated figure of 'over two hundred' protestors in Seoul's Tapgol Park, as well its being buried on page three of the newspaper, make it clear that the extent of the uprisings was not yet fully grasped. It was somehow clear to the paper's editors, though, that it was Christian missionaries who had instigated the 'seditious students' of their schools to rebel.[57]

Six days later, the extent and gravity of the situation had become clear and warranted a front-page editorial by Ume. In it, he apportions blame for the riots to 'the so-called notion of national self-determination (*minzoku jiketsushugi*) that has incited the minds of our Korean people (*waga Chōsen jinmin*)' and to those who have disseminated this notion. In this regard, while there are many culprits liable for thus 'infecting' the thinking of students and the Korean population generally – Koreans living oversees, politicians and educators – Ume argues that 'it is the religious leaders, and especially the foreign Christian missionaries that must shoulder the most serious responsibility.' Even worse, he contends, Christians, especially those in Korea, have long been engaged in the evil practice of 'advocating unpatriotic thoughts'.[58]

While the Buddhist world generally was enamoured with Wilson's Fourteen Points and supportive of the establishment of the League of Nations, it is clear from this editorial that even those on the progressive end of the spectrum found Wilson's call for 'national self-determination' troubling. It forced Japanese policymakers and intellectuals to address the question of the status of the indigenous peoples of their colonies and annexed territories. If *minzoku* – ethnic groupings – would be entitled to such self-determination, what criteria defined the borders of a *minzoku*? For some, like the prominent Tokyo Imperial University philosopher Inoue Tetsujirō (1855–1944), the answer was clear: Japanese and Koreans belonged to the same ethnic group and thus there was no scope for the latter to seek political self-determination.[59] Ume, too, is opposed to political autonomy for Korea, referring to such a notion as a 'dangerous thought' that needed to be checked before its contagion became epidemic.[60] Unlike Inoue's straightforward resolution, Ume does not address the ethnic status of Koreans directly. His referring to them as 'our Korean people', though, reveals the contours of a quandary that Japanese thinkers had been wrestling with since the early Meiji period: namely, how is one to talk about, and what is the significance of, a simultaneity of sameness ('our' *ware*) and alterity ('*Korean* people' *Chōsen jinmin*) between Japanese people and their East Asian neighbours? The term '*jinmin*' need not imply *ethnic* difference, though the use of the qualifier '*Chōsen*' denotes a distinction from 'Japanese'. While Ume does not dwell upon the ontological nature of this distinction, its political implications are clear. In a further editorial the following week, he demonstrates some sympathy for the Korean people, which was rare for the time in the Japanese press: 'However childish the Koreans may have been, were they really so foolish as to dare to wager their very lives without having any reasons whatsoever?'[61] Ume suggests that the Japanese government, both at home and in Korea, is partially to blame for the uprisings and recommends a more conciliatory approach toward the Korean people. Nevertheless, the decision to rebel against Japanese authority is 'childish'. However much Watanabe's manifesto, the 'Declaration' of the Japan Buddhist Union, or progressive Buddhist perspectives such as that of the *Chūgai nippō* might proclaim the equality of all beings based on the doctrines of innate Buddha-nature and that of the 'self being identical with all others', *in practice* the Koreans were clearly considered subordinate in terms of cultural and political maturity, and thus demands for self-determination were dismissed as foolish. Moreover, that Korean demands for self-determination could, ironically, only be seen as 'unpatriotic' – that is, towards the nation of Japan, of which Korea was now part – reveals that even progressive Buddhists saw Korean independence as not merely unacceptable, but unthinkable.

During the month of March, commentaries on the status of the racial equality proposal in the *Chūgai nippō* were conspicuously few. Editorial concerns were focused on the protests in Korea, and it is likely that Korean demands for self-determination made the Japanese case more awkward to articulate. As the protests were gradually suppressed, though, Buddhist writers again began to voice their disbelief at the initial rejection of the proposal, with Ume referring to it as 'an obvious and giant contradiction' in light of the ideals undergirding the newly established League of Nations,[62] and another contributor, Okabe Jirō, calling it 'a retrograde act that goes against the tenor of the times'.[63] The most trenchant criticism found in the pages of the *Chūgai nippō*, though, came not from a Japanese Buddhist, but from a relatively unknown French thinker and activist, Paul Richard (b. 1874), who was living in Japan at the time.[64]

The *Chūgai nippō* published Richard's address to the second meeting of the League to Abolish Racial Discrimination[65] on 23 March as the lead article on its front page, a few days later, with the title 'The establishment of a League of Asia'.[66] The piece seeks to disabuse its audience from believing that the delegates in Paris might actually bring about the League's goal of the abolition of racial prejudice. Richard warns that various prejudices – racial, ethnic, class and gender – are far too entrenched in Europe for leaders in Paris, no matter how powerful, to eradicate with the stroke of a pen. Moreover, he correctly observed that, as the proposal is not in the strategic interests of the Great Powers, one cannot hope for its being ratified. He urged the members of the League not to look to Europe *for* salvation, but rather to initiate the salvation *of* Europe from the hatreds, jealousies, chaos and darkness in which it was mired. Such salvation, he believed, could come only from Asia in the form of its spiritual teachings. Thus, he exhorted Japan to lead the way in this regard by uniting Asia both materially and spiritually in the establishment of a 'League of Asia'. Such censure of Europe by an authoritative Westerner – he was introduced in the article as a 'French Doctor of Literature' – was especially timely, given Japan's recent problems in Korea. Richard's message, *at least as it was presented to the Japanese public*, resonated well with pan-Asianist and nationalist agendas, as well as with the widespread conviction among leading Buddhists – such as Watanabe Kaigyoku – that they had something to teach the West.

Ōkawa Shūmei (1886–1957), one of the leading pan-Asianist activists in Japan, served as Richard's interpreter for the address and translator for its subsequent publication. We know that Ōkawa's translation, as it appears in the *Chūgai nippō*, is an abridged version of the address because an English translation of the French original by the well-known Indian pan-Asianist and friend of Richard's, Aurobindo Ghose, was published in 1920.[67] It is not known whether the original French text still exists.[68] While space does not permit a detailed comparison of these two versions of Richard's address, one conclusion is incontrovertible: Ōkawa's translation omits or alters every reference even slightly critical of Japanese imperialist and colonialist policies.[69] Richard was, in fact, highly critical of such policies, especially of Japanese rule in Korea. A reader of the *Chūgai nippō*, or anyone present at the original address who did not understand French, would have been unable to sense even a hint of this. One striking example of Ōkawa's misrepresentations can be seen in the comparison of his and Ghose's translations of the following passage. Ghose translated the passage thus:

Awaken her in two ways. For your work must be double: at once material and spiritual. Awaken Asia by organizing her, by uniting her. And to that end, be not masters, but allies of her peoples. Cease you also to cherish against them prejudices of race. Treat them as brothers, not as slaves. Those who are slaves liberate that they may become your brothers. Form with them all one single family.[70]

Ōkawa's version of the same passage reads:

I hope that you will awaken [Asia] by organising and uniting her materially and at the same time spiritually, and that you will establish a League of Asia. You should not engage in prejudicial treatment among Asian people. Awaken freedom and equality among them. Form one great family with them.[71]

Ōkawa omits Richard's call for Japan to 'cease' its own practice of racial discrimination vis-à-vis its colonies, as well as any suggestion that the Japanese might be 'masters' and the people in its colonies 'slaves'. Richard's pan-Asianist vision sought to unite the advances of modern science with his own religious conviction that viewed reality as a mystical monism best understood in the ancient spiritual teachings of Asia. He saw in this particularly Asian 'consciousness of Unity, of the One Soul in every being, of the One Being in all things'[72] an uncompromising ethic of racial and ethnic equality from which he could not exempt current Japanese colonial policies. It is questionable, though, whether his criticism ever reached the Japanese public. Instead, Richard ironically became a valuable, high-profile mouthpiece for Ōkawa's Japanese nationalist version of pan-Asianism.

When it became clear that Wilson's decision at the 11 April meeting of the League of Nations Commission to impose a 'unanimity rule' for the ratification of the racial equality proposal meant its de facto defeat at the Paris Peace Conference, the *Chūgai nippō* once again chose Paul Richard to deliver the most caustic criticism of this development. In consecutive front-page articles, it presented, in Japanese translation, Richard's address to the third meeting of the League to Abolish Racial Discrimination, delivered on 24 April.[73] In it, Richard reminded his audience that he had predicted this outcome a month earlier, and had warned them that the Western powers only made much of freedom and equality when it was in their own interests to do so.[74] He refers to the League of Nations as 'wolves clothed in the skins of sheep',[75] and in a compelling passage, again highlights the hypocrisy of the Western nations:

This race calls itself Christian; it adores a son of Asia. And yet if that son of Asia, if the Christ were now to come again upon the earth, he would be excluded from America, not being enough of a 'gentleman' to possess the needed number of dollars; he would be excluded from Australia, he the son of a workingman and an Asiatic, if he could not pass an examination in a foreign tongue. And in the colonies of South Africa, he could not even sit in the trams side by side with the Christian Europeans. That is how Christians would treat the Christ! And they call that civilisation – a civilisation of barbarians!⁷⁶

It was this sort of damning appraisal of the Anglo-American quashing of the racial equality proposal as one of blatant hypocrisy that became a predominant motif in the Buddhist, as well as the national, press for months and years to come.⁷⁷ Much was made of the undemocratic nature of the decision, given the fact that eleven of the seventeen members of the Commission, including France and Italy, voted in favour of the proposal.⁷⁸ Ishikawa Shuntai (1842–1931), for example, an elder statesmen from the Pure Land Higashi Honganji denomination and a close associate of Matani Ruikotsu, described Wilson's decision as the exercise of 'autocratic power' and the abandonment of justice.⁷⁹ In a *Chūgai nippō* article in October of 1919, Professor Suehiro Shigeo, Head of the Faculty of Law at Kyoto Imperial University, also decried the 'clandestine' manner in which the proposal was shelved and highlighted its hypocrisy: 'If I had to give my opinion of Mr. Wilson, I would say that while he wears a mask of justice and humanitarianism, he is a supporter of evil and deception.'⁸⁰ Suehiro linked the suppression of the proposal to American racial prejudice against its own black population, as well as to the US exclusionary policies towards Japanese immigrants in California. Regarding the former, he unsparingly concludes that American hypocrisy in this regard 'is no wonder given that [black people] are socially and politically treated as the most inferior human beings, their lynching is tolerated, and white people murder them for sport'.⁸¹ He likewise saw the US exclusion of Japanese immigrants as an 'enormous contradiction' of its so-called 'Open Door Policy'. US practice, he charged, was much more akin to a 'racially prejudiced Closed Door Policy'.⁸²

The sense of mistrust that the rejection of the racial equality proposal generated became a lens through which other events in the international political arena would be judged. Ishikawa perceived covert American action as responsible for anti-Japanese actions in Korea and Siberia. He also viewed the British as no longer reliable allies due to their refusal to temper Australian Prime Minister Billy Hughes's 'outrageous opposition' to the racial equality proposal. Like other commentators at this time, he acknowledged that the economic conflict now building momentum between Japan and the United States would continue to grow worse. However, he believed – however naively – that it would be possible to avoid outright war if only Buddhist missionaries could bring the Buddhist dharma to the United States and Britain.⁸³ Suehiro, on the other hand, harboured no such optimism. Given America's duplicitous treatment of Japan, he saw a very different future: 'When I deeply consider the future given the situation of today, a war between Japan and the U.S. is an unavoidable reality.' His prediction that this war would occur in ten to twenty years was not far off.⁸⁴

Conclusion

The willing suspension of distrust on the part of Japanese Buddhists towards the Allied Powers and their long-standing imperialist and racist modes of international engagement was exceedingly short-lived. In this way, it resembled the disappointment of the German left, which had pinned its hopes of a palatable peace settlement on the implementation of a treaty governed by Wilson's Fourteen Points. Japanese Buddhists called upon the 'peacemakers' to act with impartial justice and benevolence towards Germany and saw the seizure of German colonies, the imposition of reparations and the non-admission of Germany to the League of Nations as evidence of a vindictive justice carried out for purposes of national self-interest. They were united in their support for the racial equality proposal submitted to the League of Nations Commission by Japan and were deeply disillusioned by its abandonment. Both of these postures by the Allied representatives gave rise to accusations of hypocrisy by the Buddhist press during the months of the conference. By the time the Treaty of Versailles was signed in late June, Buddhist hopes for a new international order based no longer upon a balance of powers had been largely dashed, and the forecasts of international 'anxiety' and 'a fragile peace' found in the Japan Buddhist Union's 'Declaration' and Watanabe Kaigyoku's manifesto, respectively, were now common themes. Before Keynes had published his famous condemnation of the settlement, essays in the Japanese Buddhist press argued that the seeds of another war had already been sown.[85]

Whether one can legitimately draw causal connections between the decisions made in Paris in 1919, the international troubles of the 1920s and 1930s, and ultimately, the Second World War has long been debated. Before the ink had dried on the treaty signed in Versailles, its critics were numerous, and the predominant historiographical trend through the 1950s drew strong connections between the treaty's failures and the mid-century cataclysm. Since the 1950s, however, 'revisionist' historians have rejected this view and have instead argued that the protagonists at the Paris Peace Conference did a reasonably good job, given the difficult parameters and innumerable variables they were faced with. Ruth Henig tells us that

> the great majority of British, German, French and American historians now generally agree that the treaty was, in Niall Ferguson's words, 'relatively lenient' . . . and that, as the French historian Soutou comments, it 'would not have been easy' for the peacemakers 'to do much better'.[86]

Such debates and conclusions concerning the consequences of the treaty have focused almost entirely upon its impact on events in Europe and, to a lesser extent, the United States. This volume widens the scope of the debate to the Asian arena. This essay on the perspective of Japanese Buddhists on the Paris Peace Conference makes a modest contribution towards evaluating its ultimate impact upon the equally cataclysmic mid-century conflicts that occurred throughout Asia. What it demonstrates is that the deportment of, and decisions taken by, the Allied Powers in Paris reconfirmed and deepened a long-standing mood of mistrust towards the ultimate international designs of Anglo-American nations not only among pan-Asianists and ultranationalists but also among a moderately progressive, internationalist-leaning and cautiously optimistic sector of traditional Japanese society. Far from being 'jingoistic' and 'shrill',[87] Japanese Buddhist anxieties about a return to prewar patterns of Western imperialism were grounded in the very events playing out before the eyes of the world in Paris.

To gauge the extent to which this mood of mistrust contributed toward the rise of Japanese militarism in the 1930s is, of course, a complex task and beyond the scope of this essay. The attempt to do so, however, would comprise a necessary part of 'the truly critical examination of Japan's colonial discourse' that Sakamoto Rumi calls for in the epigraph above. Margaret MacMillan, perhaps the most widely known of the revisionist historians, rejects the attempt to draw such causal connections in the case of the European arena as mere finger-pointing and a means of avoiding responsibility. Any such attempt, she claims, is 'to ignore the actions of everyone – political leaders, diplomats, soldiers, ordinary voters – for twenty years between 1919 and 1939'.[88] Yet, such criticism smacks of caricature, seeming to suggest that historians who do see a link between decisions taken at the Paris Peace Conference and events in the 1930s and 1940s invariably view the former as necessary and/or sufficient conditions of the latter. It precludes the possibility of instead drawing the more modest, yet none the less significant, conclusion that certain decisions were indeed substantial contributing factors to a complex series of events culminating in the Second World War. Can the charges of avoiding historical responsibility not be redirected toward MacMillan's argument? Is it not irresponsible of the historian to make light of flawed and arguably disastrous decision-making by the 'peacemakers'? MacMillan writes that

> Hitler did not wage war because of the Treaty of Versailles, although he found in its existence a godsend for his propaganda. Even if Germany had been left with its old borders, even if it had been allowed whatever military forces it wanted, even if it had been permitted to join with Austria, he still would have wanted more: the destruction of Poland, control of Czechoslovakia, above all the conquest of the Soviet Union. He would have demanded room for the German people to expand and the destruction of their enemies, whether Jews or Bolsheviks. There was nothing in the Treaty of Versailles about that.[89]

As MacMillan herself acknowledges, though, there was plenty of fodder in the Treaty of Versailles for Hitler's propaganda, and the counterfactual question remains a legitimate one: would Hitler have been able to seize power without it?

Naoko Shimazu has shown that, in the case of Japan, 'by the late 1930s, the racial equality proposal became a highly useful propaganda tool used by Japanese politicians as a means of justifying whatever positions they took against the Anglo-Saxon West.'[90] Needless to say, this turn of events is rich in irony, considering that, as mentioned above, the Japanese government had abandoned its initial call in Paris for an 'equality of races' in favour of the more modest demand for an 'equality of nations'.[91] It was not this significant nuance, however, that the Japanese press accentuated and Japanese politicians exploited; it was, rather, the imperious and discriminatory manner in which the proposal was dispatched. While it may be impracticable to quantify the extent to which the rejection of the 'racial equality' proposal affected political decision-making in the 1920s and 1930s, that it did play a significant role is certain. One of the most telling pieces of evidence for the symbolic importance of this may be found in Emperor Hirohito's confidential 'monologue', recorded in the spring of 1946:

> If we ask the reason for this war, it lies in the contents of the peace treaty signed at the end of the First World War. The racial equality proposal demanded by Japan was not accepted by the powers. The discriminatory sentiment between the white and yellow remains as always. And the rejection of immigrants in California. These were enough to anger the Japanese people.[92]

'The greatest significance of this testimony', Shimazu rightly concludes, 'lies in the fact that the Shōwa Emperor recognizes the rejection of the racial equality proposal as one of the foremost underlying reasons for Japan's decisions leading to the Greater East Asia War.'[93] Revisionist arguments such as that of MacMillan minimise the significance of the psychological effects that the terms of the treaty had upon Germany, and if employed in the case of Japan, would neglect the profound extent to which Allied contradictions at the Paris Peace Conference heightened 'the tension and anxiety over the dominant West' in interwar Japan. MacMillan's monograph provides very little evidence or argument for her conclusion that the 'peacemakers' did a pretty good job under exceedingly difficult circumstances. She adumbrates such a claim in the book's last few paragraphs.[94] The preceding five hundred pages or so, though, do provide rich and vivid documentary evidence of precisely the infighting, hypocrisy and power politics based on national self-interest that Japanese Buddhist observers found so abhorrent. They, however, were much less forgiving than MacMillan of the 'peacemakers' for their knowing abandonment of universal ideals in favour of the particularist aims of realpolitik.

Acknowledgements

The author would like to thank the members of the Japan Centre of Ludwig Maximilians University Munich for their kind invitation to participate in the 'Asia After Versailles, 1919–1933' symposium. Especial thanks are in order for Professors Christoph Kleine and the editor of this volume, Urs Matthias

Zachmann. He would also like to thank Professor James McMullen of Oxford University for generously agreeing to answer some questions concerning the translations contained herein. Dr John Breen of the International Research Centre for Japanese Studies and Dr Alexander Jacoby of Oxford Brookes University made trenchant comments on an earlier draft of this essay, for which he is in their debt.

Notes

1. Tamai Kenkyūkai, *Pari kōwa kaigi*, p. 271.
2. See, for example: Tamura, '"Kokumin dōtoku" to bukkyō', pp. 21–49; Kawanami, 'Japanese nationalism and the universal dharma', pp. 105–26; Large, 'Buddhism and political renovation in prewar Japan', pp. 33–66; Large, 'Buddhism, socialism, and protest', pp. 153–71; and Ward, 'Against Buddhist unity', pp. 160–94.
3. Goto-Shibata, 'Internationalism and nationalism', pp. 66, 80.
4. Shibasaki's argument is thus summed up by Goto-Shibata in 'Internationalism and nationalism', p. 66. For the original, see Shibasaki, 'Kokusai bunka shinkōkai no sōsetsu', pp. 39–64.
5. Victoria, *Zen at War*; and Victoria, *Zen War Stories*.
6. Victoria mentions in the postscript to his second book that, due to the publication of *Zen at War*, three Zen lineages – Myōshinji, Tenryūji and Sanbō-kyōdan – have issued apologies for their wartime support of Japanese militarism. See Victoria, *Zen War Stories*, pp. 232–3.
7. Victoria, *Zen War Stories*, p. xii.
8. Victoria, *Zen War Stories*, p. xvi.
9. Victoria, *Zen at War*, p. 30.
10. Victoria, *Zen at War*, p. 79.
11. Victoria, *Zen at War*, pp. 57–63. The four figures he discusses are Shaku Sōen, Nukariya Kaiten, Ōtani Sonyū and Arai Sekizen.
12. Victoria, *Zen at War*, p. 63.
13. Victoria, *Zen at War*, p. 60; and p. 62.
14. He was born Matani Tsunemaru and his Buddhist name was Shōjun. Ruikotsu, by which he was predominantly known, is his pen name. For an account of his life and activities, see Tsunemitsu, *Meiji no Bukkyōsha*, vol. 2, pp. 379–88.
15. The contemporary Zen Nihon Bukkyōkai (Japan Buddhist Federation) was founded in 1957 and traces its roots back through the Nihon Bukkyō Rengōkai to the Bukkyō Konwakai (Buddhist Discussion Group) in 1900. Ōsawa Kōji has recently disputed this dating and claims that this latter organisation was not founded until 1912. See Ōsawa Kōji, 'Shōwa zenki no Bukkyōkai to rengō soshiki', p. 26. See also LoBreglio, 'Japan Buddhist Federation', pp. 720–1.
16. Watanabe, 'Bukkyōto no kibō', p. 1.
17. Anonymous, 'Bukkyō-to no kōwa mondai sengen keika', p. 3.
18. See Stone, 'A vast and grave task', pp. 217–33. Stone's gem of an essay is the only discussion of Watanabe in English that I am aware of. It not only describes his role in

this compilation, but also, more significantly, it contextualises his understanding of, and approach to, Buddhist doctrines and demonstrates how these were embedded in the wider social and political concerns of Taishō-period Japan.
19. Stone, 'A vast and grave task', pp. 222–3.
20. Watanabe, 'Bukkyōto no kibō', p. 1.
21. Stone, 'A vast and grave task', pp. 218–19. Originally quoted in Staggs, '"Defend the nation and love the truth"', p. 271.
22. Quoted in Stone, 'A vast and grave task', p. 227. Footnote 14 cites the original as Takakusu and Watanabe (eds), *Taishō shinshū daizōku sōmokuroku*, pp. 1–2.
23. Stone, 'A vast and grave task', p. 227.
24. Goto-Shibata, 'Internationalism and nationalism', p. 66.
25. See 'Ume', 'Bukkyō-to no sengen o yomu', p. 1.
26. Nihon Bukkyō Rengōkai, 'Nihon bukkyō-to no kōwa mondai sengen', p. 1.
27. There is no evidence that the Japan Buddhist Union produced an English translation of this manifesto. This is probably due to the standing of French at the time as the language of international diplomacy.
28. 'The hopes of Buddhists for the Peace Conference', my translation, article 2.
29. 'Japanese Buddhist Declaration on the Issue of Peace', my translation, paragraph 3.
30. 'Japanese Buddhist Declaration on the Issue of Peace', my translation, paragraph 2.
31. Anonymous, 'Sekai no heiwa o shuku-su', p. 4. Although the author's name is given, the characters are blurred and unreadable in the microfilm copy.
32. The character used for 'Ume' is 楳, a non-standard variant of the character meaning 'plum', often used in names. Staff at the present *Chūgai nippō* office were unable to answer my queries as to the identity of this editor.
33. Tsunemitsu, *Meiji no Bukkyōsha*, vol. 2. See, especially, pp. 382–3 and 388.
34. 'Ume', 'Kōwa dai-kaigi no kaikai shiki', p. 1.
35. 'Ume', 'Kōwa dai-kaigi no kaikai shiki', p. 1.
36. 'Ume', 'Kōwa dai-kaigi no kaikai shiki', p. 1.
37. 'Ume', 'Kōwa dai-kaigi no kaikai shiki', p. 1.
38. Poincaré, 'Raymond Poincaré's Welcoming Address, 18 January 1919'; original source listed as Horne, Charles F. (ed.), *Source Records of the Great War, Vol. VII*.
39. 'Ume', 'Kōwa kaigi no ankokumen', p. 1.
40. 'Ume', 'Kōwa kaigi no ankokumen', p. 1.
41. 'Ume', 'Kōwa kaigi no ankokumen', p. 1.
42. 'Ume', 'Kōwa kaigi no ankokumen', p. 1.
43. References in this paragraph are found in 'Ume', 'Kōwa kaigi no kinjō', p. 1.
44. 'Ume', 'Doitsu kokumin no kuchū', p. 1.
45. 'Ume', 'Ikyō kannen teppai', p. 1.
46. Shimazu, *Japan, Race and Equality*; see, especially, pp. 27–8, 38–67 and 83–4.
47. Shimazu, *Japan, Race and Equality*, p. 54.
48. 'Ume', 'Ikyō kannen teppai', p. 1.
49. 'Ume', 'Ikyō kannen teppai', p. 1.
50. 'Ume', 'Iburaku kannen teppai no yōkyū', pp. 1, 3.
51. 'Ume', 'Kokusai renmei to shūkyō no yūwa', p. 1.

52. 'Ume', 'Iburaku kannen teppai no yōkyū'. For a list of grievances by *burakumin* followers against the Ōtani lineage, see in this same issue: Anonymous, 'Buraku Shinshū shinto no yōkyū', p. 3.
53. See Bodiford, 'Zen and the art of religious prejudice', pp. 1–26.
54. Takashima, 'Dōhō no sabetsu-teki henken wo ikansen'.
55. For an account of his life and activities, see Tsunemitsu, *Meiji no Bukkyōsha*, vol. 2, pp. 336–47.
56. Takashima, 'Dōhō no sabetsu-teki henken wo ikansen', p. 1.
57. Anonymous, 'Chōsen no dai-sōjō to kirisutokyō no sendō', p. 3.
58. References in this paragraph are found in 'Ume', 'Chōsen no sōjō to kirisutokyō', p. 1.
59. Inoue, 'Sengo no shisōkai', p. 1.
60. 'Ume', 'Kiken shisō no bōshi', p. 1.
61. 'Ume', 'Chōsen jiken no kyōkun', p. 1.
62. 'Ume', 'Jinshu mondai no konpon-teki kaiketsu', p. 1.
63. Okabe, 'Jinshu sabetsu teppai mondai to shūkyō', p. 2.
64. See the biographical work by Richard's son, containing translations of some of his writings: Richard, *Without Passport: The Life and Work of Paul Richard*. For an account of Richard's activities in Japan, see Aydin, *The Politics of Anti-Westernism in Asia*, pp. 121–5.
65. Aydin describes the League as 'the largest Asianist pressure group aimed at influencing Japanese diplomatic attitudes during the Paris Peace Conference' (*The Politics of Anti-Westernism in Asia*, p. 143). Concerning this group, see also Torsten Weber's chapter in this volume, as well as Shimazu, *Japan, Race and Equality*.
66. Richard, 'Ajia renmei no kensetsu', p. 1.
67. Richard, 'The unity of Asia', in Aurobindo Ghose (transl.), *The Dawn over Asia*, pp. 1–10. This volume contains translations of seven of Richard's essays from the French by Ghose. The date given on page 1 for the second meeting of the League to Abolish Racial Discrimination is incorrect. It reports 22 March when, in fact, it took place on 23 March. See 'Appendix', p. 91 and Richard, 'Ajia renmei no kensetsu'.
68. I have corresponded with Michel Paul Richard, Paul Richard's son and biographer, in search of the original French texts. He is not in possession of them and does not know whether or not they are extant.
69. There is, of course, a glaring problem here when trying to decide whether to privilege Ghose's or Ōkawa's translation as being more faithful to the non-extant original. It is possible that Ghose could have wished to insert an anti-Japanese imperialism message into Richard's text; however, given Richard's statements in this regard in other places (see Aydin, *The Politics of Anti-Westernism in Asia*, pp. 121–5), this does not seem likely or plausible.
70. Richard, *The Dawn over Asia*, p. 6. See also Weber's chapter in this volume, which also refers to this passage.
71. My translation of Ōkawa's Japanese. Richard, 'Ajia renmei no kensetsu'.
72. Richard, *The Dawn over Asia*, p. 7.
73. Richard, 'Futatabi Nihon kokumin ni tsugu'.

74. Richard, 'Futatabi Nihon kokumin ni tsugu', 29 April.
75. Richard, 'Futatabi Nihon kokumin ni tsugu', 30 April.
76. Ghose's translation, in *Dawn over Asia*, pp. 14–15. Richard, 'Futatabi Nihon kokumin ni tsugu', 29–30 April.
77. Shimazu, *Japan, Race and Equality*, pp. 50–67.
78. Shimazu, *Japan, Race and Equality*, p. 155.
79. Ishikawa, 'Kaiin zanmai ni kengen seshi Taishō bukkyō', p. 4. Ishikawa was one of the first Higashi Honganji priests to go abroad, travelling through Europe and America from 1873 to 1874. At the time of this writing, he had been expelled from the Jōdo Shinshū lineage. For an account of his career, see Tsunemitsu, *Meiji no Bukkyōsha*, vol. 1, pp. 163–73.
80. Suehiro, 'Nichibei sensō no yogen', Part II, p. 2.
81. Suehiro, 'Nichibei sensō no yogen', Part I, p. 2.
82. Suehiro, 'Nichibei sensō no yogen', Part I, p. 2.
83. Ishikawa, 'Kaiin zanmai ni kengen seshi Taishō bukkyō'.
84. Suehiro, 'Nichibei sensō no yogen', 29 October.
85. John Maynard Keynes wrote *The Economic Consequences of the Peace* during the summer of 1919, and it was published in November of that year.
86. Henig, *Versailles and After: 1919–1933*, pp. 61–2.
87. Victoria, *Zen at War*, p. 30.
88. MacMillan, *Paris 1919*, p. 493.
89. MacMillan, *Paris 1919*, p. 493.
90. Shimazu, *Japan, Race and Equality*, p. 180.
91. Shimazu, *Japan, Race and Equality*, pp. 27–8.
92. Shimazu, *Japan, Race and Equality*, p. 181. The translation is by Shimazu. See also p. 231, footnote 56, which references the original as: 'Shōwa tennō no dokuhaku hachi jikan: Taiheiyō sensō no zenbō o kataru', *Bungei Shunjū*, 1990, vol. 12, pp. 94–144.
93. Shimazu, *Japan, Race and Equality*, p. 181.
94. MacMillan, *Paris 1919*, pp. 493–4.

References

Anonymous, 'Bukkyō-to no kōwa mondai sengen keika' [The development of the Buddhist declaration on the issue of peace], *Chūgai nippō* (26 January 1919), p. 3.

Anonymous, 'Sekai no heiwa o shuku-su' [Celebrating world peace], *Chūgai nippō* (29 January 1919), p. 4.

Anonymous, 'Buraku Shinshū shinto no yōkyū – Honganji ni taisuru fuhei' [Demands of Buraku (Jōdo) Shinshū followers: Grievances against Honganji Temple], *Chūgai nippō* (28 February 1919), p. 3.

Anonymous, 'Chōsen no dai-sōjō to kirisutokyō no sendō' [The large Korean riot and Christian instigation], *Chūgai nippō* (5 March 1919), p. 3.

Aydin, Cemil, *The Politics of Anti-Westernism in Asia: Visions of World Order in Pan-Islamic* and Pan-Asian Thought (New York and Chichester: Columbia University Press, 2007).

Bodiford, William, 'Zen and the art of religious prejudice: Efforts to reform a religious tradition of social discrimination', *Japanese Journal of Religious Studies*, 23:1–2 (1996), pp. 1–26.

Goto-Shibata, Harumi, 'Internationalism and nationalism: Anti-Western sentiments in Japanese foreign policy debates, 1918–22', in Naoko Shimazu (ed.), *Nationalisms in Japan* (Abingdon and New York: Routledge, 2006), pp. 66–84.

Henig, Ruth, *Versailles and After: 1919–1933*, 2nd edn (London: Routledge, 1995).

Horne, Charles F. (ed.), *Source Records of the Great War, Vol. VII* (New York: National Alumni, 1923).

Inoue, Tetsujirō, 'Sengo no shisōkai' [The postwar intellectual world], *Chūgai nippō* (29 May 1919), p. 1.

Ishikawa, Shuntai, 'Kaiin zanmai ni kengen seshi Taishō bukkyō' [A Taishō-period Buddhism that manifests the ocean-imprint meditation], *Chūgai nippō* (13 July 1919), p. 4.

Kawanami, Hiroko, 'Japanese nationalism and the universal dharma', in Ian Harris (ed.), *Buddhism and Politics in Twentieth-Century Asia* (New York: Pinter, 1999), pp. 105–26.

Large, Stephen, 'Buddhism and political renovation in prewar Japan: The case of Akamatsu Katsumaro', *Journal of Japanese Studies*, 9:1 (1983), pp. 33–66.

Large, Stephen, 'Buddhism, socialism, and protest in prewar Japan: The career of Seno'o Girō', *Modern Asian Studies*, 21:1 (1987), pp. 153–71.

LoBreglio, John, 'Japan Buddhist Federation', in J. Gordon Melton and Martin Baumann (eds), *The 21st Century Encyclopedia of World Religions* (Santa Barbara: ABC Clio Reference-book House, 2001), pp. 720–1.

MacMillan, Margaret, *Paris 1919: Six Months that Changed the World* (New York: Random House, 2001).

Nihon Bukkyō Rengōkai [Japan Buddhist Union], 'Nihon bukkyō-to no kōwa mondai sengen' [Japanese Buddhist declaration on the issue of peace'], *Chūgai nippō* (26 January 1919), p. 1.

Okabe, Jirō, 'Jinshu sabetsu teppai mondai to shūkyō' [The problem of the abolition of racial discrimination and religion], *Chūgai nippō* (27 March 1919), p. 2.

Ōsawa, Kōji, 'Shōwa zenki no Bukkyōkai to rengō soshiki – Bukkyō rengōkai kara Dai nihon senji shūkyō hōkokukai made' [The Buddhist world in the early Shōwa period and [its] formation of associations: From the Japan Buddhist Union to the Greater Japan Wartime Patriotic Association of Religions], *Musashino Daigaku Bukkyō Bunka Kenkyūsho Kiyō*, vol. XXXI (2015), pp. 21–52.

Poincaré, Raymond, 'Raymond Poincaré's Welcoming Address, 18 January 1919'. www.firstworldwar.com/source/parispeaceconf_poincare.htm (last accessed 18 July 2016).

Richard, Michel Paul, *Without Passport: The Life and Work of Paul Richard* (New York: Peter Lang, 1987).

Richard, Paul, 'Ajia renmei no kensetsu' [The establishment of a League of Asia], *Chūgai nippō* (28 March 1919), p. 1.

Richard, Paul, 'The unity of Asia', in Aurobindo Ghose (transl.), *The Dawn over Asia* (Madras: Ganesh, 1920), pp. 1–10.

Richard, Paul, 'Futatabi Nihon kokumin ni tsugu – Jinshu mondai ni tsuite' [Once again addressing the people of Japan: About the problem of race], Parts I and II, *Chūgai nippō* (29 and 30 April 1919), p. 1.

Sakamoto, Rumi, 'Race-ing Japan', in Roy Starrs (ed.), *Japanese Cultural Nationalism: At Home and in the Pacific* (Folkestone: Global Oriental, 2004).

Shibasaki, Atsushi, 'Kokusai bunka shinkōkai no sōsetsu' [The founding of the Society for the Promotion of International Culture'], *Kokusai Kankei Ron Kenkyū*, 11 (1997), pp. 39–64.

Shimazu, Naoko, *Japan, Race and Equality: The Racial Equality Proposal of 1919* (London and New York: Routledge, 1998).

Staggs, Kathleen M., '"Defend the nation and love the truth": Inoue Enryō and the revival of Meiji Buddhism', *Monumenta Nipponica*, 38:3 (1983), pp. 251–81.

Stone, Jacqueline, 'A vast and grave task: Interwar Buddhist studies as an expression of Japan's envisioned global role', in J. Thomas Rimer (ed.), *Culture and Identity: Japanese Intellectuals During the Interwar Years* (Princeton: Princeton University Press, 1990), pp. 217–33.

Suehiro, Shigeo, 'Nichibei sensō no yogen – Naiyū gaikan no Nihon no zento – Jūnen ka nijūnen ka no unmei' [Prediction of war between Japan and America: Japan's future domestic troubles and external threats; our fate in ten or twenty years], Part I, *Chūgai nippō* (28 October 1919), p. 2; Part II, *Chūgai nippō* (29 October 1919), p. 2.

Takakusu, Junjirō and Watanabe Kaigyoku (eds), *Taishō shinshū daizōku sōmokuroku* [Taishō-period Edition of the Chinese Buddhist Canon, Index] (Tokyo: Taishō Shinshū Daizōku Kankōkai, 1924).

Takashima, Beihō, 'Dōhō no sabetsu-teki henken o ikansen – Nigatsu nijūsannichi dōjō yūwakai kaisai no hi ni' [What shall we do about discriminatory prejudice toward our fellow countrymen? – On the opening day of the empathy and reconciliation conference – 23 February], Part I, *Chūgai nippō* (27 February 1919), p. 1; Part II, *Chūgai nippō* (28 February 1919), p. 1.

Tamai Kenkyūkai, *Pari kōwa kaigi to nihon no masumedia* [The Reaction of the Japanese Mass Media to the Paris Peace Conference] (Tokyo: Keio Gijuku Daigaku Hōgakubu, Seijigakka Zeminaaru Iinkaihen, 2004).

Tamura, Enchō, '"Kokumin dōtoku" to bukkyō' ['National Morality' and Buddhism], in Hōzōkan Henshūbu (ed.), *Kōza: Kindai Bukkyō* [Lectures on Modern Buddhism], vol. 5 (Tokyo: Hōzōkan, 1961), pp. 21–49.

Tsunemitsu, Kōnen, *Meiji no Bukkyōsha* [Buddhist Leaders of the Meiji Period], 2 vols (Tokyo: Shunjūsha, 1968/9).

'Ume', 'Kōwa dai-kaigi no kaikai shiki' [The opening ceremony of the great peace conference], *Chūgai nippō* (24 January 1919), p. 1.

'Ume', 'Bukkyō-to no sengen o yomu' [Reading the Buddhists' Declaration] (28 January 1919), p. 1.

'Ume', 'Kōwa kaigi no ankokumen' [The dark side of the peace conference], *Chūgai nippō* (9 February 1919), p. 1.

'Ume', 'Ikyō kannen teppai' [The abolition of the notion of heathenism], *Chūgai nippō* (18 February 1919), p. 1.

'Ume', 'Kokusai renmei to shūkyō no yūwa' [The League of Nations and the reconciliation of religions], *Chūgai nippō* (27 February 1919), p. 1.

'Ume', 'Iburaku kannen teppai no yōkyū – Dōjō yūwa taikai shokan' [Demand for the abolition of the notion that *buraku* are different: Impressions of the conference for empathy and reconciliation], *Chūgai nippō* (28 February 1919), pp. 1, 3.

'Ume', 'Chōsen no sōjō to kirisutokyō' [The Korean riots and Christianity], *Chūgai nippō* (11 March 1919), p. 1.

'Ume', 'Kiken shisō no bōshi' [The prevention of dangerous thoughts], *Chūgai nippō* (14 March 1919), p. 1.

'Ume', 'Chōsen jiken no kyōkun' [Lessons from the Korean Incident], *Chūgai nippō* (18 March 1919), p. 1.

'Ume', 'Jinshu mondai no konpon-teki kaiketsu' [The fundamental solution to the problem of race], *Chūgai nippō* (30 March 1919), p. 1.

'Ume', 'Kōwa kaigi no kinjō' [The present state of affairs at the peace conference], *Chūgai nippō* (3 May 1919), p. 1.

'Ume', 'Doitsu kokumin no kuchū' [The predicament of the German people], *Chūgai nippō* (16 May 1919), p. 1.

Victoria, Brian, *Zen at War* (New York and Tokyo: Weatherhill, 1997).

Victoria, Brian, *Zen War Stories* (London and New York: RoutledgeCurzon, 2003).

Ward, Ryan, 'Against Buddhist unity: Murakami Senshō and his sectarian critics', *Eastern Buddhist*, XXXVII:1 & 2 (2005), pp. 160–94.

Watanabe, Kaigyoku, 'Bukkyōto no kibō – Heiwa kaigi ni taishite' [The hopes of Buddhists for the Peace Conference], *Chūgai nippō* (22 November 1918), p. 1.

Chapter 7

Particularism and Universalism in the New Nationalism of Post-Versailles Japan

KEVIN M. DOAK

This chapter explores the competing tensions between new forms of particularism and universalism and how they influenced the way nationalism was understood in Japan after the Versailles Treaty. Both tendencies, while competing with and, in certain respects, symbiotically reinforcing each other, developed in a new postwar context in which ideas and ideals were given enhanced status in political life. This greater opening to the impact of ideals was connected to a sense of disillusionment with the state as the key structure of political life and to a longing for a more reliable institutional resolution to the new challenges in national and international affairs. The right resolution of these challenges, it was hoped, would end war for all times and usher in an unprecedented era of world peace. It was a heady time.

The search for forms of political life took two paths, largely, although not always, oriented in different directions: one headed down the road of internationalism, even as there was much debate as to what this 'internationalism' really meant. The other was a reappraisal of particularism, sometimes heralded as a new logic of populist democracy, at others times decried as the foundation for antidemocratic movements, as both emerged almost immediately after the end of the First World War. The intersections and divergences of particularism and universalism, especially as they influenced the politics of nationalism, shaped much of the dynamics of the political, social and intellectual life in Japan and elsewhere in the years that followed Versailles.

One useful place to begin unpacking these rival movements, and especially how they were experienced in postwar Japan, is with H. D. Harootunian's thesis of the *bunmei* (civilisation) of Meiji giving way to the *bunka* (culture) of the Taisho period (although one should note that Harootunian traces the origins of Taisho culturalism to late nineteenth-century intellectuals like Takayama Chogyū and Kitamura Tōkoku).[1] Harootunian sees a shift around the beginning of the Taisho period from overtly political concerns to internalised cultural ones. My argument builds on Harootunian's insight into the relationship between civilisation and culture, with an emphasis on these two polarities not as exclusive opposites that force one to choose between them, but as a relationship which is constantly being remade in history.

To grasp the historicity of the relationship between *bunmei* and *bunka*, it is important to extend our conceptual focus so that we can see the broader discourse as one involving shifting attitudes about universality and particularity, and what emerges in the postwar period as an integral element of that discourse – the significance of globalism and nationality. From this standpoint, we should not become distracted, at least at the outset of the discussion, by the subtleties and distinctions among such concepts as civilisation, universalism and globalism on the one hand, and culture, particularism and nationalism on the other. Inevitably, tensions will emerge among these concepts, and some might push their similarities across the broader divide between them. Yet if we are to understand how revolutionary the effects of World War I were on Japanese society and politics, it is more important to understand the inter-relationship among the core elements of each set and their shared opposition to those elements on the other end of the polarity. While there was a common foundation for universalism and particularism under the Versailles system, which I discuss below, we will miss the larger political reality of the times if we fail to grasp how meaningful the distinction between universality and particularity was for those who were working for lasting peace after the First World War.

Internationalism and particularism as products of Versailles

The impact of Versailles on the postwar order in fostering internationalism has been often noted, and it is probably the aspect of Versailles's global influence that first comes to mind. In her authoritative book, *Paris 1919*, Margaret MacMillan has described this nebulous internationalism as 'a new spirit ... [based on] the idea that there were certain things that all humanity had in common and that there could be international standards beyond those of a mere national interest'.[2] Thomas Burkman associates this 'internationalism' in Japan with the discourse on *taisei junnō*, or 'conforming to world trends' (which really meant conforming to the Versailles System). Burkman is also quite right to note that, in Japan, there was a disproportionate representation of Christians among those advocating internationalism, from the well known (Yoshino Sakuzō, Nitobe Inazō, Ebina Danjō) to the less well known (Tagawa Daikichirō, Maeda Tamon, Takagi Yasaka and others). Certainly, for some Japanese Christians (Uchimura Kanzō was a notable exception), the Versailles System and internationalism seemed a particularly welcome development. Yet, in Europe, the massive destruction of the material emblems of its civilisation and the stark barbarism of a war fought largely between self-proclaimed Christian nations were factors that spawned a widespread social rejection of Christianity as mere illusion. The postwar years in Europe were a time of atheism, socialism and Marxism, along with a growing sense of the 'decline of the West', while in Japan, ironically, Christianity grew in numbers and prominence as Japanese Christians led the way in expressing hopes for world peace under the Versailles System. Few recall today that the Japanese Prime

Minister who best represents the spirit of Versailles, Hara Kei, had been baptised 'David' in the Catholic Church.[3] These global realities of the postwar period militate against a simplistic opposition of Christianity as 'the West' versus the paganism or atheism of 'the Rest.'

There were rich contradictions within the Versailles System, and we would be remiss not to reflect first on a different, and apparently contradictory, element in this system: its enshrinement of particularism as the new logic of cultural and political identity. Benedict Anderson captured this aspect of the postwar shift toward the particular when he wrote that:

> The First World War brought the age of high dynasticism to an end. By 1922, Habsburgs, Hohenzollerns, Romanovs and Ottomans were gone. In place of the Congress of Berlin came the League *of Nations*, from which non-Europeans were not excluded. From this time on, the legitimate international norm was the nation–state, so that in the League even the surviving imperial powers came dressed in national costume rather than imperial uniform.[4]

Anderson emphasises that the League was a league of 'Nations' (not states), at least in its English inflection. This was not the case in Japan, where the League of Nations was translated as *Kokusai Remmei*, the 'International League', or better, the 'League among States'. This linguistic anomaly, although important, need not detain us here, as Anderson's point is well made. As a general proposition felt throughout most of the world, the League of Nations did promote (even if it did not very successfully embody) the proposition that the ethnic nation was the new principle of domestic political organisation and international relations in the postwar era.

In essence, the new globalising impetus of the Versailles System had within it a cancer that would prove fatal to hopes that it would bring eternal peace into the world. Writing in the early 1990s, Eric Hobsbawm identified this cancer with surgical precision when he noted that, during the Paris Peace talks,

> the basic principle of re-ordering the map was to create ethnic–linguistic nation–states, according to the belief that nations had the 'right to self-determination'. President Wilson of the USA [. . .] was passionately committed to this belief, which was (and is) more easily held by those far from the ethnic and linguistic realities of the regions which were to be divided into near nation–states. The attempt was a disaster, as can still be seen in the Europe of the 1990s. The national conflicts tearing the continent apart in the 1990s were the old chickens of Versailles once again coming home to roost.[5]

Hobsbawm gets President Wilson right. Wilson's call for populist nationalist democracy as the sole legitimating principle of the postwar world order was a radical one. On 4 July 1918, he proclaimed this radical principle, saying that world peace must be established through the settlement of every question, whether of territory, or sovereignty, of economic arrangement, or of political relationship, upon the basis of the free acceptance of that settlement by the people immediately concerned, and not upon the basis of the material interest or advantage of any other nation or people which may desire a different settlement for the sake of its own exterior influence or mastery.[6]

Of course, Wilson's ideals 'were not readily applauded in monarchist Japan'.[7] Indeed, they were, by design, incompatible with monarchist states. Popular self-determination (essentially, the principle of ethnic nationalism) was upheld as the *ex post facto* solution to the ostensible cause of the Great War: the assassination of Archduke Franz Ferdinand on 28 June 1914 by the Serbian ethnic nationalist, Gavrilo Princip. Had the ethnic Serbian nation not been subordinated by the multiethnic Austro-Hungarian Empire, there would have been no spark to ignite the World War – or so the logic went. This ethnic and antimonarchical ideology may have appealed to Wilson, Clemenceau and Orlando, but it had less lustre for Lloyd George and Saionji.

It is important to note that, in certain respects, especially regarding a critical view of the new principle of ethnic nationalism, Japan did not stand alone. Great Britain was also having problems, as a monarchy, with the new principle of national legitimacy that Wilson's ideal of 'national self-determination' unleashed. Indeed, on 21 January 1919 – only four days before the Peace Conference adopted the resolution for the creation of the League of Nations, Sinn Féin declared Ireland an independent nation, setting off a bloody struggle between Irish republicans and the British monarchy. Likewise, the Japanese Empire experienced, almost simultaneously, independence movements in Korea (1 March 1919) and China (4 May 1919). Both the Korean and Chinese nationalist movements were inspired by the language of Wilsonian 'self-determination' that was translated quite accurately into the languages of East Asia as the self-determination of *minzoku* (Chinese *minzu*; Korean *minjok*); in both places, calls for 'popular (national) self-determination' unleashed an incipient ethnic nationalism. It is not that Versailles 'invented' ethnic nationalism, but rather that the moral idealism and internationalism associated with the new world order under the League of Nations lent legitimacy to this form of ethnic nationalism (even when, ironically, the League rejected the Japanese proposal for a clause on racial equality in the League's Charter).

While it is relatively easy to understand the attraction of this new principle of ethnic nationalism in colonised China and annexed Korea, the appeal of *minzoku* as a social identity for Japanese living in a multiethnic empire requires some explanation. It does not suffice to limit our understanding of the impact of the post-Versailles principle of ethnic self-determination to anti-imperialist movements by colonised peoples in the imperial periphery. Even within the assumptions of anti-imperialism, it is important to recognise that the appeal of liberation is such that practically any group of people can – as many did – create rationales for applying 'popular self-determination' to their own situations:

ideas about internal colonisation, class exploitation, gender differences, ethnic and racial identities – all these and many other social theories provided sufficient reason (for some) to apply self-determination to various political contexts in the core 'metropole' areas, too.

To grasp the global scope of the sea change in politics that Versailles created, it helps to see how the postwar recipe for democracy – ethnic nation-states – was not limited to the future Axis Powers, but was a force unleashed on all societies. For example, in his recent and provocative book, *Liberal Fascism*, Jonah Goldberg has shown quite powerfully how the postwar revolution in political theory laid the foundations for illiberal politics – not only among the usual suspects, but even in the United States. As he notes, Wilson held a view of the state that was indebted to the same organic nationalism that Germans called the *Volksgeist* (and Japanese called the *minzoku seishin*). Goldberg writes that

> Wilson reinforced such attitudes by attacking the very idea of natural and individual rights. [. . .] 'No doubt', he [Wilson] wrote, [. . .] 'A lot of nonsense has been talked about the inalienable rights of the individual, and a great deal that was mere vague sentiment and pleasing speculation has been put forward as fundamental principle.' [. . .] The Wilsonian [. . .] progressive conception of the individual's role in society would and should strike any fair-minded person of any true liberal sensibility today as at least disturbing and somewhat fascistic. Wilson [. . .] and the vast bulk of progressives would have no principled objection to the Nazi conception of the *Volksgemeinschaft* – 'people's community', or national community – or to the Nazi slogan about placing 'the common good before the private good'. Progressives and fascists alike were explicitly indebted to Darwinism, Hegelianism, and Pragmatism to justify their world views.[8]

If such ideas could strike deeply into American political society, authorised by Wilson who personified Versailles for Americans, we should not be surprised to find similar incorporations of the 'spirit of Wilsonian democracy' at work in Japanese political circles.

For most political theorists in postwar Japan, Versailles signalled nothing less than a revolution in political theory from a universalist foundation to a particularist one. Before the First World War, civilisation and political states were the basic frame of reference; afterwards, their places were taken by culture and ethnic nationality (*minzoku*). The idea of *minzoku* seemed to many Japanese political theorists to have come out of nowhere, or more precisely, to have come directly from Versailles, if not from Woodrow Wilson himself. Looking back on that period later, at the height of the Second World War when *minzoku* ideology seemed awash over all of Japan, Social Masses Party leader Kamei Kan'ichirō asserted that 'the word *minzoku* first appeared in print in actual world politics after the Versailles Treaty.'[9] It was an exaggeration, but not by much. And like many exaggerations, it carried an element of truth.

Certainly, the principle of ethnic nationalism was central to the vision of a new, post-Versailles international order. But it was not the only principle.

Tanaka Kōtarō, professor of law at Tokyo Imperial University (and later Chief Justice of Japan's Supreme Court and Justice at The Hague), offered a trenchant analysis of the impact of Versailles in reshaping the international order. With the Second World War under way, Tanaka wrote:

> The Versailles Peace Conference tried to secure international peace by, on the one hand, devising out of the spirit of internationalism extensive peace organisations under the auspices of the League of Nations, and on the other hand accepting ethnic nationalism and establishing many independent states founded on the principle of the self-determination of ethnic minorities. [. . .] The effects of the [First] World War have produced something so important that it rivals the French Revolution. [. . .] From the late eighteenth century into the early nineteenth century, laws were codified on the basis of the philosophy of the Declaration of the Rights of Man, that is, on the principle of Natural Law. Now, the Versailles Treaty was seen as the Declaration of the Rights of Man put into international life, and it was given significance as such in international legal codes. However, just as the French Revolution ultimately failed because, as a concrete manifestation of Enlightenment Natural Law, it was found wanting at the level of the people's perception of reality, so too the League of Nations, which is the product of the Versailles Treaty, invited an unforeseen failure because of the great distance between its ideals and the reality of international life, especially because it ignored the historicity of the State.[10]

Tanaka saw the League as struggling to reconcile these two principles of (1) universality grounded in Natural Law and (2) particularity as expressed in ethnic national self-determination. The former was based on reason, the latter grounded in irrational historicism. He did not argue, however, that there was a straight line from mid-nineteenth-century mystical, romantic, ethnic nationalism to the reactionary ethnic nationalism of the post-Versailles period. Rather, the new conditions of the Versailles System meant that ethnic nationalism, influenced by racist and socialist demands for immediate political solutions in the here and now, could not fully function internationally in the form of ethnic nation–states under the new international situation. The result, and the reason for the failure of the League of Nations, was the Versailles System's quixotic attempt to particularise the universal and to universalise the particular.

Tanaka's retrospective is helpful, and it gains supporting evidence from the world events that unfolded between 1920 and 1940. Was his a unique perspective? How did the Japanese press report on the New Order as it was taking shape during and after the Versailles Treaty? Even a cursory look at the content of influential policy and academic journals in the immediate postwar years will reveal a swell of articles on the problem of *minzoku*. As early as May 1917, Professor Sakaguchi Takashi struggled with the new logic of particularism and globalism in his article on 'Minzoku, kokumin to sekai bunka'. Sakaguchi was responding to the new principles emerging in political discourse, and he explicitly separated the problems of *minzoku* and *kokumin* from the issue of race (*jinshu*), a topic on which he confessed he had little interest. Rather than remain within the framework of the prewar discourse on race and the state, Sakaguchi turned to the new interest in the particularities of ethnic cultures and the postwar universalism expressed in the idea of World Culture (*sekai bunka*). He captured the postwar sense of the interdependency of universalism and particularism well, arguing that

> [t]his trend [toward nation–states] is certainly not a rejection of global culture. It is a trend that, while encouraging the development of ethnic nations, also increasingly requires the propagation and influx of global culture for the sake of the ethnic nation itself. This is because the furthering of global culture refines the national state and its global policies and is absolutely necessary as a means of ensuring the happiness of the people of all states.[11]

Sakaguchi was hardly alone among Japanese academics and policy analysts in taking up the topic of *minzoku* and globalism. One month later, Abe Jirō published his opinion that 'ethnic nationalism opposes imperialist statism and is reconciled with the claims of cosmopolitan humanism.'[12] Abe's argument about ethnic nationalism opposing imperialism was straight out of Stalin, but how it was so easily reconciled with cosmopolitanism was never made clear.

It is, of course, one thing to *say* that particulars and universals are reconciled and another thing to demonstrate *how* they are reconciled. Sakaguchi more or less begged the question by offering a rather simplistic, functionalist argument that the more frequent the intercourse between particulars, the more they contribute to universality. Abe offers even less in terms of an argument for reconciling particulars with the universal. But his mention in passing of *minzoku shinrigaku* studies provides a clue as to what theory informed his own vague notion of an 'ideational ethnic nationalism' (*shisōjō no minzokushugi*). A few years earlier, in 1914, Matsumoto Hikojirō had introduced Wilhelm Max Wundt's *Elements of Folk Psychology* to Japanese scholars, along with Wundt's idea that ethnic national identity was largely a product of the mind. Between 1917 and 1920, a number of influential theorists writing in English added to Wundt's insight, developing what might be called the 'psychological theory of nationality'. By 1920, the two key theorists of the 'psychological theory of nationality' were W. B. Pillsbury and William McDougall. Both struggled – not too successfully – to prevent their theories from becoming infected with crude biological racism. Their intent, at least, was to see nations as unique particularities that could best be explained through the methods of psychology, which, of course, had been developed with the particularity of the individual person, not the nation, in mind. Influences from this 'psychological theory of nationalism' can be found among most major Japanese theorists working on nationalism in the post-Versailles period, including Masaki Masato, Matsumoto Yoshio, Nakatani Takeyo and Yamamoto Miono.

While the 'psychological theorists' turned optimistically to ethnic nationalism as a liberal foundation for global democracy ('liberal' because it was for them a matter of 'consciousness', and thus 'choice'), Keiō Professor Tanaka Suiichirō was not having any of it. In the December 1918 issue of the Japanese journal *Revue diplomatique*, he ignited a debate over whether this principle of ethnic nationalism was at all compatible with the spirit of the League. He acknowledged Wundt's theories, and even embraced his suggestion that the Versailles System should be based on humanism rather than the old statism of the imperial period. But Suiichirō (I use his given name to distinguish him from the other Tanaka in this chapter, Kōtarō) was 'unwilling to believe that humanism and peace were better realised through ethnic nationalism than through the political structure of the state where ethnic identities could, and should, be assimilated'.[13] Suiichirō pointed out that the League was actually a league of states (an argument that is conveyed better in the Japanese term for the league, *Kokusai Remmei*), and that 'there has not been a single example where ethnic nationalism, when carried out completely, has not destroyed an existing state.'[14] He directly contradicted Wilson's assertions by noting that if ethnic national self-determination is recognised, it would only be a matter of time until world peace, the goal of the League of the Nations, will be shattered again. Needless to say, he was prophetic in saying so, in much the same way that Tanaka Kōtarō was.

Suiichirō's thesis on the incompatibility of the League and ethnic nationalism was quickly rebuffed in the pages of the same journal by the legal scholar, Matsuda Tomoyuki. Matsuda cited Suiichirō's article by name, and countered with his own thesis on the 'harmony (*chōwa*) between the League of Nations and ethnic nationalism'. The crux of his argument was that the particularism of ethnic nationalism was a fait accompli due to the results of the war, and any effort to return to a pre-1914 theory of state supremacy was simply turning a blind eye to what history had wrought. Matsuda admitted that he accepted the League's goal of world peace only as a general ideal, and that the reality of 'justice and morality' took precedence over what he called 'peace at all costs'.[15] His focus was on the macro-level of competition between ethnic groups (both against each other and against the state), but he had less to say about justice and morality at the micro-level: for example, the rights of individuals to reside freely wherever they wished (one of Suiichirō's arguments against ethnic nationalism). In the end, Matsuda argued that lasting world peace would be established only by granting the demands of ethnic nations for independence and by states ceding their sovereign right to wage war to the League itself. Matsuda candidly admitted he had not worked out all the details of this 'harmonisation' of particularity and universality, but he was passionate about the need to make it work somehow anyway. In short, Matsuda – like many others who supported ethnic nationalism from an anti-imperialist position – was long on passion but short on details.

By the mid- to late 1920s, particularism and universalism had become deeply interwoven in Japanese discourse on nationalism and global politics. In a sense, of course, nationalism has always braided together universalism and particularism, but with the rise of ethnic nationalism as an integral element of the

Versailles System's internationalism, the relationship between universalism and particularism was completely transformed. One might even say that the previous understanding of their relationship – one in which the concrete particular forms of life point to, or were ultimately sublimated into, the universal – was now stood on its head. Rather than the direction flowing from the particular to the universal, the dominant tendency in the postwar years was to see the universal as leading toward the particular. As Matsuda implied, if the League would not use force in the service of particular ethnic nations, then it was of no use whatsoever.

A similar argument was being raised during those years by socialists and Marxists, particularly around 1922, when the Japanese Communist Party (JCP) was founded. In an issue of the leftist journal *Kaihō* earlier that year, eight leading socialists published their thoughts on the topic of 'ethnic national struggles and socialism'. Of them, Yamakawa Hitoshi's views are particularly interesting, as he was one of the founding members of the JCP and the leader of the 'Yamakawa-ism' faction of the party. In typical dialectic fashion, Yamakawa argued that socialism would both abolish competition between ethnic nations *and* exacerbate it, depending on the historical stage and political strategy of the moment. His view, which fairly represents that of most socialists at the time, is encapsulated in a plea for particularism over universalism. He argued that socialism abolishes competition between ethnic nations

> not merely because it does not suppress the divergence of particularities in humanity; rather, it is only through socialism that the various particularities of humanity are able to be developed. Conversely, when I say that socialism exacerbates the competition among ethnic nations of course I do not mean that their competition against each other for food will be more intense in a socialist world.[16]

What socialism's contribution to ethnic nationalism actually was he left unsaid. But surely Sakai Toshihiko was wrong when, in this same issue of *Kaihō*, he casually dismissed the problem of ethnic nationalism as 'nothing to worry about'.[17] What he had failed to foresee was that the problem of ethnic nationalism had so intrigued several of his co-contributors to that issue of *Kaihō* that they had, within a decade, turned to either anarchism (Iwasa Sakutarō) or national socialism (Takabatake Motoyuki, Mitsukawa Kametarō, Ayakawa Takeji). Ideas, it turned out, did make a difference.

Space is too limited to allow for a full explanation of how Marxists and socialists in the 1920s grappled with the problem of ethnic nationalism from their own ideological commitment to particularism. Here, it must suffice to note where the trajectory of leftist interest in *minzoku* took so many of them: the watershed event was the founding of the journal *Under the Banner of the New Science* in 1928 by Miki Kiyoshi and Hani Gorō. Miki made it clear that the 'new science' of the journal's title indicated a privileging of social science over natural science, precisely because he felt that social science was a science of the particular, in contrast to the universalist claims of natural science. It was in this journal that Nagashima Matao introduced his translation of Stalin's essay on nationalism, which Nagashima translated as 'On ethnicity and ethnic nationalist movements'. Even Tosaka Jun contributed an essay on character that sought to walk a fine line between the specific 'common sense' of the Japanese people while avoiding the particularism of ethnic nationalism.[18] The journal lasted only until December 1929 and, under attack by Hattori Shisō, Hani and Tosaka formed the Association for Research in Dialectical Materialism. The mainstream of leftist *minzoku* particularism, however, shifted toward national socialism after 1933, when Sano Manabu and Nabeyama Sadachika announced their move from socialism to national socialism.

It would be only too easy to conclude that the Versailles System's promotion of ethnic nationalism throughout the 1920s eventually swept universalism aside, as both the political right and left collaborated in the establishment of a particularist nationalism that came to the fore in the 1930s. This is, in fact, a common narrative in Japanese historiography on the 1930s, and there is much truth to it. But it is only part of the story. Tosaka Jun remained a courageous, if lonely, opponent of ethnic nationalism on the left. There were efforts by others who rejected neither the Meiji constitutional monarchy nor the Versailles System, and who tried in creative ways to reassess the relationship of particularism and universalism in a manner consistent with liberal, monarchical democracy. It is to one of the most important of those critics that I turn next.

Tanaka Kōtarō and Catholicism as the basis for world society

Tanaka Kōtarō presents the most interesting case of one who tried to restructure the relationship between the universal and the particular in a way conducive to democratic society. His 1927 book, *Hō to Shūkyō to Shakai Seikatsu* [*Law, Religion and Social Life*], outlined his response to the challenges of particularism and universalism as they were impacted by the new trends under the Versailles System. Each item in the title is important. 'Social life' responds directly to the kinds of concerns raised by socialists and others who sought to bring down universals to the level of particular experience, and 'law' addresses the arguments about the compatibility of ethnic nations and the League that Tanaka Suiichirō and Matsuda had debated, even as Tanaka Kōtarō seeks to provide the missing ingredient in that debate – a system of jurisprudence sufficient for the new realities of the post-Versailles world. But it was the third item, 'religion', that may be the most important for redressing the relationship of universality and particularity. Tanaka himself admitted in the Foreword to this volume that, for some time, he had not found the law to present any meaningful solution to the problems of the day. Now, the gap between the particularities of everyday life and the human need for some notion of uniform justice informed his understanding of the law as a place to enact in this world something of what the Catholic church provided as an ultimate objective for all mankind in the next world. As he titled one of his chapter subsections, 'the Church is neither a school of faith, nor a method, but the goal.' In a similar manner, the relationship of justice and reality was always a matter of particular efforts to approximate an ever-elusive universal goal. Before turning to how Tanaka sought to reconcile universal and particular as they had emerged under the Versailles System, a bit of background on how he came to this perspective may be helpful.

Tanaka wrote *Hō to Shūkyō to Shakai Seikatsu* on the heels of his April 1926 conversion to the Catholic church from Uchimura Kanzō's 'non-denominational' Christianity. Although he had broken with Uchimura in 1924, his actual entry into the church, and much of his thinking, were guided by Fr. Iwashita Sōichi, to whom he dedicated the book. Fr. Iwashita had enjoyed extraordinary global travel during the years immediately following Versailles, and that travel provided him with a lived experience that gave a concrete reality to particularism and universalism beyond the abstract discussions in political journals of the day. Tanaka himself had returned from three years in Europe in 1921. That European experience has been called Tanaka's 'artistic pilgrimage', where his exposure to European culture in the form of religious artwork enabled him to appreciate the universality of Christianity in its material particularities and not merely through the abstractions of Uchimura's lectures on the Bible.[19] Uchimura's 'churchless church' and its appeal to Japanese particularism against the West failed to provide the universal social framework that Tanaka found in the Catholic emphasis on *ecclesia*. In a sense, one can say that, for the rest of his life, Tanaka sought a means of reconciling the particularity of social community with a universal sense of justice that had applicability across social and cultural differences.

Morikawa Tamon provides keen insight into why Tanaka found the Catholic church an attractive solution to the dilemmas of particularism and universalism:

> People in the Taisho period had to discover a new standpoint following the collapse of Meiji nationalism, which had clearly constructed the way for individuals to live as a binomial of 'individual' and 'the State', and following the rise of a new place for acting called 'society'.[20]

Morikawa's comments provide insight into Tanaka's conversion from Uchimura's Christian group to the more formal ecclesiastical nature of the Catholic church, for, as Tanaka argued, 'faith is not an individualistic thing.'[21] As a jurist who believed that 'where there is society, there is law' (*ubi societas, ibi ius*), Tanaka had discovered in the Catholic church itself the global society that was a necessary precondition for a true World Law. And since World Law required a World Society, the Church as such constituted the necessary mediation between the particular individual and the universal.

Tanaka left Uchimura's 'churchless' Protestantism because he had learned in Europe that a common spirit underlay different artistic expressions and because he did not find in the individualist, even anarchic, Protestantism of Uchimura's group a satisfactory answer to the social and political concerns that he, as a student of law, had always had.[22] (Uchimura was among the most extreme of Japanese Protestants in denying the utility of institutions to address social needs.)[23] In later years, Tanaka himself reflected on the differences he felt with Uchimura's Protestantism:

> What they were mostly interested in were the ordinary affairs of human life: faith, friendship, love and marriage were the main themes. [. . .] At that time, the common characteristic was described as turning from the exterior to the interior. [. . .] In general, they had no interest in politics. [. . .] It was not that they rejected the state, but they were indifferent to the state and society and sought immediate answers to truth, goodness and beauty as they grappled directly with the affairs of life.[24]

Tanaka's retrospective on Uchimura's group almost perfectly recapitulates Harootunian's characterisation of the turn from the politics of Meiji to the culturalism of Taisho, a shift that Harootunian attributed in great measure to the Protestant Christianity of Uemura Masahisa, Kozaki Hiromichi and especially Kitamura Tōkoku.[25] In contrast, Tanaka's Catholic Christianity emphasised the importance of human institutions and the need to address social and political problems. Indeed, the more we learn about his Catholic sense of social justice, the more urgent it is to broaden our understanding of the relationship of Taisho culturalism and Christianity.

A scholar of the law with a concern for social justice, Tanaka also was drawn to Catholic epistemology: the defence of objective knowledge as attainable, and especially the position that knowledge, once obtained, is not merely for the individual but needs be applied to social problems. In contrast, much of the Protestant tradition was characterised by a subjectivism based on individual interpretation of the Bible without a mechanism for bringing those individual readings into a universal whole through the magisterium of a single, unified, global Church.[26] This was, in essence, Tanaka's response to Uchimura's own critique of the endless proliferation of denominations among Protestants: whereas Uchimura turned to the ironic project of creating his own 'churchless church' (and thus became mired in certain forms of Japanese particularism), Tanaka found Protestant Christianity too heavily invested in the particular and the subjective, and insufficiently invested in the universal and the real, and he went instead to the historical source of all denominations, the universal Catholic church. Here, he found the possibility of a universal foundation for knowledge and justice in the tradition of Natural Law.

This effort to outline such a synthetic and practical foundation for a science of social justice is evident in *Hō to Shūkyō to Shakai Seikatsu*. There, Tanaka outlined a concept of man as possessing a dual nature (*ningen no nigen-sei*), which he had learned from Fr. Iwashita. This dualistic nature of man signified the irreducible gap that always exists in this life between man as he is and man as he ought to be. Existence and Ought, *Sein* and *Sollen*, always remain in parallel relationship in this world, and anyone who is not painfully conscious of this dualism, Tanaka concluded, was 'either an angel or a beast' – in short, pure spirit without flesh or only flesh without a spirit.[27] While, on the one hand, the final resolution of this painful separation within man is possible only through the salvation promised in the Gospel, on the other hand, Tanaka argued that this salvation must begin in this world, by addressing the social structures that create either greater or lesser propensities for evil. Tanaka expressed this point quite well when he noted that

> the issue is not that the reform of institutions necessarily also restrains the external acts of human beings; rather, it comes down to the eradication of the evil that lurks in the human heart. [. . .] The spiritual salvation of an individual must be the first step toward the salvation of social life. [. . .] The existence of dualism in social life is like that in the inner life of an individual. Thus, deliverance from the suffering of this dualism is exactly the same as in the case of an individual: it cannot be achieved through one's own power or efforts, but must rely ultimately on faith.[28]

It is clear that, around the time when Tanaka left Uchimura's Mukyōkai and joined the Catholic church, he was seeking a way to address through a universal theory of justice both the sins of the individual and the problem of evil in society. Moreover, by delineating the dual nature of man, he had sketched the contours of a jurisprudence based on the Natural Law that, by recognising the difference between 'is' and 'ought', and without surrendering the reality of either, would make a powerful basis for challenging injustice anywhere in the world without necessarily eradicating cultural differences.

Natural Law: foundation for a universal theory of justice

Tanaka's interest in the Natural Law can be dated from the late Taisho period, or roughly simultaneously with his joining the Catholic church and his writing of *Hō to Shūkyō to Shakai Seikatsu*. This book was his first effort to give the Natural Law systematic treatment. Tanaka himself famously reflected later in his life that all of his vast corpus of writings can be reduced to an effort to explain this one idea: the Natural Law.[29] There is no question that his interest in the Natural Law was connected with his appreciation of the universality of the Catholic faith and the primacy it put on known and knowable truth. Tanaka read widely into Catholic Natural Law theorists, most notably Josef Mausbach and Viktor Cathrein.

In light of this eclectic reading, we might ask: how did Tanaka himself understand the Natural Law? Here is a succinct summary of his understanding of the Natural Law, taken from his 1928 book, *Hōritsugaku Gairon* [*General Principles of Jurisprudence*]:

> In its basic meaning, the Natural Law [. . .] refers to that which regulates the giving 'to each what is his'. [. . .] 'What is his' encompasses three elements in accordance with three categories of justice. As the point of departure for a principle of natural law, in the first place, 'what is his' carries the positive obligation that 'you shall give to each what belongs to him.' Secondly, there arises the negative obligation that 'you shall not commit injustice toward anyone.' As a logical and necessary conclusion of these two fundamental obligations there arise the Ten Commandments that give us [. . .] moral statements that have been substantially recognised by all ethnic groups in all times, just as the obligation to repay one's debts has been.
>
> The Natural Law is based on our reason and is a self-evident universal principle that has become our common sense. [. . .] However, determining the precise details for how this principle shall be applied to particular cases is not as self-evident as the general principle of Natural Law itself. It differs depending on each age and each place. As St. Thomas [Aquinas] perceived, when it comes to matters of human actions, the truth does not always treat all people the same in every detail, rather it is uniform only as a general principle. A just theory of the Natural Law thus only recognises universal applicability and immutability at the level of basic theory; it reserves flexibility when dealing with particulars.[30]

Not only is Tanaka's basic understanding of justice in Natural Law theory sound, but also his recognition that flexibility in application is necessary too is an expression of the traditional Catholic emphasis on the virtue of prudence. It should not be interpreted as merely opening the door to a neo-Kantian emphasis on technique, as Hanzawa has concluded.[31]

In fact, when Tanaka applied these thoughts to contemporary Japan, he strongly condemned the rise of neo-Kantian intoxication with technique as an amoral philosophy (perhaps he was thinking of Miki Kiyoshi). Tanaka saw neo-Kantian philosophy as providing legitimation for the sweeping intellectual and cultural relativism of the 1930s. It fostered a technicalism that resulted from a reliance on natural science without any universal moral principle as a guide (such as the guide Tanaka found in the Natural Law) and it meant that technological absolutism was the default position among the Japanese intellectual elite. As Tanaka noted, neo-Kantianism, when applied to questions of social justice, yielded a legal positivism that maintained 'there is no science other than the recognition of the conventional morals and laws of a given society [a view which Tanaka characterised as] a negation of the very ideas of ethics and jurisprudence.'[32] Tanaka saw such philosophical positivism as the greatest threat to the moral good of Japanese society, and he emphasised that this positivism informed movements on both ends of the political spectrum. It was, of course, found in the underlying cultural relativism of national socialism and fascism, but it also informed the Marxist rejection of universal reason and morality as the bases of social norms.

Tanaka warned against the political dangers of positivism, and by the early 1930s he was able to show how the dalliance of leftist Japanese intellectuals with neo-Kantianism during the 1920s had led to a rejection of the Natural Law and, ultimately, to a reactionary conservatism by the mid-1930s. Tanaka's analysis revealed how neo-Kantianism, in the specific case of legal theory as well as in its broader moral implications, rejected universal principles like the Natural Law in favour of a presumption of subjective determination of values and norms (in today's language, 'desire is all that matters'). This meant a retreat, in a sense, to a hyper-technical effort to transcend substantive politics, a position that left neo-Kantian theorists deeply constrained by the dominant political realities of their own time and place. Neo-Kantian jurisprudence was most closely associated with Hans Kelsen and his Japanese followers (one of whom was Yokota Kisaburō, his colleague at Teidai). But to Tanaka, neo-Kantianism simply had no foundation, no universal standard, from which to level any principled critique of violations of human rights.

What would take the place of a universal standard of justice under neo-Kantianism? According to Tanaka:

> Ultimately [. . .][neo-Kantian moral relativism] makes it impossible for anyone to criticise another's acts as fundamentally immoral or unjust. One can only affirm or negate acts based on the established morals or established laws that a given society or state has enacted from the necessities of social life in that society or state. As the place or time changes, what was unjust suddenly becomes just. [. . .] This discovery of a causal relationship between the social and economic conditions of a given society and its normative morals or laws also means there can be no science outside the perception of the established morals and established laws of a given society. This is a rejection of the very idea of jurisprudence and of the field of ethics.[33]

Tanaka ranked neo-Kantianism alongside Marxist materialism as the most popular mode of thinking among Japanese social scientists during the 1930s, and for much the same reason. Both had surrendered moral and spiritual issues at best to the technical field of material and (pseudo-) scientific method. But this was the 'at best' scenario; there was an 'at worst' one as well.

The dark side of neo-Kantian philosophy was making itself felt in the radical politics of relativism that was sweeping the world during the 1930s. Tanaka was a consistent and loud critic of the illiberal forces of cultural relativism that were on the rise in Japan. He knew something about these radical relativists and their potential for political mischief, as he had been carefully monitoring world events for years. In 1932, he had published a sharp rebuke of the rising fascism in Europe from a Natural Law perspective that emphasised the universality of human dignity and the principle of human rights.[34] He was also critical of Marxist movements that rejected universal principles of human rights and any restraint on their agendas to effect political revolution 'by all means necessary'. As noted above, by the early 1930s, Marxists in Japan and elsewhere frequently shared with rightists an embrace of the ethnic nation (*minzoku*) as the privileged 'subject' of political movements. Extreme rightists did so from an organic belief in the primacy of the eternal folk that preceded political institutions like the state; Marxists did so in light of Stalinist instrumental approaches to ethnic nationalism that grabbed any weapon that might bring down capitalist imperialism. But in either case, the subjective particularism of the *minzoku* rejected liberal political values like the universality of human rights, and Tanaka was one of the few who continued to speak out in the defence of universal standards of morality and human dignity throughout the war. He believed that to defend human rights it was necessary to defend the constitutional state (and its Article 28 that guaranteed religious freedom – an important point to someone from a religious minority like Tanaka) from those who would replace it with a romantic concept of the nation as a natural, ethnic body. Even after 1937, when he became Dean of the Faculty of Law at Tokyo Imperial University, Tanaka was an outspoken opponent of Shinto nationalists and other cultural relativists.

Tanaka's major contribution to addressing the tensions between particularist and universalist elements in nationalism came with his 1932 three-volume study, *A Theory of World Law*, which was awarded the Asahi Prize in 1935. His theory of *sekai hō*, 'World Law', made a considerable splash in the field of jurisprudence in Japan during the 1930s, with important critiques of his theory of 'World Law' published by Kamikawa Hikomatsu and Tsunetō Kyō.[35] In his magnum opus, Tanaka elaborated in greater detail the theory of World Law that he had sketched out earlier in *Hō to Shūkyō to Shakai Seikatsu*. But now, in the early 1930s, in the shadow of the assassination of Prime Minister Hamaguchi and the rise of domestic terrorist attacks on the legal order, he saw it as an urgent task to refute radical activists who believed law was a social construct that must reflect the specificities of Japanese social and cultural traditions, and to rebut Marxists whose philosophical utilitarianism held that law was merely a weapon to be used in the struggle for world revolution – or ignored altogether.

At the same time, Tanaka's concept of 'World Law' was also an effort to present an alternative to 'international law', that great misnomer for a legal norm that had evolved on the basis of the sovereignty of independent states and had proven perfectly compatible with imperialism. In contrast to international law, 'World Law' presumed the universal moral norms of Natural Law as a limitation on the kinds of contracts ('treaties') that states might establish among themselves. World Law thus sought a middle position between the Marxist instrumental legal theory that celebrated the subjectivity of *minzoku* as a tool against imperialism, and international law that maintained the sole legitimacy and sovereignty of the state and was therefore not easily dislodged from imperialism. As an intermediary position, Tanaka's 'World Law' sought – even while recognising the right to life of an ethnic nation – to subordinate the claims of ethnic nationality within the constitutional, multiethnic Meiji state, and at the same time, to hold the state accountable to universal norms of behaviour.[36] A multiethnic state, he believed, need not be an imperialist one, and must not be a culturally imperialist one.

At the core of Tanaka's theory of World Law was a distinction between the nation and the state. This distinction between the ethnic nation and the political state was hardly unique to him. What was characteristic was how Tanaka's understanding of ethnic nationality and the state reflected and paralleled his distinction between positive law and the Natural Law: in both cases, the former represents a valid expression of social consciousness, but it must be limited and guided by the universality inherent in the latter. Without the certainty of the universal values of the state and the Natural Law, both ethnicity and positive law easily could take on the fascist forms of cultural particularism and moral exceptionalism. Thus, while Tanaka was willing to accept ethnic definitions of culture when people insisted on them, he argued that the ethnic nation (*minzoku*) must be protected by, and must answer to, World Law, where a broader culture rooted in the universal dignity of all human beings must regulate the establishment of laws and the practices of all states. At stake in the rise of ethnic nationalism was not only a challenge to the constitutional state, but also a deeper challenge to the very notion of a universally applicable World Law, with its foundations and legitimacy in the Natural Law. World law and the constitutional state were conjoined, as much by their common opposition to cultural particularism and fascism as by any inherent qualities they might have shared.

It is important to emphasise that Tanaka never mistook any existing state (or even any particular codification of World Law) as equivalent to, or the full expression of, the Natural Law. There always remained a gap between the ability of positive law to approximate the Natural Law and the perfect justice of the Natural Law itself, and one could ignore that gap only at the peril of democracy and human rights. The job of the jurist – indeed, of the citizen – was to work constantly for a greater approximation of the Natural Law in both World Law and in particular national positive laws. In this way, Tanaka's theory of World Law sought to recognise both the particularism and universalism that the Versailles System had brought forth, but at the same time to hold both particularism and universalism accountable to the precepts of the Natural Law. Democracy required a delicate balancing act, but not one that was merely technical or unguided by a higher principle. The precepts of Natural Law – written on everyone's heart, regardless of cultural tradition – remained as the goal against which, and through which, the particular forms of everyday life, and man's desire for uniform and universal justice, would be measured.

Conclusion

How does Tanaka's theory of World Law help us to understand the transformation of Asia that followed from Versailles better? In the first place, his analysis of what the League made possible in terms of ethnic nationalism and internationalism was very perceptive: rather than concluding that the League was a sign of the triumph of universalism over particularism, he accepted (along with Matsuda Tomoyuki) both the League's recognition of particular ethnic cultures and their legitimate expression. But, along with Tanaka Suiichirō, Tanaka

Kōtarō also candidly admitted that the principle of ethnic national self-determination, if not placed under some broader universal framework, would ultimately pull the world apart in anarchy and war through an unbridled pursuit of particularism. In short, Tanaka saw how the League of Nations, in its assumptions that drew implicitly from Natural Law, had articulated the conditions for the possibility of world peace and also had helped to undermine those possibilities by undervaluing the historicity of the particular state. Thus, he revealed how both the idealistic 'international spirit' and the rise of ethnic nationalism of the post-Versailles period grew out of the same matrix.

But Tanaka's analysis did not remain mired in passive reflection on these dilemmas. By advocating for a jurisprudence of World Law, based on the Natural Law, Tanaka also offered a path that might have avoided the calamities of imperialism, on the one hand, and of ethnic hatreds and wars, on the other. His assessment of what would probably happen in the absence of a general embrace of World Law was prophetic. Tanaka was not without influence in the 1930s but, by his own assessment, the neo-Kantian technicalists had the upper hand; as their position solidified, the Japanese Empire led the way in creating a New Order in Asia that (while it blended elements of particularism and universalism) was largely free of the moral precepts of the Natural Law.

The significance of Tanaka's work extends beyond the period of the Versailles System, beyond Tanaka's own life, and even beyond the space of Japan or Asia. He left us an important insight into how the countervailing pulls of particularity and universality are part of our world (and still with us today); he showed us how we might celebrate our differences and our common humanity at the same time; and, most importantly, he taught us to do so while not neglecting fundamental issues of justice and human rights. If Tanaka's World Law has any meaning for us today, it is to draw from the lessons of the Versailles System to discover a way, at once both ancient and new, that enables us to live in the universal particularities of our time. With Tanaka, we can relearn the virtues of both persistence and humility in our efforts to create a just society, and recognise *our own* judicial and political systems as always imperfect – not just those of another culture or another time. In short, Tanaka's reflections on Natural Law should encourage us about what we can achieve – and the humility we need when faced with the modernist temptation to celebrate the completely unfettered individual or the absolutely autonomous nation. At such moments, Tanaka reminds us: we belong to each other.

Notes

1. Harootunian, 'Introduction', pp. 15–16 and 'Between politics and culture', passim.
2. MacMillan, *Paris 1919*, p. 493.
3. Hara was baptised in 1872, when Christianity was still illegal. Cf. Najita, *Hara Kei in the Politics of Compromise*, p. 14. Recent evidence suggests that Hara, who never spoke much about his faith, was a sincere, life-long practising Catholic. Cf. Sonoda, *Kakusareta kōshitsu jinmyaku*, p. 113.

4. Anderson, *Imagined Communities*, p. 104, cited in Doak, *Dreams of Difference*, p. xx.
5. Hobsbawm, *Age of Extremes*, p. 31.
6. Woodrow Wilson, cited in Burkman, *Japan and the League of Nations*, p. 10.
7. Burkman, *Japan and the League of Nations*, p. 10.
8. Goldberg, *Liberal Fascism*, pp. 86, 120.
9. Kamei, *Dai-Tōa minzoku no michi*, p. 301.
10. Tanaka, 'Tenkan-ki ni okeru jakkan no hōritsu tetsugaku–teki mondai' (1941), reprinted in Tanaka, *Hōritsu tetsugaku ronshū*, vol. 3, pp. 13–14.
11. Sakaguchi, 'Minzoku, kokumin to sekai bunka', p. 114, cited in Doak, 'Culture, ethnicity and the state', p.192.
12. Abe, 'Shisōjō no minzokushugi', p. 119.
13. Doak, 'Culture, ethnicity and the state', p. 193.
14. Tanaka, 'Kokusai remmei to minzokushugi', p. 23.
15. Matsuda, 'Kokusai remmei to minzokushugi no chōwa', p. 18.
16. Yamakawa, 'Shakaishugi to minzoku tōsō', p. 121.
17. Sakai, 'Sonna ni shinpai suru koto wa nai', pp. 126–7.
18. Cf. Doak, 'Under the banner of the new science', pp. 232–56.
19. Hanzawa, *Kindai Nihon no Katorishizumu*, pp. 31–4.
20. Morikawa, 'Tanaka Kōtarō no kaishū', p. 18.
21. Tanaka, *Hō to shūkyō to shakai seikatsu*, p. 78.
22. Hanzawa, *Kindai Nihon no katorishizumu*, pp. 131–3.
23. Cf. Burkman, 'Japanese Christians and the Wilsonian world order', pp. 42–3.
24. Tanaka, *Watakushi no rirekisho* (1961) and 'Kyōyō ni tsuite', *Gendai seikatsu no ronri* (1951), cited in Hanzawa, *Kindai Nihon no katorishizumu*, p. 126.
25. Harootunian, 'Between politics and culture', p. 124; also Harootunian, 'Introduction'.
26. Hanzawa, *Kindai Nihon no katorishizumu*, p. 118.
27. Tanaka, *Hō to shūkyō to shakai seikatsu*, pp. 37, 39, 271, cited in Hanzawa, *Kindai Nihon no katorishizumu*, p. 146.
28. Tanaka, *Hō to shūkyō to shakai seikatsu*, pp. 64, 291, cited in Hanzawa, *Kindai Nihon no Katorishizumu*, p.147.
29. Tanaka, *Hō tetsugaku ronshū*, vol. 3, 'Preface', cited in Hanzawa, *Kindai Nihon no katorishizumu*, pp. 176–7. Tanaka conveys the point through this humorous anecdote drawn from the painter Wilhelm von Kügelgen's autobiography. There was a painter famous for his paintings of church bells, but who would not paint any other subject matter. One day, a man ordered a painting of a knight from him but when the painting was done, lo and behold, it was not a knight but yet another church bell. When the customer complained that it was a church bell, and not a knight as he had ordered, the painter replied, 'But it kind of looks like a knight, doesn't it?' Tanaka concludes that his thirty-year-long obsession with the Natural Law makes him something like this painter.
30. Tanaka, *Hōritsugaku gairon*, pp. 62–4, cited in Hanzawa, *Kindai Nihon no katorishizumu*, pp. 182–3.
31. Hanzawa, *Kindai Nihon no katorishizumu*, pp. 192–7.

32. Tanaka, 'Gendai no shisō-teki anākii to sono gen'in no kentō', *Kaizō* (1933), reprinted in Hayashi (ed.), *Shin hoshushugi*, p. 248.
33. Tanaka, 'Gendai no shisō-teki anākii to sono gen'in no kentō', in Hayashi (ed.), *Shin hoshushugi*, p. 248.
34. Cf. Tanaka, 'Fashizumu to katorikku no tachiba', *Yomiuri Shimbun* (May 1932).
35. Kamikawa, 'Kokusai remmei to sekai-hō no kensetsu'; Tsunetō, 'Sekai-hō no honshitsu to sono shakai-teki kiso', in Tsunetō, *Hō no kihon mondai*. From the date of publication, it is apparent that Kamikawa must be reviewing Tanaka's earlier work on *sekai-hō* (that is, *Hō to shūkyō to shakai seikatsu*). In English, there is a brief discussion of Tsunetō's critique of Tanaka in Kobayashi, 'Rōyama Masamichi's perception of international order', pp. 139–41, 149–50. In Japanese, see Kiriyama, 'Tsunetō Kyō no sekai-hō ron to Tanaka Kōtarō no "Sekai-hō no riron"', pp. 198–222.
36. Tanaka, *Sekai-hō no riron*.

References

Abe, Jirō, 'Shisōjō no minzokushugi' [Ideational ethnic nationalism], *Shisō* [Thought] (June 1917), pp. 99–120.
Anderson, Benedict, *Imagined Communities: Reflections on the Origin and Spread of Nationalism* (London: Verso, 1983).
Burkman, Thomas W., 'Japanese Christians and the Wilsonian world order', *The Japan Christian Quarterly*, 49:1 (Winter 1983), pp. 38–46.
Burkman, Thomas W., *Japan and the League of Nations: Empire and World Order, 1914–1938* (Honolulu: University of Hawaii Press, 2008).
Doak, Kevin, *Dreams of Difference: The Japan Romantic School and the Crisis of Modernity* (Berkeley and Los Angeles: University of California Press, 1994).
Doak, Kevin, 'Culture, ethnicity and the state in early twentieth century Japan', in Sharon Minichiello (ed.), *Japan's Competing Modernities: Issues in Culture and Democracy, 1900–1930* (Honolulu: University of Hawaii Press, 1998), pp. 181–205.
Doak, Kevin, 'Under the banner of the new science: History, science and the problem of particularity in early twentieth century Japan', *Philosophy East & West*, 48:2 (April 1998), pp. 232–56.
Goldberg, Jonah, *Liberal Fascism: The Secret History of the American Left from Mussolini to the Politics of Meaning* (New York: Doubleday, 2008).
Hanzawa, Takamaro, *Kindai Nihon no katorishizumu: Shisōshi-teki kōsatsu* [Catholicism in Modern Japan: An Intellectual Inquiry] (Tokyo: Misuzu Shobō, 1993).
Harootunian, Harry D., 'Between politics and culture', in Bernard S. Silberman and Harry D. Harootunian (eds), *Japan in Crisis: Essays on Taishō Democracy* (Princeton: Princeton University Press, 1974), pp. 110–55.
Harootunian, Harry D., 'Introduction: A sense of an ending and the problem of Taisho', in Bernard S. Silberman and Harry D. Harootunian (eds), *Japan in Crisis: Essays on Taishō Democracy* (Princeton: Princeton University Press, 1974), pp. 3–28.
Hayashi, Kentarō (ed.), *Shin Hoshushugi* [Neo-conservativism], (Gendai nihon shisō

taikei [Series on Contemporary Japanese Thought], vol. 35 (Tokyo: Chikuma Shobō, 1963).

Hobsbawm, Eric, *The Age of Extremes: A History of the World, 1914–1991* (New York: Pantheon, 1994).

Kamei, Kan'ichirō, *Dai-Tōa minzoku no michi* [The Road Forward for the Ethnic Nations of Greater East Asia] (Tokyo: Seiki Shobō, 1941).

Kamikawa, Hikomatsu, 'Kokusai remmei to sekai-hō no kensetsu' [The League of Nations and the construction of world law], *Kokka Gakkai Zasshi* [Journal of the Association of Political and Social Sciences], part 1 (1 April 1930), pp. 1–22.

Kiriyama, Takanobu, 'Tsunetō Kyō no sekaihō ron to Tanaka Kōtarō no "Sekai-hō no riron"' [Kyo Tsuneto's Theory of World Law and Kotaro Tanaka's Theory of World Law], *Hōgaku Zasshi* [Journal of Law and Politics of Osaka City University], 54:1 (August 2007), pp. 198–222.

Kobayashi, Hiroharu, 'Rōyama Masamichi's perception of international order from the 1920s to 1930s and the concept of the East Asian community', in Dick Stegewerns (ed.), *Nationalism and Internationalism in Imperial Japan: Autonomy, Asian Brotherhood, or World Citizenship?* (London and New York: RoutledgeCurzon, 2003), pp. 135–66.

MacMillan, Margaret, *Paris 1919: Six Months that Changed the World* (New York: Random House, 2001).

Matsuda, Tomoyuki, 'Kokusai remmei to minzokushugi no chōwa' [Harmony between the League of Nations and ethnic nationalism], *Gaikō Jihō* [Revue Diplomatique] (February 1919), pp. 12–23.

Morikawa, Tamon, 'Tanaka Kōtarō no kaishū: Uchimura to no ketsubetsu to 'tasha' [Kotaro Tanaka's conversion: The break from Uchimura and 'Being Other'], *Nihon shisōshi kenkyū* [Studies in Japanese Intellectual History], 38 (2006), pp. 17–38.

Najita, Tetsuo, *Hara Kei in the Politics of Compromise: 1905–1915* (Cambridge, MA: Harvard University Press, 1967).

Sakaguchi, Takashi, 'Minzoku to kokumin to sekai bunka' [Ethnic nation, civic nation, and world culture], *Nihon shakai gakuin nenpō* [Annals of the Japan Sociological Academy], vol. 5 (1917), pp. 97–114.

Sakai, Toshihiko, 'Sonna ni shinpai suru koto wa nai' [There's nothing to worry about], *Kaihō* [Liberation] (January 1922), pp. 126–7.

Sonoda, Yoshiaki, *Kakusareta kōshitsu jinmyaku: Kenpō kyūjō wa kurisuchan ga tsukutta no ka* [The Secret Network of the Imperial Household: Was Article 9 of the Constitution Written by Christians?] (Tokyo: Kōdansha, 2008).

Tanaka, Kōtarō, *Hō to shūkyō to shakai seikatsu* [Law, Religion and Social Life] (Tokyo: Kaizōsha, 1927).

Tanaka, Kōtarō, 'Fashizumu to katorikku no tachiba' [Fascism and the Catholic position], *Yomiuri Shimbun* (May 1932).

Tanaka, Kōtarō, *Sekai-hō no riron* [A Theory of World Law], 3 vols (Tokyo: Iwanami Shoten, 1932–4).

Tanaka, Kōtarō, *Hōritsu tetsugaku ronshū* [Essays on Legal Philosophy] (Tokyo: Iwanami Shoten, 1952).

Tanaka, Suiichirō, 'Kokusai remmei to minzokushugi' [Ethnic nationalism and the League of Nations], *Gaikō Jihō* [Revue Diplomatique] (December 1918), pp. 21–39.

Tsunetō, Kyō, *Hō no kihon mondai* [Basic Problems in the Law] (Tokyo: Iwanami, 1936).

Yamakawa, Hitoshi, 'Shakaishugi to minzoku tōsō' [Socialism and the ethnic national struggle], *Kaihō* [Liberation] (January 1922), pp. 121–5.

Chapter 8

Versailles and the Fate of Chinese Internationalism: Reassessing the Anarchist Case

GOTELIND MÜLLER

The Versailles Peace Conference (1919) is a very familiar topic in China to this day, not least due to the fact that in middle school all Chinese children are confronted with a narrative in their history textbooks that stresses the conference as a typical example of how China has been bullied by Western imperialist powers. Let us first look at the description in a widely used textbook on modern Chinese history:

> After the end of World War I, from January to June 1919, the victorious countries including the imperialist powers Great Britain, the US, France and Japan opened the so-called 'Peace Conference' in French Paris, but in fact it was a booty-sharing conference to newly distribute the colonies. During World War I China had also participated in fighting Germany, and as a victorious country sent her delegates to participate in the conference. The Chinese delegates proposed to the assembly righteous demands like the abolishment of all privileges imperialism [held] in China, abrogating the [Japanese] 'Twenty-One Demands' and regaining sovereignty of Qingdao. But the conference was manipulated by countries like Great Britain, France and the US and rejected the just demands of China. Without reason it even handed over to Japan the sovereignty over Shandong which had been occupied by Germany before the war. When the news arrived in China, it made the fire of rage squeezed in the Chinese people's hearts erupt like a volcano![1]

The world history textbook, taking up the issue from an international perspective, adds the information: 'The Chinese delegates refused to sign the "Versailles Peace Treaty".'[2] And the Washington Treaty of 1922, which completed the so-called Versailles–Washington Treaty System and finally redressed the problems left unsolved for China by the Versailles Treaty, is evaluated as follows:

> In 1922, the delegates of nine powers signed the 'Nine Powers' Convention'. This convention declared to respect the integrity of Chinese sovereignty, independence and territory and to observe the principle of 'open door' and 'equal opportunity' for all countries in China. In reality, this was [only] to serve America's expansionism in China.[3]

The above quotations represent the common Chinese narrative of the Versailles conference, which highlights two points in particular: on the one hand, China was victimised by the Japanese, who forced their territorial ambitions in Shandong on to the other delegates at the Peace Conference. Thus, Japan's aggression is presented as logically in line with the infamous Twenty-One Demands of 1915, to be followed later by the Japanese invasion of Manchuria in 1931, linking up to the final outbreak of the second Sino-Japanese War (or rather, in Chinese terminology, the 'war of anti-Japanese resistance', *kangri zhanzheng*).

On the other hand, Western – or, more specifically, US – hypocrisy is 'exposed' in this narrative. For all the hopes that US President Wilson had raised with his slogans of democracy and 'self-determination' in all those feeling 'oppressed', in reality these words were counter-evidenced by his 'deed' in accepting Japan's demands during the Peace Conference. To Chinese eyes, Versailles is defined above all by the Shandong Question, exemplifying Chinese victimisation. Consequently, one finds little interest in how the Shandong Question historically evolved, how far Chinese warlords were 'guilty' because of their secret agreements with the Japanese, or how the role of the Chinese delegates – very much contested at the time – should be evaluated. In today's presentation, what counts is only that, in the end, the Chinese delegates did not sign – a token of 'desperate resistance', though without any substantial gain for China. The fact that, with the Washington treaties (which the Chinese delegates did sign), Shandong was finally returned to China is barely worth a mention in today's textbooks – though they do briefly touch on this conference in world history classes, as seen above, bespeaking a one-sided interest in 'victimisation history'.

As for historical scholarship in and on China, May Fourth is predominantly treated as the hour of the birth, or, at least, the moment of take-off, of Chinese nationalism.[4] Thus, the common historiographical reading of the protest movement is a 'nationalist' or, in official Chinese parlance, a 'patriotic' one,[5] being directed against Japan and the Westerners who did not give China its due at Versailles (and against those Chinese who did not stand up against this treatment). In the Chinese Communist Party (CCP)'s view of history, May Fourth constitutes the 'awakening' of the Chinese 'masses' (*qunzhong*), integrating students, workers, shopkeepers and even consumers who would boycott Japanese (and US) goods for some time. Thus, May Fourth has been viewed as a catalysing event for Chinese nationalism/patriotism to this day. And after the perceived disillusionment with the self-declared (but 'unmasked') 'liberal' West, interest in the alternative – that is, the Soviet Union – appears logical.[6] Consequently, the May Fourth movement is also interpreted as mid-wife at the birth of the CCP, which then supposedly embodies Chinese nationalism.

In recent years, Bruce Elleman has published a book on the so-called Shandong Question, with the explicit objective of redressing Wilson's negative image in China, arguing that Wilson was in fact adhering to his stated vision of a more egalitarian new world after the nightmare of World War I. However, on discovering the secret Chinese–Japanese agreements of 1918, by which Japan had secured Chinese acceptance of her claims in return for providing loans, he had no chance of legally countering Japanese pressure. Thus, Elleman argues, the Chinese actually defeated themselves at Versailles[7] and later conveniently put the blame on President Wilson. Elleman, however, argues that, for all his idealism, Wilson unconsciously helped China's Communist transformation because of his poor sensitivity to public relations, allowing the Soviets to capitalise on this event and on the 'distorted' view of what actually happened. Thus, again, the conference seems to lead rather straightforwardly to Chinese Communism, though only at the cost of historical misunderstanding.

Keeping all these prevailing nationalism-oriented evaluations in mind, I would like to turn to the opposite question of how Chinese internationalism fared and how it was de facto affected by Versailles, looking especially at one of the currents that was most internationalist of all and quite influential at the time: the Chinese anarchists. What was their internationalism like before Versailles? How did China react to the conference and what about the impact on Chinese anarchist internationalism afterwards? Finally, I will try to draw some conclusions from the anarchist case, questioning the validity of the above-mentioned established historiographical readings of the impact of the events of May Fourth on China and the supposedly straightforward connection to Chinese nationalism.

Chinese anarchist internationalism before Versailles

Anarchism not only negates the validity of the state and is thus by definition beyond national boundaries,[8] but also, in East Asia, it was historically perceived in an international(ist) way.[9] In the beginning, anarchism was perceived as being mixed up with 'nihilism', terrorism and various brands of socialism associated with late nineteenth-century events in Russia and Western Europe. Since the Japanese wrote early and repeatedly on those topics, much of the printed information in Chinese was taken (if not translated) from Japanese, especially after the turn of the century, when information on 'anarchism' intensified. This close relationship between Japanese and Chinese anarchism would, incidentally, be a characteristic throughout the following decades. It is only with the second half of the first decade of the twentieth century, however, that one may meaningfully talk of an anarchist 'movement' in East Asia.[10] The Chinese 'movement' actually had two starting points: one in Tokyo with a close connection to Japanese 'comrades', led by Kōtoku Shūsui,[11] and the other in Paris with connections to the circle around the journal *Les Temps nouveaux* and Jean Grave.[12] Both groups not only were interested in anarchism as a political 'theory' but also found in its Kropotkinian version a new world view.[13] Thus, they both took up a whole range of cultural questions, such as proposing new ways for the sexes to relate to each other[14] or offering a critique of social etiquette or of received economic relations.

Even language and script were on the agenda, and East Asian anarchism was, throughout its existence, closely connected to the Esperanto movement (though there were, of course, also non-anarchist Esperantists in East Asia).[15]

With this breadth of impetus, Chinese anarchism was, in fact, already taking up many of the cultural implications of May Fourth, and thus one can safely say that much of what was declared as 'new' at the time of the 'New Culture Movement', which blended with the more political May Fourth movement, had already been spelled out in the last decade or so of the Qing dynasty.

Interestingly, the anarchist Paris group presented a more 'nationalist' picture with some involvement with the Revolutionary Alliance (and later, the National People's Party) of Sun Yat-sen,[16] compared to the highly idealist Tokyo group, which – for several reasons – did not visibly bestow its heritage on the later Chinese anarchist movement.[17]

With (Liu) Shifu, the embodiment of Chinese anarchism, now finally on Chinese soil after the founding of the Chinese Republic, Chinese anarchism 'matured'. Shifu was a remarkable internationalist, even though he himself had not spent a lot of time in foreign countries as other Chinese anarchists had.[18] He was a deeply convinced Kropotkinian and used the internationalist language Esperanto to keep up an exchange with anarchists abroad. Again, he showed the typical breadth of anarchist activities, reformulating all aspects of life in his somewhat unique 'puritanical' understanding of anarchism.[19] Furthermore, the especially close relationship to Japanese anarchists is demonstrated in his asking Ōsugi Sakae, the leading Japanese anarchist after Kōtoku's execution in the High Treason Affair, to help him with his journal, 'People's Voice' (*Minsheng*). Ōsugi did indeed help by sending his close collaborator, Yamaga Taiji (who was a knowledgeable typesetter), to get Shifu's journal started.[20]

Anarchist internationalism had already had to face a big challenge with the outbreak of World War I, when the old master, Kropotkin, sided with the Allies and nearly split the movement. Bitter accusations were made of him having forsaken internationalism, and in China Shifu was greatly shocked by his idol's position, citing eminent anarchists Errico Malatesta and Emma Goldman's criticisms of Kropotkin.[21] Young Shifu died soon after, however, and the Chinese anarchist movement went through a time of great difficulty until just before May Fourth.

One of the topics thrown up consistently was the language issue, and thus Esperanto remained a 'signifier' of anarchist activities. When Chen Duxiu launched the journal of the New Culture Movement, 'New Youth' (*Xin Qingnian*), language soon became one of the issues that had to be tackled. In 1918, controversial discussions about Esperanto found their way into this flagship periodical, and even some non-anarchists were fascinated by the international language.[22] Anarchists, in turn, used this opportunity to unite around this common topic, thus gaining new visibility through the widely circulated journal and soon bringing out a host of new – though often short-lived – independent publications themselves.[23] Thus, internationalism at this time was strongly connected to the issue of Esperanto as a more egalitarian means of communication, redressing the East Asian 'linguistic disadvantage' without having to choose a language attached to one nation or other. Esperanto thus embodied the ideal of true internationalism, being a 'foreign language' for everybody, but at the same time 'modern' in the sense of being rational and free from the inconsistencies typical of historically received languages. Like science, which had a comparable reputation for being international and which was one of the catchwords of May Fourth, Esperanto was considered a similar endeavour in the field of language.

Interestingly, discussion of Esperanto in *Xin Qingnian* suddenly died down in early 1919, which leads one to speculate whether news about Versailles could have influenced this sudden decline (after all, the language issue did not play any part in these international talks), removing, for the moment, the vigour of internationalism. It reappeared very soon in various journals, however, suggesting that the negative influence was only temporary.

Chinese reactions to the Versailles Peace Conference

How exactly did the Chinese react to Versailles? Basically, there are two important areas to look at: one in France and the other in China.

As far as France is concerned, there were quite a number of Chinese living and/or studying there. And, of course, the Chinese delegation was present, representing the 'official' northern government (but also including delegates from the rival southern government in Canton), which meant that the delegation felt pressure from the Chinese in Paris on top of the pressure from Beijing (and Canton). Chinese anarchists had, in fact, already been involved for a decade in bringing a considerable number of young Chinese to France. The 'Paris group' members had developed various 'study in France' programmes, as well as a 'work and study' programme for poorer (or idealistic) students to finance their studies themselves by working in France.[24] At the time of the Versailles conference, some rather intellectually and ideologically engaged Chinese in France followed events through what was to be learned from the press, and even protested and physically pressured the chief Chinese delegates into not signing. Members of the delegation also debated hotly among themselves, as suggested by the memoirs of China's 'star' diplomat, young Wellington Koo (Gu Weijun),[25] and the memoirs of China's 'first woman lawyer' and member of the delegation, Sorbonne-trained Zheng Yuxiu.[26] (The latter, incidentally, had attended an anarchist 'study in France' preparatory programme in China before attending the Sorbonne.) One important Chinese observer present at the conference (though not part of the official delegation) was leading 'conservative' intellectual Liang Qichao. His powerful pen was feared, and his comments on the devastation he saw in Europe after World War I also influenced Chinese public opinion to a considerable degree. He furthermore published his sceptical evaluations of the on-going negotiations in Versailles in Western media as well, and sent home a couple of highly influential telegrams to his political friends, who would circulate them in the Chinese press.²⁷ Obviously, the Chinese delegates were under great pressure from different sides and were forced into not signing the treaties in the end.

Tightly interwoven with protests by those Chinese in France were the reactions at home in China. The present-day Chinese middle-school textbook on modern Chinese history, mentioned above, narrates these events to Chinese pupils as follows:

> On May 2, 1919, the Beijing 'Morning Post'²⁸ published an article ... stating bitterly: 'Jiaozhou is lost, Shandong is lost, the country is no country any longer!' When the student delegates of Beijing University and other [universities] realised that this meant that Chinese diplomacy at the Paris conference had failed, they decided to call an emergency meeting to discuss what countermeasures should be taken. On the evening of May 3, over 1000 student delegates of Beijing University and other universities in Beijing assembled in the aula of the Law Faculty of Beijing University. Upon hearing the report of the 'Beijing Gazette's' chief editor Shao Piaoping on the failure of Chinese diplomacy, the feelings of the mass grew agitated. One student of Beijing University bit his middle finger on the spot, tore his sleeve and wrote with his own blood the four big characters 'Return us Qingdao'. This agitated the students even more. The next day, the May 4ᵗʰ movement exploded.²⁹

Since the secret agreements of September 1918 between China and Japan, which had accepted Japan's claims to Shandong, were not known to the general public, the totally unexpected turn the Shandong Question had taken during the negotiations led to uproar in China. Furthermore, American propaganda had been directly involved in heightening Wilson's appeal to China and the high hopes of the Chinese for the Peace Conference.³⁰ When news broke in China of the downhill developments at the Versailles talks regarding Chinese aspirations, the May Fourth demonstrations were immediately sparked and would soon spread beyond Beijing to Shanghai and to more and more places, involving people from 'all walks of life'.³¹ As Wagner has shown,³² this was orchestrated and channelled by intellectuals and was less spontaneous than is usually assumed (or described in the Chinese 'standard narrative' quoted above). Furthermore, the design clearly followed the Korean March First Movement. Rage was now directed towards the 'scheming' Japanese, Chinese 'traitors' and the 'betrayal' of Wilson, whose idealistic words seemed to be 'unmasked' by the United States not helping China at the conference table in the end. Clearly, China had been bullied once again.

The immediate targets of the rage were – as with Korea's March First Movement – pro-Japanese Chinese officials: that is, the so-called 'national traitors' involved earlier in negotiating the secret loans. And for the present, obviously, Chinese diplomacy was held as chiefly responsible for this 'bad' final outcome for China at the conference. The Chinese government could save the situation (and itself) at home only by dismissing some of the pro-Japanese ministers and by urging their delegates at Paris at least not to sign.³³

Liang Qichao, for his part, commented on the conference, at first expressing his disappointment with the Chinese side as well with the secret treaties – fully realising how little hope there was even for friendly nations to help China under these circumstances – but then moving on to criticise the West and its values.[34] In the end, Liang was not a neutral observer, but rather had his own political agenda. To bolster his claims, he extensively quoted sceptical Western observers, who judged not only World War I itself but also the issue of how it was addressed within the Versailles Treaty to be highly problematic, foreshadowing worse things to come. This, in turn, sparked a whole 'conservative' wave in China to reassert 'Asian values'; in contrast to the more 'progressive' reactions, however, this remained a minor current.[35]

Basically, it is clear that Chinese officials were held at first to be the main 'culprits' behind the diplomatic disaster in Versailles; it was only with time, by means of the media and by the actions of the Chinese government to appease the public, that blame was 'shifted' more pointedly to 'the West', or to Wilson personally as 'betraying' China,[36] thus broadening the issue into a more general question of China's position and destiny on the world stage.

Chinese anarchist internationalism after Versailles

Versailles did, in fact, for a short time shake up Chinese beliefs in 'the world'. Yet, for all the rage expressed during May Fourth, nationalism was only one 'child' produced (or at least 'adopted') by this movement, and was a rather slow-growing one at that. Internationalism in China was by no means dead after Versailles – as testified by the fact that respect for and envy of Japan continued, notwithstanding any protests. The 'other', 'liberal' side of May Fourth has been acknowledged in the West,[37] mainly with a view to its cultural and literary implications (though, of course, downgraded in the People's Republic of China, or PRC). Adding to this 'liberal' cultural trend, the early 1920s in China were also the heyday of internationalism. In China, even though Wilson's dreams were, to a certain extent, discredited, internationalism of various brands was still attractive,[38] since China wanted to take a more active role in her own future. For so many decades she had only watched others decide her fate. Thus, World War I and its aftermath were also heeded as an alarm call for more positive action on the part of China.[39] For the anarchists, the outcome of Versailles only reinforced their already engrained positions: governments are not to be trusted. But this only demonstrated just how insignificant national boundaries were: 'comrades' are everywhere, so 'true' commonness did not depend on which country one belonged to.[40] Even world Communism was perceived in those early years as 'internationalist' and only in time did it become exclusively 'centred' on Moscow.

For the anarchists, the early 1920s marked a peak in their influence,[41] and for them there was no break in internationalism at all after Versailles, which for them represented only governments. Even throughout the early 1930s, a special and strong connection remained specifically with Japanese and Korean anarchists. When Ōsugi was murdered in the wake of the Great Kantō earthquake of 1923, for example, big commemorative services were held and commemorative editions of journals were produced in China too. And, in the late 1920s, Japanese anarchists were active in educational projects established by Chinese anarchists,[42] and Korean and Chinese anarchists worked together, mainly in Shanghai, to help the 'movement' in both countries.[43] The connection with Western anarchists remained intact as well.[44] In the mid-1930s, there were still Chinese anarchists who were considering helping their comrades in the Spanish Civil War, though at home they already had their backs to the wall.[45] Thus, Versailles did not curb their enthusiasm; rather, it reinforced it. If governments or the League of Nations ran into difficulties, this only proved the 'egotism' of states, as Kropotkin had always taught. Certainly, in China, the reorganisation of the Guomindang (GMD) along Leninist lines in 1923/4 and the uneasy position of the anarchists between the two political parties – the big GMD and the still small CCP (which, since 1924, were more or less cooperating in the first united front) – also made nationalism a physically ever-stronger force. However, the key points in time when Chinese nationalism really took off were the 'anti-imperialist' May Thirtieth incident of 1925[46] and the Northern Expedition of 1926–8, moving on under the label of National Revolution. The falling-out of the GMD and the CCP in 1927, bloodily ending the first united front and forcing the CCP underground, made nationalism a visibly contested issue and also led to a serious split in the anarchist movement, from which it was never to recover fully.[47] Thus, one may summarise, it was not by events at Versailles that Chinese internationalism in general and anarchist internationalism in particular were fundamentally challenged, since internationalism peaked in the years immediately after the conference. Rather, the tide turned in the mid-1920s.

Conclusion

Did Versailles not affect Chinese internationalism at all, then? As already stated, as far as Chinese anarchists are concerned, the Peace Conference did not curb their internationalism in the slightest, since Versailles involved only 'treaties' signed (or not) by nation–states. For the non-anarchists, Versailles challenged internationalism to some extent, but basically it only took out the idealism connected to it, realising that powers and interests had not perished with the war. However, the wheel of time was not to be turned back. Even though Wilson appeared to have been unsuccessful, his 'liberate yourself' message still had some indirect impact on a broader worldwide audience – what has been termed the 'Wilsonian moment' by Erez Manela.[48] The world had changed after World War I, and in China internationalism coexisted with – if not dominated – nationalism, which was supposedly 'begotten' by (or took off with) May Fourth, until well into the 1920s, when nationalism finally gained the upper hand. But even then, internationalism was not dead, and among those trying to adhere to it for as long as possible were the anarchists.

Thus, not only is today's official PRC portrayal of May Fourth (briefly introduced above) clearly one-sided, but in non-Chinese scholarship as well it has been acknowledged how difficult it is to dispense with these established views of May Fourth as the crucial historical juncture for the development of nationalism in China.[49] This has much to do with a teleological view of history looking at only those currents dominating in the long run. The 1920s (especially the early 1920s) are also (unofficially) remembered in China as 'golden' in terms of an internationalist window, which was to remain open until much later. The long-term writing-out of Chinese anarchism and its role in Chinese history on and *after* May Fourth and the singular concentration on the founding of the CCP in 1920/1 as historically 'significant' are two of the key factors contributing to this historically misguided evaluation.

Notes

1. *Yiwu jiaoyu kecheng biaozhun shiyan jiaokeshu. Zhongguo lishi. Banianji, shang ce*, p. 46. At the time of writing (2009), this textbook on modern Chinese history is the most commonly used one in China.
2. *Yiwu jiaoyu kecheng biaozhun shiyan jiaokeshu. Shijie lishi. Jiunianji, xia ce*, p. 15. At the time of writing, this textbook on modern world history is the most commonly used one in China.
3. *Shijie lishi*, pp. 17–18.
4. For a 'classical' Western treatment, see, for example, the sections on May Fourth in Fairbank (ed.), *Cambridge History of China*, vol. 12. See also Zhang, *China in the International System*, pp. 74–8. It is mainly in the literary field that this reading has been challenged, focusing on May Fourth as a cultural movement. (For a fairly recent example, see Dolezelová-Velingerová and Král (eds), *The Appropriation of Cultural Capital*.) For an overview of some newer Western scholarship on the May Fourth movement, see Ip, Hon and Lee, 'The plurality of Chinese modernity'.
5. The common Chinese characterisation of the May Fourth movement is therefore *wusi aiguo yundong* (May Fourth patriotic movement).
6. The Soviets, for their part, were aware of this chance to enhance their public relations and launched the Karakhan Declaration on 25 July 1919, amidst Chinese frustration over 'the West'.
7. This, in fact, had already been argued in Chow Tse-tsung's 'classic', *The May Fourth Movement* (1960). Whereas Elleman (*Wilson and China*, 2002) mainly used Western-language archival diplomatic sources, Chow used a host of Chinese press material. Elleman's assessment has, to a certain degree, been challenged as one-sided because of its narrow focus on the Shandong Question by Xu, *China and the Great War*, esp. pp. 271–2 and 280.
8. Basically, the anarchists – at least the 'mainstream' ones of the time – did question all kinds of 'boundaries'. Therefore, they did not even value highly issues of *minzu*

('nation' in an 'ethnic' sense) per se, which Kevin Doak has pointed out elsewhere in this volume as a possible alternative point of reference to the 'state'. In other words, to them, ethnic 'boundaries' were as arbitrary (or irrelevant) as boundaries between states.
9. The term 'internationalist' is used here since it was popular with the anarchists themselves, though one might argue that, in fact, it is a misnomer since anarchists, in negating/transcending 'national boundaries' (which theoretically would be the precondition for inter-nationalism), are rather 'cosmopolitan'. However, the term 'cosmopolitan' retained a 'bourgeois' connotation (not least because of Marx's nineteenth-century attacks on it), whereas 'internationalism' had a 'progressive' ring and therefore was preferred by anarchists, as by Communists. For careful historical analyses of the terms and their usage, see Friedemann and Hölscher, 'Internationale, International, Internationalismus'; and Busch and Horstmann, 'Kosmopolit, Kosmopolitismus'.
10. For a survey of the Chinese movement in the English language, see Zarrow, *Anarchism and Chinese Political Culture* (focusing on the early anarchists); and Dirlik, *Anarchism in the Chinese Revolution*. A more recent and extensive treatment, in terms of both coverage and approach, is available in German (Müller, *China, Kropotkin und der Anarchismus*).
11. For an English treatment of Kōtoku, see Notehelfer, *Kōtoku Shūsui: Portrait of a Japanese Radical*.
12. Grave has left behind an interesting memoir: *Quarante ans de propagande anarchiste* [1930] (1973).
13. A synopsis of the reception of Kropotkin's writings in Japan and China is included in Müller, *China, Kropotkin und der Anarchismus*, pp. 633–90.
14. Cf. Müller, 'Knowledge is easy – action is difficult'.
15. See Müller and Benton, 'Esperanto and Chinese anarchism, 1907–1920'; Müller and Benton, 'Esperanto and Chinese anarchism in the 1920s and 1930s'.
16. The rationale was a 'first step in the right direction': that is, Sun's aims were seen, from an evolutionary perspective, as one step further towards anarchy. For a perception of the Chinese anarchists in Paris from the side of the French anarchists, see Grave, *Quarante ans*, p. 541.
17. This 'idealism' was at least the articulated stance of the Tokyo group. Since the Tokyo group's core members 'defected' to the Qing soon after, there is some speculation about their motives.
18. For Shifu, see Krebs, *Shifu: Soul of Chinese Anarchism*.
19. This was noted by the Japanese anarchist Yamaga Taiji, who worked with Shifu and was surprised by the difference in lifestyle between Shifu and Japanese anarchists. With Shifu, a certain Buddhist underpinning is discernible, which contrasted with the decidedly 'materialist' undercurrent in Japanese anarchism.
20. For an English-language treatment of Ōsugi, see Stanley, *Ōsugi Sakae*. For Yamaga, see Mukai, *Yamaga Taiji*.
21. A reflection of this crisis is *Minsheng*, no. 22 (9 August 1914). (See *Minsheng* [1992].)

22. One of the more vocal ones was Sun Guozhang, teaching Esperanto at Beijing University.
23. For details, see Müller and Benton, 'Esperanto and Chinese anarchism, 1907–1920', pp. 58–63 and 'Esperanto and Chinese anarchism in the 1920s and 1930s', pp. 174–80.
24. Some Chinese Communists who would later become prominent participated in this programme, including the Premier of the People's Republic of China, Zhou Enlai, and Mao's 'successor', Deng Xiaoping. The latter programme did not attract a substantial number of students until late 1919, however.
25. A Chinese translation of the relevant section on the Versailles conference appeared in Wellington Koo's memoirs: Gu, *Gu Weijun huiyilu*, vol. 1, pp. 172–215. (One may note that, with hindsight, Koo's presentation – well aware of the 'popularity' of not having signed in the end – nevertheless tends to play down the arguments between the Chinese delegates around the decision at the time.)
26. See Madame Wei Tao-Ming [= Zheng Yuxiu], *My Revolutionary Years*, pp. 114–25.
27. *Liang Qichao nianpu changpian*, pp. 879–84. See also Liang's summary after the conference in his 'Ouyou xinying lu' [1920] (1999).
28. This newspaper belonged to Liang Qichao's faction.
29. *Yiwu jiaoyu kecheng biaozhun shiyan jiaokeshu. Zhongguo lishi. Banianji, shang ce*, p. 46.
30. Instrumental for American propaganda in China were US journalist Crow and US ambassador Reinsch. Crow had a Chinese translation of Wilson's Fourteen Points already prepared and circulated in 1918. Thus, it was American propaganda that suggested to the Chinese that Wilson's points were significant for them too (see Crow, *China Takes Her Place*, pp. 113–15, and Crow, *I Speak for the Chinese*, pp. 27–9. For the general context, see also Creel, *How We Advertised America*, pp. 358–63). For an analysis of American propaganda in China, see Matsuo, 'American propaganda in China'; Schmidt, 'Democracy for China'; and Yamagoshi, 'The media wars'.
31. As Bryna Goodman has pointed out, merchant-led native-place organisations were already politically active well before May Fourth, thus paralleling the students rather than being 'instigated' by them. See Goodman, 'New culture, old habits', esp. pp. 92–4.
32. Wagner, 'The canonization of May Fourth'.
33. For an evaluation of the problematic position the Peking government was in, see Fung, 'Reinterpreting the events of May Fourth'.
34. His 'Ouyou xinying lu', referred to above, expressed these views and was circulated widely. It influenced, for example, advocates of a newly developing trend toward a Chinese 'third way', like Liang Shuming. As is well known, Liang Qichao's group was also instrumental in inviting foreigners critical of Western contemporary civilisation to China in the early 1920s.
35. The 'conservatives' have become a rather popular academic topic in recent years after *Limits of Change* (1976), the early ground-breaking volume edited by Charlotte Furth.

36. The first accusations pointing at Wilson himself, however, appeared as early as May 1919. (See Schmidt, 'Democracy for China', p. 19, citing the Shandong newspaper, *Jinan ribao*, 16 and 17 May. See also Xu, *China and the Great War*, pp. 267–8, for further examples.) But the May Fourth slogans of the time did not mention him as the primary target. Rather, the main thrust of the movement aimed at internal Chinese issues, looking for a way for China to take more positive action.
37. See, for example, its characterisation as 'enlightenment': namely, in Schwarcz, *The Chinese Enlightenment*.
38. Besides the anarchists, Communists as Christians advocated some kind of internationalism at the time; even in politically 'conservative' circles, a desire to link up with like-minded worldwide trends may be observed, expressing itself, for example, in invitations to foreigners to come to China for lecture tours and so on.
39. This holds true even on a diplomatic level. See Xu, *China and the Great War*, pp. 271–7.
40. For example, in the first new 'common platform' of Chinese anarchists, the journal *Jinhua*, founded in January 1919 and prohibited in the wake of the May Fourth demonstrations, the French anarchist Jean Grave had been presented with his own critical views on the postwar order as a kind of anarchist 'counter-proposal' to what was going on in Versailles. See 'Timin' (1919).
41. See Müller, *China, Kropotkin und der Anarchismus*, pp. 415–512, for a detailed account.
42. Besides Yamaga Taiji, Iwasa Sakutarō and Ishikawa Sanshirō were long-term Japanese 'comrades' who joined in these educational projects.
43. Some glimpses of Sino-Korean anarchist cooperation are offered in Shimada, 'Bakin to Chōsen-jin'.
44. For example, Jean Grave and the Reclus family retained their long-standing contacts with Chinese anarchism. Emma Goldman occasionally remained in touch as well, and Chinese anarchists time and again linked up with local anarchists when in foreign countries or – when at home – wrote letters (often in Esperanto).
45. The famous Chinese writer and one-time anarchist and Esperantist, Ba Jin, for example, took a keen interest in the developments in Spain (see, for example, his letter to 'E. G.' – that is, Emma Goldman – in Ba Jin, *Sheng zhi chanhui*, p. 66, or his edited volume on Durruti as mentioned in *Ba Jin nianpu*, vol. 1, pp. 488–9 and 500–1, as did some other young anarchists around Lu Jianbo, incidentally an active Esperantist as well).
46. For a fairly recent general assessment of this particular event and its context in a Western language, see Osterhammel, *Shanghai, 30. Mai 1925*. See also Perry, 'Popular protest in Shanghai, 1919–1927'.
47. For a more detailed account, see Müller, *China, Kropotkin und der Anarchismus*, pp. 547–629.
48. Manela, 'Dawn of a new era', and Manela, *The Wilsonian Moment*.
49. See Dolezelová-Velingerová and Wang, 'Introduction', p. 23.

References

Ba Jin, *Sheng zhi chanhui* [Life Confessions] (Shanghai: Shangwu Yinshuguan, 1936).
Ba Jin nianpu [Chronology of Ba Jin] (Chengdu: Sichuan Wenyi, 1989).
Busch, H. J. and Axel Horstmann, 'Kosmopolit, Kosmopolitismus', in Joachim Ritter (ed.), *Historisches Wörterbuch der Philosophie* (Darmstadt: Wissenschaftliche Buchgesellschaft, 1976), vol. 4, pp. 1155–67.
Chow, Tse-tsung, *The May Fourth Movement: Intellectual Revolution in Modern China* (Cambridge, MA: Harvard University Press, 1960).
Creel, George, *How We Advertised America* (New York and London: Harper & Brothers, 1937).
Crow, Carl, *I Speak for the Chinese* (New York and London: Harper & Brothers, 1937).
Crow, Carl, *China Takes Her Place* (New York and London: Harper & Brothers, 1944).
Dirlik, Arif, *Anarchism in the Chinese Revolution* (Berkeley: University of California Press, 1991).
Dolezelová-Velingerová, Milena and Oldrich Král (eds), *The Appropriation of Cultural Capital: China's May Fourth Project* (Cambridge, MA: Harvard University Press, 2001).
Dolezelová-Velingerová, Milena and David Der-wei Wang, 'Introduction', in Milena Dolezelová-Velingerová and Oldrich Král (eds), *The Appropriation of Cultural Capital: China's May Fourth Project* (Cambridge, MA: Harvard University Press, 2001), pp. 1–27.
Elleman, Bruce A., *Wilson and China: A Revised History of the Shandong Question* (Armonk: M. E. Sharpe, 2002).
Fairbank, John K. (ed.), *Cambridge History of China*, vol. 12: *Republican China, 1911–1949, Part 1* (Cambridge: Cambridge University Press, 1983).
Friedemann, Peter and Lucian Hölscher, 'Internationale, International, Internationalismus', in Otto Brunner, Werner Conze and Reinhart Koselleck (eds), *Geschichtliche Grundbegriffe*, vol. 3 (Stuttgart: Klett, 1982), pp. 367–97.
Fung, Allen, 'Reinterpreting the events of May Fourth: Power and politics in mid-1919', *Papers on Chinese History*, vol. 2 (Spring 1993), pp. 54–77.
Furth, Charlotte (ed.), *Limits of Change: Essays on Conservative Alternatives in Republican China* (Cambridge, MA: Harvard University Press, 1976).
Goodman, Bryna, 'New culture, old habits: Native-place organization and the May Fourth Movement', in Frederic Wakeman Jr and Wen-hsin Yeh (eds), *Shanghai Sojourners* (Berkeley: Institute of East Asian Studies, 1992), pp. 76–107.
Grave, Jean, *Quarante ans de propagande anarchiste*, ed. by Jean Maitron (Paris: Flammarion, reprint 1973 [1930]).
Gu, Weijun [= Wellington Koo], *Gu Weijun huiyilu* (Wellington Koo Memoir) (Beijing: Zhonghua Shuju, 1983).
Ip, Hung-Yok, Tze-ki Hon and Chiu-Chun Lee, 'The plurality of Chinese modernity: A review of recent scholarship on the May Fourth Movement', *Modern China*, 29:4 (2003), pp. 490–509.

Krebs, Edward S., *Shifu: Soul of Chinese Anarchism* (Lanham, MD: Rowman & Littlefield, 1998).
Liang, Qichao, 'Ouyou xinying lu' [Impressions from travels in Europe (1920)], in *Liang Qichao Quanji* [Liang Qichao Complete Works] (Beijing: Beijing Chubanshe, 1999), vol. 5, pp. 3000–10.
Liang Qichao nianpu changpian [Long Version of the Chronology of Liang Qichao], ed. by Ding Wenjiang and Zhao Fengtian (Shanghai: Shanghai Renmin Chubanshe, 1983).
Madame Wei Tao-Ming [= Zheng Yuxiu], *My Revolutionary Years: The Autobiography of Madame Wei Tao-Ming* (New York: Charles Scribner's Sons, 1943).
Manela, Erez, 'Dawn of a new era: The "Wilsonian Moment" in colonial contexts and the transformation of world order, 1917–1920', in Sebastian Conrad and Dominic Sachsenmeier (eds), *Competing Visions of World Order: Global Moments and Movements, 1880s-1930s* (New York: Palgrave Macmillan, 2007), pp. 121–49.
Manela, Erez, *The Wilsonian Moment: Self-determination and the International Origins of Anticolonial Nationalism* (Oxford: Oxford University Press, 2009).
Matsuo, Kazuyuki, 'American propaganda in China: The U.S. Committee on Public Information, 1918–1919', *The Journal of American and Canadian Studies*, vol. 14 (1996), pp. 19–42.
Minsheng [People's Voice] [1913–21], complete reprint, ed. by Hazama Naoki (Kyoto: Hōyū, 1992).
Mukai, Kō, *Yamaga Taiji: Hito to sono shōgai* (Yamaga Taiji: The Man and his Life) (Tokyo: Seigabō, 1974).
Müller, Gotelind, *China, Kropotkin und der Anarchismus: Eine Kulturbewegung im China des frühen 20. Jahrhunderts unter dem Einfluß des Westens und japanischer Vorbilder* (Wiesbaden: Harrassowitz, 2001).
Müller, Gotelind, 'Knowledge is easy – action is difficult: The case of Chinese anarchist discourse on women and gender relations and its practical limitations', in Mechthild Leutner and Nicola Spakowski (eds), *Women in China: The Republican Period in Historical Perspective* (Münster: LIT, 2005), pp. 86–106.
Müller, Gotelind and Gregor Benton, 'Esperanto and Chinese anarchism, 1907–1920: The translation from diaspora to homeland', in *Language Problems & Language Planning*, 30:1 (Spring 2006), pp. 45–73.
Müller, Gotelind and Gregor Benton, 'Esperanto and Chinese anarchism in the 1920s and 1930s', in *Language Problems & Language Planning*, 30:2 (Summer 2006), pp. 173–92.
Notehelfer, F. G., *Kōtoku Shūsui: Portrait of a Japanese Radical* (Cambridge: Cambridge University Press, 1971).
Osterhammel, Jürgen, *Shanghai, 30. Mai 1925: Die chinesische Revolution* (Munich: dtv, 1997).
Perry, Elizabeth J., 'Popular protest in Shanghai, 1919–1927: Social networks, collective identities, and political parties', in Nara Dillon and Jean C. Oi (eds), *At the Crossroads of Empires: Middlemen, Social Networks, and State-building in Republican Shanghai* (Stanford: Stanford University Press, 2008), pp. 87–109.

Schmidt, Hans, 'Democracy for China: American propaganda and the May Fourth Movement', *Diplomatic History*, 22:1 (Winter 1998), pp. 1–28.

Schwarcz, Vera, *The Chinese Enlightenment: Intellectuals and the Legacy of the May Fourth Movement of 1919* (Berkeley: University of California Press, 1986).

Shimada, Kyōko, 'Bakin to Chōsen-jin' [Ba Jin and the Koreans], in *Aiura Takashi sensei tsuitō Chūgoku bungaku ronshū* (Collections of Essays on Chinese Literature in Memoriam of Professor Aiura Takashi) (Tokyo: Hatsubaijo Tōhō Shoten, 1992), pp. 179–236.

Stanley, Thomas A., *Ōsugi Sakae: Anarchist in Taishō Japan. The Creativity of the Ego* (Cambridge, MA: Harvard University Press, 1982).

'Timin', 'Gelafu zhi heping lianhe jihua' [Grave's plans for a peaceful alliance], *Jinhua* [Evolution], no. 1 (1919), pp. 14–15.

Wagner, Rudolf, 'The canonization of May Fourth', in Milena Dolezelová-Velingerová and Oldrich Král (eds), *The Appropriation of Cultural Capital: China's May Fourth Project* (Cambridge, MA: Harvard University Press, 2001), pp. 66–120.

Xu, Guoqi, *China and the Great War: China's Pursuit of a New National Identity and Internationalization* (Cambridge: Cambridge University Press, 2005).

Yamagoshi, Toshihiro, 'The Media wars: Launching the May Fourth Movement. World War I and the American Propaganda Activities in China, Led by P. S. Reinsch and Carl Crow', www.geocities.jp/crow1919jp/may_4th/english/may4th_e.html (last accessed 25 July 2016). (Original Japanese version appeared in *Tōyō Bunka*, 73, 1994, pp. 49–63)

Yiwu jiaoyu kecheng biaozhun shiyan jiaokeshu. Zhongguo lishi. Banianji, shang ce [Provisional Textbook According to the Curriculum Standards for Compulsory Education: Chinese History. Class 8, vol. 1], 2nd edn (Beijing: Renmin Jiaoyu, 2006).

Yiwu jiaoyu kecheng biaozhun shiyan jiaokeshu. Shijie lishi. Jiunianji, xia ce [Provisional Textbook According to the Curriculum Standards for Compulsory Education: World History. Class 9, vol. 2], 2nd edn (Beijing: Renmin Jiaoyu, 2008).

Zarrow, Peter, *Anarchism and Chinese Political Culture* (New York: Columbia University Press, 1990).

Zhang, Yongjin, *China in the International System, 1918–1920: The Middle Kingdom at the Periphery* (New York: St Martin's Press, 1991).

Chapter 9

The Impact of Versailles on Chinese Nationalism as Reflected in Shanghai Graphic and Urban Culture, 1919–31

HIROKO SAKAMOTO

Nationalism and the New Culture and May Fourth Movements

Following its inauguration as the first Asian republic in 1912, China was profoundly affected by the outbreak of the First World War in the early days of its national formation. The impact was further amplified by the Russian Revolution, which followed a few years later.[1] Japan had made Korea its protectorate in 1905 as a foothold for the invasion of Manchuria, before annexing the country in 1910. Furthermore, when the First World War broke out, Japan moved quickly to appropriate German interests in the Shandong Peninsula by taking advantage of the diminishing presence of the Western powers, who were now preoccupied with the war in Europe. After the murder of a German missionary in the Shandong Peninsula in 1897, German troops had occupied Jiaozhou (Kiaochow) Bay in Tsingtao (Qingdao), and then the city as a whole on the pretext of protecting German missionaries. Since 1898, Tsingtao had been a leased territory of Germany. Now, however, Japan declared war against Germany in August 1914 when the war broke out, ostensibly citing the Anglo-Japanese Alliance. In addition, in September of the same year, Japanese troops landed in Shandong, claiming that the province was under German rule, despite China having already declared its neutrality in the war. In the following month, Japanese troops occupied Jinan, and in November, Tsingtao. These actions prompted local Chinese to start organising a movement for regaining their territory. In January 1915, Japan served the Twenty-One Demands to China, which were accepted by the then government of Yuan Shikai on 9 May. The day soon became known as National Humiliation Day in China. In August 1917, shortly before Germany's surrender, China entered the war. There were growing expectations among the Chinese that the return to China of the rights to the Shandong Peninsula would be decided at the Paris Peace Conference, given that US President Woodrow Wilson had announced his Fourteen Point peace programme upholding the principles of self-determination and of fair solutions to colonial problems.

When the Peace Conference opened in Paris in 1919, however, the Racial Equality Proposal put forward by Japan was defeated on 11 April due to the strong opposition of the United Kingdom and its dominions such as Australia and South Africa, which were concerned with their own immigration policies, and also of the United States, which had its own problem of discrimination against black Americans and was pushing ahead with policies aimed at rejecting Asian immigrants. Although the Proposal, according to Naoko Shimazu, was intended to improve Japan's international standing and to free Japanese nationals from existing, and future, discriminatory measures,[2] China supported the Japanese proposal. Following the defeat of the proposal, Wilson, on 28 April, supported Japan's demand that Japan continue in possession of the German concessions in Shandong. As expected, when the news reached Beijing, it caused an uproar among students and many other Chinese. The May Fourth Movement began, demanding the restoration of Chinese territory.

Initially, the Movement was started by students in Beijing, Tianjin and Shanghai. These students and young intellectuals were the so-called 'New Youth', who came of age during the New Culture Movement, which had started around 1915. As they grew up, they had benefited from the further, albeit incomplete, dissemination of education after the establishment of the Republic of China, as well as the beginnings of the formation of a standard national language, the development of highly commercialised print media, and the wider circulation of newspapers and magazines. The New Culture Movement challenged some of the traditional attitudes and systems of belief, such as the monopolising of knowledge by the male elite, based on the Confucian system (which was supported by the civil service examinations), prejudice against physical labour (according to Mencius, only those who use the mind will become rulers), and prejudice against women (as it was the accepted Confucian belief that women ought to obey their father, husband and [first] son as they grew older, and Chinese women were subjected to the practice of foot-binding). Thus the Movement defied the traditional Confucian belief system and opened the way for a more egalitarian and democratic society. Students formed their own societies, which, in turn, built up a wider communication network. They boycotted classrooms, demonstrated on the streets, and sent their members to various places to educate local people. Their activities led to the campaign to reject Japanese goods and to use Chinese goods instead, and also influenced workers and business people.

On 3 June 1919, the Chinese government arrested a number of students. In response, on 5 June, large-scale strikes started in Shanghai and beyond, taking three forms: students' strikes, the closing of shops and workers' strikes. Nearly 100,000 workers are believed to have taken part. The strikes spread to over one hundred cities in more than twenty provinces. Hence the New Culture Movement and the May Fourth Movement were intertwined. During this process, Chinese nationalism, which was forged in response to the situation created by the Paris Peace Conference, transcended regional differences, and this nationalism inevitably contained anti-imperialist aspects.

When the closing of shops began to reach Beijing, the government yielded, releasing the students and sacking three governmental leaders who were thought to be pro-Japanese. The Prime Minister also stepped down. On 28 June, the Chinese delegates in Paris refused to sign the Versailles Peace Treaty. The impact of the Anti-imperialist Movement was not restricted to Chinese domestic politics and diplomacy, however. For instance, some students at girls' schools also formed their own campaign groups, which would mean that the Movement penetrated into individual homes even more deeply. The Movement also helped to raise women's awareness as Chinese, tapping into their desire for fuller emancipation. They also took part in the movement to boycott Japanese goods and to use Chinese goods, contributing to the development of a truly national movement (Figure 9.1).

After the 1911 Revolution, the Women's Suffrage Society was formed by members of the Chinese Socialist Party and other organisations. The Nanjing Provisional Government began to draft a National Constitution immediately after the establishment of the Republic of China. The Representatives of Women, led by Tang Qunying and others, petitioned the government to grant women voting rights. Song Jiaoren and other leaders, however, prioritised the formation of the Nationalist Party by amassing forces against Yuan Shikai, dropping the clause for gender equality from the platform of the Chinese Alliance. As a result, the Provisional Constitution, which reflected the principles of the Republic of China at that time and was promulgated in March 1912, proclaimed that 'the people of the Republic of China are equal, regardless of their race, class, or religion,' but omitted 'gender equality'. The rights of women had fallen victim to political manoeuvring. In the first general election, held in February 1913, women were excluded.

Furthermore, when he came to power in November 1912, Yuan Shikai dissolved the Nationalist Party, depriving its members of their eligibility to become members of the National Assembly, which was subsequently dissolved in early 1914. Yuan abolished the Provisional Constitution and announced a New Constitution, which expanded the President's power. Prior to the announcement of this new constitution, Yuan's government had promulgated the regulations intended to extol public morality, which set the criteria to reward those who practised filial piety, and model wives for their chastity and loyalty. These model women included those who did not marry before the age of fifty after being widowed before they had reached thirty; those who were killed while resisting rape, or committed suicide after experiencing such violence; and those who committed suicide after the death of their husbands. The government's attempts to control individual sexuality were not restricted to women. For instance, a series of oppressive penal bills included one that would revive historically cruel punishments for male adultery, although these punishments were in the process of being reformed from the late Qing period onwards.[3] These measures imply an attempt to construct a mechanism to suppress individual sexuality. Hence the policy of the new government shortly after the 1911 Revolution included anti-feminist measures, prompting some women to demand liberation

Figure 9.1 Women students taking part in a demonstration, *Shenbao*, 27 May 1919.

openly. Their activities were strengthened during the New Culture Movement, and they were able to participate in the May Fourth Movement as Chinese demanding recognition of their rights.

Because its ideological foundation was to challenge the old ethical standards, the New Culture Movement entailed criticism of traditional gender-based norms of behaviour. In other words, the movement was recognisably feminist, and those who were involved in this movement pitted the 'new' against the 'old' inherent in Chinese culture. Nevertheless, this dichotomy inevitably sparked debate concerning West and East. Such radical pro-Western intellectuals as

Chen Duxiu would employ very strong language in order to defeat their opponents, and Chen's friend, Zhou Zuoren, explained the rabidity as follows: 'Even the slightest compromise was perceived as a sign of accepting the opponent and a failure to continue our attack [on the old system].'[4] Feminist assertions were also entangled within such intense cultural debate.

The decline of the New Cultural Movement was most explicitly addressed by Liang Qichao in a series of essays he began to publish in 1920 under the title 'A Reflection on a Journey in Europe' (*Ouyou xinying-lu*). He wrote these essays after travelling in war-ravaged Europe after the First World War, between 1918 and 1920, after experiencing the collapse of the Qing Dynasty and losing the political battle after the establishment of the Republic of China. On the way, he heard about the victory of the new Soviet power in the Russian Civil War. Liang defines the basis of modern European civilisation as that of a material civilisation obsessed with the applicability of scientific methods and approaches, although China had used Europe as a model since the reform movement period of the late 1890s. The series expresses a deep disillusionment with European civilisation, and signals the decline of the New Culture Movement, accompanied by doubts about materialism that became apparent around the time of the establishment of Soviet power. In this sense, the publication of the series was extremely significant. Around the same time, Liang Shuming was trying to reassess Asian culture by comparing Europe and India at Beijing University, the stronghold of the New Culture Movement, while facing the severe criticism of Hu Shi, the founder of the movement. Liang Shuming's view contains elements that emphasise the superiority of Asian culture, and could antagonise those who advocated the fuller introduction of Western culture, while Liang Qichao called for more moderate politics and integration and harmonisation of Eastern and Western culture. It was against this backdrop that the debate on 'science or philosophy' took place in 1923, mostly among Liang Qichao's students.

In this way, the Chinese nationalism of this period branched out into camps focusing on anti-imperialism and on Chinese traditions, thus complicating its character. Such complex nationalism could surface in very simple forms. Nevertheless, it also penetrated into Chinese society through new forms of urban and popular culture. I will now turn to cartoons and popular magazines published during this period in Shanghai, a cosmopolitan 'colonial modern' city with large foreign concession districts, and examine how they, while cosmopolitan in style, express Chinese nationalism. I will also investigate them from a feminist viewpoint.

Newspaper advertisements and cartoons during the New Culture and May Fourth Movements

In 1919 alone, about 200,000 emigrants left the British Isles for non-European regions, lured by demands for engineers and white-collar workers, which were advertised in newspapers, or through personal connections.[5] One of these migrants was Richard Maurice Tinkler, who was barely twenty years old. He was born to a lower middle-class family in a small town in Lancashire. He responded to a newspaper advertisement for officers for the Shanghai Municipal Police (SMP). Tinkler arrived in Shanghai by boat on 15 August 1919, disembarking at the French Concession. Two weeks later, he sent the following letter to one of his aunts:

> Shanghai is the best city I have seen and will leave any English town 100 years behind – that's not exaggerated. It is the most cosmopolitan city of the world bar none and the finest city of the Far East. At night it is lit up like a carnival, and an orchestra plays in the Public Gardens along the river front. (Fountains beautiful trees etc.) Of course, it is not a bit like a European city of the same population, as say Manchester. There is a splendid electric car service and everyone seems to own one of the latest type of American cars. We go about in rickshaws mostly and thro' out the East they grow to be a habit with everyone.[6]

In his later life, Tinkler faced many difficulties, the hardest of all being the Sino-Japanese War. He was killed in 1939 by a Japanese soldier in the middle of a strike at the factory where he was an employee in Shanghai. It was undeniable, however, that Shanghai was a mesmerising cosmopolitan city when Tinkler arrived there. The city was flourishing against the background of the growth of a capitalist economy supported by overseas Chinese entrepreneurs and the inflow of global capital into the concessions from the imperial powers. By the 1930s, until the anti-Japanese war got into full swing, Shanghai had developed into one of the most mature urban cultures the world had ever seen, despite being a quasi-colony. Shanghai had a cluster of international urban spaces, which had a mutual influence on one other. At the early stage of its development, the appearance of workers' communes and new feminist movements led by female students, who developed their own culture as 'modern girls', was particularly noticeable.

Modern cartoons and advertisement drawings are commercial arts that are part of urban culture, formed through the integration of heterogeneous cultural forms. I will give representative examples of the period of the New Culture and May Fourth Movements, a period that has a strong correlation with the Paris Peace Conference, the event that initiated 'the political season' in China. In the third part of the chapter, I will introduce examples from the time when urban culture matured, after the Chinese Nationalist Party had unified China and Chinese capital began to grow, and compare these examples with ones from the late 1920s.

Shanghai Puck (*Shanghai Poke*) was a pioneering cartoon magazine from the period of the New Culture and May Fourth Movements. The original *Puck* was published by Joseph Keppler, an Austrian who had emigrated to the United States in 1867. The American *Puck* was published in colour between 1871 and 1918. Inspired by the US *Puck*, *Tokyo Puck* was published in 1905 and

Osaka Puck in 1906. *Shanghai Puck* appeared in September 1918, although the American *Puck* itself was discontinued in this year. Because contemporary Chinese newspapers and magazines tended to be visually dull, carrying mainly letters, *Shanghai Puck* attracted wide attention and its first issue sold more than 10,000 copies.

The publisher of *Shanghai Puck* was Shen Bochen (1889–1920), whose real name was Shen Xueming. He was born in Zhejiang Province and worked as a shop assistant and then as a cartoonist for the major newspapers, *Shenbao* and *Shishi Xinbao*. He had visited Japan as a member of a group of journalists observing the Japanese newspaper business in 1917. *Shanghai Puck* was published by a company that he set up with his brother, Xueren, and Shen drew most of the cartoons carried in the magazine himself. Figure 9.2 depicts a sword, with the word 'democracy' inscribed on it, stabbing the Russian and German Emperors, reflecting the October Revolution in Russia in 1917 well before the appearance of similar depictions in other magazines. The return of Tsingtao, then a leased territory of Japan in Shandong, was also a major theme for many cartoons and texts.

Shanghai Puck was terminated after the fourth issue, when Shen Bochen died in 1920 at the age of thirty-two. Figure 9.3 shows one of his cartoons that appeared in the *Shishi Xinbao*, with the caption 'Unless animalistic desires are removed, no just principle will emerge, and evil is so big as to block the Way.' In

Figure 9.2 'Not exactly, but almost' by Huang Wennong, *Shanghai Puck*, vol. 1, no. 1 (1918).

Figure 9.3 *Shishi Xinbao* (Shanghai), 11 May 1919.

this picture, the artist presents the redistribution of economic and other interests among the imperial powers at the Paris Peace Conference as subhuman.

The restoration of Chinese territory was also one of the major themes in newspapers. In these papers, one of the frequent themes of advertisements is a call for boycotting foreign goods advertised by Chinese companies. During the First World War, Chinese companies grew in various forms of light industry, such as textiles. Among the advertisements in newspapers, the most prominent were for items for personal consumption, such as cigarettes and medicine, where advertising images played an important part.

During the May Fourth Movement, advertisements by Chinese cigarette companies emphasised patriotism and the purchase of Chinese goods. One advertisement urges the reader to smoke Shandong Taishan Tobacco Brand if they need to smoke after 'strikes at schools, shops and factories'.[7] A Chinese Industrial Tobacco Company's advertisement boldly asserts, 'Rise up now, comrade!'[8] Nanyang Brothers Tobacco Company was particularly skilful at emphasising patriotism, using the Great Wall as a key image (as shown in Figure 9.4) and inserting such phrases as 'A single cigarette will determine the future of business, and influence patriotism and the concession issue.'[9]

Nanyang Brothers Tobacco Company was the successor of the Canton Nanyang Tobacco Company, established in 1905 in Hong Kong by the Cantonese Jian Zhaonan and his brother, Yujie. The brothers had cut their professional teeth in Japan, where they secured funding. When the boycott of American goods started in China in response to the reported mistreatment of Chinese labourers in the United States, the pair had moved to Hong Kong. Jian Zhaonan registered their company as Japanese, because that was common practice among overseas Chinese entrepreneurs at that time, and he also wanted to do business in Japan. He himself legally acquired Japanese citizenship so that he

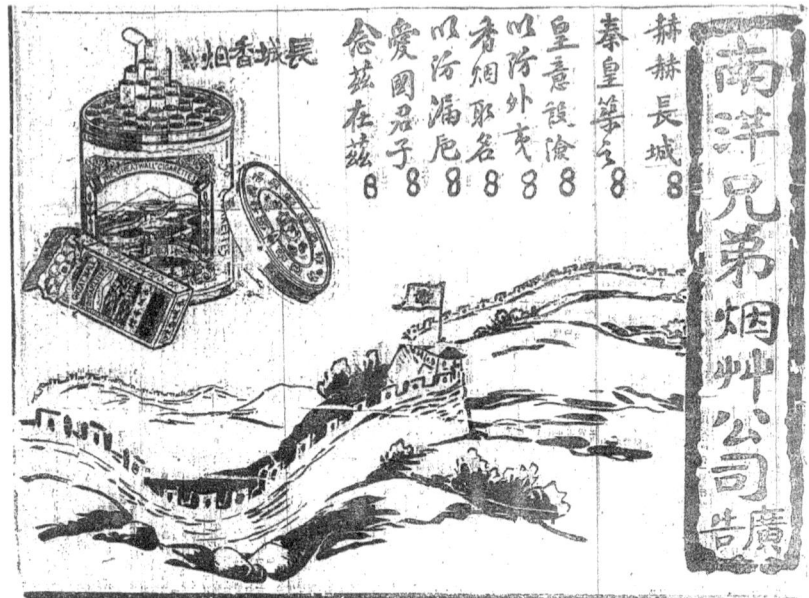

Figure 9.4 *Shibao* (Shanghai), 27 April 1919.

had dual nationality, a fact that his business enemies would use later to criticise him when Chinese nationalism was gaining momentum.

Meanwhile, British American Tobacco (BAT) was established in 1902 in London as a global trust funded by major British and American tobacco companies. The company absorbed other American and Chinese companies in Shanghai, and began to produce cigarettes in various parts of China. As BAT quickly began to dominate the Chinese market, the brothers' company could not survive the competition and went bankrupt. Thanks to new funds from one of their uncles, however, Jian Zhaonan restored the company, though on a smaller scale, and renamed it Canton Nanyang Brothers Tobacco in 1909. The firm grew rapidly after the fall of the Qing Dynasty and during the First World War. In 1916, the company built a factory in Shanghai, and in 1918 relocated its headquarters there from Hong Kong. BAT was producing and selling the largest volume of cigarettes in China at that time, thanks to cheap labour, abundant resources and nationally organised sales campaigns. Canton Nanyang Brothers Tobacco was the only Chinese company that could compete against BAT. As a result of competition with Chinese agents of BAT, Canton Nanyang Brothers Tobacco was accused of being funded by Japanese capital and suffered badly from the boycott in the wake of the May Fourth Movement.[10] The company was even compelled to place an advertisement in the major newspapers, saying that it was genuinely a Chinese company, accompanied by a certificate issued by the US Consulate General to this effect.[11] Jian Zhaonan was also forced to forfeit his

Japanese nationality.[12] Nevertheless, the fortunes of Canton Nanyang Brothers Tobacco subsequently improved, while BAT suffered serious business losses during the anti-imperialist May Thirtieth Movement in 1925.

Many of the earlier cigarette advertisements highlight images of machismo and 'Big China' as an expression of patriotism. This may reflect the political climate of the time, when even the Nationalist Party did not think that it was necessary to give women voting rights. Interestingly, however, women who smoked began to appear in advertisements such as those used for the campaign to promote Chinese goods (Figure 9.5). From the late 1920s onwards, there are more women smoking in advertisements as modern girls. In the countryside of Northeast China, older women smoked habitually. However, smoking was taboo for women in big cities, as it was thought to be inappropriate for them. The appearance of women smoking may therefore signal that change was under way.

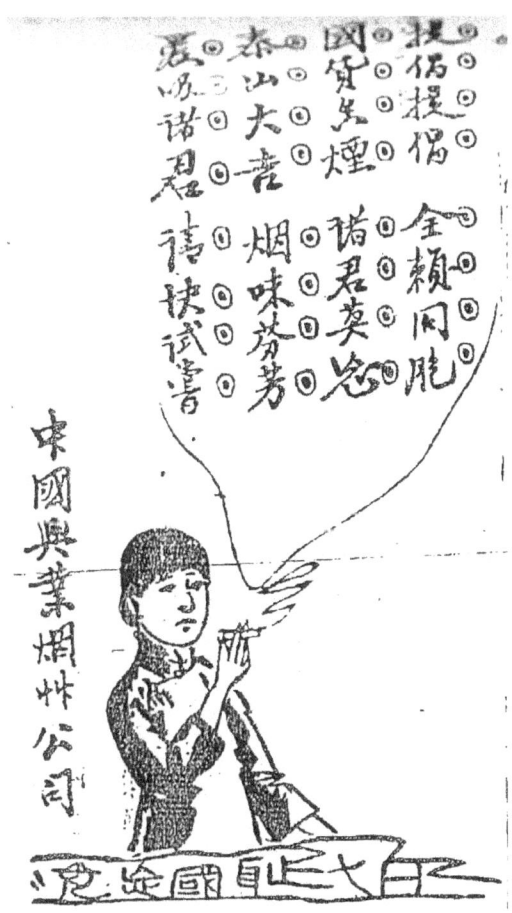

Figure 9.5 *Shibao* (Shanghai), 18 May 1919.

Meanwhile, the requirements for the modern army to be kept healthy, and for the people to be informed of the importance of sanitation and hygiene, necessitated the use of Western medicine in addition to traditional Chinese medicine. This was reflected in the personal use of medical and other therapeutic drugs, although traditional ideas of self-nurturing based on Taoism remained influential in Chinese society. During the educational reform after the establishment of the Republic of China in 1912, Chinese medicine was dropped from the formal teaching curriculum, when epidemics of disease were rampant. Doctors of Chinese medicine protested, and there was a campaign to revive Chinese medicine. Also, the relative merits of Chinese and Western medicine constituted part of the cultural debate between East and West. Nevertheless, the emphasis on Western medicine in medical training was preserved. Even prominent intellectuals known for their traditional views shunned Chinese medicine as being based on superstition and ignoring anatomy. However, a majority of the population were too poor to visit a doctor, and also traditional Chinese drugs could be more effective than Western drugs, depending on the nature of the disease. Chinese-style drugs remained popular. Following the mass production and commercial sale of therapeutic drugs, both Chinese and Western, ordinary families would buy those drugs for home use. One of the drugs that entered the Chinese market on a large scale was Jintan.

Jintan was produced and marketed by Morishita Nan'yōdō, which was founded by Morishita Hiroshi as a family-run business selling drugs in Osaka in 1893. Morishita advertised his products aggressively. He made a considerable profit from the sale of Dokumetsu, a drug for treating syphilis, in 1903. When he was sent to Taiwan as a soldier, Morishita witnessed local people keeping a 'refrigerant' in their mouths to fend off contagious diseases. The experience prompted him to develop a new kind of all-purpose medicine, using herbs obtained from the Chinese mainland. He started to sell the small, coated pill called Jintan to the general public in 1905, and renamed his company Morishita Hiroshi Yakubō.

The name Jintan has Confucian and Taoist origins, and its trademark man, wearing the so-called 'Kaiser' moustache associated with the German Chancellor, Bismarck, and the popular ceremonial morning coat, was a symbol of upward mobility and success, implying a connection with the imperial court. Morishita's intention was to transmit the image of a diplomat who endorsed the drug. Most Chinese took the figure with the Kaiser moustache to be a military officer, however. One noticeable strategy of Morishita Hiroshi Yakubō was to spend nearly one-third of its profits on advertisements. The company advertised its products in newspapers and on street billboards, posters pasted on telegraph poles, banners at the entrances of pharmacies, billboards erected in the fields along the main railway lines, and poles built specifically for advertising Jintan all over Japan. As a result, the name of Jintan became well known. In 1907, the company established a department exclusively for export business. It expanded its sales network in China, using four hundred post offices to which the company entrusted the handling of its mail orders. Around the same time, it opened overseas offices in Tianjin, Hankow and Shanghai, where Japanese staff were stationed.

Billboards and posters for Jintan were used in China, as well as in Korea. In late 1908, the *Gonglun Xinbao* in Hubei Province carried an advertisement with the following caption, 'An irreplaceable miracle family drug, Jintan for overcoming all serious illnesses',[13] which accompanied the Kaiser-moustached figure. The poster first began to appear at the company's office at the Xuanwu Gate in Beijing, then in the main stations and ports, on the walls of residents' homes along the main railway lines, and even on traffic signboards.

Such extensive exposure also provoked strong anger among the Chinese, however. Huang Chunan from Zhejiang Province was one of those who were offended by Jintan's large-scale marketing campaign. Huang was a descendant of the well-known reformer, Huang Zongxi, of the late Ming and early Qing period, and was originally a doctor of Chinese medicine. He later, in 1890, turned to Western drugs, running a pharmacy called the Great Eastern Dispensary in the French concession. Huang produced his own Jintan-like drug following the old remedy described in the *Romance of Three Kingdoms*, as developed by the legendary hero Zhuge Liang so that soldiers could endure a series of battles and overcome summer heat and illnesses. Huang named the drug Rendan, which was a homonym of Jintan in Chinese, although the first Chinese character of its name differed from that of Morishita Jintan. At the same time, Huang founded a business called the Dragon and Tiger Company, and registered the drawing of a dragon and tiger as the trademark of his Rendan. In 1911, he started to sell Longhu (Dragon and Tiger) Rendan. He inserted an advertisement in the *Shenbao* with a caption running 'Dragon and Tiger Rendan is the only irreplaceable energy pill, suitable for both travel and home use, a panacea for emergency, a treasure and Saviour.' However, Huang's Rendan was no rival to Morishita Jintan, which had already established a stable sales network and excelled in its advertising strategies, including the deployment of many sandwich men on the streets. In 1915, Huang abandoned his company and renamed it Zhonghua, affiliating it to the Great Eastern Dispensary. He continued to advertise his product under the name Zhonghua, however. The business grew to become one of the leading companies selling Western medicine in China. Huang expanded his business to include the Great World Entertainment Centre and a film company.

Huang's fortunes turned around when the campaign started to reject Japanese goods during the May Fourth Movement.[14] Morishita Jintan's image, with its strong links to the Japanese imperial army, was undoubtedly affected negatively. Dragon and Tiger Rendan began to make itself known, and received support from Chinese entrepreneurs. In its advertisements in early May 1919, however, Morishita Jintan began to use a Chinese couple. In one design, the man with the Kaiser moustache and morning coat recommends Jintan to the Chinese woman, in an apparent effort to placate the Chinese, who were calling for the boycott of Japanese goods (Figure 9.6).

Figure 9.6 *Dagongbao* (Tianjin), 6 May 1919.

Jintan was confronted by other imitators, however, such as Chundan and Lingdan, the latter advertised as 'made of patriotism'. One of the strongest rivals was Zhuge Liang Dan, sold by the Beijing Huamei Pharmacy. Its label carried the message 'Use Chinese Goods and Regain Profits' in bold letters, followed by such messages as 'researched by its owner paying no attention to cost and labour, using purely Chinese ingredients', and having a 'cooling effect stronger than any foreign product'. The remedy incorporated the idea of using Zhuge Liang's story from Dragon and Tiger Rendan, and taking the image of Zhuge Liang as the logo. The Kaiser moustache and morning coat of the Jintan gentleman were now challenged by the Chinese national hero, Zhuge. The caption to the image of Zhuge runs as follows: '[the drug] saves and resuscitates life, as if [it is the] manifestation of spiritual and religious power, penetrates through holes in the joints where internal energy travels [according to Taoist medical theory], with a force like the splitting of bamboo.' The message also incorporates Jintan's slogan, 'Spiritual home medicine, resuscitating life from death', but also emphasises the Chinese national character using Taoist theory (Figure 9.7).

This situation forced Morishita Jintan to respond. In June, the company began to include a notice in its advertisements. The notice says:

Figure 9.7 *Shenbao*, 7 June 1919

Jintan is a product based on a secret method developed by a renowned Japanese medical doctor. Our Jintan is made from valuable ingredients and through a carefully planned production line. Its spiritual merits will be enormous. Recently, however, shameless profiteers have begun to make and sell fake products using a very similar name, intending to deceive customers and make a huge profit. Please make sure that you buy the right product.[15]

At the same time the company brought a lawsuit through the East Asian Company, a trading company established by Japanese businessmen in 1905 to promote the export of their products and their production and sale in China and Korea, to the Chinese court, claiming that their copyright was infringed by those companies that used similar names to Jintan, and seeking an injunction from the Chinese government's to terminate production. The court battle lasted for ten years and ended in 1927, with the plaintiff losing the case. The case is said only to have increased the popularity of Chinese Rendan.

The Chinese Chemical Industry Company, which produced insecticidal fumigants and other kinds of insecticide, also emphasised that their products were made by a Chinese company in their advertisements. In one example, the image used is of the Detachment of Women, who are said to have helped the first emperor of the Tang Dynasty to unify the country, together with the caption that the Detachment will eliminate all ugly pests, thus emphasising an image of feminist resourcefulness (Figure 9.8). It is interesting that the advertisement presents the idea of 'Chinese-made' women, who, at the same time, are depicted as independent and strong; women's independence is implicitly addressed within the nationalistic paradigm.

Shanghai cartoons (1928–30) – growth of urban cartoon culture

The ripples of the Shandong Problem lingered on and political instability continued. One group that took part in the New Culture Movement turned Bolshevik, and in 1921 around fifty individuals formed the Chinese Communist Party under the influence of the Communist International (Comintern). Anti-imperialist workers' strikes also began to become more frequent, as the development of capitalism led to an increase in the number of labour disputes. When military force was used to suppress a dispute at a Japanese-run factory in Shanghai in 1925, it led to the May Thirtieth Incident, triggering a nationwide anti-imperialist struggle. The number of Party members grew to several tens of thousands, nurturing a distinctively left-leaning political culture. In Shanghai, which was awash with globalised capital because of the many foreign settlements and investments by overseas Chinese, cosmopolitan urban culture of the 'colonial modern' variety flourished in the 1930s, making the city distinctly alien to the Chinese countryside. Together with the spread of Marxism, cartoon culture was part of this flourishing urban culture, which included a strong cosmopolitan outlook.

Figure 9.8 *Shenbao*, 22 May 1919.

Cartoon culture in China entered one of its most exciting periods in 1928, the same year as Japanese troops occupied Jinan (the so-called second Shandong Expedition) after a military confrontation between Japanese and Chinese troops. In Japan, a group of cartoonists led by the avant-garde cartoonist Okamoto Ippei had formed the Tokyo Cartoon Society (Tōkyō manga-kai) in 1915. In 1927, following in the footsteps of the Tokyo group, young avant-garde cartoonists in Shanghai formed their own Cartoon Society. Among them was Ye Qianyu (1907–95), who was born in Zhejiang Province. Still in his early twenties, he was a precocious young man, a dropout who moved from one job to another. Other members included an employee of the Nanyang Tobacco Company, a known left-wing cartoonist. Many had a keen interest in the problems facing Chinese women. From 1928 onwards, they produced and published the weekly *Shanghai manhua* (Shanghai Sketch; 110 volumes in total, published by Zhongguo Meishu Kanxingshe) with the photographer Lang Jingshan (1892–1995), who also hailed from Zhejiang Province, and his friends. This magazine is said to have been the start of a golden era for cartoon and magazine culture in the mid-1930s. The cost of publication of every issue was shared by several members of the group, supplemented by advertisement fees that they collected by drawing material themselves.

As it was sold in Shanghai, this cartoon magazine also contained information about entertainment and fashion. One selling point was the presentation of modern girls, who were eye-catching with their anti-Confucian images and who typically wore short hair, tight dresses and sophisticated accessories, even smoking cigarettes. The magazine also contained messages that were anti-Japanese, anti-imperialist and critical of military factions. Although only about 3,000 copies were published, the real readership is estimated to have been much larger, since it was customary at the time for one copy to be circulated among a number of people.

Most *Shanghai manhua* cartoonists were themselves would-be 'modern boys', who strongly disliked traditional Confucian culture. Some of their work even reveals their envy of those 'modern girls', who were now freed from the foot-binding practice and in full control of their own bodies. Some cartoons exhibit their admiration for these women and even their desire. At the same time, their work also transmits an anticipation or even a fear of the reversal of traditional gender roles. Such anticipations or fears are seen in cartoons in which girls are depicted as much bigger than boys, or where boys worship modern girls, or are controlled by them. In these cartoons, women take the initiative in defiance of their conventional gender roles. From such depictions, it is not so difficult to construe that these male cartoonists now see the women as possessed of a will of their own. At the same time, their work also communicates scepticism about Western material culture after the First World War. Such scepticism is seen in cartoons that mock modern girls' fashions and consumer culture at the time of national crisis. Yet, around this time, pictures of Paris fashion models and Hollywood actresses were also produced en masse, sending subliminal messages to Chinese consumers about the superiority of 'white' actresses and models, and thus shaping their aesthetic sensibilities. Discernible here is the impact of Social Darwinism and the racial prejudices resulting from perceived evolutionary ranking, combined with the new genetics and eugenics, in the period of early globalisation.[16]

On the other hand, it is difficult to sense the same degree of intensity as in the 'political season' of a decade earlier, when many advertisements called for the purchase of Chinese goods. This is so even when the same pages may carry the horror of the occupation of Jinan by Japanese troops. Instead, the dominating image is of women, smoking, flirting and dancing. For instance, the caption to one such advertisement says, 'A Beautiful Woman is Worth a Beautiful Capstan Cigarette.'[17] Even the Nanyang Brothers Tobacco Company, which had been involved in the aggressive patriotic campaign during the May Fourth Movement, uses an image of modern girls with short hair, manicured nails and earrings, smoking a cigarette, while at the same time proclaiming that domestic cigarettes taste better (Figure 9.9). Compared with advertisements from almost ten years previously (Figure 9.5), the woman in this picture is much more urbanised. This group of young graphic designers may harboured had similarly strong patriotism to those of a decade earlier. Their work, however,

Figure 9.9 *Shanghai manhua*, vol. 12 (7 July 1928).

also demonstrates a certain awareness of the autonomy of cultural production, which cannot be submerged by the domination of state or politics, for this generation grew up while the New Culture and May Fourth Movements were in full swing. Their awareness of the autonomy of cultural activities is in keeping with the cosmopolitan outlook of those intellectuals who took part in the New Culture and May Fourth Movements. They were closely following the new artistic trends in Europe, the United States, Southeast Asia, Japan and Mexico, and were in tune with the New Culture Movement, and also with the Mass Education Movement, which Y. C. James Yen (Yan Yangchu) and his friends started after studying in the United States or living in France during and after the First World War.

The *Shanghai manhua* photographer Lang Jingshan was also the advertising agent in China for the company that sold the home medicine Tiger Balm, and which was run by an overseas Chinese based in Singapore. Perhaps that is why this magazine did not carry advertisements for Jintan or other fake Jintan-like products. However, Morishita Jintan did appear in a cartoon (Figure 9.10). The caption to this cartoon reads,

> The moustached Jintan man tells the wife of a businessman [meant to suggest Morishita], 'Don't cry, Madame. While I am being boycotted, please wash away my entire body, paint me over, and wait until things calm down, my face regains its past beauty, and business returns to normal.'[18]

In this highly skilled cartoon, the boycott of Japanese goods is implied in the moustached Jintan man's words to the wife of President Morishita. In terms of the composition of gender and nationalism, it is interesting that a Japanese woman is shown in tears as her husband faces ruin. This may express the common image of Japanese men, who were stereotyped as either violent soldiers or politicians, or powerless and miserable commoners oppressed by the military.

The cartoonist who drew this caricature of Jintan was Huang Wennong, the oldest member of the Shanghai group. Huang was a chief critic of Japanese aggression, Western imperialism and military elements in *Shanghai manhua*, akin to Shen Bochen, who voiced his opinions in *Shanghai Puck*. Clearly, the members saw themselves as successors to *Shanghai Puck*, and they devoted one page in volume 18 of the magazine in August 1928 to the work of Shen Bochen.

Huang Wennong was born to a poor family in Shanghai. At the age of sixteen, he began work as an apprentice at the Shanghai Zhonghua Book Company and learned how to draw. He was then hired by the important general magazine, *Dongfang zazhi* (Eastern Miscellany), as a commissioned cartoonist. He was producing a number of caricatures at the time of the May Thirtieth Incident in 1925. While Huang was working at the Publicity Department of the Police, however, Jiang Jieshi (Chiang Kaishek) carried out an anti-Communist coup d'état in 1927. As a result, Huang lost his job and was thrown into hardship. Figure 9.11 was published in 1929. Although its publication was delayed due

VERSAILLES AND SHANGHAI GRAPHIC/URBAN CULTURE   231

Figure 9.10 Huang Wennong, *Shanghai manhua*, vol. 5 (19 May 1928).

Figure 9.11 Huang Wennong, *Shanghai manhua*, vol. 75 (28 September 1929).

to the fear of censorship, Huang's anger at Jiang is apparent as Jiang's fist epitomises authoritarian rule (fist in Chinese being a homonym for the word for 'power grabbing'). In drawing many caricatures with strong political messages, however, Huang was an exception in *Shanghai manhua*. Often his work is critical of Japan's attempt to control Manchuria and the Shandong Peninsula, and also of those Chinese who lived far from these regions and were indifferent to the situation. Nevertheless, Chinese nationalism alone cannot explain the full range of Chinese realities that Huang was trying to expose.

Ye Qianyu, for example, caricatures nationalist rigidity in a drawing entitled 'Chinese Treasures'. These are 'men's queue, women's foot-binding, the smoking and distribution of opium'.[19] The renewed endorsement of traditional Chinese practices was to start as the New Life Movement in the latter half of the 1930s. Chinese nationalism always contained a deep concern for what was essentially Chinese, and could become reactionary, as Ye's cartoon points out.

Conclusion

Chinese nationalism has a long history. Nevertheless, it has also absorbed various heterogeneous cultural influences, especially during the early stages of globalisation. From the opening of the Paris Peace Conference to the conclusion of the Versailles Peace Treaty, anti-imperialism emerged as a major issue but cosmopolitan cultural influences were also noticeable. The issue deepened the awareness of the country's past and future. Decreasing during this period was the unexamined absorption of anything European or American. In other words, the simplistic dichotomy between Chinese traditions and European modernity was now challenged, although the view continued to influence the Chinese.

Gender constitutes a challenge to this conventional dichotomy, as we have seen in urban visual forms of popular culture such as cartoons and advertisements. It was during this period, and in the context of the weakening paradigm of East–West confrontation, that Chinese women were given an opportunity to learn how to regain their rights and participate in political activities.

Coda

On 15 May 2010 the *Tōkyō shinbun* carried a short piece that read:

> Morishita Jintan has decided to enter the Chinese market for the first time in 65 years, it was learnt yesterday. The company stopped marketing Jintan in China after the war because the refrigerant had been used by soldiers of the Japanese Imperial Army and this association deeply alienated Chinese consumers. However, the recent rise in awareness of a healthy lifestyle among the Chinese has prompted the company to consider marketing the item as a health product in the country. The company will link up with a local Chinese company, and will start marketing the product in Beijing, Shanghai and other Chinese cities within this fiscal year. The company hopes to sell

health items or supplements worth more than 1 billion yen. The company started to sell Jintan in 1905 domestically, and in China in 1908. Its unique taste was loved by many Chinese. Its logo, a man with a Kaiser moustache and in a morning coat, was a familiar figure in China. However, the company withdrew from the Chinese market, and the product's association with the Japanese Imperial Army has long prevented the company's return. Yet, as new generations have replaced the old, strong reactions against the product have weakened. It does not mean however that there is no animosity. According to a spokesman of the company, 'We will study carefully Chinese consumers' response, concerning the sales of Jintan and the use of the company's logo.'[20]

Despite its Confucian or Taoist name, Jintan was always associated with Japanese militarism. One wonders whether the moustached Jintan man in a morning coat will regain his popularity after sixty-five years, or merely become another symbol of the anti-Japanese movement. Today's Shanghai is a megacity even larger than what it was in 1919. Has its urban culture become so thoroughly cosmopolitan as to be capable of producing similar caricatures of Jintan as were produced by the Shanghai cartoonists of the 1920s? Jintan's re-entry into the Chinese market, and its fortunes, will test the waters.

(Translated from the Japanese by Hiromi Sasamoto-Collins)

Notes

1. For the impact of Versailles on the formation of Chinese nationalism, see Sakamoto (ed.), 'Sekai taisen to kokumin keisei'. For a concise analysis of the topic, see Sakamoto, 'Kaisetsu' [Introduction], pp. 1–22.
2. See Shimazu, *Japan, Race and Equality*.
3. See Ono, *Goshi jiki kazoku-ron no haikei*.
4. Zhou Zuoren, 'Qian Xuantong', pp. 365–6.
5. Bickers, *Empire Made Me*, p. 32.
6. Bickers, *Empire Made Me*, p. 39.
7. *Shenbao*, 25 May 1919.
8. *Shenbao*, 15 May 1919.
9. *Shibao*, 23 June 1919.
10. The competition between Nanyang Brothers Tobacco Company and BAT has already been studied in detail by various authors. See, for instance, Cochran, *Big Business in China*, and Cox, *The Global Cigarette*, Ch. 6.
11. *Shenbao*, 25 May 1919.
12. *Xinwenbao* (28 May 1919). See also Cochran, *Big Business in China*, p. 115.
13. *Gonglun xinbao*, 14 February 1909.
14. Sherman Cochran has studied the competition between Huang Chunan's company and Morishita Jintan, with a special focus on advertising (Cochran, *Chinese Medicine Men*). In Chapter 2, 'Advertising Dreams', Cochran shows that 'Ailuo brain tonic', one of the leading products of Huang's company, the Great Eastern Dispensary, was able to compete against Western products, thanks to successful marketing in

which he employed commercial artists who drew traditional paintings of beautiful women. His product could not compete against Morishita Jintan, however. Cochran concludes that it was not nationalism but the sales network and advertising methods that determined the sales of those products.
15. *Dagongbao*, 26 June 1919.
16. For a study of the depictions of modern girls in *Shanghai manhua* and its sequel *Shidai manhua*, see Sakamoto, 'Manga hyōshō ni miru Shanhai Modan Gāru', pp. 117–50.
17. *Shanghai manhua*, vol. 5 (1928).
18. Huang Wennong, *Shanghai manhua*, vol. 5 (19 May 1928).
19. *Shanghai manhua*, vol. 73 (1929).
20. *Tōkyō shinbun*, 15 May 2010.

References

Primary sources

Periodicals:
Dagongbao (Tianjin)
Gonglun xinbao (Shanghai)
Shanghai manhua
Shanghai puck (*Shanghai Poke*)
Shenbao (Shanghai)
Shibao (Shanghai)
Shishi xinbao (Shanghai)
Tōkyō shinbun
Xinwenbao (Shanghai)

Secondary sources

Bickers, Robert, *Empire Made Me: An Englishman Adrift in Shanghai* (New York: Columbia University Press, 2003).
Cochran, Sherman, *Big Business in China: Sino-Foreign Rivalry in the Cigarette Industry, 1890–1930* (Cambridge, MA: Harvard University Press, 1980).
Cochran, Sherman, *Chinese Medicine Men: Consumer Culture in China and Southeast Asia* (Cambridge, MA: Harvard University Press, 2006).
Cox, Howard, *The Global Cigarette: Origins and Evolution of British American Tobacco, 1880–1945* (Oxford: Oxford University Press, 2000).
Ono, Kazuko, *Goshi jiki kazoku-ron no haikei* [The Background of the Debate on the Family during the May Fourth Movement] (Kyoto: Dōhōsha shuppan, 1992).
Sakamoto, Hiroko, 'Manga hyōshō ni miru Shanhai Modan Gāru' [Shanghai Modern Girls as depicted in cartoons], in Ruri Itō, Hiroko Sakamoto and Tani Barlow (eds), *Modan Gāru to shokuminchi-teki kindai: Higashi-Ajia ni okeru teikoku, shihon, jendā*

[The Modern Girl and Colonial Modernity: Capital, Empire and Gender in East Asia] (Tokyo: Iwanami Shoten, 2010), pp. 117–50.

Sakamoto, Hiroko (ed.), 'Sekai taisen to kokumin keisei – Go-shi shin-bunka undō' [The First World War and national formation – The May Fourth and New Culture Movements], *Shinpen genten Chūgoku kindai shisōshi* [New Edition of Primary Sources of Modern Chinese Thought], vol. 4 (Tokyo: Iwanami Shoten, 2010).

Sakamoto, Hiroko, 'Kaisetsu' [Introduction], in Hiroko Sakamoto (ed.), 'Sekai taisen to kokumin keisei – Go-shi shin-bunka undō' [The First World War and national formation – The May Fourth and New Culture Movements], *Shinpen Genten Chūgoku Kindai Shisōshi* [New Edition of Primary Sources of Modern Chinese Thought], vol. 4 (Tokyo: Iwanami Shoten, 2010). pp. 1–22.

Shimazu, Naoko, *Japan, Race and Equality: The Racial Equality Proposal of 1919* (London and New York: Routledge, 1998).

Zhou Zuoren, 'Qian Xuantong', in Chen Zishan and Yan Kun (eds), *Fanhou suibi: Zhou Zuoren zixuan jingpin-ji* [Collected Works of Zhou Zuoren], vol. 2 (Shijiazhuang, Hebei: Hebei Renmin Chubanshe, 1994), pp. 365–6.

Index

Abdülmecid, Hindli, 60
Abdülmecid Efendi, 70
Abe Jirō, 181
Aden, 28
advertisements, 217–26, 228–9
aesthetics, 4
Afghanistan, 57, 61, 64
Africa, 30, 36, 55
Aga Khan, 66
agriculture, 26; *see also* grain; rice
Aj, 130
Akçura, Yusuf, 58–9
Albania, 57
Ali, Abdullah Yusuf, 62
Ali, Syed Ameer, 67
All Asia Association, 84–5
All Asian League, 85; *see also* Asian League
All Asian Peoples' Congress, 85–6
Allenby, Edmund, 62
Amritsar massacre, 36, 137n
Anand, R. P., 137n
anarchism, 5, 183, 186, 197–205
Anatolia, 35, 66, 67
Anderson, Benedict, 177
Andra Patrika, 129
anti-Asian discourses, 78–9
anti-British movements, 38
anti-colonialism, 3, 5, 35, 55–6, 60, 81
anti-democratic movements, 175
anti-imperialism
  Asianism, 88
  in cartoons, 228
  Chinese internationalism, 204
  Chinese nationalism, 214, 216, 221, 226, 228, 233
  Japanese Buddhist perspectives, 151
  Muslim Asia, 64

anti-Japanese movements, 27, 37, 38, 40, 80, 83, 228, 230
anti-Qing movement, 27
anti-Westernism, 5, 83–4, 163–4, 167, 197, 228
Arab populations, 35, 63, 65–6, 70
Arita Hachirō, 116
Armenia, 65–6
armistice shock, 25
Arslan, Shakib, 62, 67, 70
Asia as method, 77
Asian League, 78, 81, 84, 162
Asian Values debate, 7, 90n
Asianism, 77–90
Asia's Fifteenth Point, 4
Associated Press, 108
Ataturk, Mustafa Kemal, 62
Aurobindo Ghose, 162
Australia, 82, 164, 213

Ba Jin, 208n
Baker, Ray Stannard, 105
Balachandran, G., 39, 45
balance of powers, 144, 157, 165
Balfour, Arthur, 2
Balfour Declaration, 69
Balkan Wars (1912–1913), 58, 59
Bandung Conference (1955), 71
bank failures, 42, 47
Bank of England, 40, 41
Bank of Japan, 40, 42
Barthold, Vasili V., 60, 61
Bergère, Marie-Claire, 27
Big China, 221
Big Four/Council of Four, 1–2, 105, 112–15
billboard advertising, 223
Bolsheviks, 55, 56, 64–5, 106, 226
Bombay, 31, 32

237

Bombay Chronicle, 125
Bonsal, Stephen, 113
boom-and-bust cycles, 23, 24, 25, 26, 39–49
Bose, Rash Bihari, 79, 85, 87
Bose, Subhas Chandra, 130
boycotts, 58, 198, 214, 219, 223
Britain
   Allied Powers' treatment of Germany, 155–9
   Amritsar massacre, 36, 137n
   British pound exchange rates, 29
   and Communism, 38
   gold standard, 41, 47
   and India, 27, 29, 41, 45, 61, 64, 124–30, 132–4
   and Japan, 164
   mandate system, 66, 69
   and Muslims in Asia, 58–9, 61, 62, 63, 64, 66, 69, 70
   and the Ottoman Empire, 59, 60, 61–2, 64–5
   and pan-Islamism, 62, 64–5, 69
   and the racial equality clause, 213
   rice controls, 37, 38, 39
   in satirical sketches, 130
   trade tariffs, 27
   treatment of exported labour, 28, 29
   and Turkey, 67
   universal male suffrage, 106
British American Tobacco, 220
bubble-and-boom *see* boom-and-bust cycles
Buddhism, 144–67, 206n
burakumin liberation, 159–60
Burma, 36–7, 38, 39, 44
Bush, George, H. W., 7

Caliphate question, 56, 57, 60, 63, 66, 67–8, 69–72
Canton Nanyang Brothers Tobacco, 220–1
capital, 27, 45
capitalism, 27, 217, 226
Carr, E. H., 4
Carthaginian peace, 2
cartoons, 217–33
Catholicism, 184–7
censorship, 233
Ceylon (Sri Lanka), 45
Chatterjee, Atul Chandra, 126
Chen Duxiu, 200, 216

Chiang Kai-shek (Jiang Jieshi), 87, 120n, 230, 233
China
   Asianism, 79, 85, 87–8
   boom-and-bust cycles, 44
   capitalism, 27
   Chinese exported labourers, 28, 37
   Chinese medicine, 222
   currency, 40
   depression (1920), 44, 45, 47
   Five Year Plans, 27
   and France, 201
   industrialisation, 28
   inflation, 40
   internationalism, 197–205
   intra-Asian trade, 27
   and Japan, 43, 80, 87, 197, 198, 199, 202, 212, 219, 223–4, 226, 233–4
   Japanese Buddhist perspectives, 154
   nationalism, 80, 81, 87, 198–205, 212–34
   at Paris Peace Conference, 2, 36, 110, 198, 201, 214
   rice trade, 37
   service industries, 28
   and silver, 27–8, 29
   silver-standard currencies, 29, 37, 42, 47
   strikes, 36
   unification, 87
   and United States, 197, 198, 202, 219
   universalism, 5
   women in, 4, 213, 214–15, 217, 221, 226, 228–9, 233
   see also May Fourth Movement
Chinda Sutemi, 109, 110–11, 114, 115, 116, 159
Chinese Chemical Industry Company, 226
Chinese Communist Party (Guomindang), 85, 87, 198, 204, 205, 226
Chinese language, 86
Chinese Nationalist Party, 85, 88, 214, 217, 221
Chow Tse-tsung, 28, 205n
Christianity
   and anarchism, 208n
   as basis for world society, 184–7
   and internationalism, 176
   and Islam, 62

in Japan, 151, 160, 163–4, 176–7
and Muslim Asia, 65–6
Chūgai nippō, 144, 146–7, 151, 152, 155–64
cigarette manufacture, 40, 219–20, 229
Civil Disobedience Movements, 124, 133
civilisation and culture, 175–6, 216
Clemenceau, George, 1, 109, 111, 113–14, 127, 178
Cold War, end of, 7
Committee on Public Information (CPI), 105
common sense, 4
Communism, 27, 35, 38, 64, 106, 198, 199, 203, 204
Communist Party of the Indies (PKI), 38
Confucianism, 213, 222, 228
Congress of Vienna, 105–6
Conyngham Greene, William, 110, 111
cosmopolitanism, 58, 114, 181, 206n, 216–17, 226, 230, 233
cotton, 27, 31, 40
Council of Four/Big Four, 1–2, 105, 112–15
Council of Ten, 112
Covenant of the League of Nations, 4, 72n, 80, 117, 127, 132–3
crash (economic) of 1920, 40–6
credit, 24, 29, 41
Creel, George, 105
cultural relativism, 188–90
currency, 27–8, 29, 39–40, 43; *see also* gold; silver

Dagongbao, 224
Dai Jitao, 79
Das, Taraknath, 79, 129–30
Day of National Humiliation, 83, 212
death rates, 3, 32
debt accumulation, 26–30
decolonisation, 55, 57, 71, 81–2, 84
deflation, 25, 26, 39, 40–7
democracy, 6, 25, 33, 164, 179, 213
Deng Xiaoping, 28
depression
 1920 onwards, 23, 25, 33, 40–9
 1927, 43
 1929 onwards, 26, 43, 45, 46
diplomacy, 101–18
drought, 24, 31, 32, 45
drugs (medications), 222–3, 230
Duranty, Walter, 101

Dutch disease effect, 31
Dutch empire, 25, 38, 61, 71

East Asian Company, 226
economics
 boom-and-bust cycles, 23, 24, 25, 26, 39–49
 boycotts, 58, 198, 214, 219, 223
 crash (economic) of 1920, 40–6
 deflation, 25, 26, 39, 40–7
 embargoes, 24, 25, 29, 39, 41, 47
 exchange rates, 29, 41
 export boom and accumulation of debts, 24, 26–30
 free-market economics, 38
 inflation, 24–6, 29–30, 34, 36, 44
 shocks 1918–20, 24
Efendi, Abdülmecid, 70
Egypt, 35, 36, 64, 67, 68, 70
El Niño, 24, 31, 32
Elleman, Bruce, 198–9
embargoes, 24, 25, 29, 39, 41, 47
English language, 86, 107
Enlightenment, 151
Esperanto, 86, 200–1
ethnic cleansing, 66
ethnic nationalism, 5, 178–84, 189–90, 192
Eurocentricity, 2–3, 7–8
Europeanisationism, 77
exchange rates, 29, 41
export booms, 24, 26–30, 39–40, 43, 44

Faisal, King, 70
famine, 31, 32, 45
fascism, 88
Federal Reserve Bank of New York, 40
feminism, 215–16, 217
Fifteen Years War (1931–45), 78
Fifth Point, 2
financial bubble, 25, 39–40
Five Year Plans (China), 27
flooding, 45
flu pandemic, 24, 28, 30–1
Foch, Ferdinand, 158
food riots, 32, 37–8; *see also* rice riots
Fourteen Points, 1, 130–1, 159, 161, 165, 212
France
 Allied Powers treatment of Germany, 155–9
 Arab provinces, 65

France (cont.)
    and China, 201
    inflation, 44
    mandate system, 66
    media at the Paris Peace Conference, 111
    racial equality clause, 164
    in satirical sketches, 130–1
    treatment of exported labour, 28
    universal male suffrage, 106
    and Wilsonianism, 101
French Revolution, 3, 5, 6, 180
fuel prices, 31
Fukuyama, Francis, 7
'Funeral Procession of Wilson's 14 Points', 130–1

Gallipolli, 28
Gandhi, Mahatma, 33, 66, 129, 130
Gaspirali, Ismail, 59
gender relations, 4, 25, 34, 214–15
Gérard, Auguste, 119n
Germany
    Allied Powers treatment of, 155–9
    Hitler, 47, 166
    Japanese Buddhist perspectives, 151, 154–9, 165
    and the Ottoman Empire, 58, 60, 61, 62
    and pan-Islamism, 65
    and the Paris Peace Conference, 35
    in Shandong, 212
globalisation
    and Asianism, 77, 80, 84, 88, 90
    early period of, 228
    global governance, 127
    globally synchronous boom-and-bust, 46–9
    and the media, 105
    and universality, 176, 181
Goh Tun-ban, 38
gold
    gold-restoration depression, 41
    gold-standard countries, 26, 29, 40, 41, 42, 47
    and India, 29–30, 45
    and Japan, 29, 47
    restrictions on, 24, 25, 39
Goldman, Emma, 200, 208n
Gonglun Xinbao, 223
Gotō Shinpei, 117
Government of India Act (1919), 128–9
grain riots, 33; see also rice riots

grain supply shock, 24, 31
Grave, Jean, 199, 208n
Great Alliance of Asian Peoples, 85
Great Depression, 26, 43, 45, 46
Great Destruction, 3
'Great Three', 1–2
Greater Asianism, 68, 88
Greece, 66
Greene, William Conyngham, 110, 111
Gu Weijun (Wellington Koo), 110, 201
Guomindang (Chinese Communist Party), 85, 87, 204, 205, 226

Hani Gorō, 183, 184
Hara Takashi (Hara Kei), 33, 109, 111, 112, 115, 117, 177
'hard money', 26
harvest failure, 24, 30, 31–2
Hattori Shisō, 184
Hawtrey, Ralph, 39
Henig, Ruth, 165
Hibiya Riot, 111–12, 117–18
Hilmi, Şehbenderzade Ahmed, 60
Hindu, The, 132, 133
Hindu nationalism, 66
Hirohito, Emperor, 167
historical memory, 117–18
Hitler, Adolf, 47, 166
Hobsbawm, Eric, 177–8
Home Rule League of Annie Besant, 127
Horiuchi Kensuke, 116
House, Edward, 105
Hu Shi, 216
Huang Chunan, 223
Huang Gongsu, 87
Huang Wennong, 218, 230, 231, 232
Huang Zongxi, 223
Hughes, Billy, 82, 164
human rights, 7, 148, 151, 189, 190, 192
humanism, 181, 182
humanitarianism, 6, 148, 150, 151, 157
Hungary, 35
hyperinflation, 47
hypocrisy, 6

ideational changes, 4–5, 28, 35, 48
identity
    and ethnic nationalism, 182
    Japanese Buddhist perspectives, 156, 161
    minzoku, 178

multiplicity of Muslim wartime
    identities, 57–64
  pan-Islamic identity, 57–64
Ijūin Hikokichi, 109, 110–11
illiberal politics, 179
Imazato Juntarō, 84, 87
imperialism
  and Asianism, 85, 88
  Chinese internationalism, 197
  cultural imperialism, 151, 154
  and ethnic nationalism, 181, 190, 192
  imperial decline, 55–6
  Japanese Buddhist perspectives, 144, 145, 158, 166
  see also anti-imperialism
import substitution, 27, 33
India
  Asianism, 86
  boom-and-bust cycles, 44
  and Britain, 27, 29, 41, 45, 61, 64, 124–30, 132–4
  deaths in World War I, 3, 32
  and the depression (1920), 41–2, 45
  exported labourers, 28–9
  famine, 31–2
  food riots, 32–3
  gold market, 41–2
  industrialisation, 27
  influenza pandemic, 24, 30–2
  intra-Asian trade, 27
  Khilafat Movement, 5, 56, 57, 66–7, 69
  and the League of Nations, 5, 124–34
  monetary system, 29–30
  Muslims in, 61–2, 63, 64, 68, 69, 70
  nationalism, 81
  at the Paris Peace Conference, 2, 124–5
  popular revolts, 35, 36, 124, 129, 132–4
  rice riots, 24
  service industries, 28
  strikes, 36
  transportation bottlenecks, 24
Indian Emigrant, 128
Indian National Congress (INC), 127, 130, 132, 133, 134
Indochina, 44
Indonesia, 36, 38, 44, 68, 71
industrialisation, 26, 27, 28, 33, 36
inflation, 24–6, 29–30, 34, 36, 44
influenza pandemic, 24, 28, 30–1
Inoue Enryō, 150
Inoue Tetsujirō, 161
interest-rate hikes, 40

International Women's Day, 34
internationalism
  and anarchism, 199, 200–1, 203–4
  and Asianism, 78, 88, 89
  Chinese internationalism, 197–205
  and Esperanto, 201
  Japanese Buddhist perspectives, 144, 145
  and the League of Nations, 5, 80
  Muslim Asia, 56, 67
  pan-nationalism, 55, 56, 58, 60
  as product of Versailles, 80, 175, 176–84, 192
  and World Law, 190
intra-Asian trade, 26–7, 36–7, 43
Iran, 57, 70–1
Iraq, 28, 35, 64, 67
Ireland, 35, 178
Iriye, Akira, 80
Ishikawa Shuntai, 164
Islam *see* Muslim Asia
Istanbul, 66, 67–8
Italy, 35, 58, 60, 106, 164
Itō Miyoji, 109
Iwasaki Isao, 84
Iwashita Sōichi, 185, 186

Jalllianwala Bagh massacre *see* Amritsar massacre
Japan
  advertising in, 222
  anarchism, 199, 204
  anti-Japanese movements, 27, 37, 38, 40, 80, 83, 228, 230
  Asianism, 78–9, 82, 84–5, 87–8, 89, 90
  boom-and-bust cycles, 26, 40, 44, 46, 47
  Buddhist perspectives, 144–67
  and China, 43, 80, 87, 197, 198, 199, 202, 212, 219, 223–4, 226, 233–4
  currency, 40
  debt accumulation, 29
  deflation, 40, 41
  diplomacy, 101–18
  economic collapse (1920), 42–3
  gold outflow to, 39
  as great power, 107, 109, 112–15, 117
  industrialisation, 27, 28, 33, 36
  inflation, 39–40
  influenza pandemic, 30
  intra-Asian trade, 27
  Japanese 'stage' at Paris, 106–9

242 INDEX

Japan (*cont.*)
  and League of Nations, 6, 47, 80–1, 88
  Manchurian Incident, 6, 47, 88, 198
  media in, 218
  Meiji period, 110, 146, 150, 161, 175, 184, 185, 186, 190
  militarism, 145, 158, 166, 234
  minzoku, 178–9, 180–1, 183–4, 190–1, 205n
  national revolts, 36
  nationalism, 87, 145, 175–92
  at the Paris Peace Conference, 2, 106–18
  and the racial equality clause, 4, 212–13
  rice riots, 24, 30, 33, 38–9
  rice trade, 37
  service industries, 28
  stereotypes of, 230
  strikes, 36
  Taishō chic, 4
  Taishō period, 4, 146, 175, 185, 186, 187
  and United States, 39, 164
  universal male suffrage, 106
  universalism, 5
  wage increases, 46
Japan Buddhist Union, 147, 152–4, 161, 165
Japanese Communist Party, 183
Japanese language, 86, 107, 177
Jerusalem, 58, 62, 66
Jian Yujie, 219
Jian Zhaonan, 219, 220
jihad, 60, 61, 64
Jinan, 227, 229
Jinhua, 208n
Jintan, 222–6, 230
Johnston-Reed Act (1924), 83
justice, concepts of, 156, 185, 187–91, 192

Kaihō, 183
Kamei Kan'ichirō, 179
Kanokogi Kazunobu, 117
Katō Takaaki, 109, 114, 117
Keenleyside, T. A., 133, 140n
Kelsen, Hans, 189
Kemal, Mustafa, 64, 65, 66, 68
Keppler, Joseph, 217
Keynes, John Maynard, 116, 165
Khilafat Movement, 5, 56, 57, 66–7, 69
Kitamura Tōkoku, 186
Kokusai Press Service, 108

Komura Jutarō, 110, 112
Kondratiev, N. D., 46
Konoe Fumimaro, 6, 146
Korea
  advertising in, 223
  anarchism, 204
  independence, 35, 80
  and Japan, 79
  Japanese Buddhist perspectives, 154, 160–1
  March First Movement, 25, 80, 178, 202
  rice, 39
Koselleck, Reinhart, 119n
Kōtoku Shūsui, 199, 200
Kratoska, Paul, 39
Krishnavarma, Shyamji, 136n
Kropotkin, Peter, 199, 200, 204

labour, exports of, 28–9, 37
Lang Jingshan, 228, 230
language, 86, 107, 162–3, 177, 200–1
Lansing, Robert, 103, 105
Lausanne Treaty, 56, 67–8
Lawrence of Arabia, 63, 93n, 109
League for the Promotion of the Abolishment of Racial Discrimination, 81, 82
League of Asia, 162; *see also* Asian League
League of Nations
  Arab nationalism, 63–4
  and Asianism, 80
  and ethnic nationalism, 182, 184, 192
  and India, 124–34
  and Japan, 80–1, 88
  Japanese Buddhist perspectives, 157, 161
  Manchurian Incident, 6, 47
  mandate system, 66, 117
  'nations' versus 'states', 177, 182
  and the 'new diplomacy', 5
  and the racial equality clause, 4, 115, 159–64
  and universalist principles, 180, 191–2
League to Abolish Racial Discrimination, 115, 162, 163
Lenin, Vladimir Ilych, 48, 55
Li Dazhao, 79
Liang Qichao, 201, 203, 216
Liang Shuming, 216
liberalism, 45, 203
Libya, 58, 61

livelihood crises, 30–9, 48
Lloyd George, David, 1, 62, 109, 113–14, 137n, 159, 178
long-term effects of Paris Peace Conference, 7–8, 165–6, 176
long-wave economic cycles, 46–7

Machida Affair, 160
MacMillan, Margaret, 7, 166, 176
Mahendra Pratap, 79
Mahratta, 128
Makino Nobuaki (Baron), 107, 109, 110, 111, 112, 114, 115, 116, 159
Malaya
  boom-and-bust cycles, 44
  economic collapse (1920), 43, 44
  end of commodity-export boom, 43
  Muslims in, 61
  national revolts, 36–7, 38
  rice riots, 38
  rice trade, 37
malnutrition, 31, 32
Manchukuo, 88
Manchuria, 6–7, 43, 87, 212, 233
Manchurian Incident, 6, 47, 88, 198
mandate system, 56, 58, 64, 65–8, 117, 157
Manela, Erez, 3, 4, 48, 204
Mantoux, Paul, 113
manufacturing boom, 26
March First Movement, 25, 80, 178, 202
marine insurance, 28
martial law, 112
Maruyama, Masao, 88, 89
Marxism, 79, 176, 183, 188, 189–90, 226
Mass Education Movement, 230
masses, increasing importance of, 4
Matani Ruikotsu, 146, 147, 155
Mathews, Basil, 68
Matsuda Tomoyuki, 182, 183, 184
Matsui Keishirō, 109, 110–11, 115
Matsumoto Hikojō, 181
Matsuoka Yōsuke, 108, 109
May Fourth Movement
  in advertising, 229
  anti-Japanese boycotts, 40
  and Asianism, 80
  Chinese nationalism, 2, 178, 198, 200, 202, 203, 204–5, 213

and cultural outlooks, 230
and internationalism, 5
livelihood crises, 35, 36
political shocks, 25
in Shanghai graphic and urban culture, 212–26
strikes, 36
women in, 4
May Thirtieth incident, 204, 221, 226
McDougall, William, 181
Mecca, 58, 63, 70, 71
media
  and anarchism, 200, 201–2
  and Asianism, 79, 83
  Chinese nationalism in, 212–34
  and diplomacy, 101, 105–6, 107, 108
  emergence of mass media, 4
  India in the League of Nations, 124, 125–6, 128–33
  Japan, 108–9, 115–16, 218
  Japanese Buddhist perspectives, 144, 146–7, 150–1
  minzoku, 180–1
  and nationalism, 48
  at the Paris Peace Conference, 4, 108–9, 111, 115–16
  and racial discrimination, 115
  and Woodrow Wilson, 101, 103–5
medicine, 222, 230
Medina, 58, 63, 71
Meiji period, 110, 146, 150, 161, 175, 184, 185, 186, 190
Mexico, 29
Micronesian Islands, 102
Miki Kiyoshi, 183, 188
militancy, labour, 34
militarism, 158, 166, 234
Mills, I. D., 30
Minsheng, 200
minzoku, 178–9, 180–1, 183–4, 190–1, 205n
Miyazaki Tōten, 82
modern day effects of Paris Peace Conference, 7–8, 165–6, 176
Modern Review, 129–30
monarchist states, 178, 184
Mongolia, 35, 87, 145
Montagu, Edwin, 127
Montagu–Chelmsford Reforms, 128–9
morality, 88, 182, 188, 190, 214
Morikawa Tamon, 185
Morishita Jintan, 222, 225, 230, 233

muhajirs, 64
Muslim Asia, 55–72
Muslim League, 127

Nabeyama Sadachika, 184
Nagashima Matao, 184
Nakano Seigō, 108, 116
Nallino, Carlo Alfonso, 60
Nanigawa Arata, 82
Nanyang Brothers Tobacco Company, 219–20, 228, 229
national awakening movements, 25, 34–9
National Humiliation Day, 83, 212
National Revolution, 204
nationalism
  Arab, 63, 71
  and Asianism, 88
  China, 80, 87, 198–205, 212–34
  ethnic nationalism, 5, 178–84, 189–90, 192
  India, 124, 126–7, 128–34
  Japan, 87, 145, 175–92
  livelihood crises, 38–9, 48
  Muslim Asia, 55–6, 57
  pan-Islamism, 64, 71
  pan-nationalism, 55, 56, 58, 60
  and the Paris Peace Conference, 80
  popular movements, 178
  versus regionalism, 5
  Tanaka Kōtarō, 3, 180, 182, 184–92
  and Wilsonianism, 3
natural law, 151, 180, 186, 187–91, 192
Nazi party, 35
Nehru, Jawaharlal, 130
Nehru Report, 132
neo-Kantianism, 188–9, 192
neo-Wilsonianism, 7
New Constitution (China), 214
New Culture Movement, 200, 212–33
'new diplomacy', 2, 5
New Life Movement, 233
'New Order in East Asia', 5
New World Order, 7
New York Times, 101
news shocks, 35
Nicolson, Harold, 110
Nine Powers Convention, 197
Nitti, Francesco Saverio, 102
Nizam of Hyderabad, 70
Non-Cooperation Movement, 124, 129–30

Ogawa Heikichi, 81
Okabe Jirō, 162
Okamoto Ippei, 227
Ōkawa Shūmei, 162–3
Ōki Enkichi, 81
Ōkuma Shigenobu, 79, 82
Olmstead, Albert T., 61
Olympians *see* Big Four/Council of Four
Open Door, 116, 164
Orientalism, 90n
Orlando, Vittorio Emmanuele, 109, 113, 178
Ōsawa Kōji, 168n
Ōsugi Sakae, 200, 204
Ōtani Sonyū, 146
Ottoman Empire, 1, 2, 55–6, 57–68, 69–72; *see also* Caliphate question; Khilafat Movement; pan-Islamism; Turkey
over-production, fears of, 45–6
Ōyama Ikuo, 82

Pakula, Hannah, 120n
Palestine, 69
pan-Africanism, 55, 57
Pan-Asian Conferences
  Kabul (proposed), 87–8
  Nagasaki (1926), 85, 87, 90
  Shanghai (1927), 78, 87, 90
pan-Asianism, 5, 55, 77–90, 159, 162, 163, 166
pandemics, 24, 28, 30–1
Pan-Islamic Congress (1907), 59
pan-Islamism, 5, 55, 56, 57–72
pan-nationalism, 55, 56, 58, 60
pan-Turkic ideals, 58–9
Paris Peace Conference, 1–8
  cartoons, 219
  China at, 2, 110, 197, 198, 201, 214
  Japanese Buddhist perspectives, 144–67
  Japanese 'stage' at Paris, 106–9
  news shocks, 35
  photographs, 107, 109
  seating arrangements at, 107
  Wilson's public performance, 102–6
particularism, 175–92
Paşa, Hamdi, 60
patriotism, 111, 198, 219, 221, 225, 229
perfomativity of diplomacy, 106–9, 112, 117

Permanent Mandates Commission, 66
Perry, Elizabeth, 34–5
Philippines, 43–4
photographs, 107, 109
Pillsbury, W. B., 181
Poincaré, Raymond, 155–6
Poland, 35
political shocks, 25, 48–9
'popcorn' effect, 35
popular revolts
  1918–20, 30–4
  India, 35, 36, 124, 129, 132–4
  Japan, 178
  Muslims in, 63
  pan-Islamic activism, 64
  see also March First Movement; May Fourth Movement; rice riots
populism, 177
Portsmouth peace negotiations, 110, 112, 116
positivism, 188–9
Praja Bandhu, 128
Pratap, Mahendra, 87
price fixing, 38
profiteering, 32
propaganda
  and Asianism, 82
  and China, 202
  Indian self-rule, 133
  pan-Islamism, 59–60, 61
  pan-nationalist ideals, 60
  as part of peace diplomacy, 108
  and racial equality, 167
  and the Second World War, 166
  and Woodrow Wilson, 101
Protestantism, 185–6
Provisional Constitution (China), 214
psychology, 181
public performance at Paris, 106–9, 112, 117
Punjab, 36

race, and the Lausanne Treaty, 67–8
racial discrimination, 83–7, 89, 159–64
racial equality clause
  Asianism, 78, 79, 80–1, 82, 89
  versus 'equality of nations', 159, 167
  failure of, 6, 117, 163, 212–13
  iconic status of, 4, 102
  Japanese Buddhist perspectives, 151, 154–5, 159–64, 165, 167
  public relations disaster, 115–16

railways
  and food riots, 33
  and the influenza pandemic, 30, 31
  inter-Asian railway, 87
  and the Ottoman Empire, 63
Rajakāran, 125
Rash Bihari Bose, 79, 85, 87
Realpolitik, 68, 89, 107, 167
regionalism, 5, 10, 56, 58–9, 67, 71, 78, 88
relativist politics, 188–9
religion, 184–7; *see also* specific religions
restorative policies, 47
revanchism, 84
revisionist perspectives, 165, 167
Revolutionary Alliance, 200
Revue diplomatique, 182
rice prices, 42
rice riots, 24, 30, 33, 37–9, 112, 117
Richard, Paul, 81–2, 162–3
Rida, Rashid, 70
Riza, Muhammad, 70–1
Rowlatt Acts (1919), 137n
Roy, M. N., 64
Ruikotsu (Matani), 146, 147, 155
Rumi Sakamoto, 144, 166
rupee exchange rates, 41–2
Russia, 35, 59, 60, 90n
Russian Revolution, 25, 34, 212, 218
Russo-Japanese War (1904–5), 111, 117, 146

Said, Edward, 90n
Saionji Kinmochi, 109–10, 111, 112, 178
Saitō Hiroshi, 116
Sakaguchi Takashi, 180–1
Sakai Toshihiko, 183
Samne, George, 61
Sampad Abhyudaya, 125
Sāndesh, 128
Sano Manabu, 184
Sarekat Islam, 38
Sastri, Srinivasa, 136n
satirical sketches, 130
Saudi, 70, 71
Scheidemann, Philipp, 158
Schneider, N. C., 135n
Schumpeter, J. A., 46
science, 183–4, 188, 201, 216
Second World War, 166–7

246 INDEX

self-determination
  Asianism, 89
  and China, 198
  India, 126, 127–8, 129
  and internationalism, 177
  Japanese Buddhist perspectives, 161
  Muslim Asia, 65
  and the new world order, 6, 55
  and Woodrow Wilson, 48
Sen'ō Girō, 145
Servant of India, The, 133
service industries, 28
Sethna, P. C., 136n
Sèvres Treaty, 56, 66, 67
Shakib Arslan, 62, 67, 70
Shandong province
  and Chinese internationalism, 197, 198–9, 202, 212, 213, 218, 226, 233
  influence on May Fourth movement, 2, 5
  and Japanese diplomacy in Paris, 102, 117
Shanghai manhua, 228, 229, 230, 231, 232, 233
Shanghai Puck, 217–18, 230
share prices, 42, 45
shared sociality, 114, 120n
Sharif Hussein, 63, 65, 69–70, 71
Shen Bochen (Shen Xueming), 218, 230
Shenbao, 215, 218, 225, 227
Shibao, 220, 221
Shibasaki Atsushi, 145
Shifu (Liu), 200
Shigemitsu Mamoru, 116
Shimazu, Naoko, 159, 166–7, 213
Shintoism, 159, 190
shipping, 27, 28, 31
Shishi Xinbao, 218, 219
Siam (Thailand), 2, 37, 38, 43, 44
silence, 110, 115
silk, 28, 39, 42, 45
silver
  and China, 27–8
  exchange rates, 41
  falling prices of, 42
  inflation, 40
  pressures on price of, 29
  restrictions on, 24, 25, 29, 39
  silver-standard currencies, 29, 37, 42, 47
Simon Commission, 132
Singapore, 61

Sinocentricity, 77
Sino-Japanese War, 198, 217
Smuts, Jan, 65
social justice, 186, 188–91
socialism, 25, 176, 183–4, 199
Society of Reformists of the Foreign Ministry, 116
soldiers, exports of, 28–9
Song Jiaoren, 214
Soong Meiling, 120n
sovereignty, 55, 67, 125, 190; *see also* nationalism
Soviet Union, 198; *see also* Russia
specie embargoes, 29
specie flows, 39–40, 48
Sri Lanka (Ceylon), 45
stock exchanges, 42, 45
Stoddard, Lothrop, 67
Stone, Jacqueline, 150
strikes, 25, 30, 32, 33–4, 36, 226
subaltern actors, 55
Suehiro Shigeo, 164
Sugita Teiichi, 81
Sukarno, 68, 71
Sun Yat-sen, 38, 68, 79, 83, 88, 200
Supreme Council, 156
swadeshi (self-sufficiency), 33
swaraj (self-rule), 124, 130, 132, 133; *see also* self-determination
Swarajya, 125, 126
synchronicity of economic phenomena, 46–9
Syria, 35, 67

Tagore, Rabindranath, 83
Taikai (League for the Promotion of the Abolishment of Racial Discrimination), 81, 82
taisei junnō, 176
Taishō period, 4, 146, 175, 185, 186, 187
Taiwan, 39, 79, 154
Takahashi Korekiyo, 111
Takakusu Junjirō, 147
Takashima Beihō, 160
Takeshita, Vice-Admiral, 116
Takeuchi Yoshimi, 77–90, 90n
Tamils, 33, 37–8
Tanaka Giichi, 87, 111
Tanaka Kōtarō, 3, 180, 182, 184–92
Tanaka Suiichirō, 182, 191
Tang Qunying, 214
Taoism, 222

tariffs, 27
tea, 28, 45
Temps nouveaux, Les, 199
textile industries, 27
Thailand (Siam), 2, 37, 38, 43, 44
theatre of power, peace conference diplomacy as, 106–9
Thompson, Charles T., 108
Tiananmen Gate student demonstrations, 35
Tiger Balm, 230
Tilak, Bal Gangadhar, 127
Times, The, 111
Tinkler, Richard Maurice, 217
tobacco companies, 219–20, 229
Tokyo Cartoon Society, 227
Tokyo group, 200, 227
Tomlinson, B. R., 33
Tooze, Adam, 49n
Tosaka Jun, 184
Toynbee, Arnold J., 61, 62
trade surpluses, 27, 29, 43
trade unions, 34
transcendentalism, 112
transportation bottlenecks, 27, 31
Treaty of Lausanne, 56, 67–8
Treaty of Portsmouth, 112, 116
Treaty of Sèvres, 56, 66, 67
Treaty of Washington (1922), 197, 198
Triple Intervention, 117
Tsingtao, 212, 218
Turkey
  Arab nationalism, 63, 71
  Muslims in, 57, 67–8, 69–72
  and pan-Islamism, 64–5
  see also Ottoman Empire
Turkish War of Independence, 2, 56, 67–8, 69
Twenty-One Demands, 80, 197, 198, 212

Uchida Yasuya, 109, 111
Uchimura Kanzō, 176, 185, 186
Ukraine, 35
unanimity rule, 163
Under the Banner of the New Science, 183
United States
  and China, 197, 198, 202, 219
  and diplomacy, 102–6
  illiberal politics, 179
  influenza pandemic, 30
  and Japan, 39, 164
  Johnston-Reed Act (1924), 83

mandate system, 65–6
  at the Paris Peace Conference, 66, 111
  and the Philippines, 43–4
  propaganda, 101–2
  and the racial equality clause, 213
  racial exclusion legislation, 83, 84
  role in depression (1920), 40–1, 45
universal male suffrage, 106
universalism
  Japanese Buddhist perspectives, 144, 145
  Japanese nationalism, 175–92
  and national protest movements, 35
  pan-Islamic activism, 64
  Western rhetoric of, 5, 55
urban cartoon culture, 226–33
urbanisation, 36, 45
utilitarianism, 190

Versailles, metonymic use of, 16n
Vienna system, 26
Vietnam, 37, 38
Vijiaraghavachariar, Chakravarti, 132–3
Vittorio Orlando, Emmanuele, 109, 113–14, 178
'Vive Wilson', 103
Volksgeist, 179
Vyanga Chitravali: Caricature Album, 130, 131

wage increases, 36, 40, 46
Washington Treaty (1922), 197, 198
Watanabe Kaigyoku, 147–51, 153–4, 161, 162, 165
Wellington Koo, V. K., 110, 201
white supremacy, 67–8
Willingdon, Viscount, 125–6
Wilson, Woodrow
  and China, 198–9, 202
  and diplomacy, 101
  Fourteen Points, 1, 130–1, 159, 161, 165, 212
  and Japan, 213
  at the Paris Peace Conference, 102–6, 109, 113–14
  petitioned by India, 127–8
  and the racial equality clause, 82, 159, 164
  and self-determination, 55, 127, 177–8, 198
  unanimity rule, 163
  views of the state, 179

Wilsonian Moment, 5, 48, 204
Wilsonianism
  Buddhist perspectives, 144
  'dark Wilsonianism', 6
  Eastern Europe, 56
  in Japan, 179
  and the mandate system, 66, 67
  modern manifestations of, 7
  and nationalism, 3
  neo-Wilsonianism, 7
  and the new world order, 3–4
  pan-Asianism, 57
  public performance at Paris, 102–6
  in satirical sketches, 130–1
  self-determination, 55, 127, 177–8, 198
Witte, Sergei, 110
women
  anarchists, 201
  in China, 4, 213, 214–15, 217, 221, 226, 228–9, 233
  and inflation/deflation, 34
  and popular revolts, 34
  wives uprising, 34
  women's rights, 25, 34
  women's suffrage, 4, 214, 221
workers' revolt, 25
World Culture, 181
World Law, 190–1, 192
World Society, concepts of, 185–7
World War II, 166
Wundt, Wilhelm Max, 181

Xin Qingnian, 200, 201
Xu Guoqi, 16, 28

Yamaga Taiji, 200
Yamagata Aritomo, 111
Yamakawa Hitoshi, 183
Yan Yangchu, 230
Ye Qianyu, 227–8, 233
'Yellow Peril' discourse, 78, 151
Yen, Y. C. James, 230
Yokota Kisaburō, 189
Yoshino Sakuzō, 82
Young, Governor, 37
Yuan Shikai, 212, 214

Zheng Yuxiu, 201
Zhongguo Meishu Kanxingshe, 228
Zhou Enlai, 28
Zhou Zuoren, 216

EU representative:
Easy Access System Europe
Mustamäe tee 50, 10621 Tallinn, Estonia
Gpsr.requests@easproject.com

www.ingramcontent.com/pod-product-compliance
Lightning Source LLC
Chambersburg PA
CBHW051113230426
43667CB00014B/2567